CRYSTAL
BASICS

"Nicholas Pearson's *Crystal Basics* leaves no stone unturned! As a crystal healing instructor, I look forward to recommending this as a resource to my students for years to come. Not only does Nicholas share a bountiful directory of 200 crystals and their uses (including a very useful appendix of properties sorted by body, mind, and spirit), but he also introduces the reader to the physics and metaphysics of crystal energy in a way that's easy to understand for beginners and thought-provoking for seasoned crystal workers. Nicholas also describes *how* the reader can work with crystal energies for powerful transformation as well as the best practices to care for your crystals. This book is a true gem!"

ASHLEY LEAVY, FOUNDER OF THE LOVE & LIGHT SCHOOL
OF CRYSTAL THERAPY AND AUTHOR OF *COSMIC CRYSTALS*

"Thorough, concise, and clear—*Crystal Basics* is an excellent resource for anyone who wishes to have a solid foundation in the practical, scientific, and mystical exploration of healing crystals."

KRISTA N. MITCHELL,
AUTHOR OF *CRYSTAL REIKI* AND *CHANGE YOUR ENERGY:
HEALING CRYSTALS FOR HEALTH, WEALTH, LOVE & LUCK*

"Finally, this is the book the crystal community has been waiting for! *Crystal Basics* delves deep into the relationship between how minerals are formed and their metaphysical properties. With his wealth of knowledge, Nicholas guides you step-by-step through every aspect of working with crystals. This comprehensive book is an excellent primer and practical guide to the fascinating world of crystals and crystal healing for beginners and beyond."

ETHAN LAZZERINI, AUTHOR OF *CRYSTAL GRIDS POWER*
AND *PSYCHIC PROTECTION CRYSTALS*

"Nicholas Pearson's knowledge of geology and gems shines through the pages of *Crystal Basics*. This book is full of valuable information that will satisfy rock enthusiasts, especially the section on how and why crystals work."

MARGARET ANN LEMBO, AUTHOR OF *THE ESSENTIAL GUIDE TO CRYSTALS, MINERALS AND STONES* AND *ANIMAL TOTEMS AND THE GEMSTONE KINGDOM*

"A must-have for your library! Nicholas Pearson's knowledge on crystals is quite impressive. *Crystal Basics* delivers a magnitude of information for crystal enthusiasts of all skill levels. This will be my new 'go-to' crystal book!"

ELIZABETH GARDIEPY, AUTHOR OF *CRYSTAL SKULL MAGICK*

"*Crystal Basics* is a comprehensive guidebook to the amazing powers of crystals and how they intensely impact you in a positive, beneficial way. Pearson showcases the intimate connection between you and crystals for healing all levels of your mind, body, and soul. Written in an easy-to-read style, this illuminating book will enrich your holistic crystal practices."

MELINDA CARVER, AUTHOR OF *GET POSITIVE LIVE POSITIVE*

"I've collected more than three dozen crystal and gemstone books over the past 40 years. If I could only keep one, this would be it. *Crystal Basics* by Nicholas Pearson covers almost anything and everything that you would want to know about the mineral kingdom and crystal healing. There is such a wealth of information that is shared in *Crystal Basics*—mineral science, basic practices and procedures using crystals, great crystal meditations, and how to make crystal elixirs and unique crystal layouts for healing. The instructions for making your own crystal grids are fun and easy. And, to top it all off, there is a large section on the use and healing properties of 200 gemstones. All the best is included in one book. There is even a section on energy healing."

REV. OJELA FRANK, MSC, LMT, FOUNDER OF AUMAKHUA-KI® ENERGY BALANCING & MEDITATION AND AUTHOR OF *CRYSTAL THERAPEUTICS*

CRYSTAL
BASICS

The Energetic, Healing, and
Spiritual Power of
200 GEMSTONES

NICHOLAS PEARSON

Destiny Books
Rochester, Vermont

Destiny Books
One Park Street
Rochester, Vermont 05767
www.DestinyBooks.com

Destiny Books is a division of Inner Traditions International

Note to the reader: *This book is intended as an informational guide. The remedies, approaches, and techniques described herein are meant to supplement, and not to be a substitute for, professional medical care or treatment. They should not be used to treat a serious ailment without prior consultation with a qualified health care professional.*

Cataloging-in-Publication Data for this title is available from the Library of Congress

ISBN 978-1-62055-934-5 (print)
ISBN 978-1-62055-935-2 (ebook)

Printed and bound in the United States by Versa Press, Inc.

10 9 8 7 6 5 4 3

Text design and layout by Virginia Scott Bowman
This book was typeset in Garamond Premier Pro and Avenir with Hermann, and Tide Sans used as display typefaces
Photographs and illustrations by Steven Thomas Walsh unless otherwise indicated

To send correspondence to the author of this book, mail a first-class letter to the author c/o Inner Traditions • Bear & Company, One Park Street, Rochester, VT 05767, and we will forward the communication, or contact the author directly at **www.theluminouspearl.com**.

Contents

▲ ▲ ▲

PART ONE
How and Why Crystals Work

▲ ▲ ▲

PART TWO

A Directory of Crystals and Stones

11 Two Hundred Gemstones for Healing   196

Agate *(Blue Lace Agate • Botswana Agate • Crazy Lace Agate • Fancy Agate •*
Fire Agate • Flower Agate • Moss Agate • Pink Agate • Snakeskin Agate
• Tree Agate • Turritella Agate) •

Amazonite • Amber •

Amethyst *(Chevron Amethyst • Lavender Quartz) •*

Ametrine • Angelite •

Apatite, Blue *(Golden Apatite • Green Apatite • Red Apatite) •*

Apophyllite • Aquamarine •

Aragonite *(Blue Aragonite • Brown Aragonite • Green Aragonite •*
Aragonite Sputnik • White Aragonite) •

Aventurine, Green *(Blue Aventurine • Peach Aventurine) •*

Azurite • Barite • Black Onyx • Bloodstone •

Calcite *(Blue Calcite • Golden Calcite • Green Calcite •*
Mangano Calcite • Optical Calcite • Orange Calcite •
Red Calcite • Yellow Calcite • Zebra Calcite) •

Carnelian • Cavansite • Celestite •

Chalcedony *(Black Chalcedony • Blue Chalcedony • Grape Chalcedony • Pink*
Chalcedony • White Chalcedony) •

Chalcopyrite • Charoite • Chrome Diopside • Chrysocolla • Chrysoprase •

Citrine • Creedite • Danburite • Dioptase •

Dumortierite • Emerald • Epidote •

Fluorite *(Blue Fluorite • Blue John Fluorite • Green Fluorite • Purple Fluorite •*
Rainbow Fluorite • Yellow Fluorite) •

Fuchsite • Galena •

Garnet *(Almandine Garnet • Black Garnet • Green Garnet •*
Hessonite Garnet • Rainbow Garnet • Rhodolite Garnet) •

Heliodor • Hematite • Hiddenite • Howlite • Iolite • Jade •

Jasper *(Dragon's Blood Jasper • Green Jasper • Leopardskin Jasper • Mookaite •*
Ocean Jasper • Picture Jasper • Polychrome Jasper • Poppy Jasper •
Red Jasper • Silver Leaf Jasper • Yellow Jasper) •

Jet • Kunzite •

Kyanite, Blue *(Black Kyanite • Green Kyanite • Orange Kyanite)* •

Labradorite • Lapis Lazuli • Larimar • Lepidolite • Magnetite •

Malachite • Moldavite •

Moonstone *(Rainbow Moonstone)* •

Obsidian, Black *(Apache Tears • Mahogany Obsidian • Platinum Obsidian •*
Rainbow Obsidian • Snowflake Obsidian) •

Opal *(Black Opal • Blue Opal • Dendritic Opal • Ethiopian Opal • Fire Opal •*
Green Opal • Pink Opal • Purple Opal • White Opal • Yellow Opal) •

Peridot • Petalite • Petrified Wood • Phenakite •

Pietersite • Prehnite • Pyrite •

Quartz *(Amphibole Quartz • Elestial Quartz • Garden Quartz • Herkimer*
Diamond Quartz • Lemurian Seed Crystal • Lithium Quartz • Phantom Quartz
• Rose Quartz • Rutilated Quartz •
Scepter Quartz • Smoky Quartz • Spirit Quartz • Tangerine Quartz •
Tibetan Quartz • Tourmalinated Quartz • White Quartz) •

Rhodochrosite • Rhodonite • Ruby *(Ruby in Zoisite)* • Sapphire • Scapolite •

Selenite *(Desert Rose Selenite • Golden Selenite • Satin Spar Selenite)* •

Seraphinite • Serpentine • Shungite • Smithsonite • Sodalite • Spinel •

Stilbite • Sugilite • Sunstone • Tanzanite • Tektite •

Tiger's Eye *(Blue Tiger's Eye • Red Tiger's Eye)* •

Topaz, White *(Blue Topaz • Golden Topaz)* •

Tourmaline *(Black Tourmaline • Blue Tourmaline • Brown Tourmaline •*
Green Tourmaline • Pink Tourmaline • Watermelon Tourmaline) •

Turquoise • Unakite • Vanadinite • Vesuvianite •

Wulfenite • Zincite • Zircon

Conclusion

▲ ▲ ▲

Acknowledgments

NO BOOK IS THE EFFORT of a single person, and much gratitude is owed for all the effort and inspiration that has brought this book to fruition.

First and foremost, thank you to my partner and photographer, Steven, for helping make this book beautiful and for your relentless support in this and all projects.

Many thanks to the fabulous and talented team at Inner Traditions (not least of all my incredible editor, Jamaica) for once again helping my dreams become reality.

Thank you to all the students and clients who have inspired this work; you showed me the need for a text like this to serve as a complete primer to working with the mineral kingdom.

I send my love and gratitude to Miranda and the wonderful team at Avalon in Orlando, Florida, for all the help you offered in providing stones to photograph and giving me the opportunity to share the material in this book with you and our local community.

To everyone else who has in any way contributed your support, encouragement, insight, and love: thank you for all that you do and all that you are.

INTRODUCTION

What Is a Crystal?

CRYSTALS HAVE SKYROCKETED to the forefront of popular culture today. They are no longer relegated solely to the realms of the mystical and arcane. Those who wear them or carry them aren't outsiders any longer. We see healing stones being carried by contestants on reality television, while rocks and minerals have taken center stage in both fashion and interior design, accenting the necklines of models and gracing the homes of celebrities. Gemstones have infiltrated cartoons, graphic novels, and all other corners of society today. But what really are crystals, and what makes them so popular?

The word *crystal* is defined as a solid whose components are arranged in a highly ordered, repetitive structure, forming a crystal lattice that extends in all directions. When given adequate space during the formation process, crystals also exhibit geometric faces that reflect the internal symmetry and coherence of their composition. For many of us, the word *crystal* conjures images of transparent crystals of quartz—or perhaps it evokes polished gemstones and brightly colored mineral specimens. However not all crystals are necessarily geologic in origin, nor does their crystallinity seem apparent at first.

All around us there are crystals. Tiny crystals of gypsum—better known as selenite in its gem-quality form—comprise the drywall (or plasterboard) that probably lines the walls of your home or office. Crystalline ice cools your favorite beverages on a hot summer's day. Metals like copper, iron, and aluminum are smelted from ore-bearing rocks and minerals with crystalline compositions, just as glass is also derived from once crystalline sources. Everywhere we go we find evidence of the mineral kingdom, from the brick and pavement at our feet, to the pigments adorning the billboards that tower above us. Crystals are even within us; they are part of the human body, in the form of certain organic compounds that are crystalline in structure and are necessary for life.

In most books on crystals today, words such as *crystal, mineral, rock, gem,* and *stone* are thrown around without much understanding as to what they really mean. It's helpful to examine these terms more closely to help us better understand the tools offered by Mother Nature.

▸ A **crystal** is a homogeneous solid substance with a repeating symmetrical structure. This structure is called a *crystal lattice.* Crystals' external forms are outlined by regular geometric planes. Examples of common crystals include quartz, snowflakes, and even the salt and sugar with which we cook.

▸ A **quasicrystal** meets only some of the above criteria, and this may be solid or liquid. Liquid crystals such as those used in the screens of many electronics (as well as those found in living tissue) are considered a *liquid crystal mesophase;* that is, in a state between liquidity and crystallinity. Water in its most natural, perfected state exists as a liquid crystal mesophase.

▸ A **mineral** is a naturally occurring, inorganic crystal. That means that minerals must be formed by nature, from nonliving sources, and exhibit homogeneous compositions and symmetrically repetitive structures. Minerals can be macrocrystalline, usually exhibiting a visible crystal structure, or they may be microcrystalline, meaning they are composed of many microscopic crystals that have grown together. Pyrite, calcite, diamond, topaz, and beryl are some minerals with which you are probably familiar.

▸ When a substance meets some, but not all, of the criteria of a mineral (which include the natural, inorganic origin and regular composition and structure that are the hallmarks of crystallinity), it is called a **mineraloid.** Obsidian and opals are classic, well-known mineraloids; they lack the crystal structure necessary to be deemed proper minerals. Similarly, the apatite in our bones and the aragonite in pearls are considered mineraloids because they are made by organic processes.

▸ **Rocks** are aggregates of one or more minerals (or mineraloids). Rocks vary in composition, appearance, texture, and structure. They are formed by many different processes, which are categorized as being igneous, sedimentary, or metamorphic in nature. Rocks such as granite, schist, rhyolite, and basalt are usually composed of several minerals that form together, whereas rocks like quartzite, marble, and limestone are principally formed from a single mineral species (though they may have traces of other minerals too).

▸ **Stone** is a more nebulous term. It often connotes a small, hard fragment of rock. Sometimes *stone* is used to refer to rocks that have been somehow affected by humankind, either by moving them (such as the standing stones in megalithic monuments) or by shaping (like stone tools or gemstones). *Stone* can refer to materials that are homogeneous or heterogeneous in nature: both rocks and minerals. The word *stone* seldom refers to euhedral (meaning "well formed") crystals; that is, those that exhibit crystal faces.

▸ The word **gemstone** (or simply **gem**) refers to any rock, mineral, mineraloid, or crystal used for ornamental purposes. Many gemstones are single minerals, like amethyst and topaz, while others are actually rocks, such as jade and lapis lazuli. Gems may even include organic "stones" such as amber, jet, and pearl.

THE BIRTH OF CRYSTALS

Rocks and minerals are formed by geologic activity in and on the earth's crust. The collective processes that create rocks and minerals are called the *rock cycle*. The rock cycle includes three main categories of rock and mineral genesis: igneous, sedimentary, and metamorphic.

Igneous rocks are formed when molten rock cools. They fall into two categories: intrusive and extrusive. Intrusive rocks are those that result from the cooling of magma within the crust. Because this magma is insulated by the surrounding rock, intrusive rocks cool more slowly, forming larger component minerals. Extrusive rocks, on the other hand, are the product of lava that has breached the surface, such as in volcanic eruptions. They cool much more quickly than their intrusive counterparts, thereby exhibiting finer-grained textures with tiny crystal structures. Rocks like granite, gabbro, and rhyolite are common examples of igneous formations.

Other igneous, or primary, processes result in an array of common crystals used in healing. The three main actions that form igneous rocks and primary minerals are liquid magmatic, hydrothermal, and pneumatolytic. Quartzes (including agate and chalcedony), obsidian, zircon, peridot, garnet, sodalite, prehnite, danburite, and apophyllite are examples of stones typically formed by primary processes.

Sedimentary rocks are made from other rocks and minerals that are cemented together or somehow rearranged. They may be the result of chemical or mechanical weathering, whereby rocks are broken down by the influence of their environments; these rock fragments are transported, deposited, and eventually *lithified*—turned into stone. Limestone, sandstone, and shale are sedimentary rocks that you may already know.

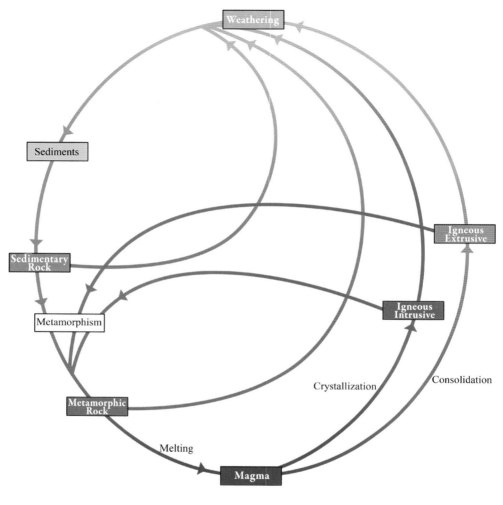

The rock cycle

Some common minerals are the result of certain sedimentary (or secondary) processes. Calcite, selenite (gypsum), turquoise, celestite, aragonite, rhodochrosite, aventurine, and howlite are a few examples of healing stones formed in this way.

Metamorphic rocks are also birthed from other rocks, either sedimentary or igneous. They are subjected to heat or pressure (or a combination of the two), which causes their constituents to rearrange themselves. Metamorphic rocks are often bent and twisted, or they may display bands called *foliation;* they are reinvented by the moving of mountains or by heat escaping from neighboring magma. Marble, gneiss, schist, and quartzite are common metamorphic rocks.

Even the gemstone lapis lazuli is a metamorphic rock. Commonly occuring minerals formed by metamorphic (tertiary) processes include garnet, kyanite, serpentine, charoite, sunstone, emerald, and jade.

There are many stones in our toolboxes that can be formed from any of the above processes. Hematite, calcite, tourmaline, garnet, and aventurine may result from more than one of the three formation processes. Sometimes we have to dig deeper into the provenance, or origin, of our beloved healing stones to better understand where they come from and how they are formed. This, in turn, points us toward the spiritual gifts and healing energies that they offer us.

WHY CRYSTALS MATTER

Mother Nature has blessed us with the gifts of her mineral kingdom. Rocks and minerals comprised the very first tools that early humans used. Our ancestors hunted with flint arrowheads, cut through plants and flesh with sharpened obsidian, and left their art on the stone walls of caverns. Today we use rocks and minerals in art, architecture, science, medicine, industry, and, of course, in our eternal spiritual quest.

This begs the question as to why crystals are so intimately connected to humankind. Rocks and stones have been praised for eons, and this is surely due to more than just their ubiquity. No matter where we turn, people all over the globe have cultivated mystical and spiritual relationships with the mineral kingdom. Ancient people living in the Anatolian peninsula (modern-day Turkey) and Central America carved obsidian mirrors for peering into other worlds. Gemstones such as lapis lazuli, jade, and quartz have been discovered in the tombs of kings and commoners alike, to accompany the dearly departed to their final destination. These examples of ancient uses of gemstones remind us that there is something primal and universal about connecting with crystals.

Our planet will continue to reveal new mineral treasures, and humanity will seek out rocks, minerals, ores, and other crystalline treasures to use in new and innovative ways. Crystal healing offers humankind one of many avenues for co-creating with the mineral kingdom. Currently, our world is faced with troubles the likes of which we have never known, and the mineral kingdom is offering a helping hand on the road back to wellness and transformation. We can take a page from the books of our ancestors by learning how to more effectively connect with the mineral kingdom.

Throughout this book you'll find practical, hands-on information for using crystals in your life. The book is divided into two sections: a primer on the basics of working with crystals and a directory of two hundred stones commonly used in crystal healing. The first part opens with a discussion of how and why crystals work, beginning with a look at crystal structure and mineral composition. It also includes advice for selecting crystals for your toolbox, as well as detailed instructions for cleansing and programming crystals. Part 1 details dozens of applications for your crystals, ranging from meditation and building crystal grids to therapeutic applications like healing layouts and clearing the aura. Treat the techniques in this book like recipes; as you gain experience working with your beloved crystals, you will feel empowered to adapt the instructions to suit your needs.

The crystal directory that composes part 2 of this book includes many of the most popular healing stones available today, listed in alphabetical order. Each entry includes the chemical formula (and important trace elements), hardness, crystal system, related chakras, and a brief summary of the physical, psychological, and spiritual healing properties of each crystal. It would be impractical to describe the benefits of these stones in great detail, so I've distilled some of the more prominent effects to inspire your work with your own crystals.

Together, the human and mineral kingdoms can facilitate deep healing, shift consciousness, and help transform the planet. May the wonder and beauty of the mineral kingdom kindle your inner flame, offering you the tools you need to transform your life.

PART ONE

How and Why Crystals Work

1

Exploring Crystal Energy

THE EXPRESSION *CRYSTAL ENERGY* is heard everywhere these days, especially in the metaphysical community. We talk about stones that are brimming with positive energy, as well as those that transform our energy. Some practitioners describe how to recharge their crystals' energy, while others might try to seek a scientific model for how this otherwise mysterious force impacts our lives. In my own quest to understand the mineral kingdom I've searched high and low for the mechanisms responsible for the hows and whys of crystal healing.

EVERYTHING IS ENERGY

For starters, the world around us is not as solid as it appears. If we magnify any object, we see that the atoms of which it consists are mostly empty space. Each atom is made of tiny particles that remain in motion, and if we continue to magnify those atoms there will be tinier particles that compose it. Even *those* particles can be broken down into smaller units too. If we continue to do this, the smallest fundamental units of matter don't always behave like how we expect solid matter to act.

The same is true of energy such as light. Light is made of packets of energy called *photons*. Each photon emits its own energy signature. These units sometimes behave like matter, and they have measurable mass; other times they behave like waves, and they have momentum. Curiouser still is the fact that what we find when we examine them depends on what we *expect* to find. Seeking particles, we will see particles, while an expectation of waves produces waves. The observer and the observed are intrinsically linked.

Matter thus produces fields of energy such as electromagnetic fields (EMFs) according to its composition and structure. All vibration produces waves, which means that everything in the universe is generating waves of energy. These energy fields expand from their point of origin, moving at the speed of light. The closer you are to the source of an energy field, the easier it is to detect, and it diminishes in strength as you move farther away. Fields such as these are generated by the tissues in your body as well as by your electronics and appliances. Weaker fields are made by other objects in your environment. Everything under the sun—including the sun itself—has its own unique energy. It is theorized that psychically sensitive people can perceive these fields of energy and, with practice, can "read" or interpret them.

Crystals, then, are not simply inert matter magically endowed with healing qualities. Each crystal has a precise composition and orderly arrangement of atoms, ions, and molecules that yield an energy field that is just as orderly. Before we dive into how to use crystal energy for our own physical, psychological, and spiritual well-being, it is helpful to learn *how* and *why* crystals are so therapeutic.

Frequency, Amplitude, and Wavelength

There is one last important topic to cover before breaking down the basic energies of crystals, and that is the subject of *frequency* versus *amplitude*. These two terms describe the shape and pattern of a wave. In the figure below you can see the familiar S-shaped curve of a sine wave plotted on the axes of a graph. One complete cycle in the sine wave is called a *period*. The wave itself is measured in several different waves, including its frequency, amplitude, and wavelength.

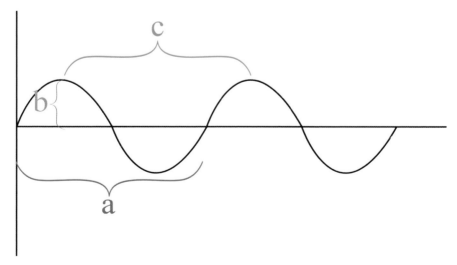

A sine-wave graph displaying (a) frequency,
(b) amplitude, and (c) wavelength

The *frequency* of a wave is the number of times the entire pattern repeats within a certain unit. Traditionally, this measurement is given in cycles per second, known as *hertz*. The *amplitude* of a wave is the distance from the center line; it is one-half the entire height of the wave. *Wavelength* is a measurement of the distance between two equal points on the wave, such as between the crests or troughs. For our purposes, frequency and wavelength will have similar functions,* so we'll simplify by discussing only the frequency and amplitude.

The frequency of a wave amounts to its unique signature, while its amplitude is the strength of that signal. To use a radio to illustrate this point, the frequency is the station to which you listen, while the amplitude represents its volume. In many metaphysical circles we pay a lot of attention to the frequency that we tune in to, but we often forget about amplitude. To return to our radio analogy, it's like turning the dial to your favorite station but forgetting to raise the volume enough for it to be audible.

The human energy field is composed of many different frequencies (hopefully) working in harmony. The spectrums of energy that we produce are influenced by what we think and eat, what we say and do, where we go, and with whom we spend our time. That means that our fundamental frequency and amplitude are constantly changing. Rocks and minerals, on the other hand, generate very stable energy waves because of their coherent structure and composition. They influence us through a process called *entrainment,* whereby two vibrating systems (in this case, fields of energy) synchronize and assume the same pattern or period. We will explore this in greater detail a little later.

ESSENTIAL CRYSTAL FUNCTIONS

The regularity and precision of crystal lattices endow the mineral kingdom with a number of basic universal functions. These mechanisms can be viewed as the essential ways that crystals interact with energy, both measurable and subtle. In short, all crystals have the following attributes:

---

*The frequency and wavelength of a wave of energy are proportional. The shorter the wavelength, the higher its frequency. In other words, a shorter wavelength means that a wave will have more cycles in one unit. Lower-frequency waves therefore have fewer repetitions and produce longer wavelengths.

- ▶ Coherence
- ▶ Amplificaton
- ▶ Reflection and refracttion
- ▶ Information storage
- ▶ Transmiting and receiving
- ▶ Translation

These essential crystal functions serve as the foundation for all the healing benefits that we experience when we work with crystals. Virtually all of these functions hinge on the coherent structure—and subsequently coherent energy—of crystals, so we will begin our exploration of the essential crystals functions there.

Coherence

The predominant feature of any crystal—whether solid or liquid, in your body or in the ground—is its innate order and perfection. These traits amount to a state known as *coherence*. In short, we could define coherence as "the quality of forming a unified whole." On a physical level this refers to the organization of a crystal's lattice: the arrangement of its atoms, ions, and molecules in an orderly fashion. Every group of components that represents the most fundamental unit of crystallinity, sometimes called a *unit cell,* repeats throughout the entire structure of a crystal. Using quartz as an example, the silica base forms a tetrahedron, a Platonic solid that resembles a pyramid with a triangular bottom; this tetrahedral unit repeats throughout the entirety of the crystal's physical structure, with virtually no deviation.

Looking at the physical structure of any mineral (as all minerals are crystalline), they exhibit the same degree of coherence in their makeup. This coherent structure is what results in most of the other measurable qualities that minerals have, such as their physical properties (like hardness and density), optical properties (like refractive index), and even magnetism, luminescence, and unique mechanical properties.

Since all forms of matter generate energy fields, the energies that surround your favorite stones are naturally influenced by the coherent internal order of their crystal lattices. Thus we can conclude that coherent structures will generate coherent energy fields. This isn't limited to the fields generated by crystals either; the coherence that crystals generate is made use of in laser technology and a number of other applications in science and industry too. Again returning

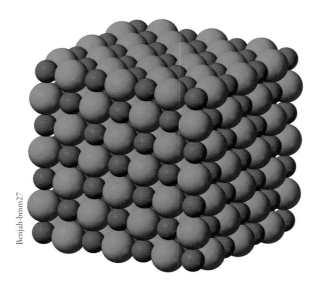

Benjah-bmm27

An example of a crystal lattice

to the example of quartz, when light enters the crystal, the lattice of the mineral actually organizes and aligns the photons (packets of light energy) so that the electric and magnetic waves from which light is composed are all unilaterally aligned. This process is called *polarization*.

When we work with crystals, we are benefiting from their innate perfection. The sea of vibrations through which we navigate each day is largely incoherent. Even the fields emitted by all the cells, tissues, organs, and systems of your body can be fraught with incoherent patterns. The reason that crystals are so helpful is that they train these incoherent fields by allowing their coherent, ordered energy to serve as a template for them. This action of entrainment occurs whenever two resonating fields interact; the field with the greater amplitude (or volume) "wins" by bringing the lesser amplitude into harmony with it.

Coherence is the single most important feature of working with crystal energy. On a physical level, quartz and other minerals clearly entrain the measurable fields of energy that our bodies produce. In other words, the orderly energy fields of crystals instill order on our own energy fields. Furthermore, this state of order and harmony is also imposed over the nonmeasurable or subtle energies. This is the primary mechanism behind healing with the gifts of the mineral kingdom.

Amplification

Coherent fields naturally project a louder and clearer message; this is why so many people find that quartz in particular amplifies energies. To illustrate this, imagine stepping into a crowded room and trying to listen to everyone's conversations at once. You'd probably pick up very little from this, and the sound would be a dull cacophony of white noise. Now, imagine if everyone began to recite the same words at exactly the same time; the message would be clearly audible *and* it would appear to increase in volume, as a coherent signal projects farther. This is the difference in the average field of energy and that of a crystal. It is the principle of cohering signals that allows crystals to apparently amplify signals (such as how quartz can magnify our intentions or amplify the effects of other stones). In truth, amplification ends up as a side effect of coherence.

Reflection and Refraction

When someone says the word *crystal,* it probably conjures images of transparent quartz or perhaps clear glass such as leaded-glass. The world of precious gemstones is populated by transparent stones too, and their relationship with light is one of the most important factors in humankind's long obsession with the crystal world. There are many properties that can factor into the optics of any crystal, but the two most important for understanding how crystals work are reflection and refraction. These two terms describe the behavior of a material in relation to light, and this influences how it interacts with other energy too.

Reflection occurs when incoming light bounces off a surface. If you play with your favorite crystal under full sunlight, there will come a moment when you feel you might blind yourself as you turn it in the light. This is the critical angle of reflection. Virtually all materials reflect visible light, in addition to many other wavelengths in the electromagnetic spectrum, of which light as we see it is only the minutest fraction. It is due to the reflection of specific wavelengths of light that we perceive all the color in the world; objects appear to be a certain color because they reflect photons of that particular color's wavelength, which is then received by your retina. Thus all substances must reflect something for us to see them.

With crystalline substances, the reflection takes place on a level deeper than just the physical. Crystals are tools for contacting higher consciousness because they reflect this consciousness back at us. The reason for this is because their highly ordered, coherent state is able to reflect back our own highly ordered, coherent state. However, more than likely, when we work with crystals, our experience will not be all rainbows and sunshine—it is more than probable that you will see some shadow in there too. This is because our imperfections (or at least our perceived imperfections) stand in the way of seeing our true nature: that we are utterly perfect beings created in divine love.

Refraction, on the other hand, takes place when light or other energy is bent as it travels. We often think of beautiful prismatic rainbows when we think of refraction, but the word *refraction* includes so much more. Magnifying glasses, burning globes, even funhouse mirrors all refract visible light because they change the angle by which this light travels. Crystals are also known for their refraction, and we see this best in transparent examples of minerals.

As light and other energy moves through a given medium, the angle is bent according to the arrangement of the molecules in that substance. If you've ever marveled over the way a straw appears to bend at a curious angle when seen in a glass of water, this is refraction in action. Refractive functions in crystals result in a redirection. The key word I associate with this is *focus*. Crystals are catalysts for change because they can improve the quality of our focus as well as shift that focus onto the right path. Energetically speaking, crystals reflect and refract energy such that they can direct the flow, bringing light, nourishment, and awareness to areas that need healing or change. When we work with crystals in a therapeutic setting, they help to focus and redistribute the flow of energy to the recipient's benefit.

The key to all of this is understanding that all materials interact with energy, both subtle and measurable forms of it. The measurable frequencies can be mapped out on the electromagnetic spectrum, including visible light, infrared (heat), X-rays, microwaves, radio waves, and more. However, science is beginning to apprehend that this gradient of energies doesn't include *all* the forces at work in our universe. Those that cannot be measured yet are referred to as *subtle energy*. If crystals interact with known energies in precise and predictable ways as a result of their inner and outer perfection, then they will similarly affect the spiritual energies that we haven't yet learned how to quantify.

The optical properties of crystals become a powerful metaphor when we talk about how crystals of all sorts interact with subtle or spiritual energy. Crystals, like the minerals and gemstones that are commonly used in healing practice, are such profound catalysts because they direct light, both visible and spiritual, where we most need it, often by illuminating the aspects of our psyche, body, and spirit that require deep healing.

Information Storage

I can remember reading about the use of quartz in electronics and computers since the very beginning of my interest in crystals. Many books and articles claimed that it was thanks to quartz that these devices had memory. I parroted this idea many times as I embarked on my journey with crystals; that is, until I learned better.

Crystals are amazing tools with many practical uses in science and industry. They can be used in crystal radios, as oscillators in watches, and in the world of optics, for many purposes. They are not, however, even remotely responsible for the data storage that your computer, smartphone, or any other device has. Maybe you are as surprised to learn this as I was. The truth is that quartz *is* used in electronics—it's cut into oscillators (as described in the section below) that translate or transduce one kind of energy into another, such as mechanical force into electricity and vice versa. Computer memory, on the other hand, owes to many other substances. The first hard drives used a metallic, magnetic substance to retain information. Metals can be more or less crystalline, so it's not wrong to think that crystals have a role in computer memory. Subsequent iterations of computer memory technology made use of the metal sili**con,** which isn't to be confused with quartz, which is sili**ca** (alpha silicon dioxide). Quartz contains silicon, but it also contains oxygen. Pure silicon is used because it is synthesized in a laboratory to be especially helpful for the specific purpose of data storage. Nowadays, computing technologies like quantum computing take advantage of new crystalline materials such as lithium niobate for storing information.

I don't bring this up to nullify the idea that crystals can—and do—store information. Rather, it's good to start with the facts and work our way forward from there. So before going any further with crystals, let's talk about digital information. One way to conceptualize what it is, is to think of it in terms of energy. All information is coded energy. When we speak, we convey information through the energy of sound. When we read, our brain translates what some arbitrary symbols mean and interprets them as the sounds, and therefore the ideas, they represent. Similarly, when computers store information they are doing so energetically.

Since all information is essentially a form of energy (and we already know that crystals have very special means of working with various types of energy), then it isn't too far a stretch to think that they store data too: to wit, crystals interact with the information carried by the energy fields they meet. Tiny imperfections in the crystal lattice act as storage cells, in which free-roaming electrons, photons, and other tiny particles become trapped. These pockets of energy are set in motion whenever we expose the crystal to the right energy source.

Sound, mechanical force, vibration, light, and even ionized breath can be sources of energy, or information, that cause the crystal lattice to squeeze or deform or otherwise set those trapped particles free. Crystals work as information storage tools because of the odd juxtaposition of their innate perfection—their coherency—with their minute imperfections, called *lattice defects*.

To take advantage of this, you must understand that information can only be reached via the same frequency with which it was installed in your crystal. Thus you must be in the same state of consciousness, the same frame of mind, so to speak, as the moment the information was imparted to the crystal. Crystals witness and record the energy of their environs, such as via their formation processes and from their experiences with humans too. The energy fields they meet are imprinted in the defects of the crystal lattice. Since each of these patterns of energy has its own frequency and wavelength, each one is a different channel on the cosmic radio. This is in part why two different people can access two very different expressions of the same crystal. Our individual state of being determines what we can connect with in the crystal, *regardless of our intention.* In this case, using the radio station as a metaphor, you can't just change the frequency or the station by merely intending to; you have to actually adjust the dial.

We take advantage of the storage capacity of crystals in a variety of ways. Programming, dedicating, and charging a crystal with our intention is an aspect of this. When we do so, we are uploading our direction or goal into the crystal's lattice. The crystal will then be able to broadcast this particular frequency within its highly ordered energy field.

Transmitting and Receiving

Much of what we accomplish through our work with crystals is a direct result of their ability to transmit and receive signals. Crystals and crystalline materials

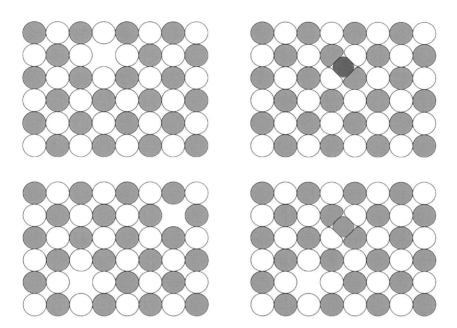

Examples of lattice defects

act as antennae that are attuned to precise frequencies, thereby allowing them to broadcast their signal outward. Likewise, they can receive energies, especially when the incoming frequencies are enharmonic to the crystals' own. As you may have already guessed, both transmission and reception are a function of a crystal's coherence.

Many years ago I learned from one of my teachers, Naisha Ahsian (now known as Samaya K. Aster), that rocks and minerals are *electromagnetic oscillators*. This means that they vibrate at specific frequencies, contingent on such factors as their chemical composition, crystal structure, and other physical properties that we will explore in depth in chapter 2. In our electronics we find quartz oscillators used as timekeeping tools; the precision with which they vibrate allows clocks to stay synchronized. This is an example of how oscillation relays information—in this case, the passage of a predetermined amount of time. The intrinsic order and perfection of any given stone means that it always oscillates at the same frequency, and this frequency is akin to the signal that the stone broadcasts wherever we place it and however we put it to use.

Thanks to minute defects in their lattices, crystals can also receive information or energy. These vacant places hold an energetic imprint of the fields that crystals encounter. An unprogrammed crystal or gemstone will thus absorb or record the energies it meets, while one that has been programmed will be less likely to do so unless the ambient energy field resonates enharmonically with the crystal itself. When we program a crystal (see chapter 5 for instructions on programming crystals), we imbue the stone with a specific set of frequencies to broadcast. In doing so, we allow the crystal to transmit these energy frequencies so that they will manifest in our lives.

A crystal lattice works like a fractal antenna, which repeats a fractal (or self-similar) pattern in its construction. These coherent, periodic geometries resemble the unit cells that make up crystal lattices. Fractal antennae are used in cell phones and microwave communication devices today; it is thanks to advances in this type of technology that today's cell phones no longer have external antennae like those of the past. Fractal antennae are also able to operate on many different frequencies simultaneously, whereas traditional antennae cannot. Because of this, crystals can send and receive several different frequencies at once, enabling them to connect with us on more than one level. This may explain why they are such multidimensional catalysts for healing and transformation.

Translation

Crystals are natural translators. No, they won't interpret a foreign language for you while on holiday, but they can help to translate one form of energy into another. This process is more appropriately referred to as *transduction*. With quartz (and a variety of other crystals, including those in your bones), the most commonly seen form of transduction is piezoelectricity. Other forms of energy translation include *pyroelectricity* and optical phenomena like *thermoluminescence, triboluminescence*, and *fluorescence*.

There are myriad misconceptions surrounding piezoelectricity in the crystal community. To begin, let's take a deeper look at what this property really is. Piezoelectricity is derived from the Greek word *piezein,* "to squeeze." To produce piezoelectricity, a crystal lattice must first be mechanically deformed by applying pressure such as squeezing, pressing, or striking. Quartz and other minerals produce an electrical charge under these conditions. To produce energy that can be measured with scientific equipment, a generous amount of force must be applied—in other words, it isn't something you can do with your bare hands. Once that mechanical stress is released and the crystal lattice returns to its normal shape, the substance becomes electrically neutral once again.

Many books on crystals toss around the word *piezoelectricity*, thinking that it explains how and why crystals heal. The truth is that there is never enough electricity being generated during a therapeutic application of crystals to produce any significant (or even measurable) effects. We know from our discussion above that the real reason why crystals work on us is because of the coherency of their structure and composition, and the resulting coherence this produces in their energy fields has a corresponding effect on our physical and subtle-energy bodies.

In any instance of transduction via crystals, one form of energy is being translated into another. Quartz watches take advantage of this principle by sending a minute electrical charge from the watch's battery into a small wafer of quartz crystal. This tiny crystal responds to the electricity by converting it into mechanical energy; as a result, it oscillates or vibrates at a precise rate. Your watch counts the number of oscillations and measures time with it. (This is similar to how quartz is used in most electronics. It isn't actually used to store information in your computers—a persistent crystal myth!)

The transductive quality that quartz and other minerals possess is what permits them to regulate and adapt their message or vibration to the task at hand. Spiritually speaking, when we input energy while co-creating with crystals via programming, setting an intention, visualization, and so on, the crystal translates this raw fuel into the appropriate form of energy needed to bring our intention to fruition. This does not necessarily mean that we cause the crystals to vibrate from piezoelectricity, although this may happen to a tiny degree that science hasn't yet measured. Instead quartz can apply its translation skills to all spectrums of energy, even the energies of the subtle or spiritual kind.

One of the bonuses of this quality of translation is that the energy fields of crystals are highly ordered. Thus, even if we connect with them while our consciousness is in a less-than-ordered state, the crystal will cohere the energy or information that we share with it. The mineral kingdom, composed of unimaginable crystalline treasures, has a tool for every task and a medicine for every ill that we face. Crystals can thus help us translate our goals into coherent messages to be sent to the universe so that we can achieve tangible results.

CRYSTALS AND
THE HUMAN BODY

To really appreciate the influence of crystals we need to look at the inherent crystallinity of the human body. Our physical form is more crystalline than we might imagine. The crystalline order found in living organisms is, in fact, one of the hallmarks of life itself. Examples of crystals and quasicrystals abound in our physical form, and this serves as the platform for how we can be healed and transformed by the energy of our healing stones. The collective system of crystalline materials in the body is sometimes referred to as the *liquid crystal body matrix.**

To give you an idea of the level of crystallinity within your own body, let's start with some of the more obvious examples. Your teeth and bones contain hydroxylapatite, a calcium phosphate mineral that provides durability and rigidity to the skeletal system. Hemoglobin, the compound in red blood cells, has more than one crystal form, depending on whether it carries oxygen or carbon dioxide. DNA, the biological blueprint found in every cell of your body, has a regular, repetitive structure that echoes the principles of crystallinity itself. Subtler evidence of your inner crystallinity can be found in your connective tissues and both your extracellular and intracellular fluids. Collagen fibers and other forms of connective tissue exhibit the long-range order of crystals, which provides them with their structural integrity, flexibility, and sensitivity. Lipid molecules in cell membranes, muscle proteins, and the water molecules in every cell of your body exist as a liquid crystal mesophase.

The liquid crystal matrix of your body exhibits many of the same characteristics as the crystals we use in healing. For starters, we can see evidence of transduction throughout the body. Your bones and collagen tissue are piezoelectric. Every step you take causes minute deformations of the physical structure of bone tissue in your feet and legs, and this results in a small electrical charge being generated. Your DNA is triboluminescent, which means that when it unwinds, tiny amounts of light are discharged as its structure is deformed for replication or protein synthesis. The liquid crystal matrix in your body is luminous in a very real and measurable sense.

---

*For a thorough discussion of the liquid crystal body matrix, please see my book *The Seven Archetypal Stones,* pp. 209–12; and Robert Simmons, *Stones of the New Consciousness,* pp. 31–35.

Thanks to this crystalline substrate, your body can send and receive energy and information. Not only does this happen in the form of chemical and electrical signals sent respectively via hormones or nerve cells, the body transmits other forms of messages as well. The electrical charges created by piezoelectricity are carried throughout the body, and the light generated by the DNA in the nucleus of your cells is also used for communication from one cell to the next. The larger energy fields of your heart and brain are also cohered, amplified, and transmitted by the liquid crystal body matrix.

Researchers have even found evidence that our tissues store memory, a result of their crystalline makeup. Connective tissue and the proteins in muscles retain a memory of physical injury and trauma, and it is probable that this extends to psychological and spiritual pain. If you've ever heard the expression "issues in your tissues" before, now you can see that there is a clear model for how and why we repress our psychological baggage and in turn cause physical conditions to arise from nonphysical causes.

Liquid Crystals and Structured Water

One of the most important substances in the human body is water. Water is dihydrogen oxide, or H_2O, and virtually every biological process in your body relies on or takes place in an aqueous solution. I'm sure you've heard the oft-quoted statistic that the human body is approximately 70 percent water by volume. However if we tallied up the total number of all the different molecules contained in the human body, we would see a different picture of just how important water truly is. Because water molecules are so tiny, they constitute at least 99 percent of our makeup by molecular count.

Water is the undisputed elixir of life, and in its perfect state it exists as a liquid crystal mesophase. Most of the water we encounter today is in a disordered, chaotic state (sometimes called *bulk water*), while the crystalline, organized form of water is called *structured water.* So that all the subcellular components of your body work properly, they are held together by a matrix of structured water. In other words, if the water in your cells isn't crystalline, your cells cannot perform their necessary duties.

Water molecules are *polar molecules,* meaning that although their net electrical charge is neutral, opposite ends of the molecules have mildly opposing electrical charges. This permits molecules of water to form weak bonds, called *hydrogen bonds,* which cause water to arrange itself in unique geometric forms at the most basic level. Thus water generally exhibits some degree of order; the shape of these liquid crystals can resemble the unit cells of any of the seven crystal systems.

Water molecules respond to the energies they meet, both subtle and gross. These energy fields either cause water to organize itself and demonstrate the properties of a liquid crystal, or they break down the organization of the water molecules, reverting the water to its bulk state. Many of us have seen the striking images of water crystals (in the form of ice) taken by Japanese scientist Dr. Masaru Emoto. His experiments, though controversial, illustrate that water itself has a memory, and that this memory influences the inherent crystallinity of water molecules.

Marcel Vogel, a visionary scientist and researcher who worked for IBM for twenty-seven years, is considered the father of liquid crystal technology. He observed liquid crystals in the laboratory setting for decades, and he continued to do so after retiring from the scientific arena to study crystal healing and psychic phenomena. Vogel is considered a forerunner of the modern crystal-healing movement, and he incorporated his scientific expertise into his work with crystals as healing tools. He also studied the effects of consciousness on crystal forms long before Dr. Emoto did, and he drew several important conclusions about the relationship between water, crystals, and consciousness.

From a structural level, Vogel noted the striking resemblance between molecules of quartz (SiO_2) and water (H_2O). These compounds have molecules with similar proportions and are both polar. His research suggests that this similarity allows these two compounds to have enharmonic energy fields—they are naturally in sync with each other.

Since we know that water molecules have a memory and that their organization (or lack thereof) can be influenced by electromagnetic fields, it stands to reason that the coherent, high-amplitude fields generated by quartz in particular (and other crystals more generally) can bring water molecules into a coherent state. Thus crystals can help transform bulk water into structured water. Marcel Vogel documented this in his personal experiments many times over. It is this transformation from bulk water to a liquid crystal mesophase that may initiate positive changes at the subcellular level in our body. The intrinsic order of the mineral kingdom is transferred to us through entrainment. This means that the energy fields produced by crystals, when coupled with a focused intent, can actually reorganize the water molecules of which we are made. Ultimately this

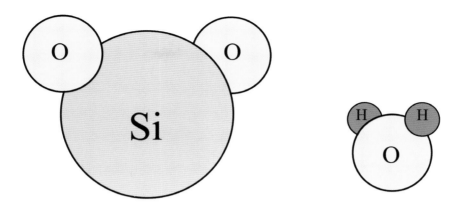

Note the similarity between molecules
of quartz (left) and water (right).

means that as we work with crystals, we become more crystalline ourselves, and this increased coherence improves our overall health and well-being. When we augment the liquid crystal matrix of the body, it becomes better equipped to maintain our health on every level.

Energy Transcends Pathology

There is another mechanism at work in crystal healing that I'd like to address. Although the changes in the liquid crystal body matrix are likely to be more than enough to cause healing to occur, another model for crystal healing works more on the electromagnetic level. With this model, the crystal's energy field more directly influences the human energy field, which works its way down to our physiology.

Earlier we touched on the idea of entrainment. To refresh your memory, when two vibrating systems such as electromagnetic fields meet, they will attempt to synchronize. This synchronization, called *entrainment,* is an exchange of information. The field with the higher amplitude will bring the lower-amplitude field into harmony with it. You've probably experienced this happening firsthand. Imagine that you're having a pretty good day, but someone walks into the room in a foul mood—perhaps seething with anger or morbidly depressed. Suddenly it feels like the happiness has been sucked out of the room. Or maybe you've been having an off day, but someone's kindness, enthusiasm, and positivity felt infectious, and you couldn't help but feel better. This is entrainment in action.

Lower-amplitude energy always yields to the higher-amplitude field. If we look at a crystal's energy field, it is innately more coherent than our own, and the "volume," or amplitude, of coherent fields is generally greater than that of incoherent ones. This means that when we work with crystals, their highly ordered energy fields are exchanging information with our own energy fields. If we supply them with enough focused, conscious intention, then their amplitude inevitably exceeds that of the human energy field, and we are necessarily brought into harmony with the energy of the crystal. You might experience warmth, tingling, a sense of calm, or any number of physical, psychological, or spiritual sensations that accompany this shift.

Something remarkable begins to happen when we change the human energy field: our consciousness changes along with it. This equates to a change in mood. Any significant change in mood causes a chain reaction that changes our biochemistry, as different neurotransmitters are released. These changes in our chemistry yield changes in heart rate, blood pressure, metabolism, and other systems of the body. Thus energy does influence the physical body. By using this model, we can explain how crystals affect change at every level of our being, including the physical, psychological, and energetic.

WE ARE LITERALLY MADE OF CRYSTALS

Crystal energy may at first seem to be nebulous and hard to categorize. However when we turn to the measurable and identifiable properties that crystals demonstrate, it is much easier to translate these qualities to the spiritual effects that crystals have. In this chapter we have examined how the basic qualities exhibited by crystals are functions of their inner and outer order, their coherence. We learned that the essential functions of all crystals include cohering and amplifying, reflecting and refracting, transmitting and receiving, translating, and storing energy and information.

By looking at our own bodies through the lens of crystallinity, we find that many of our tissues display the same basic functions as crystals and that we are literally made of crystals, both liquid and solid. By partnering with the mineral kingdom intentionally, we can influence the level of coherency and crystallinity in our bodies, thereby steering us toward health and well-being on every level of existence.

Crystals are powerful tools that can transform our lives. Though we've looked at crystals from a broad perspective in this chapter, the essential functions and healing mechanisms discussed here apply to virtually every healing stone that you will meet. However the individual makeup and structure of these stones differ, and from these differences are born the wide array of healing properties espoused by the many types of crystals used in healing. In the following chapter we will dive deep into the factors that determine what each stone offers us in terms of its formation process, composition, crystal structure, hardness, and color.

2

Decoding Crystals

YOU MIGHT BE WONDERING WHY all stones don't produce the same results if they all use the same mechanisms discussed in the previous chapter. The answer lies in the individual character of each stone's energy field—something that results from all the other properties of a given rock or mineral, such as its composition, crystal system, habit (outer form or external morphology), hardness, specific gravity, diaphaneity, purity, mass, and even color. Each of these properties defines the individual qualities of the energy field a crystal or stone produces, but their innate coherency is the underlying attribute that unites them all.

The two primary drivers of a crystal's energy are its composition and its structure. The former describes the ingredients of the mineral, and the latter dictates how those ingredients come together. Most branches of mineral science organize various minerals according to the chemical bases from which they are made, such as oxides, carbonates, silicates, and halides. The crystal systems reflect the seven fundamental types of symmetry displayed by the internal lattices of a crystal. A rock or mineral's healing qualities are also influenced by its formation process, hardness, transparency, morphology, and any other associated minerals or trace elements. To a lesser extent, quality, mass, color, and other factors play a role in a crystal's energy too.

In this chapter we will dive deep into the primary factors that influence the energy and function of every stone in your collection. We'll start with formation processes and then examine how a crystal's structure and composition determine the energies we experience from it. From there we'll take a brief tour through color and hardness. After exploring each of these properties, we'll take a look at a couple of minerals, both familiar and unfamiliar, to do our best to put all the information into practice.

FORMATION PROCESS

One of the first things I will research when I meet a new rock or mineral formation is its formation process. We briefly touched on the three formation processes—igneous, sedimentary, and metamorphic—in the introduction. These principles of formation often relate to the big picture of how a stone's energy is expressed.

A rock or mineral's formation process can usually provide an idea of the level of its action. Igneous minerals work on the level of an issue's root cause, while sedimentary stones typically reflect surface-level concerns. Metamorphic stones are related to processes of change and transformation. A clear understanding of how your favorite stones are formed can provide insight into where they direct their healing energy; the precise nature of their energy is more clearly discerned by examining their structure and composition.

It's important to note that there are minerals that are formed by more than one of the three formation processes, though typically just one process per stone.* Chalcedony, aventurine, and garnet are good examples of this. We have to look into the provenance of the individual specimens with which we are working to better understand this. Garnets that result from igneous activity will have a more fiery energy than those that result from metamorphism, for example. Online resources such as mindat.org can help you locate the formation process of many of the mineral specimens in your collection.

Igneous Rocks and Primary Minerals

Igneous rocks and their constituent minerals are the result of *primary formation processes*. They generally result from the cooling of molten rock (called the *liquid-magmatic process*), though primary minerals frequently emerge from hydrothermal and pneumatolytic processes, in which mineral-rich waters and vapors, respectively, deposit fresh crystal formations. Common igneous rocks include granite, rhyolite, basalt, pumice, scoria, obsidian, pegmatite, and andesite. Primary minerals include most varieties of quartz (agate, clear quartz, amethyst, smoky quartz, citrine, chalcedony, etc.), apatite, lepidolite, topaz,

---

*Sometimes rocks and minerals are subjected to partial metamorphism and thus may retain most of the characteristics of their parent rock while still portraying the energies of metamorphic rocks too.

peridot, the feldspar group (amazonite, moonstone, sunstone, labradorite, etc.), garnets, fluorite, and many more minerals. Upward of 65 percent of the earth's crust is composed of igneous rocks.

Igneous rocks and primary minerals are the start of the rock cycle, the very first rocks to emerge from the earth's primordial magma. Thus they represent new beginnings and fresh starts. Primary minerals provide the spark of inspiration needed to get the ball moving when we feel stale or stagnant. These rocks and minerals also provide stability and tenacity. Their fiery origins point to their ability to burn off disharmonious energy patterns too. These stones resonate with the idea of pure potential; engaging with them facilitates the recognition and manifestation of your own potential. Igneous rocks and minerals often catalyze the realization of your own growth and healing. They inspire learning, growth, creativity, and freedom. They can be used to break through limiting circumstances, just as lava bursts forth from the earth's crust during a volcanic eruption. Igneous rocks and minerals can assist in transforming disorders of the metabolism and digestive systems. They are also able to penetrate the causal level of long-standing illnesses and conditions, reaching into the source of any issue at hand.

Sedimentary Rocks and Secondary Minerals

Sedimentary rocks and minerals comprise the group formed by *secondary formation processes*. They are referred to as "secondary" because they are made from the breakdown of extant rocks and minerals that are reformed as sedimentary formations. The stages of sedimentary rock formation are weathering, transportation, sedimentation, and lithification. Sandstone, shale, limestone, chalk, conglomerates, and breccias represent the most common sedimentary rocks. Secondary minerals include calcite, aragonite, azurite, selenite, anhydrite, halite, dolomite, pyrite, malachite, chrysocolla, and opal.

Sedimentary rocks and secondary minerals are broken down and put back together as a result of interacting with their environment. These stones can provide insight into how our own environs are influencing our lives. Sedimentary rocks also have a strong relationship with memory and karma, as their strata hold the records of the planet's history. These stones reach into the subconscious mind, helping us come to terms with old patterns buried in the subconscious. Because sedimentary stones are the product of breaking down other stones, they can help us dissolve and dismantle situations. They form only on or at the surface of the planet and thus relate to more superficial conditions in the human body such as skin issues, mild injuries, and colds and flu. They can help us manage environmental sensitivities such as allergies.

Metamorphic Rocks and Tertiary Minerals

Metamorphic rocks are formed when heat and pressure transform igneous and sedimentary rocks into new substances. The forces applied to these stones cause their constituents to reorganize themselves into new minerals that take new shapes. Collectively, the processes of metamorphism are called *tertiary formation processes*. Gneiss, marble, quartzite, schist, and slate are among the most well-known metamorphic rocks. Examples of tertiary minerals include garnet, kyanite, amphiboles, serpentine, lazurite (the main component in lapis lazuli), rhodonite, emerald, and many others.

Metamorphic rocks and tertiary minerals are the preeminent stones of transformation. They support the internal processes required for positive change to be made in our lives. These rocks and minerals come to our aid when the pressures of life feel overwhelming, and they stimulate self-reflection so that we can find what we need to change so as to leverage these periods of transition for self-actualization. Tertiary stones also promote strength, courage, and stamina; we can work with them to provide a sense of safety and protection while we grow. In the physical body we can use metamorphic rocks to knit together broken tissues, to treat conditions of the circulatory system, and to deal with psychosomatic illness.

THE SEVEN CRYSTAL SYSTEMS

Crystal systems fall into seven categories: cubic, tetragonal, orthorhombic, trigonal, hexagonal, monoclinic, and triclinic. These categories are classified as such according to the relationships of their crystal axes based on the shapes of the crystal lattices. Fourteen different lattice patterns are organized into the seven crystal systems, while those mineraloids that do not exhibit a crystal lattice belong to an eighth category, amorphous. Generally speaking, minerals that share a crystal system will often exhibit similarly shaped crystals.

While a stone's formation process indicates the level to which it might direct its energy, the crystal system indicates the mechanism or overall activity of its energy. The geometry (or lack thereof) encoded in each of these groups of stones represents the direction and focus of the crystal's energy; in this way the crystal systems are the personality types of the mineral kingdom.

Two minerals with the same chemical composition will be distinguished by their crystal structure. Calcite and aragonite, for example, share the formula $CaCO_3$. Calcite, however, is a trigonal crystal, while aragonite is orthorhombic, so they have different crystal structures, which results in different crystal shapes, colors, and optical phenomena.

Some stones in your healing toolbox will be combinations of different minerals that express different crystal systems, such as rutilated quartz (quartz is trigonal; rutile is tetragonal) and lapis lazuli (pyrite and lazurite are cubic, while calcite is trigonal). Rocks are often composed of minerals of different crystal systems, so one can look at which minerals are the most prevalent to identify the crystal system that will have the greatest influence over its healing qualities.

Cubic Crystal System

The cubic crystal system is also called *isometric,* meaning "equal measure." Crystal lattices that form this group have three equal axes that meet at ninety-degree angles (right angles). Cubic crystals are the most regular and symmetrical of all the crystal systems. Energetically they engender stability, order, and structure. Cubic crystals have an overall settling and grounding influence, and they also promote organization. Overall, cubic crystals help us at the most fundamental level of our being, helping us build a foundation to wholeness.

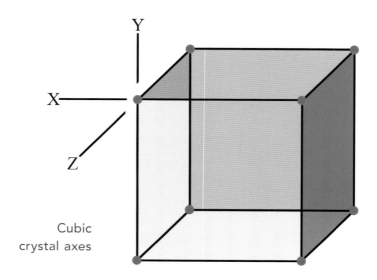

Cubic
crystal axes

Cubic crystals do not distort light that moves through their lattices; they leave it just as it is. This represents how cubic crystals can be used to promote contentment and consistency when we use them in healing. These stones can teach us the value of nonattachment and inaction at the right time. Crystals with cubic structures also tend to help enforce healthy boundaries. They consolidate our energy and help draw it inward to repair imbalances. Cubic crystals support manifestation by drawing our focus and energy to the material plane, but this can occasionally result in becoming overly materialistic if not countered. These crystals also tend to promote greater focus and drive, and they motivate us to stay the course.

Applied to our physical well-being, cubic crystals are helpful when treating conditions such as insomnia, indigestion, and injuries to the face or jaw. Cubic minerals often relate to themes of structure, and they may be used to improve or correct imbalances of our physical structure, such as the skeletal system, as well as the cellular structures. Cubic minerals are adept at correcting damaged DNA, and they support healthy fetal development.

Cubic crystal structures activate the root chakra. Common examples of minerals with a cubic crystal structure include diamond, garnet, fluorite, halite, lapis lazuli, magnetite, several native metals (gold, silver, iron, and copper to name a few), pyrite, and sodalite.

Tetragonal Crystal System

The tetragonal crystal system is characterized by three axes that meet at right angles; two are of equal length, while the third axis is longer. The tetragonal crystal system has fewer mineral species than any of the other crystal systems. Generally speaking, these crystals balance opposite forces, and they exert a stabilizing influence that mitigates vacillation and inconstancy.

Tetragonal crystals work as reflectors; they reveal the areas of our lives that need greater balance. Tetragonal minerals can absorb and transmute negative or disharmonious forces. When we work with them for healing, they can lift guilt and shame while helping us understand how these emotions have arisen. Many tetragonal minerals inspire creativity and attract new opportunities; they help us achieve a balance between the heart and the mind, thereby leading to greater self-awareness and a sense of sovereignty.

Tetragonal minerals foster a sense of resolution. They can help us through moments when we feel utterly depleted, rerouting our efforts away from trying

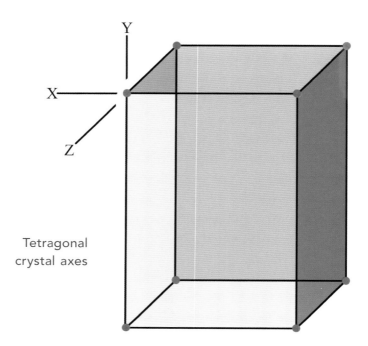

Tetragonal
crystal axes

to be productive and toward healing and wellness. These crystals help us find a better balance between giving and receiving. They are protective, though they have a tendency to reinforce barriers that we may already have in place. It is necessary to practice vulnerability when working with tetragonal crystals so as not to feel alienated or aloof. Tetragonal minerals also deepen our attunement to higher planes of consciousness and facilitate contact with the higher self.

For our physical health, tetragonal minerals tend to act on the lungs and respiratory system, as well as on the large intestine and processes related to physical growth and metabolism. Tetragonal minerals help us balance taking care of our body while attending to other areas of our life. They have an overall rejuvenating effect on the body and mind. Tetragonal crystal structures also activate the sacral chakra. Common tetragonal minerals include apophyllite, cassiterite, cristobalite, rutile, vesuvianite, wulfenite, and zircon.

Orthorhombic Crystal System

Orthorhombic minerals exhibit three axes, each of different lengths, which all meet at right angles. Orthorhombic minerals represent the still point where order and chaos meet. They tap into the creative potential of the universe for

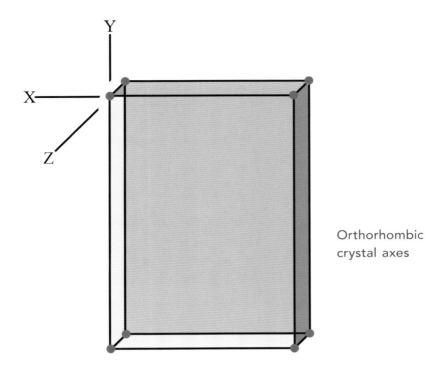

Orthorhombic
crystal axes

the act of random creation. Minerals belonging to the orthorhombic group often have four faces along the length of the crystal, parallel to the central axis of their form. Sometimes these minerals, like aragonite, form crystal shapes that mimic hexagonal prisms but are in fact composed of three crystals with rhombic cross-sections.

Working with orthorhombic crystals brings greater perspective and a dynamic sense of balance. These crystals help clear away and purify old patterns, especially those that keep us locked in a state of imbalance. Their energies tend to be more projective than receptive, and they influence the bigger picture. Minerals with orthorhombic structures help you see how and where you fit into the universe, and they encourage you to have the motivation and drive to improve your station in life. Orthorhombic stones help you focus on the tasks that matter the most, allowing you to make the greatest change with the least amount of effort. These minerals can also help in cases of indecision, providing an impartial and disciplined energy. They are also protective and help you release old worldviews and programming that holds you back.

Crystals with an orthorhombic structure can improve the function of the circulatory system, balance the body's temperature, and alleviate conditions affecting the joints and mobility. These stones are particularly useful for treating conditions of the spine, and they may improve the health of the nervous system and small intestine.

Orthorhombic crystals activate the third eye chakra. Some of the more common orthorhombic minerals include chiastolite (andalusite), barite, bronzite, cerussite, chrysocolla, danburite, hemimorphite, marcasite, peridot, prehnite, topaz, and zoisite (tanzanite, thulite, etc.).

Monoclinic Crystal System

The monoclinic crystal system has three axes of unequal length, not unlike the orthorhombic system. However in this crystal system, two of the axes meet at right angles, while the third is anything but 90 degrees. They often exhibit crystalline forms derived from the parallelogram. These crystals have an energy that is directional and that generates forward momentum.

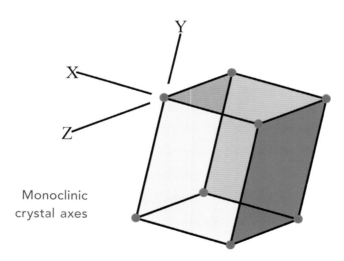

Monoclinic
crystal axes

Monoclinic crystals drive us forward in our growth by clearing the path for us, helping to keep us focused on what lies ahead. They offer an encouraging energy and help us strive to attain our dreams. These crystals enhance our perception, enabling us to see into the truth of things. Monoclinic crystals are gently protective and purifying, thereby helping us face our fears and feel safe while doing so. They are also effective for resolving guilt and shame.

Sometimes monoclinic minerals can make us feel rushed or impatient.

Because they are so focused on the future, they sometimes cause us to overlook destructive behaviors in the present. For this reason it is necessary to temper the use of these stones with regular meditation and self-care.

Working with monoclinic minerals targets the extremities of the body. These stones initiate detoxification, and they can help us examine the link between repressed emotions and our physical health. Monoclinic minerals are adept at soothing tension held in the body, and they can resolve conditions that involve the connective tissues.

Monoclinic crystals stimulate the throat chakra. Some examples of monoclinic minerals include azurite, howlite, jade (both nephrite and jadeite), kunzite, lepidolite, malachite, moonstone, muscovite (mica), orthoclase feldspar, selenite, and staurolite.

Triclinic Crystal System

Triclinic crystals are characterized by three axes of unequal lengths, none of which meet at right angles. On the surface, triclinic crystals appear to have the least amount of symmetry. Their seemingly hidden coherence and order help us reach into the unseen world. Because of this, triclinic minerals often help us discover how our beliefs and attitudes—conscious or unconscious give rise to our challenges in life.

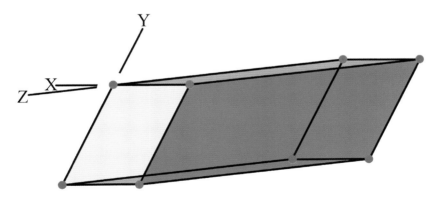

Triclinic crystal axes

Triclinic minerals assist in integrating new and different states of energy. They are the stones of ascension, allowing the body, mind, and spirit to access and anchor higher states of being. Minerals with triclinic structures deepen intuition, expand the senses beyond the physical plane, and help us forge a deeper relationship with our spirit guides and guardians. Because they reach into the unseen world, triclinic crystals also reveal past-life memories, karma, and childhood trauma so that they can be transformed.

The triclinic stones usher us toward a state of completion. These crystals also help balance opposing polarities, such as yin and yang, masculine and feminine. They represent the ability to break free from limiting expectations, whether our own or those of our loved ones or society. Triclinic minerals are the stones of reinvention; they can initiate profound transformation to enable us to become more truly who we are meant to be.

Triclinic crystal structures affect us more at the soul level than the physical level. These stones can reveal the karmic implications behind a physical illness or injury, and they can help the soul become more anchored in the physical body. Triclinic crystals often support the health of the endocrine and reproductive systems too.

Triclinic minerals open the crown chakra. Ajoite, amazonite, kyanite, labradorite, larimar, rainbow moonstone, rhodonite, sunstone, turquoise, and ulexite are examples of triclinic minerals.

Trigonal Crystal System

Trigonal minerals are among the most common stones we use in our healing toolboxes. They have four axes; three are of equal length and form angles of 120 degrees from one another. The fourth axis may be longer or shorter, and it is perpendicular to the other axes. The trigonal crystal system is a subset of the hexagonal crystal system, wherein its members exhibit threefold rather than sixfold symmetry. Many are hexagonal in cross-section, while most others are rhombic.

The fundamental symbol of the trigonal crystal system is the triangle, representing its triune symmetry. Trigonal crystals help us simplify life inside and out. They have a regulating influence that helps rein in our energy and resources and redirects our focus when needed. Trigonal minerals boost personal energy, and they radiate or broadcast our intentions in all directions. These stones are dynamic tools for healing.

Trigonal minerals reset the metabolic processes in the physical body, allowing the body to reboot itself. They are ideal for correcting a variety of physical imbalances, as they offer a mediating point between deficiency and excess.

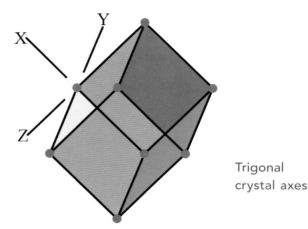

Trigonal
crystal axes

These minerals are usually the most adept at supporting the immune system.

Trigonal minerals strengthen the solar plexus chakra. The most well known of the trigonal minerals is quartz (including agate, chalcedony, jasper, amethyst, rose quartz, etc.), although some other common trigonal minerals are calcite, dioptase, dolomite, hematite, ruby, sapphire, and the tourmaline group.

Hexagonal Crystal System

Hexagonal minerals have four axes. Like trigonal minerals, three of the axes are arranged at 120-degree angles from one another, while the fourth is perpendicular to them. True hexagonal minerals display sixfold symmetry and thus have

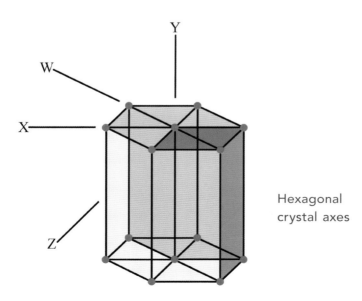

Hexagonal
crystal axes

great order to their crystalline forms. These crystals are masters of efficiency and growth.

The energy of hexagonal crystals is expansive and balancing. They help to balance masculine and feminine polarities within us, and they stimulate growth. Hexagonal minerals help us cultivate an inquisitive, creative state of being. These stones help us explore ourselves and the universe. They have a way of helping us understand how we fit into the bigger picture, and they sharpen our intuitive faculties as we explore life. Hexagonal stones also facilitate meditation and spiritual development.

When we work with hexagonal minerals they open our heart and help release barriers to love. These stones foster healthy, authentic communication, and they can deepen our relationships with everyone we meet. Many hexagonal crystals boost self-love and help us cultivate love and compassion for those around us. Hexagonal crystals ensure a reciprocal balance of communication and resources in our relationships. They emphasize themes of service and help us put our gifts into the world in a practical way.

Hexagonal minerals relate to the physical as well as the spiritual heart, and thus they can be used to treat disorders such as arrhythmia, high blood pressure, and irregular heartbeat. Hexagonal crystals are excellent pain relievers, and they may alleviate cramps and tightness, especially in the hands and feet. Use these stones for the health of the liver, gallbladder, and muscle tissue.

Hexagonal crystals open the heart chakra. Apatite, beryl (such as aquamarine, emerald, heliodor, and morganite), covellite, graphite, sugilite, vanadinite, and zincite are minerals with hexagonal crystal structures.

Amorphous, the Noncrystal System

For our purposes, the amorphous group serves as the eighth and honorary crystal system. However, by their very nature, amorphous materials are noncrystalline, as they lack crystal lattices altogether. This makes the stones in this group mineraloids, as crystal lattices are a requisite for being a mineral.

Because they lack a distinct crystal structure, these gemstones boast energies that work on a primal, ineffable level. Amorphous stones sit on the cusp of crystallinity; some, like obsidian and tektites, are natural glass, which is considered a supercooled liquid rather than solid matter. They represent the primordial void of creation. These noncrystalline stones are catalysts for profound growth; they impose no agenda and allow energy to pass freely and rapidly. Like water,

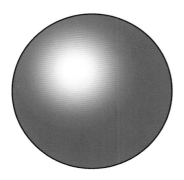

Some amorphous stones, like opal, have spherical units, so the circle or sphere is sometimes used to represent the amorphous group.

amorphous mineraloids symbolize change and flux; they therefore have a resonance with our emotional body and can help us examine the emotional makeup of the subconscious mind.

Amorphous stones impart flexibility. They enable us to adapt and evolve at a rapid pace. Many of them reflect back to us the nature of the true self, and they help us observe this without judgment. Amorphous stones also release deeply seeded behavioral conditioning. They calm the spirit and allow us to dream of infinite possibilities.

Stones with an amorphous structure relate to the fluids of the body. They can be used to treat conditions of the circulatory system, lymphatic system, and urinary tract, as well as to hydrate mucous membranes, tear ducts, and skin. These stones are sometimes used to treat conditions affecting the brain and nervous system, including seizures and migraines.

Strictly speaking, amorphous stones do not relate to any of the seven main chakras by structure alone; however, they may influence any chakra because of their adaptable and mutable energy. Many amorphous mineraloids are used in healing today, including amber, fulgurite, jet, obsidian, opal, shungite, and tektite (moldavite, indochinite, Libyan desert glass). Several popular artificial stones are also noncrystalline, such as goldstone, opalite, and brightly colored slag (usually sold as obsidian); each of these is in fact man-made glass.

MINERAL COMPOSITION

When I meet a new rock or mineral, my very first question is always, "What's in it?" We often get the most immediate idea of what energy a crystal offers us by looking at its composition.

The very first correlations I made between mineral science and crystal healing resulted from paying attention to the composition of stones. I've always been a voracious reader, and in my college years I dove into as many books on crystals as I could find. At the same time I was working part-time in an earth science museum on campus, which happened to be home to one of the largest mineral collections in the southeastern United States. I noticed that different authors from different time periods often used similar language when describing minerals with similar compositions: iron-bearing stones are strengthening, silicates are amplifying, and lithium stones are soothing. In many cases it was apparent that these writers weren't familiar with the science behind the stones; they were tapping into their energy from an intuitive rather than an analytical perspective. This prompted me to start researching the connections between composition and structure, and shortly thereafter I found other authors who had also pursued this idea.

Learning the chemical composition of the stones in your toolbox can be an enlightening experience. Oftentimes we find ourselves repeatedly drawn to minerals with common elements, like my friend who just couldn't get enough copper minerals, or a student who was amazed to learn that some of her favorite new additions—adamite, smithsonite, and zincite—all contained zinc. Just like our bodies have cravings for certain foods rich in particular vitamins, our nonphysical bodies will crave specific energies, such as those represented by the composition of many of our beloved crystal healing tools.

Proportion is something to consider when working with the composition of your favorite stones. Both rhodochrosite and morganite obtain their characteristic pink color from manganese; however, there is significantly more manganese in rhodonite ($MnSiO_3$) than in morganite, a variety of beryl whose color is derived from only trace amounts of manganese. So if you need a strong manganese energy, look to minerals with a higher concentration of the element rather than those with tiny amounts; the same is true for other chemical elements whose energy you are looking to work with.

A complete look at the energetic signatures of every element on the periodic table is outside the scope of this work. The elements listed below make up many of the most popular stones in our collections.

Aluminum (Al)

Aluminum is a very common mineral-forming element. It is used for greater mental focus, and it can calm and clear the mind. This element fosters greater understanding of beliefs and mental patterns that shape our reality. Aluminum-bearing minerals help us shift perspectives and see life from a new vantage point. These stones soothe frayed nerves, assuage fear, and help to eliminate guilt. They also allow us to access higher states of consciousness. This element breaks down barriers between spirit and matter and stimulates past-life recall, clairaudience, and better connection to your spirit guides.

Aluminum-bearing rocks and minerals treat disorders of the mind and brain, stimulate memory, and improve sleep. These stones also help reduce upset stomach and counteract physical weakness.

Beryllium (Be)

Beryllium is a fairly rare element in the earth's crust. It is nourishing to the feminine, receptive energies within us. Many beryllium-bearing minerals have strong spiritual qualities, and this element may catalyze our evolutionary processes. These stones foster deep insight and make us more perceptive. Beryllium-rich stones also help us create and achieve our goals.

Beryllium is soothing and balancing to the physical body. Minerals containing this element treat conditions of the female reproductive system and stimulate an underactive thyroid. They support hormonal balance in men and women alike.

Boron (B)

Boron is classified as a nonmetal, but it displays many of the properties of metals. It is balancing psychologically and helpful in treating cases of nervousness, fear, and panic. Boron-rich stones invite greater harmony, and they help us believe and trust in the goodness of the universe. They also help us feel as if we are in control of our lives.

Boron-rich minerals can treat conditions of the eyes, skin, and intestines. They have a detoxifying effect, and they also support the function of the kidneys and other eliminatory organs.

Calcium (Ca)

Calcium is a vital component of the body's structure, and in mineral form it supports themes of structure. It is sometimes binding and limiting energetically, helping us enforce healthy boundaries and break bad habits. This mineral-forming element also counteracts confusion and fear. Minerals that contain calcium allow us to process and integrate our emotions, beliefs, and experiences by making nebulous patterns feel more solid.

Calcium minerals may also improve musculoskeletal health and circulation. They are used for treating pain and injury, anxiety, and insomnia. These minerals regulate the heartbeat, encourage healthy cellular metabolism, and support healthy replication of the DNA.

Carbon (C)

Carbon is the quintessential element of organic compounds, yet it is common in the world of rocks and minerals as an inorganic compound. Carbon builds the bridge between the biological and mineral kingdoms. Carbonates—minerals containing a carbon and oxygen base—stimulate and stabilize growth. Carbon offers structure, helping to bring order out of chaos.

Carbon often relates to cleansing and detoxification in its mineral form. Minerals that contain pure carbon compounds have a filtering effect on the body, mind, and spirit, while carbonates may help us examine the subconscious so that we can choose to let go of outdated beliefs and feelings that limit us.

Chlorine (Cl)

Chlorine is deeply cleansing. It releases tension and constriction, both in the mind and the body. It can also lessen sensitivity, helping us become more resilient when faced with stress and challenging people or situations. Minerals containing chlorine (or chloride, an ion of chlorine) promote optimism and a sense of freedom. They assist digestion and the assimilation of nutrients.

Chromium (Cr)

Chromium, whose name derives from the Greek word for "color," often produces vividly colored minerals. Being regenerative, this element stimulates growth on all levels. Many chrome-bearing minerals relate to the heart chakra, and chromium indeed helps to open and activate this energy center. Chromium has a shielding effect on the energy field. It strengthens the ability to receive intuitive information, such as through clairaudience, and fosters independence, discipline, and drive to further the quest of self-realization.

Chromium-bearing minerals help the body regulate blood sugar, cholesterol, and hormonal balance. Just as it relates to the metaphorical, spiritual heart, this mineral-forming element helps to heal and balance the physical heart and is used in the treatment of all kinds of cardiovascular conditions. Chromium also supports metabolism and weight loss.

Copper (Cu)

Copper is a highly energetic mineral-forming element. Pure copper is an excellent conductor of electricity, and minerals containing copper help to conduct life force and other spiritual energies. In astrology, copper is connected to Venus, relating to matters of love, beauty, and the arts. This metal is connected to the archetypal Great Mother, and thus stones containing copper help us tap into the Divine Feminine. Copper-bearing minerals provide emotional relief, and they emphasize the theme of cooperation, thereby facilitating empathy, understanding, and cooperation. Copper stimulates dreaming and creativity, and it helps us cultivate love for all beings.

Working with copper-bearing minerals can reduce pain and treat some conditions of the circulatory system such as anemia and varicose veins. Copper minerals also help in the treatment of inflammation and arthritis. Note that some copper minerals may be toxic if mishandled.

Fluorine (Fl)

Fluorine is often found in minerals as the anion fluoride. It has an overtly mental energy that enables us to break free from limiting habits and beliefs. It stimulates and expands the mind, fostering flexibility, learning, and a quick wit. Ultimately, fluorine-bearing minerals initiate a sense of spiritual freedom.

Fluoride-bearing minerals support the health and well-being of the skeletal system. They treat sharp pains and stimulate the kidneys. They may also be used to treat conditions affecting the mucous membranes, skin, and nervous system.

Hydrogen (H)

Hydrogen is the single most abundant chemical element in the universe. On earth, much of our hydrogen is available as water, and in minerals it is usually present as water (H_2O) or hydroxide (OH). Water in a crystal's composition points to a relationship with the emotions. Minerals containing water can help clarify unseen thoughts and feelings lurking below the surface of the conscious mind. These stones can cleanse and clear on the physical, psychological, and spiritual levels.

Hydroxide, on the other hand, is not quite water since it lacks a hydrogen atom. When present in minerals, hydroxide has a purgative effect, and hydroxide-bearing stones can flush out hidden conditions. (See also *oxygen*.)

Iron (Fe)

Iron is traditionally connected to the planet Mars and is thus related to themes of conflict, ambition, and strength. Iron-bearing rocks and minerals have a descending effect on the energy field, making them excellent allies for grounding. Many iron-rich stones support personal power and confidence. Because of their grounding, descending effects, iron-bearing minerals can help us when we are too mentally focused; they help us get back in touch with our bodies and be more present in the world around us.

Traditionally, iron and iron-rich minerals have been used to treat conditions of the heart and circulatory system (anemia, low blood pressure, clots, etc.), reproductive organs, and immune system, as well as for general pain.

Lead (Pb)

Lead is ascribed to the influence of Saturn in astrology, making it the element of karma. Lead has a slackening effect on the body, mind, and spirit; it slows down cycles to enable us to investigate them more consciously. Lead can be grounding, but it lacks the stability and strength of iron. Lead can prevent the intrusion of foreign energies into the human energy field. Working with lead-based minerals yields self-control and strengthens your sense of duty. Lead lightens the mood and helps us break bad habits, release dogmatic beliefs, and escape from restricting influences.

Lead-bearing minerals are used to treat cases of poisoning, especially from heavy metals. These stones can also target diseases that affect the stomach, intestines, and circulatory system. Rocks and minerals containing lead can slow the development of chronic illness. Exercise caution, as lead minerals are usually toxic if mishandled.

Lithium (Li)

Lithium is truly the metal of the New Age. It expands consciousness, soothes turmoil, and helps one find greater emotional balance. Lithium tends to activate the higher heart chakra, located in the area of the thymus, and it grants buoyancy to our mood. Lithium minerals can unlock higher states of consciousness, unwind tension, and improve the memory. They promote acceptance and surrender, and they teach humility and devotion. Lithium minerals are among the deepest and most insightful spiritual healers in the mineral kingdom.

Lithium minerals are sometimes used to treat psychological disorders (anxiety, bipolar disorder, depression, PTSD), high blood pressure, muscle spasms, neurological disorders, and conditions of the kidneys and liver. Lithium-bearing stones can break down calcifications and deposits in the body, particularly in the joints and blood vessels. They can also be helpful in treating or supporting people with autism.

Magnesium (Mg)

Magnesium is an abundant mineral on earth. It restores movement to stuck and stagnant energies and emotions. It supports an open heart and helps us release emotional burdens. Many magnesium minerals impart resilience and help us tackle our fears head-on. They invite a positive attitude, lower stress, and evoke good cheer.

Magnesium-bearing minerals have a cooling effect on the body. Use them to treat high blood pressure, anxiety, constipation, asthma, muscle cramps, pain, and numbness. Magnesium minerals are sometimes used to prevent clotting and improve circulation. Stones containing magnesium may alleviate stress-related conditions, especially those affecting the digestive system.

Manganese (Mn)

Manganese is grounding and protective, particularly for the heart chakra and the emotional body. It helps us feel more secure with our emotions, thereby reducing anxiety, irritability, and overreactive emotions. Manganese-bearing minerals encourage empathy, generosity, and trust. They deepen our affection and help us release emotional wounds and psychological baggage.

In the body, manganese-rich stones can be used to treat conditions such as diabetes, arthritis, infertility, dizziness, and fatigue. They may help relieve the symptoms of allergies and accelerate the healing of wounds. Manganese-bearing minerals can also be used to treat heart conditions, stimulate growth, and increase fertility.

Nickel (Ni)

Nickel is a metal that is resistant to corrosion. Its toughness represents its ability to confer confidence and self-esteem; we are less likely to be broken down or harmed by the outside world if we are more confident. Nickel-bearing minerals thus assuage fear, sadness, and irritability; they also help promote a sense of belonging. Rocks and minerals containing nickel invite creativity and innovation, and they feed the inner child.

Nickel-bearing minerals can be used to promote the absorption of iron, and they help regulate the viscosity of blood. Minerals with nickel are sometimes used to treat skin conditions, headaches, and diseases of the liver. They also regulate digestion, metabolism, and detoxification.

Oxygen (O)

In the mineral kingdom, oxygen bonds with many other elements to produce a wide array of minerals. Oxygen often relates to themes of breath and spirit. It can be spiritually nourishing and is extremely centering. Oxygen delivers the energies of other mineral-forming elements to the body at a cellular level. The oxygen content of minerals inspires alertness and creativity, and it reduces inflexibility of the mind and the emotions. It is gently grounding, centering, and purifying.

On the physical level, minerals containing oxygen provide metabolic support at the cellular level. They also support healthy cell division and can eliminate metabolic wastes. Oxygen in minerals supports the health of the lungs and reduces shortness of breath, such as during bouts of asthma and anxiety.

Phosphorus (P)

Phosphorus means "light bearer" in Greek. This substance ushers light into the body, mind, and spirit. Minerals rich in phosphorus illuminate the root causes of imbalance and enable us to store vital energy (life force, or *chi*), thus preventing or treating burnout and exhaustion. Minerals containing phosphorus reduce irritability and anger while promoting hope and sensitivity. Phosphorus boosts perception and awareness on all levels, particularly psychic skills. Stones containing this element often expand the consciousness and facilitate rapid spiritual growth.

Phosphorus-bearing minerals such as the phosphate group are adept at treating conditions affecting the teeth and bones. They bolster the immune system, help us overcome fatigue, and ease muscular strain. Phosphorus stones can also be used to treat conditions affecting the sensory organs.

Potassium (K)

Potassium helps us break down old, disharmonious patterns and discover the lessons within them. This can jump-start the healing process by allowing us to extract only the helpful part of a situation while releasing the rest. Potassium minerals bring movement and freshness to stagnant energies, especially in the mental and emotional bodies. These stones increase self-worth and contentment while simultaneously vanquishing anger, fear, restlessness, and victimhood. Potassium-bearing minerals invite us to take action guided by the wisdom of the heart. This results in heightened intuition and a sense of greater freedom.

Potassium stimulates the endocrine system and nourishes muscle tissue. Minerals containing potassium are sometimes used to treat fluid buildup, much the way they treat stagnant energies. They relieve fatigue, cramps, weakness, and depression and stimulate the pineal gland.

Silicon (Si)

Silicon is an abundant mineral-forming element, most commonly available as silica (a compound of silicon and oxygen). Silica is the universal amplifier of the mineral kingdom, providing clarity to any situation in which it is used. It amplifies the effects of other elements in a mineral's composition, including trace elements present in very minute amounts. Silicon-bearing minerals open the mind, promote learning, and draw inspiration. They allow us to keep one foot in the material world and the other in the spiritual, helping us reconcile the differences between the two as we encounter them. Minerals with silicon offer stability, determination, and an overall sense of well-being.

Silicon-bearing minerals expedite and clarify the healing process overall. They are used to strengthen bones, teeth, hair, and nails as well as to treat conditions of the nervous system, sensory organs, and immune system. Silica is particularly helpful in reducing the effects of the aging process.

Sodium (Na)

Sodium can be cleansing, catalyzing, and initiatory. Minerals rich in sodium can help you explore new paths while providing structure and organization. Sodium-bearing minerals initiate emotional release, enable higher reasoning, and help you achieve your potential.

Sodium in mineral form has a drying effect on the body, therefore it regulates fluid retention, mucous production, and swelling. Sodium minerals improve digestion, stimulate the kidneys, and help maintain the pH of the body.

Sulfur (S)

Sulfur scrubs our energy field of stale energies, foreign attachments, and toxic patterns. It is strongly protective, and stones containing sulfur can heal and prevent leaks and tears in the aura. Stones containing sulfur often work to dispel illusion and confusion, and they help us confront our shadow self. Sulfur-bearing minerals are also stimulating, and they can help us become more receptive to nourishing energies. These stones can also help us face our fears.

Sulfur-bearing minerals are strongly detoxifying. They can be used to treat infection (especially fungal infections), inflammation, and afflictions of the digestive system. Sulfur minerals are warming and boost the metabolism.

Titanium (Ti)

Titanium boosts psychic receptivity and enhances communication. It bolsters our sense of self-worth and protects our vital energy. Minerals containing titanium typically help us overcome fears, limitations, and feelings of inadequacy and codependence. These stones engender honesty and bestow independence.

Titanium minerals offer a regenerative influence on the physical body, repairing damage from illness and injury, and they can be used to treat male sexual dysfunction. These stones have a tonifying effect on the muscles and can improve posture. Titanium-bearing stones protect against harmful radiation.

Zinc (Zn)

Zinc-bearing minerals often relate to creativity and sexuality. Energizing and enlivening, they are used to treat feelings of weakness and exhaustion. Minerals containing zinc strengthen courage, promote abstract thinking, and instill spontaneity. When you feel truly stuck, zinc minerals initiate transformation and can help you find creative solutions to life's problems. Zinc also improves communication skills.

Zinc-rich minerals exert a warming influence in the body. They boost the body's ability to absorb nutrients, improve immune function, and support the sensory organs. Additionally, zinc minerals treat conditions affecting the skin, hormonal balance, mucous membranes, and the reproductive system.

THE MOHS SCALE
OF HARDNESS

One of the defining characteristics of a mineral is its *hardness,* a measure of its resistance to abrasion. The most common method of measuring the hardness of a stone is by means of the Mohs scale of hardness, named for nineteenth-century German mineralogist and geologist Friedrich Mohs. The Mohs scale describes the relative hardness of minerals, ranking common minerals on a scale from 1 to 10, with 1 being the softest and 10 the hardest. Minerals with a higher degree of hardness can be used to scratch those with a lower ranking. The standard minerals used are

10 diamond
9 corundum (ruby and sapphire)
8 topaz
7 quartz
6 orthoclase feldspar
5 apatite
4 fluorite
3 calcite
2 gypsum (selenite)
1 talc

In crystal healing, the softer minerals tend to work more effectively on acute conditions. They also tend to have gentler effects when used over longer periods of time. Many soft stones are somewhat porous, so energetically they act as sponges that soak up stagnant or disharmonious vibes. Those with a hardness below 4 often work more readily with the nonphysical anatomy, regulating the flow of light and energy through the aura and chakras. These softer stones often provide an energetic cushion when we experience bumps along life's path.

As the hardness increases, the intensity of a mineral's effects also increases. The hardest minerals are closest to the expression of the absolute will of the Divine, as seen in diamond's representation of Divine Will. Generally, harder minerals also express energies closer to absolute truth, as opposed to relative truth like what we experience here in the material plane. As the hardness decreases, minerals translate absolute truth and Divine Will into more tangible lessons for us to incorporate into our daily lives. Harder minerals also support healing of chronic conditions, as they have the durability that allows them to penetrate to the causal level of illness and injury. Softer minerals tend to require more frequent cleansing than harder minerals.

Knowing a mineral's hardness is helpful for both mundane and metaphysical purposes. For example, on a practical level very soft minerals should not be stored with harder ones, as they can get scratched or otherwise damaged. Many people like to use selenite to cleanse or energize other stones, but you can see that its hardness (or rather, softness) of 2 on the Mohs scale leaves it susceptible to being damaged by common stones, such as members of the quartz family. To prevent mishaps consult the crystal directory to double-check the hardness of your crystals before storing them together.

When making crystal elixirs, hardness and chemical composition are important factors to consider, as soft stones more readily interact with water, and they may even crumble or dissolve, thereby increasing the risk of making toxic components more abundant if the elixir is used internally or externally. Always be sure to exercise caution with softer minerals, especially those that contain toxic elements like lead, arsenic, mercury, copper, or others.

COLOR

For many beginners as well as advanced practitioners, color is our primary way of relating to the energy of rocks and minerals, and it certainly serves as our primary means of decoding a stone's properties. The most common models attribute the seven colors of the rainbow to the chakra system, thereby lumping all blue stones with the throat chakra and all yellow stones with the solar plexus chakra. To a certain degree this works, but color plays a much subtler role than many crystal healers might think.

For starters, the meaning of colors is not universal. Different cultures assign different values to the same color, and those meanings change over time. For example, at one point male babies were wrapped in pink and females in blue, but this, as we know, has changed over the years and now pink is viewed as a stereotypically feminine color and blue masculine. Furthermore, color and its effects are deeply entrenched in one's psyche. If I love lime green more than any other color, I will find it empowering, soothing, and joyful. However someone who despises lime green may feel uncomfortable, resentful, or otherwise upset by it.

The matter is further complicated when we look at the mechanisms responsible for color in minerals. Some minerals are colored by the elements from which they are normally composed, such as the element iron making hematite metallic gray, or copper making azurite blue. Other minerals get their hues from only trace amounts of ancillary substances. For example, amethyst contains only a negligible amount of iron in its crystal lattice, yet it is enough to transform otherwise colorless quartz into a violet gemstone.

Many rocks and minerals are found in a wide range of colors, such as fluorite, calcite, agate, jasper, chalcedony, and crystalline quartz, to name a few. The various colors of these stones are separated by the addition of a few stray particles here and there in the crystal lattice, meaning they are more alike than they are dissimilar. I learned from crystal healing expert Naisha Ahsian many years ago that color only accounts for approximately one-fourteenth (approximately 7 percent) of a stone's total energy. That means that nearly 93 percent of its energy is influenced by factors other than its color—chiefly its chemical composition, crystal structure, formation process, hardness, and other factors.

I like to think of color as the icing on the cake when we are interpreting the effects of a stone. Because we accumulate meanings associated with colors as we grow, the color of gemstones often imparts profound effects despite the relatively small role that it plays in the crystal's overall energy. Use the following interpretations as a starting point for understanding how color works in crystal healing.

Black

Many black stones are rich in metals such as iron and manganese, which accounts for their strengthening and grounding properties. These stones also represent self-reflection, and they are excellent tools for confronting the shadow self and for initiating self-control. Black stones tend to be protective, shielding, and introspective. Black stones can help detoxify the physical body.

Blue

Blue stones represent movement and flux, and they are often attributed to the throat chakra and its themes of communication and connection. Blue stones often present a more mental energy; they are cooling to the mind and the emotions. Blue inspires peace, hope, and serenity. Shades of blue-green and turquoise can bring clarity to the emotional body, often by bringing the emotions into the realm of conscious awareness. In the physical body, blue stones are often used to alleviate inflammation, fever, and pain, and they support the health of the nerves and blood vessels.

Brown

Brown stones espouse an earthy vibe, and they focus on themes of stability, security, and patience. Brown is a color that relates to the natural world, and stones in this color family often provide a connection to the conscious forces in nature, such as the devas. Brown stones offer steady growth and support for steady, continuous changes. These stones can be gently grounding and protective.

Gray and Silver

Gray stones initiate states of balance; they mediate between extremes. Gray stones cloak the energy field, and so they are helpful in dreamwork and for developing shamanic practices. Gray instills a sense of impartiality and fairness. Silver stones also typically relate to the moon and to intuition, in addition to the properties already listed for gray stones.

Green

Green symbolizes growth, renewal, and regeneration. Green stones are therefore employed for physical healing as well as for abundance, luck, and harmony. These stones provide a sense of structure, expansion, and innovation. Green stones often invite compassion and an outward expression of love. In the physical body, green stones can be used to treat conditions affecting the heart, lungs, and immune system; they are adept in situations of infection and abnormal growths.

Indigo

Indigo deepens self-awareness by stimulating the intuition and psychic awareness. Indigo-colored stones tend to deepen the scope of one's conscious awareness, facilitating contact with the higher mind. These stones support mental growth, and they are excellent for strengthening the memory and improving study skills. Indigo invites order and structure. Stones of this color are the most nourishing to the skeletal system, including the bones, cartilage, and ligaments.

Orange

Orange incites a fiery energy, one of passion, creativity, and sensuality. Orange stones mobilize us, inviting us to take decisive action. They clear stagnant energy and remove energetic blockages. Orange stones promote enthusiasm and ameliorate the effects of trauma by freeing us from the past. Orange provides both the stamina and the impetus to initiate positive change. Physically, orange stones can assist in overcoming lethargy, poor digestion, and low libido.

Pink

Pink stones tend to work toward our emotional well-being. They are often gentle and soothing stones that foster a sense of self-love. Pink nurtures the heart, provides reassurance, and boosts self-esteem. Pink stones may help cultivate love and romance. These stones also soothe the inner child and encourage compassion, empathy, and trust. Pink can be used to invite harmony and diffuse tense situations. In the body, pink stones alleviate pain, bring warmth to cold extremities, and neutralize psychosomatic conditions.

Red

Red stones exude confidence, strength, and passion. They often work on a more instinctual level as they root us in the material plane and enable us to draw strength from our primal, vital essence. Red stones offer mobility, determination, and motivation. They counteract timidity, fear, and a sense of inadequacy. Red stones can help jump-start creative endeavors and sidestep procrastination. They can be used for treating low energy, congestion, pain, poor circulation, and weakness. They support the health of the circulatory systems and muscle tissue.

Violet and Purple

Violet and purple are intensely spiritual colors. These colors heighten the psychic senses, enhance meditation, and help one see the big picture. Violet stones highlight limiting forces and empower us to transmute or transcend the obstacles in our lives. Violet encourages problem-solving skills, dispels illusion, and releases guilt. In the body, purple and violet can break down barriers to our overall well-being. Stones of this color nourish the nervous system, pituitary and pineal glands, and the sensory organs, and they can be used to treat headache, vertigo, and other conditions affecting these systems.

White and Colorless

White and colorless stones are among the most versatile. White light is composed of all colors, and white stones therefore represent unlimited potential. They can be used to initiate purification, diffuse excess energy, and deflect unwanted vibrations. White is fairly protective since it reflects all colors, and white stones can help us detach from painful or confusing circumstances. Clear and colorless stones bring clarity and perspective. They can be used to break down blockages and amplify one's intentions. In the physical body, these stones balance the fluids, support the body's detoxification processes, and help us resolve confusing symptoms.

Yellow and Gold

Yellow stones strengthen the ability to let go. They unwind tension and invite optimism and charisma. Yellow is the color associated with happiness, wealth, and joy. Stones of this color offset worry, stress, and lack of attention. Yellow stones treat the digestive system, the organs of elimination (skin, kidneys, bladder, lungs, colon, liver), and some conditions of the nervous system. Yellow lifts depression and elevates mood. Golden stones express a more refined energy than yellow, and they help to spiritualize the focus of yellow's themes. Gold stones are additionally more projective in their energy, and they help us understand value and attract prosperity.

DIAPHANEITY, PLEOCHROISM, CLEAVAGE, LUMINESCENCE

Rocks and minerals have so many defining characteristics that it is challenging to reduce them to just their formation process, crystal system, composition, hardness, and color. Properties such as diaphaneity, cleavage, color changes, luminescence, and many others are often important tools for gaining insight into the healing properties that any particular stone offers. Although a complete discussion of each of these factors is beyond the scope of this book, following is a brief overview of some of the more common mineral properties you'll encounter.

> ▸ *Diaphaneity* refers to how light travels through a stone. Opaque stones allow no light to enter; they often have a grounding or stabilizing energy.

Translucent stones allow some light to pass through; these stones may point to the subconscious mind and the emotions. Transparent stones are completely see-through, and they direct their focus toward the conscious mind and the spirit.

▶ Some crystals have unusual relationships with light. Some, like alexandrite, will change color in different types of light. Others, including tanzanite, kunzite, and iolite, exhibit a property called *pleochroism,* wherein they appear to change color when viewed from different angles. These stones often have a dominant color and secondary or tertiary colors that allow the crystal to work on more than one level of our makeup at once. Crystals with color changes of either variety are often multidimensional healing stones.

▶ A mineral's *cleavage* describes its tendency to break into smooth planes along weak bonds in its structure. Stones such as calcite and fluorite have perfect cleavage in three planes, and they always cleave into the same shapes—rhombohedrons and cubes or octahedrons, respectively. Those stones with perfect cleavage provide perfect templates for our own healing, showing us that when we feel as if we are breaking apart, we are actually revealing our innate perfection.

▶ Many minerals exhibit different varieties of *luminescence,* including fluorescence, phosphorescence, triboluminescence, and thermoluminescence. Rocks and minerals with these optical properties quite literally emanate light, and they can bring hidden or suppressed energies into view. These stones are often profoundly healing at the spiritual level because they remind us to shine as brightly as they do.

Whenever you are getting to know a new stone in your toolbox, be sure to research its chemical, optical, and physical properties thoroughly. You'll surely find hidden gems that point you toward its healing energies.

THE CONSCIOUSNESS OF STONES

It would be really simple to say that the healing qualities of rocks and minerals can be neatly explained by factors like formation process, crystal system, composition, hardness, and color, but it's not as formulaic as this. The truth is that though there are apparent patterns, there is something more to the process of evaluating how and why crystals work.

There is consciousness in everything, from human beings to the tiniest grains of sand. The mineral kingdom too has its own consciousness, a quality of subtle energy that lacks anything quantifiable. However it is at this level of consciousness that stones initiate their deepest transformational gifts. Crystals, gemstones, rocks, minerals, and fossils all have distinct personalities and purposes. They exist on Planet Earth to contribute to the total evolution of our world, just the same as every plant, animal, person, or microbe does. We are all in this together. To really comprehend how crystals heal and what energies they offer, we have to meet them on this level—we have to treat them with respect, reverence, and trust. They, in turn, will treat us the same way.

This explains why two pieces of quartz with the same chemical composition, the same crystal system, the same hardness, as well as the same color, refractive index, specific gravity, and the same mechanical, optical, electrical, and physical properties, will exhibit markedly different energies. The souls of these stones are different, and that means that they will have different influences over our lives.

PUTTING IT ALL TOGETHER

I am often asked *how* we know what effects certain crystals exhibit. People who are new to the world of crystal healing may at first rely on color, shape, or historical clues to learn how to use their beloved stones, but we can dig deeper and learn to apply the information outlined in this chapter to get a feel for what an unknown stone will offer us. Essentially, once you learn to think more critically about the inner workings of rocks and minerals, and combine this with your own intuition and insights, you can figure out what properties they have without relying on books to tell you. Let's consider a couple of examples.

Decoding Rhodonite

Rhodonite is a popular mineral that is available as tumbled stones, beads, carvings, fine mineral specimens, and jewelry. It is one of my favorite stones to work with for my personal healing, and I find that so many of my students and clients benefit from rhodonite too. Let's start with an overview of rhodonite's information.

Formula: $MnSiO_3$
Hardness: 5.5–6.5
Crystal system: triclinic
Formation process: metamorphic (tertiary)
Color: usually pink to red, often mottled with black inclusions of manganese oxide (MnO)

Rhodonite

For starters, rhodonite is a *manganese silicate.* The silica base works to expand and amplify the manganese in this mineral's composition. From the previous discussion on chemical composition, we can see that the mineral manganese works predominantly on the emotions and the heart chakra. Thus rhodonite is grounding, and it targets conditions such as anxiety, fear, irritability, and perhaps depression. Since manganese-bearing minerals encourage empathy and release old emotional baggage, we can surmise that rhodonite will be an effective tool for treating emotional wounds. The additional manganese oxide inclusions will make this stone especially stabilizing to the emotional body.

If we look to rhodonite's crystal system, we see that it is *triclinic.* Triclinic crystals are the masters of reinvention; they integrate new and higher energies. That makes rhodonite the perfect stone for emotional transformation. As a triclinic mineral it helps us to be complete as we are, recognizing our inherent emotional wholeness so that we will no longer rely on external validation for our sense of well-being.

Rhodonite is a *tertiary mineral,* meaning it is formed by metamorphic processes. Metamorphic rocks and minerals assist in transformation. They enable us to find the stamina and dedication needed for healing and metamorphosis. The formation process of rhodonite resembles the body's process of healing wounds; thus it is often used to speed up recovery from injuries like cuts, scrapes, and other wounds.

As a relatively hard stone, rhodonite is an excellent tool for long-term healing, as it can reach into the roots of chronic conditions. Rhodonite's color palette also indicates an emotional connection, as pink and red stones tend to work on the heart and teach us about love.

By examining each of these characteristics, it is possible to understand why rhodonite is considered such a capable healer of the heart. To learn more about rhodonite and its healing properties, see the listing for this mineral in the directory of crystals in part 2 of this book.

Decoding Plumbogummite

Chances are, plumbogummite is something you've never heard of in the crystal healing milieu. I hadn't heard of it either until my dear friend Sharron showed me a specimen for the very first time. It's a relatively rare mineral, one not commonly used in healing, which is why I've chosen it for this exercise. Let's look at some basic information.

Formula: $PbAl_3(PO_4)_2(OH)_5 \cdot H_2O$
Hardness: 4–5
Crystal system: trigonal
Formation process: sedimentary (secondary)
Color: usually blue, gray, purplish, or green; occasionally yellow

Botryoidal plumbogummite

Plumbogummite typically forms as crusts or masses in oxidation zones. It rarely exhibits crystals, but when it does they are usually hexagonal prisms. Most specimens that I have seen are bluish gray or greenish. It forms beautiful pseudomorphs as it replaces minerals such as pyromorphite. Plumbogummite is toxic due to its lead content, and so it must be handled with care.

Plumbogummite is a phosphate mineral. All phosphates are balancing, light-bringing stones. The presence of phosphorus also indicates that plumbogummite offers hope and sensitivity, and it boosts psychic senses. Its aluminum content relates to the mind, and aluminum points us to the true self. The lead content and sedimentary origin both hint that plumbogummite is a capable karmic healing stone. This mineral also contains water and a significant amount of hydroxide, which tells us that it has a special relationship with the emotions. Putting all of this together, plumbogummite works to bring light to the darkest corners of the mind and causal body. It breaks down, releases, and transmutes the old karmic and emotional patterns that we have accumulated and that prevent our expressing our true nature. As it does this, plumbogummite begins to heighten our psychic sensitivity.

As a secondary mineral, it relates to one's relationship with the environment. Because it belongs to the trigonal crystal system, it has a focusing and rejuvenating effect. Plumbogummite can help us examine how the people around us might be holding us back or throwing us off course; it can help us moderate how much we invest in others' dramas and remind us to take time for our personal spiritual development.

Plumbogummite has a soft-to-moderate hardness; therefore it is likely to work as well on chronic conditions as it does on acute scenarios. Its color range is often bluish to grayish green (sometimes with tinges of purple). Depending on the exact shade, we can surmise that plumbogummite aims its energy toward healing the mind. Bluer shades will tend to focus on the conscious mind, while grayish ones represent the subconscious. The purple undertones remind us that there is a spiritual cause for every condition we experience.

Overall, plumbogummite is a powerful catalyst for personal transformation. Its energy is direct and focused, and it works to bring our hidden nature to the surface for deeper healing. Plumbogummite is a powerful stimulator of the higher mind and psychic abilities, but it can be too stimulating for constant use. Work with this stone with caution, because it can initiate rapid and unexpected release.

3

The Human Energy Field

EVERY HUMAN BEING, like all living things, is enveloped by a sheath of energy. This field consists of both measurable energy generated by the physical body and subtle energy generated by the spiritual anatomy. The human energy field (HEF) both surrounds and interpenetrates the physical body. Our overall health and well-being are reflected in and affected by this dynamic field of energy. There are many systems for classifying and comprehending the major components of the HEF; in this chapter we will explore some of its elements and learn how to assess the health of the HEF.

BIOLOGY AND SPIRIT

Recall from chapter 1 that all matter produces measurable fields of energy made up of frequencies in the electromagnetic spectrum. Living tissue is no exception to this rule. Not only do all of the vibrating particles from which we are made contribute to our electrical fields but so do the activities of our cells, tissues, and organs. The heart and brain are two of the largest drivers of these electromagnetic fields, with the heart being many times more potent at generating electromagnetic energy than the brain. Other biological processes also contribute to the measurable energies found in the HEF, including the function of the nervous system, cellular metabolism, the piezoelectricity of our bones, and the biophotons emitted by our DNA. Literally and metaphorically, every part of us is bathed in energy.

Unlike the highly ordered, coherent, and predictable electromagnetic fields produced by rocks and minerals, biological systems produce energy fields that are anything but consistent. Each component of the body's electromagnetic field contributes its own frequency and amplitude, which collectively creates our base resonant frequency and amplitude. Our energy fields are in a constant state of flux; they are affected by what we eat, think, wear, say, and do, as well as by where we go and with whom we spend our time. Music, color, scent, and other

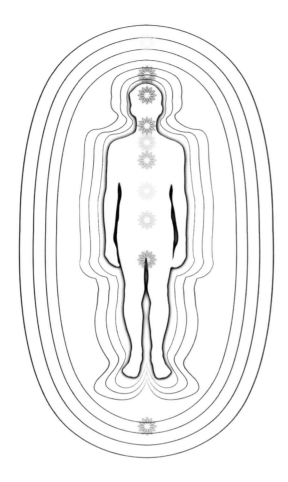

The human energy field

factors in our environment can influence the HEF too. These energy fields are sensitive to other energies, such as those generated by crystals or by other people. So in a way they serve as nonphysical sensory organs. I'm sure you've had the experience of feeling when someone is staring at you or felt the energy of a room change when someone with a certain kind of energy walks in. This is the result of the HEF exchanging information with your environment.

In addition to the measurable energies that make up the HEF, there are numerous subtle or spiritual forms of energy present. These energies include our life force, or vital energy, as well as the other animating forces of the body, mind, and soul. These subtle energies are created, organized, and processed by our subtle anatomy much the way our physical anatomy generates electromagnetism.

The main components of our subtle anatomy include the *aura,* the *chakras,* the *tanden,* the *nadis,* and the *meridians.* The aura consists of the combined layered fields of subtle energy that surround the physical body. Chakras are non-physical organs that are usually depicted as wheels or vortices of energy that correspond to specific points in the body. The tanden (or *dantien* in Chinese) are three energy centers in the body similar to the chakras; they are responsible for conserving, transforming, and directing the life force and nourishing the soul. Nadis are vessels through which subtle energy flows throughout the physical and subtle bodies, not unlike how veins and arteries transport blood to the physical body. Meridians are similar to nadis in that they are pathways along and within the physical body through which the life force flows. Twelve of these meridians correspond to organs of the body.

Since different cultures have conceptualized the HEF in different ways, modern-day interpretations of the subtle anatomy often draw from a variety of sources. As we continue to refine our perception and understanding of subtle energies, our models for the subtle anatomy will continue to develop too.

THE AURA

The term *aura* usually refers to the subtle or spiritual energies that contribute to the HEF, in contrast to the measurable energies emitted by our physical body. The aura is usually pictured as round or egg-shaped, but it is actually in the shape of a torus. The torus is somewhat like a donut, and the physical body occupies the hollow space in the middle. The aura is a complex system consisting of individual fields that are layered around the body, like a Russian nesting doll. These fields are called *subtle bodies,* and each one governs a different aspect of our being. As you move outward from the physical body, each layer of the aura becomes less dense. The aura serves to store and process information and energy as well as offering a defense against foreign energies, much in the way that your physical body has an immune system.

There is no single definitive system for classifying the subtle bodies; different systems use different models, and it seems that no two agree. Because the aura is composed of subtle energy, there is no scientific equipment* that can

---

*Certain forms of technology exist for visualizing the aura and chakras, including Kirlian photography and biofeedback-driven equipment. Kirlian photography is a means of capturing the etheric body on a photographic plate. Modern-day aura cameras use biofeedback metrics to visualize the aura. Though these may help us map out the energies that constitute the aura, they do not in fact photograph the aura itself.

reliably measure it. Some systems use only four bodies: the physical, emotional, mental, and physical. Others use up to twelve. Each system is a means of conceptualizing an otherwise abstract, metaphysical concept. The following list of bodies, from the physical to the subtle, is what I use in my practice.

- ► Physical body
- ► Etheric body
- ► Astral body
- ► Emotional body
- ► Mental body
- ► Intuitive body
- ► Causal body
- ► Soul body

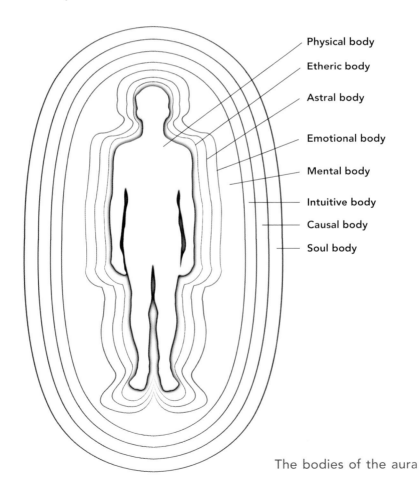

Physical body
Etheric body
Astral body
Emotional body
Mental body
Intuitive body
Causal body
Soul body

The bodies of the aura

Etheric Body

The etheric body, also called the *supraphysical body,* is the energetic template of the physical body. It is the densest layer of the aura and lies closest to the physical body, usually from two to three inches away from the physical body. This layer of the aura is the most nourishing to the physical body. The etheric body contains memories of illness, injury, imbalance, and trauma sustained at the physical level. A healthy supraphysical body is indicated by physical health, youthfulness, and strength in the body. When unhealthy or imbalanced, this body can cause physical illness, injury, and fatigue. Consciously changing the patterns in the etheric body results in changes in the physical body.

Some of the most nourishing stones for the etheric body are aquamarine, carnelian, chrysoprase, clear quartz, Herkimer diamond quartz, kunzite, nephrite jade, pietersite, prehnite, rainbow moonstone, shungite, and white topaz.

Astral Body

The astral body contains the idealized blueprint for our self-image. Some sources consider it to lie between the mental and the intuitive bodies, whereas others place it between the etheric and the emotional bodies. Because of this, we experience our astral body in dreams, astral travel, and deep meditation. The image of the astral body reflects how we feel and think about ourselves and not necessarily who we really are. Other people's perception of us is also influenced by the patterns contained in the astral body. The astral body is influenced by the transits of stars, planets, and luminaries in the heavens above us. It also serves as the boundary between individual identity and collective identity; for this reason we often form cords and entanglements with others on the astral level.

Gemstones such as apophyllite, citrine, clear quartz, danburite, green jasper, labradorite, lapis lazuli, malachite, moonstone (adularia), pietersite, rhodochrosite, rose quartz, and turquoise fortify the astral body.

Emotional Body

The emotional body is the container of our emotional patterns. Of all the bodies, this is the one that exhibits the greatest amount of movement and change. This body is among the most sensitive to the world around us, as it responds to our perceptions and experiences with pure emotion. An out-of-balance emotional body is generally indicated by psychological conditions, including depression and anxiety, as well as a general sense of being emotionally ill at ease.

The emotional body is supported by stones such as agate, calcite, chrysocolla, lepidolite, morganite, opal, pink chalcedony, pink tourmaline, rhodonite, rose quartz, ruby, spinel, and many more.

Mental Body

The mental body stores thoughts, beliefs, and intellectual patterns. This layer of the aura is home to logic and reasoning, language skills, and our internal dialogue. Through the efforts of the mental body we interpret events and experiences according to our belief system. A healthy mental body yields a sharp mind and quick wit and allows us to learn new information and skills easily. An imbalanced mental body makes us feel like we're in a mental fog; it may also impede memory and recall, making learning difficult and affecting communication skills.

Stones for the mental body include amazonite, apatite, aquamarine, blue chalcedony, blue lace agate, calcite (especially blue, green, and gold), citrine, clear quartz, fluorite, howlite, lapis lazuli, pyrite, scapolite, smoky quartz, sodalite, topaz, and yellow jasper.

Intuitive Body

Also called the *psychic body,* the intuitive part of the aura interacts with the world around us through symbols, images, and forms. The intuitive body is the home of our psychic senses as well as our visualization skills. This body, like the astral body, is especially active in the dream state. Clear intuition, perception, the ability to interpret psychic information, and a healthy imagination are hallmarks of a healthy intuitive body. When this body is out of balance we experience infrequent, fragmentary, or misleading psychic impressions, and we often have difficulty visualizing.

Some of the most effective stones for working on conditions of the intuitive body include amethyst, azurite, charoite, iolite, lapis lazuli, purple fluorite, purple opal, selenite, sodalite, sugilite, tanzanite, and tiger's eye.

Causal Body

The causal body is sometimes referred to as the *memory body* or the *karmic body.* It is our personal storehouse of karma, or the law of cause and effect. The causal layer of the aura is tasked with storing, sorting, and stabilizing karmic patterns. This layer also contains the ancestral or genealogical karma that we inherit from our families and communities. A healthy causal body resolves and releases karma easily, thereby allowing any karmic debts or credits to flow. An unhealthy causal body results in repeated karmic lessons, difficulty with memory and recall, and reliving past traumas. Changes we make to our karma by releasing or transmuting it are also stored in the causal body.

Stones for the causal body include dumortierite, heliodor, jade, kyanite, lapis lazuli, leopardskin jasper, opal, phantom quartz, and rhodochrosite.

Soul Body

The soul body is sometimes known as the *divine body* or the *ketheric template*. It contains and integrates the patterns of all the other bodies. It is the body of the higher self and the soul. The soul body is the first spark of our identity created by Source. Our soul body knows no separation; it is innately one with everything, including the Divine Mind that created us. There is rarely any imbalance in the soul body itself, although we can cut ourselves off from our divinity and alienate ourselves from the soul body's unity and unconditional love. When this happens we may experience hopelessness and despair, as well as lose our sense of purpose.

To connect more deeply to the soul body, consider working with stones such as ametrine, celestite, danburite, elestial quartz, emerald, kunzite, moldavite, selenite, seraphinite, and tanzanite.

THE CHAKRA SYSTEM

The chakra system as we know it in the West is inspired by ancient Vedic teachings. The word *chakra* (properly pronounced with a hard *ch,* as in *change*) means "wheel" in Sanskrit. Early texts describe the chakras as gateways through which consciousness passes on our journey of spiritual development. These were often visualized as lotuses with varying numbers of petals, and texts from different times and regions ascribed to the chakras different colors and locations.

Over the past two hundred years the Western chakra system has become more codified. Today chakras are recognized the world over as subtle organs within the HEF. Chakras are usually described as swirling wheels or vortices of energy that are rooted in the energy channels known as *nadi* that run along the spinal column and extend outward into the aura. Each of the chakras helps to absorb, process, transform, and release life-force energy in different ways. The most well-known systems list seven major chakras, generally depicted in the seven colors of the rainbow (a practice that dates to the 1970s); however, it is claimed that there are as many as hundreds of minor chakras.

Each chakra is connected to a different aspect of our physical, psychological, and spiritual well-being. The locations, colors, and themes associated with the chakras all provide clues as to how the chakras affect our overall health and personal development. The chakra system is a helpful model for us to understand in crystal healing because the chakras function as target points at which crystals and gemstones can be applied. Chakras are energy pathways—doorways to the inner workings of the HEF; thus applying stones to and around these centers enables the practitioner to nourish, balance, and transform the chakras and the HEF as a whole.

Before delving into the roles of the chakras themselves, one more note is required. The chakra-color correspondences propounded by the Western chakra system is quite recent in origin. It serves as a helpful and effective way for many crystal therapists to select crystals that relate to the issues associated with specific energy centers. Remember, however, that rocks and minerals have been used for their energetic properties for tens of thousands of years, while the color correspondences of the Western chakra system are less than fifty years old. A stone's color *can* be an indication of which chakra it supports, but *color accounts for only one-fourteenth of the total energy of a stone.* Thus, when pairing crystals with the chakras they treat, we are not limited by color alone.

The Major Chakras

The modern chakra system consists of the following seven energy centers. In ascending order these are the root, sacral, solar plexus, heart, throat, third eye, and crown chakras.

Root Chakra

The root chakra, also called the *base chakra,* resides at the base of the spine (sometimes visualized at the perineum). In the Western chakra system it is represented by the color red. The root chakra governs survival, strength, and grounding. It also relates to themes of abundance, motivation, sexuality, and kundalini energy. Physiologically, it is the chakra that oversees those parts of us related to survival, strength, and movement, such as the musculoskeletal system, circulatory system, metabolism, and reproductive system.

Some of the most important stones for the root chakra include black

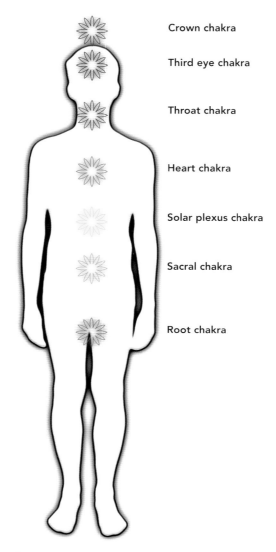

Crown chakra

Third eye chakra

Throat chakra

Heart chakra

Solar plexus chakra

Sacral chakra

Root chakra

The seven major chakras

onyx, black tourmaline, bloodstone, garnet, hematite, jasper, obsidian, pyrite, red calcite, ruby, and smoky quartz. When treating the root chakra, it is often difficult—if not altogether invasive—to place a stone directly on it. Instead pick two stones of the same variety that are of similar size and place them on the thighs or hips on either side of the groin. Alternatively, place these two stones below the soles of the feet to treat the root chakra more indirectly.

Sacral Chakra

The sacral chakra, sometimes called the *sexual chakra,* rests one-and-a-half to two inches below the navel. It is associated with the color orange and with themes of connection, sexuality, vitality, passion, creativity, fertility, and identity. It is the chakra that enables us to access our more primal emotions. In the physical body, the sacral chakra governs the reproductive organs, kidneys, and bladder.

Stones associated with the sacral chakra include brown aragonite, carnelian, calcite (especially yellow and orange), fire agate, fire opal, mahogany obsidian, mookaite jasper, smithsonite, tangerine quartz, vanadinite, wulfenite, and zincite. Much like the root chakra, the sacral chakra may need to be treated indirectly, either above or to the sides, to avoid inappropriate contact.

Solar Plexus Chakra

The solar plexus chakra is located just below the sternum. It is depicted as yellow or golden yellow in Western chakra systems, and it represents personal power, will, manifestation, self-esteem, and the intellect. This chakra also supports the digestive system, adrenal glands, diaphragm, and the eliminatory organs (skin, urinary tract, liver, and lungs).

Some of my favorite stones to use for the solar plexus chakra are amber, apatite, aragonite, blue lace agate, citrine, elestial quartz, golden calcite, jasper, malachite, pietersite, prehnite, pyrite, rhodochrosite, sunstone, topaz, and tiger's eye.

Heart Chakra

The heart chakra resides in the center of the sternum, and it is depicted as green and/or pink in the Western chakra system. This chakra is associated with love, relationships, emotions, balance, and compassion. Physically, the heart chakra is linked to its namesake, the heart, and the rest of the circulatory system. It also supports the immune and respiratory systems, as well as the thymus gland (though many practitioners ascribe this organ to a minor chakra; see page 71). The heart chakra is the energetic bridge between the upper and the lower chakras, and it serves as the primary driver of the entire HEF.

Heart chakra stones include agate (moss, pink), aquamarine, aventurine, calcite (mangano, red, green), chrysoprase, danburite, dioptase, emerald, kunzite, lapis lazuli, Lemurian seed quartz, lepidolite, opal, rhodochrosite, rhodonite, rose quartz, ruby, spinel, sugilite, and tourmaline (pink, green, and watermelon).

Throat Chakra

The throat chakra, depicted as blue or turquoise, is located at the throat itself. It is the center of communication, and it is also responsible for self-expression, truth, and projecting our mental energy into the world of form. In the body, the throat chakra rules the mouth, throat, vocal cords, nervous system, sensory organs, and the thyroid.

Among the most effective throat chakra stones are amazonite, aquamarine, aragonite, barite, blue chalcedony, celestite, chrysocolla, kyanite, lapis lazuli, larimar, ocean jasper, rutilated quartz, sapphire, sodalite, and turquoise. Treating the throat chakra directly can be uncomfortable; stones may also roll off the throat. Try using lightweight specimens placed at the base of the throat/neck instead.

Third Eye Chakra

The third eye, or brow, chakra, lies in the center of the forehead, just between and above the eyebrows. Often visualized as indigo or purple, this chakra is the seat of our intuition. The brow chakra supports the higher function of the mind, as well as dreaming, intuition, insight, understanding, and a sense of purpose. Physically speaking, this is the chakra responsible for the brain and pineal gland, sinuses, and the sensory organs of the head, especially the eyes.

Many stones serve to support the well-being of the third eye chakra, including amethyst, angelite, apophyllite, azurite, barite, blue apatite, charoite, fluorite, howlite, iolite, magnetite, moldavite, moonstone, pietersite, scapolite, sodalite, sugilite, and tanzanite.

Crown Chakra

The crown chakra is the energy center atop the skull. It is traditionally depicted as violet in the Western chakra system, but it is also associated with white, golden white, and sometimes pink. The crown is the center of our divine connection and our spiritual journey. This chakra facilitates spiritual growth and self-realization or enlightenment. It also rules the brain, nervous system, pituitary gland, and the subtle anatomy of the entire HEF.

For the crown chakra, consider working with amethyst, ametrine, angelite, apophyllite, aquamarine, botswana agate, calcite (optical and golden), charoite, clear quartz, danburite, fluorite, labradorite, moldavite, phenakite, opal, rainbow moonstone, selenite, seraphinite, sugilite, and turquoise. When treating the crown, crystals can be placed on a pillow above the head, as close to the client as possible.

Minor Chakras

Both traditional and modern texts indicate that there are dozens, if not hundreds, of other energy centers in the body. Some of the more commonly recognized ones include those in the hands and feet, as well as centers that lie roughly at the midway points between each of the seven main chakras. Others, such as the soul star and earth star chakras, are not on the physical body at all but instead are found in the subtle bodies of the HEF. Of all the minor chakras that have been explored in the past few decades, the three that I use most regularly are the earth star, higher heart, and soul star chakras.

Earth Star Chakra

The earth star chakra is located at the bottom of the HEF, approximately twelve to eighteen inches below the feet. It is sometimes visualized as black or metallic gray to black; some practitioners visualize it as a deep red or crimson color. This chakra offers profound grounding, and it helps to nourish and revitalize the entire being with telluric energies. The earth star chakra also contains information about our past lives, karmic patterns, DNA, and the soul's origins. Tapping into this energy center can evoke a better understanding of your soul's purpose on earth.

Barite, black tourmaline, elestial quartz, hematite, magnetite, petrified wood, shungite, and tourmalinated quartz are chief among the stones for the earth star chakra.

Higher Heart Chakra

The higher heart chakra is located between the heart chakra and the throat chakra, roughly at the thymus gland. It is also known as the *thymus chakra* and the *witness point*. Sometimes this chakra is visualized as a bluish green color (a shade between the heart and throat chakras' colors) or as a bright pink or lilac. It serves as a window into the overall health and well-being of the HEF. When stimulated, the higher heart chakra allows our consciousness to tap into new levels of unconditional love and compassion. It can also help to unify our inner masculine and feminine energies. This chakra also supports the function of the thymus gland, the immune system, the upper respiratory system, and the lymph

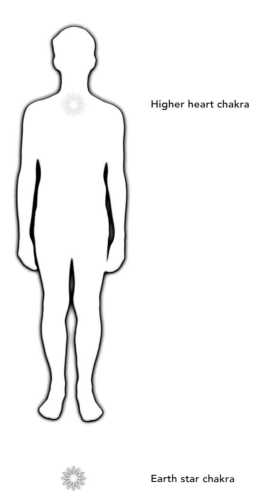

Soul star chakra

Higher heart chakra

Earth star chakra

Three of the minor chakras

nodes. It is a window through which we can integrate the energies of new gem-stones, either in meditation or during a healing layout.

All lithium-bearing stones correspond to the higher heart chakra, including lepidolite, lithium quartz, kunzite, sugilite, and some tourmalines. Additional higher heart stones include dioptase, emerald, Lemurian seed quartz, and turquoise.

Soul Star Chakra

The soul star chakra is the complement to the earth star; it can be found approximately six to twelve inches above the crown chakra, at the top of the HEF. This chakra is often visualized as white, golden white, or a prismatic white that contains all seven colors in it, like a sparkling diamond. When fully activated, the soul star heightens your relationship with the universe, and it permits your consciousness to transcend the ego. The soul star is the gateway through which the soul enters the body, and stimulating this chakra can provide a conscious awareness of the soul's relationship with the entire cosmos.

The crystals most effective for healing and activating the soul star chakra are charoite, Herkimer diamond quartz, Lemurian seed quartz, phenakite, selenite, tanzanite, Tibetan quartz, and tourmalinated quartz.

◆ Scanning the Aura

Learning to sense the aura in a tangible way can help you become a more sensitive and effective crystal healer. You can practice scanning the aura with your hands, a pendulum, dowsing rods, or a crystal. Although tools are not necessarily needed, I find that using a crystal often makes this process much easier for people who do not consider themselves to be sensitive to subtle energy. For this exercise choose a natural or polished crystal point or wand, preferably one that you can hold comfortably in the hand with the two ends clasped between the thumb and forefinger as pictured below.

Hold the crystal as shown here to scan the aura.

Hold the crystal so that one of the c-faces (i.e., the sides of the crystal, so-named because they are parallel to the central axis, or c-axis, of the crystal) faces the body of the client. Sweep along the person's midline in a slow and deliberate fashion. Sweep on either side of the midline, moving farther out with each consecutive pass. As you scan the aura, pay attention to any sensations, internal or external, that arise. You may feel changes in temperature, tingling sensations, or perhaps a stickiness or resistance in the energy field. Alternatively, you may have internal impressions, such as symbols, images, colors, or emotions that arise as you scan. Each of these represents the health of the person's energy field.

Wherever you locate a pattern of disharmony, make note of it so that you can revisit it during the healing session, such as with the exercises described in chapter 10 or by selecting crystals that correspond to the part of the aura affected by the disharmonious energy.

You can scan various layers of the aura by holding the crystal at different distances from the body. Start closer to the body with either the etheric or astral body, roughly three to six inches away from the physical body. Most people will feel these the strongest, as they are the densest layers of the aura. With practice, you will be able to scan the other subtle energy bodies too.

◆ Dowsing the Chakras

Evaluating the health of the chakra system offers significant clues about how to approach a treatment. This information can help you select the crystals that you'll use for layouts, grids, elixirs, and other treatment methods, and it may also help you understand some of the deeper meaning behind symptoms present in the client's mind, body, and energy field. While there are many methods for assessing the chakras, my favorite technique is a simple one: dowsing. To perform this exercise, all you'll need is a pendulum. If using a crystal or gemstone pendulum, ensure that it is properly cleansed beforehand (see "Cleansing Crystals" in chapter 5).

If the person is lying down, begin by holding your pendulum over the earth star chakra. Hold the intention that the pendulum's movement will indicate the overall health of the energy center and wait for it to exhibit consistent movement. Note the direction and relative speed of the pendulum's movement as well as anything else you observe. Gently move the pendulum toward the root chakra, allowing it to come to a stop before moving again. Observe the pendulum's swing, and repeat for each of the remaining chakras. Jot down your impressions and proceed with your treatment. Repeat after the treatment is finished.

A pendulum can be used to dowse the health of the aura and chakras.

The pendulum's movement is open to interpretation, but here are some general patterns that I have observed:

- Generally speaking, a circular movement is healthier than a side-to-side or up-and-down motion.
- The direction of the pendulum's swing (clockwise or counterclockwise) indicates the direction in which the chakra itself is spinning. Neither is better than the other, and the direction will periodically change throughout the day—sometimes even by the end of the treatment.
- Small circular patterns represent closed or underactive chakras. Larger circles indicate a chakra that is more open and active. Closed and underactive chakras can be opened with the appropriate stones; check the lists above or the crystal directory in part 2 of this book, or simply use your own intuition to select the right stones.
- Overactive chakras cause the pendulum to move in very large circles, often at a very fast speed. This can be countered with stones that regulate the function of the affected energy center as well as with sufficient grounding stones.

- Irregular shapes, such as ovals or shapes other than circles, can indicate a damaged or blocked chakra. These may require more work than a simple laying-on-of-stones.
- If you are having trouble observing any movement over one of the chakras, it may be off-center and in need of correction. Try moving the pendulum around the area to detect where it has moved.
- Generally speaking, a pendulum will move up and down the central nadi (parallel to the spine) between the chakras. Deviation from this movement may indicate an obstruction in the HEF.

You can perform the same technique on yourself, but it will require some adaptation. You'll have to forego dowsing the earth star and soul star chakras, as they will be outside of your reach. Instead of holding the pendulum over your body while lying down, hold the pendulum in front of your body while standing upright. With a clear intention you can produce the same results, even though the pendulum is essentially rotating in front of the chakra vortexes rather than moving with them from above.

Regular practice will help you develop a visual and kinesthetic lexicon for your pendulum's movement. I have also found that using the pendulum as a diagnostic tool has helped me visualize and sense the subtle anatomy through other means; knowing exactly how wide a chakra is open and where it is located allow me to psychically see the vortex of energy that is causing the pendulum to move. Document your experiments with this technique so that you can see how crystal healing is affecting the energy anatomy over time.

◆ Chakra Balancing with a Pendulum

In addition to being a useful diagnostic tool, a crystal pendulum can provide energetic support to the HEF and help correct imbalances to the subtle anatomy. After performing the previous exercise to discern where there are areas of disharmony in your client's chakra system, the pendulum can be employed to correct minor imbalances. In addition to working on the chakras themselves, the pendulum can be used to provide healing to other parts of the HEF. This exercise is a simple way to prepare the subtle anatomy for deeper work with crystal layouts and other healing methods.

Ensure that your pendulum has been cleansed and programmed before use. Hold the pendulum as still as possible over the chakra. Observe its swing without any conscious intention or judgment. Visualize a brilliant, prismatic white light entering your own crown chakra as you inhale. Allow it to continue downward to your heart and out along your arm as you exhale. Send this healing light down through the pendulum and out the crystal at its base. As you maintain this visualization to direct healing energy through the tool, continue to observe the swing of the pendulum. Once the pendulum's behavior indicates that healthy movement has been restored to the chakra or other target area, move on to the next pattern of disharmony. If no significant change is made, note the area and follow up with specific treatments via laying-on-of-stones, crystal grids, or other techniques.

When you have treated all of the areas indicated by the pendulum, cleanse it immediately as it can pick up and store the energy being released by the person's energy field during this exercise.

4

Building a Collection

ONE OF THE MOST EXCITING PARTS of working with crystals is adding new tools to your collection. Shopping for crystals can be both enjoyable and overwhelming if you do not know where to begin, so it's always a good idea to educate yourself about the market beforehand.

There are many places to shop for crystals. Metaphysical and spiritual bookstores, body-mind-spirit expos, and local rock shops are all great places to start. Many communities have a local gem and mineral club that offers educational and networking opportunities, and most will also host a rock and mineral show with a wide variety of vendors. These local events often have the best prices for rocks, minerals, fossils, lapidary rough, crystals, gemstones, and jewelry. Don't forget to check out science museum gift shops either. There's always the internet too.

When looking for stones to round out your toolbox for crystal healing, consider how you will want to use them. Are you looking for something wearable, or do you want a loose stone to lay on the body or carry with you throughout the day? Do you need multiples of the same stone to make crystal grids, or will a single, large specimen of rough stone suffice for your sacred space? Do you have a good variety of different colors, shapes, and sizes in your collection?

HELPFUL CONSIDERATIONS

There are many factors to consider when purchasing stones, including size, shape, quality, provenance, and (perhaps most important) price. Each of these will influence what you buy and how it can be used. Let's take a closer look at these factors.

Size

Despite what you may have read elsewhere, size does indeed matter when it comes to crystals—but not always the way you might expect. Larger stones usually produce a greater amplitude and thus have a louder or more forceful energy. Many people try to discredit this idea by comparing stones like rhodizite and moldavite, which pack a powerful punch even when tiny, to more common crystals, like agate or amethyst. However this is a case of comparing apples to oranges; a piece of moldavite that weighs 100 grams is going to feel much different from one that weighs only 4 or 5.

Just because larger stones have a more intense energy doesn't mean that they are always appropriate. If we continue with the analogy of sound, you don't need to shout at the top of your lungs to be heard by someone standing right next to you. Small stones are appropriate for most of our everyday applications. However greater mass will increase the range of a crystal's energy; this means that for larger grids or more immediate results when we practice laying-on-of-stones, bigger stones may occasionally be necessary. Naturally, small stones are easier to carry, wear, and place on the body, so we should consider practicality above all else when assessing the size that we need.

Shape

There are many who believe that rough or natural specimens are inherently more powerful than their polished counterparts. Conversely, some schools of crystal healing subscribe to the belief that a stone's healing benefits are only unlocked when cut and polished into the correct shape. From our perspective, the fundamental energy of a rock or mineral is not determined by its external shape but instead by the principles of its inner world, such as its composition and structure. No amount of polishing alters the fundamental composition or molecular structure of a gemstone, so the same fundamental energy is present regardless of the outer shape.

There is an expression often used in design that states that "form follows function." This is true of our crystal tools too. Naturally terminated crystal specimens and polished crystal wands have an inherently directional quality to them. Spheres distribute their energy in a softer, more diffuse manner. Tumbled stones may seem gentler than rough stones with crystal faces and jagged edges, while crystal clusters radiate energy wherever their crystals face. Though these differences may account for our perception of a crystal's energy, they do not change the fundamental energy itself. Thus a crystal's shape only influences the way that stone's energy is delivered.

From a practical perspective, shape can have a big impact on how we use our stones. Perfect spheres do not lay on the body comfortably for crystal healing treatments, and rough stones can be uncomfortable to carry in one's pocket. Therefore we have to base our decisions on how we want to use our crystals. This encourages many crystal lovers to collect several iterations of their most beloved stones so that they can be prepared for a variety of scenarios.

Crystal Shapes

When starting out, the variety of rocks, minerals, crystals, and gemstones can be staggering. In addition to the sheer number of different stones, there is a wide range of shapes, sizes, and forms in which each one can be found. Here is a helpful guide to some of the more common natural and polished forms that you'll encounter as you build your crystal toolbox.

Crystal shapes (from left to right, starting at the top left): egg, rough, heart, point, skull, cluster, tumbled, pyramid, sphere

Egg: Eggs represent fertility, creativity, and growth. Stones carved into this shape can be gently anchoring, and they make excellent massage tools.

Rough: Rough stones are unpolished and uncut. They may exhibit crystal faces or have only indistinct, broken surfaces. Rough stones tend to have a less refined energy than polished ones, and they may be more grounding than some polished shapes.

Heart: Gemstone hearts are tokens of love, affection, and emotional balance. Many lie flat on the body for use in healing, and smaller specimens fit into the pocket nicely.

Point: This is the classic crystal shape. Crystals with a single termination, or point, direct energy through their point. They may be natural or polished into this shape.

Skull: Skulls carved from crystals and gemstones are powerful tools for expanding the consciousness, deepening spiritual practice, and communing with nonhuman intelligences, such as guides, ancestors, devas, and star beings. Crystal skulls are dimensional doorways, and they bring healing on the soul level.

Cluster: Many mineral species form as groups of crystals attached to a common matrix or base. These clusters disperse their energy in many directions and are helpful for uplifting the vibes in a whole room or for harmonizing groups of people.

Tumbled: Tumbled stones are irregular, rounded shapes produced by a machine called a rock tumbler. These are among the most readily available and affordable shapes on the market, and they are perfect for carrying in the pocket, placing on the body, or adding to a crystal grid.

Pyramid: Pyramids are popular shapes for gemstones, and they simultaneously offer an anchoring and uplifting influence. Pyramid-shaped stones can support manifestation, confer protection, and help align the entire energy field.

Sphere: Spherical stones emit a gentle, pervasive energy that flows evenly in all directions at once. Spheres are balancing, nourishing, and unifying. Small spheres of exceptional quality are powerful healing tools used in the systems of healing called *gemstone therapy* and *gemstone energy medicine*.

Wand: Crystal wands may be natural or polished, and they come in a wide variety of shapes, sizes, and materials. Wands can be used to activate crystal grids, cut cords, or direct energy in a healing session or in meditation and ritual.

Double-terminated: Double-terminated crystals exhibit points at each end. They are able to send and receive energy from each termination, and they help link energies, such as harmonizing two chakras or connecting two crystals in a grid. Double-terminated crystals are most effective when they are naturally occurring, but many polished options are available too.

Obelisk and generator: Obelisks are usually polished pillars with square bases and pyramidal terminations. Generators are polished crystal points with flat bases that stand upright (though there are other configurations often referred to as generator crystals too). These shapes are sometimes called *towers,* and they exhibit the same directional flow of energy as crystal points. They are wonderful for broadcasting an energy or intention long distance, such as in crystal grids.

Cabochon: A cabochon is gemstone cut with a dome-shaped top and a flat underside. Though originally made for jewelry, they are excellent healing tools because they lie flat on the body.

Many other crystal shapes are available, from carved deities and animals, to exquisite flames and free-form sculptures. Each shape will offer its own symbolism and purpose, which can be explored through meditation, research, and experimentation.

Quality

Of all the parameters we can use to evaluate our stones, quality is often overlooked until our collections become more sophisticated. The overall quality of a rock, mineral, or gemstone can have a big influence on its energy. Let's take a gemstone like aquamarine as an example. The more perfect the stone, the more precise its energy will be. An imperfect stone will be filled with inclusions of other substances. These foreign materials aren't inherently helpful or harmful, but they do produce their own energies, thereby making an impure and imperfect stone more likely to have an energy signature that is hazy or imprecise.

Examples of different levels of quality of rhodonite (clockwise from top left): lower quality from Peru, low quality from Brazil, fine quality from Australia, gem quality from Brazil, medium quality from Afghanistan

Perfect stones express greater coherence, and they will have a more laserlike effect when used for healing.

Quality parameters differ from one stone to the next. What is desirable in lapis lazuli, for example, may be inappropriate for diamond. Color, clarity, and crystal form (or the polished shape in the case of gemstones) all play a role in determining the quality of a given stone. Translucent and transparent stones are valued for having clear interiors, and colored stones are graded by the intensity of their color. The presence or absence of mineral inclusions also influences the overall quality; this differs for each species of mineral.

Naturally, higher-quality stones command higher prices, and we must account for this accordingly. High-end specimens of much smaller size can command much higher value than large stones of lesser quality. Sometimes the mineral inclusions in less-than-perfect stones have an energy that we desire, such as the iron needed to transform clear quartz into amethyst. At other times they may detract from the goals we have in working with certain stones. When adding new tools to your collection, quality may take a backseat to other factors—especially when you're just starting out. However, as many of us grow our collections, we look to adding finer specimens to our toolboxes.

Provenance

Among mineral collectors, the provenance, or origin, of a specimen can make a substantial difference in its value. Historic mining locations often produce unique crystal shapes or mineral combinations; specimens from these locations are esteemed not only for their rarity and beauty but also for being tangible pieces of history. From an energetic perspective, two specimens of the same mineral will have different personalities if they come from different places. Quartz from Hot Springs, Arkansas (USA), has a markedly different energy from quartz from Minas Gerais, Brazil. The geology of each region on the planet creates unique vibrations among the stones that are commonly available.

Another aspect of provenance reflects not only where a stone was discovered but also how it got to you and by whom. Were the minerals mined in an environmentally conscious way? Were the people who mined them treated ethically, and were they paid fair wages? Were the stones bought and sold many times along the links of the chain that brought them to the store shelves before you? It may be impossible to know the answers to these kinds of questions for the vast majority of tools that you'll encounter, but looking for ethically sourced stones makes a big difference in the world. Gemstones like diamond, jade, and lapis lazuli often come from conflict-laden regions, and the sales of these gemstones can encourage the proliferation of violence and oppression.

Wherever possible, get to know your suppliers and their wares. If we demand justly sourced healing tools, the market will deliver them. This helps to support indigenous peoples worldwide who are responsible for the mining and polishing of much of the world's rocks, minerals, and gemstones. If we are attracted to crystals for their spiritual potential and healing energies, then we need to look for tools that reflect the change we want to see in the world and not just their metaphysical energies.

Price

It should probably go without saying that price is an important consideration in buying new crystals. The price of rock, mineral, and gem is sometimes subjective, as it fluctuates with changes in availability, demand, and taste. Size and quality impact the prices of stones considerably, as can provenance.

Price usually has the final say in whether we can bring a new stone home with us. No one should go broke trying to add new crystals to their healing toolbox. That said, the advice that one of my dear friends and mentors has always shared rings true: it's never the rocks you buy that you'll regret—it's the ones you don't buy. Some stores may have layaway options; vendors at shows may be willing to haggle on prices from time to time. If something is really the right tool for you, there is usually a way to bring it home.

Buyer Beware!

Buying crystals is not always a straightforward venture. Part of assessing the value of stones, not to mention their quality and provenance, is knowing what is natural and what is not. These days, artificial and treated stones abound on the market, and it can be hard to tell the difference between them. Here is a handy synopsis of the more common ones that you'll likely encounter.

These are examples of treated, simulated, and synthesized stones: (top row, left to right) dyed Brazilian agate, dyed howlite, dyed crackle quartz treated with thermal shocking, crackle agate dyed and treated with thermal shocking (often sold as fire agate), heat-treated citrine, aura quartz coated with titanium via vapor deposition; (bottom row, left to right) simulated aura quartz coated with teflon, artificially grown bismuth crystals, goldstone (a man-made glass), opalite (man-made glass), green "obsidian" (man-made glass), and simulated malachite made of resin

- **Treated** stones are altered in some way by humankind to improve or change their appearance. Gemstones have undergone treatments to raise their value for centuries, if not millennia, although in recent decades the range and frequency of treatments used has skyrocketed. In the metaphysical market, crystals and healing stones are often heated, dyed, irradiated, stabilized, or otherwise changed to make them more beautiful. *It is important to note that some of these treatments render the finished rock or gem nontherapeutic.*

- Stones that are **heat-treated,** like the citrine pictured on page 85, are generally still of therapeutic value, though they work more gently than their natural counterparts. Crackle quartz (also called *fire-and-ice quartz*) and some agates exhibit a special kind of heat treatment called *thermal shocking,* wherein the stones are rapidly heated and cooled to cause iridescent fissures to snake their way through the stone; these are often dyed bright colors.

- **Dyed** gemstones should be used with caution, if at all. They should *never* be placed in your drinking water, and they may stain skin or clothing when worn. Howlite and magnesite are frequently dyed to resemble more expensive minerals, like turquoise. Other stones, such as jade, quartzite, chrysocolla, and many others, are dyed to improve their appearance and command a higher market value.

- Other stones are **irradiated** to change their appearance. Such gemstones are also not generally of therapeutic grade, and many may still be radioactive. Commonly irradiated stones include smoky quartz, blue topaz, and some varieties of aquamarine and citrine found in fine jewelry.

- **Stabilized** stones are imbued with a filler material, such as wax, plastic, or resin, to make them more durable for use in jewelry. Tumbled stones and polished minerals are also sometimes stabilized. Turquoise is the most often seen stone that has undergone this treatment, though you may also find polished specimens of chrysocolla and malachite that are similarly stabilized. These stones may also be injected with dye during the stabilization process, and they may not be of therapeutic quality.

- One category of treated stones stands above the rest, both in popularity and their mesmerizing appearance; these are **aura crystals.** These stones are the result of a process called *vapor deposition* or *precious metal anadonization*. Natural crystals are coated in a superficial layer of metals, like gold, platinum, titanium, nickel, iron, or niobium, to create eye-catching, iridescent finishes. These crystals have passionate fans and ardent opponents. Personally, I do not often use them in my healing practice, although I do have several beautiful specimens in my collection. Nowadays, aura quartz can be simulated with cheap resins and pigments and with teflon, so one must be careful when buying these crystals, as they may not be therapeutic quality.

• **Synthetic** stones are man-made counterparts to natural stones. They are grown in a laboratory, and they are often used in jewelry as cheaper, more perfect alternatives to natural stones. Synthetic quartz is used in our electronics, and synthetic corundum (sapphire and ruby) is used in watch faces, smartphones, and laser technology. Because synthetic crystals have the same components and crystal structure as their naturally occurring equivalents, they may be used in healing; however, you may find that they feel somewhat empty or quiet energetically until they have been properly cared for. Synthetic quartz is often sold on the metaphysical market as "Siberian quartz" and is in bright colors. Synthetic bismuth and zincite crystals are also popular, and they are effective tools for healing.

• **Artificial** or **simulated** stones are materials that do not occur in nature. Many times they are made to mimic the look and feel of natural stones, but they are not made of the same substances. The most common artificial stones available today are really only man-made glass, and these include opalite, goldstone, andara glass, and fancifully colored "obsidian." Similarly, materials like blueberry "quartz" and cherry "quartz" are in fact nothing more than glass. These stones do not have a crystalline structure, nor are they as mineral-dense as natural glasses like obsidian and tektite. Personally, I find the majority of the materials to be vibrationally neutral and nontherapeutic. They are best appreciated for their beauty and not their healing potential. Other artificial stones can be made of resin, ceramic, plastic, and similar materials; naturally these have no place at all in crystal healing. Malachite, amber, and jade are often simulated with resin or plastic. Some artificial stones are crystalline, like silicon carbide (also called *carborundum*); these crystals do not occur in nature, but they do have the coherent energy of natural stones.

One last cautionary category exists: stones that have been renamed. Crystal miners, distributors, and vendors of all varieties have rebranded old stones to make them more interesting and to command a higher price. Beware of stones with the trademark symbol (™) or copyright symbol (©) appearing alongside their names, as these almost always indicate that a material has been given a more interesting name. These stones are not necessarily any more or less effective than their more truthfully labeled counterparts, but they will command a higher price—sometimes by a factor of ten or more! Low-quality quartz, granite, and other rocks are renamed with magical, metaphysical-sounding names to make them appeal to the healing market. Always do your research to make sure that you know what you are buying.

When purchasing crystals, don't be afraid to ask about their provenance. By learning where they come from and whether they've been altered, you can become a more discerning buyer.

BUILDING A HEALING TOOLBOX

Ultimately the goal in learning how to source the right stones is to have the right tools for the right task. No matter how beautiful or eye-catching our collection, the goal of the crystal healer is to have viable tools for energy medicine. Once you have acquainted yourself with where to shop and how to store your stones (see the section "Storing Crystals," page 95), the next step is to build a healing toolbox.

There are many approaches one can take to building a versatile collection of crystals. Many budding crystal healers rely on color to help them curate their collections; having all the colors of the spectrum represented in your collection allows you to work on a wide array of issues. Another approach is to collect samples of all seven crystal systems (don't forget the amorphous stones). Conversely, you might choose to aim for a diverse assortment of mineral-forming elements.

Choosing the Right Stones

When it comes to selecting the right stones, there are many ways to narrow down the selection process. First and foremost, many crystal healers and collectors use a prescriptive route, which means they look up crystals that correspond to the issue they are looking to resolve or the goal they want to manifest. Although this is a viable way to choose, it can be limiting, as it causes you to rely on an external source for validation and wholly sidesteps your own intuition and autonomy. Instead of merely relying on crystal books (even the one you're reading now), the best bet is to seek the stones with which you have a special connection.

One popular way of choosing crystals is via dowsing. A pendulum or a dowsing rod can be used to answer yes/no questions, such as "Is this the crystal that will benefit this situation?" or "Is this the stone that I need?" Dowsing can also reveal the changes in your energy field and chakras when you hold or work with your stones. It is a helpful tool for those who may not be as sensitive to the energy of the mineral kingdom, and it is also a helpful diagnostic tool.

Applied kinesiology, also referred to as *muscle testing,* is an invaluable way to check for the compatibility between your own energy and that of the crystal (or virtually anything else for that matter). There are several methods available, some of which require a partner to use effectively. My favorite technique is one that I first learned in gemstone therapy, a healing modality that uses high-quality gemstone spheres. Another method that many of my students find helpful is the body pendulum.

◆ *The Pull-In Test*

The pull-in test is one of my favorite ways to decide which stones to work with for myself. It can be used to select the right crystal to add to your toolbox or which one might be appropriate to wear or carry throughout the day. This method can be used for single specimens (like tumbled or rough stones carried in the pocket), pieces of jewelry, or virtually any other form of crystal.

Start by laying out the stones from which you are choosing before you. Take a couple of deep breaths and quiet your mind. When you are ready to test the stones, hold the first one cupped in one or both hands; extend your hands in front of you, roughly level with the thymus gland, located at the center of your sternum, just above the inward dip. The energy center associated with this organ, the higher heart center, is an energetic window into the overall health and well-being of your energy field.

Gently begin to pull the stone toward you, allowing the stone to guide your hands as you draw it closer to your body. As your hands approach your body, you may find that you feel resistance, as if your hands have hit an invisible cushion. Sometimes it may feel like the stone is drawn to you as if by a magnet. In other instances the stone will take a circuitous path rather than moving directly toward the thymus. Whatever sensations you might experience, allow the stone to guide the motion however it needs to. If it feels as if the stone has hit a barrier or if it feels repelled by you, move on to the next stone. The stone or stones that are most readily drawn to the body reflect the energies of which you are in greatest need.

Note that the results of this method will vary from day to day as well as from one stone to another. Just like we have unique cravings for different foods, our energy field will respond to the energies of gemstones differently as it changes each day. Some stones may be readily accepted one day but pushed away the next.

◆ The Body Pendulum

For many people who are less sensitive to energy, the body pendulum is a simple and effective technique. When trying to determine which crystal to buy, or perhaps which one to wear or carry on a particular day, the body pendulum offers a simple yes/no answer without the use of any external tools.

As with the pull-in test, start by laying out the stone(s) you wish to test. Take a moment to breathe deeply and clear your mind. Hold the stone you are testing to your center of gravity (your solar plexus), and ask a clear and concise yes/no question, such as "Is this the best stone for me to wear today?" or "Is this the best piece of red jasper to add to my healing kit?" After the question has been formed, wait for your body's response.

If you feel yourself leaning forward, the answer is *yes.* If you feel yourself leaning backward, the answer is *no.* Oftentimes these shifts in direction will be very slight, but palpable nonetheless. These tiny motions are an example of applied kinesiology, and they are unconscious movements. Many people who are skeptical when I teach this technique are amazed at how quickly they master it. The more you practice, the faster the responses will come, and you may even find that you do not have to ask a question—merely holding the stone to your solar plexus triggers the response as your body responds to the energy of the stone.

It is also possible to decide which crystal to purchase or put to work based solely on psychic or intuitive feedback. As we build our relationship with our stones, we usually become more sensitive to their energies, and we can simply sense which ones are the right tools. Many times we are drawn straight to the right stone for us; we may not even realize this is a form of psychic feedback from the stone. It might be the way it sparkles or an attraction to its color or texture, but whatever it is, the stone will find a way to communicate in a language that we can perceive. If you are shopping for crystals, take a step back from all the stones on display and allow your gaze to wander over all the treasures before you. There's a good chance that you'll be inexplicably drawn to exactly the stone you need.

As you gain more experience, you may find yourself using a much less intuitive approach to choosing your crystals. Instead you might start to look for more refined additions to your collection. Exquisite minerals often increase in value over time, and they are a beauty to behold. Striking mineral specimens are often powerful healing tools (though a crystal does not necessarily have to be gorgeous to be effective). I can vividly remember the point in my crystal journey when I pulled back on the number of stones that I bought in favor of aiming for higher-quality tools. Part of that resulted from all the experience I had gained working in the mineral science field in a museum setting—when you are armed with knowledge and experience, it helps you to become a more discerning buyer. In part, though, this shift was born of necessity—I already had more small crystals than I could count!

These days I find myself occasionally at odds with myself when shopping for crystals: the intuitive part of me is drawn to the energy of one crystal, while the collector is looking for the textbook-perfect specimen. In the end I know that both options will do the job effectively, so I try to weigh my options carefully.

Uncomfortable Gems
with Uncomfortable Truths

Most crystal lovers settle into a rhythm for choosing new stones. Perhaps we read about something amazing in a book, or we simply fall in love with something because of its amazing color. There may be times when we hunt down a stone based on the recommendations of a friend or colleague. More than likely, though, what we are really seeking is a stone that shares a certain feeling with us.

Even if it might be hard to put into words, you've surely felt that sensation. A new stone gives you that warm-and-fuzzy feeling that lets you know it's the perfect companion. A stone like this is bound to be the right one to help you grow, right?

What if the opposite were true? Imagine, if you will, that the crystals and gemstones that provide you with that warm-and-fuzzy feeling are affirming some energy, lesson, or message *that you have already integrated.* These stones feel so nice because they aren't upsetting the apple cart. They emphasize some part of you that has already achieved growth and learned a lesson.

Now, what about those stones that make you feel uncomfortable? You know the ones—they might give you that sensation of butterflies in the stomach, or maybe a headache. Perhaps they just leave you feeling unsettled. For many crystal lovers, their first encounter with a stone like this might be a high-consciousness stone like moldavite or phenakite, but many of us feel this same way with seemingly ordinary stones. I had a friend in high school who couldn't go near chrysocolla. I myself had difficulty with gem-quality indigo sodalite. These are the stones we tend to overlook in our work, and they usually aren't the ones we are eager to wear all day long.

You might be wondering what we're supposed to do with these stones and what they have to offer us. The fact is that the stones that make us the most uncomfortable are the ones that represent the lessons we have yet to master. They are the ones that vibrate enharmonically with an energy that is *outside* of us. That's what makes us feel downright icky sometimes when holding a stone. Our natural inclination is to reach for the stones that resonate with our "home" vibration and to avoid those that take us outside of it. However, it is those strange, energetically foreign crystals that can assist you with your greatest growth potential.

Working with these stones can be challenging. I remember when I first got a necklace made of therapeutic-quality indigo sodalite spheres. I was so eager to wear it that I put it on right away and immediately went to work. Within a couple of hours I had to take it off and stow it in my bag, as I wasn't quite myself. I'm sure that you may have had a similar experience. So what do we do with these stones? Use them in short bursts in a safe space. Wear or carry them in small increments, and gradually build your tolerance. Meditate with them and use them in self-therapy. Experiment. Cleanse them frequently. The protocol won't be the same for all of us. You'll need to forge a relationship with your stones and see where it leads you. The more respectfully and open-mindedly you approach the stones you are repelled by, the more likely you are to learn their inner teachings.

The next time you visit your favorite crystal shop, keep this in mind as you select new tools to take home. Don't just go for the newest, sparkliest, and warm-and-fuzziest crystals. Pay attention to the stones that make you want to turn and run the other way. They may be difficult to get to know at first, but they can become your greatest allies and teachers in time.

Shopping for Someone Else

Over the years I have heard so much conflicting advice on how to select stones for someone else. They have ranged from the idea that the most powerful tools for healing must be given as gifts—you cannot buy them for yourself—to the principle that you must only ever purchase your own crystals because it is such a personal experience. Naturally the truth lies somewhere in the middle of these extremes.

The bottom line is that it's perfectly acceptable to buy crystals for other people. When I shop for others or when I consult with clients who are looking for crystal gifts, I always make an effort to connect with the recipient of the gift. If you are shopping for a loved one, picture them in your mind or reflect on their name; you may also want to think of what positive influence you want to bring to their life with a new crystal or gemstone. Then look over the variety of stones or jewelry available and see what stands out.

Provided we approach shopping for others with the same openness as when we seek out stones for our personal collection, then we will achieve the same results. Giving crystal gifts is both meaningful and transformational, for both the giver and the receiver.

Crystal Starter Kit

On a weekly basis I see people who are overwhelmed with the sheer number of crystals that are available to them. When you are just starting out it can be helpful to have a template for what constitutes a well-rounded set that will cover all the bases for crystal healing. Following are some guidelines for compiling a basic working set of crystals for healing.

- Clear quartz points (at least six)
- Grounding stones (at least four)
- Higher-consciousness stones
- Crystal wand(s), natural or polished
- Two or more tumbled or rough stones in each color of the spectrum
- Crystal clusters
- A pendulum

With the above stones you'll be able to create layouts on and around the body, build crystal grids, dowse the overall health of the human energy field, and perform a variety of specific therapies. Wands can be used to remove blockages, cut cords, activate grids, and extract foreign energies. Clusters can scrub the aura as well as lend an uplifting energy to the room. Having an assortment of clear quartz crystals enables you to make simple crystal grids as well as create layouts around the body. An assortment of colors (and presumably mineral content) allows you to have a broad range of energies represented in your collection. Similarly, have a selection of both grounding stones (such as petrified wood, hematite, black tourmaline, shungite, smoky quartz, garnet, pyrite) and higher-consciousness stones (such as moldavite, phenakite, rhodizite, herderite, selenite, etc.), which will allow you to facilitate deeper, longer-lasting shifts in consciousness.

Your toolbox will transform over time. It will change as you change and as your collection grows. What begins as a basic set may become more refined over the years, and you may find some of the more unusual stones joining some of the basic ones listed here. These days there are some stones that are indispensable in my personal healing kit, whether working on myself or my clients. Invariably you're likely to find some combination of aquamarine, obsidian, lapis lazuli, pietersite, malachite, shungite, citrine, Lemurian seed crystal, laser wand, kyanite, calcite, and selenite in my toolbox when I teach or meet clients for treatments. Generally speaking, I like to connect with the person receiving the treatment and select crystals that meet their specific needs; however, there are some tools that I use almost universally. Experiment with the crystals in your collection to find the perfect working set for you.

STORING CRYSTALS

When you're first starting out on your crystal journey, storing your crystals may not be much of a challenge. However, as your collection grows, you'll need a way to keep your beloved mineral treasures safe and sound. The most important considerations for storing your crystals are safety and accessibility. It is important to ensure that you have easy access to your healing tools while preventing any unexpected accidents.

There are different approaches to storing crystals that vary according to tradition and culture. For example, many Native traditions stress the importance of keeping crystals wrapped in cloth or some other form of protection until they are to be used; they are never displayed for all the world to see. Other spiritual traditions may encourage displaying crystals, such as by placing them on your altar. Many crystal lovers recommend storing stones in natural materials to allow your crystals to breathe energetically. This allows their energies to still be broadcast into the room around them. Storing in materials like plastic, however, has a bit of a dampening and insulating effect on crystals; this mitigates their ability to project their energy into the room around them—which is helpful if you find yourself very sensitive to crystal energy. Plastic containers also insulate your stones from outside energies, and they are durable and affordable too.

Rocks and minerals of all sizes make attractive additions to your home, garden, and office decor. Be mindful of exposure to light and moisture if you leave your stones on display. A sunny windowsill may seem like the perfect home for your favorite crystals, but you'll find that many colored stones, like amethyst, citrine, rose quartz, fluorite, calcite, aquamarine, and kunzite will lose their color from prolonged exposure to sunshine. Crystals that are kept outdoors are also subject to changes in temperature, precipitation, and other factors, so be sure to use stones of adequate hardness. The humidity of the bathroom or kitchen may not be suitable for water-sensitive stones like halite or selenite.

When storing your crystals, it's a good idea to double-check their hardness and avoid storing softer stones with harder ones, as they stand a good chance of getting damaged. Similarly, rough stones and crystal points may not be appropriate to mix with tumbled and polished stones. Many collectors and crystal healers use plastic or wooden boxes with small compartments to organize their collections; though I prefer natural materials, I use mostly plastic for my smaller stones. Beautiful cabinets, glass cases, and other displays can protect specimens large and small from dust and moisture while allowing you to enjoy their beauty around the clock. Delicate specimens may need to be stored separately or wrapped in cloth or acid-free, undyed tissue paper when not in use. Cloth pouches are handy ways to store crystals between use or to protect them when you carry them with you.

However you store your crystals, be aware about where you place them. Sometimes tuning in to a crystal will help you find the perfect place to put it. When we engage with our crystals in a conscious, meaningful way like this, our precious stones will support us and maintain the energetic integrity of our environs wherever we keep them.

Cleaning Crystals

Early in my metaphysical studies as a teen I learned that dirt and dust accumulate disharmony. No matter how you store your crystals, gemstone jewelry, and mineral specimens, they will eventually need to be cleaned; this benefits not only their beauty but improves their energy. Many crystal books give advice for cleansing the energy of your stones but neglect to offer advice about physically cleaning your collection. Some cleaning methods may also damage your beloved tools.

Generally speaking, dirt and dust can be removed with a cloth, soft-bristled brush, water, or a can of compressed air. I would follow the same guidelines given in chapter 5 about energetically cleansing your crystals with water, and be sure to avoid using water on soft, porous, soluble, friable (easily crumbled), or otherwise delicate minerals. For those that are water-safe, you can use a mild detergent when necessary, but tepid water usually does the trick. Prolonged exposure can damage some specimens that are otherwise safe to take a quick rinse, so always exercise caution. Once clean, always be sure that your stones are thoroughly dry before putting them away.

For those rocks and minerals that cannot be immersed, many can be wiped clean with a soft cloth or dusted with a brush or a can of compressed air. Fragile specimens should be handled with caution, as even these methods can damage some crystal formations. Avoid using cleaning chemicals unless you really know your crystal chemistry.

Jewelry, on the other hand, requires a different kind of upkeep. Metals like silver will benefit from regular polishing, but some gemstones are too sensitive to be cleaned with traditional polishing creams and dips. Always consult with someone with experience, such as a jeweler or gemologist, if you are uncertain.

5

Foundational Practices

THERE ARE SEVERAL IMPORTANT STEPS to master before you dive into working with crystals for healing. Cleansing, dedicating, and programming your crystals are chief among these practices. With so many ways to approach each of these important steps, I've dedicated this chapter to exploring each one from multiple angles. You'll find a good mix of theory and practice throughout, thereby empowering you to choose the right techniques for you.

CLEANSING CRYSTALS

If we recall the essential functions of crystals from chapter 1, we will remember that crystals retain memories of their experiences, much like we humans do. These memories are imprints of the energies that the crystals have experienced. This energy is inherently neither good nor bad; it either supports your intention or it doesn't. When a stone is saturated with energy that impedes our ability to manifest our goals, it needs to be energetically cleansed.*

Cleansing crystals is an essential step to building a relationship with them. Cleansing new crystals is important because they have been handled by many people on their journey to you. Not everyone involved in the process of mining, preparing, shipping, distributing, and selling crystals is conscious of their own energy and how it affects crystals. Even though many conscious retailers will cleanse crystals when they arrive, customers in their stores will also leave an energetic mark on the stones they handle. Cleansing your new crystals gives you an opportunity to wipe away the energetic debris that your tools have accumulated and start with a blank slate.

When we cleanse our crystals the benefits are really twofold. On the surface, a crystal that is clean and clear is ready to do its work, whether for personal

---

*Note that I use the term *cleanse* to indicate energetic or spiritual purification of a stone. When referring to the physical removal of dirt, dust, and such, from a stone, I use the term *clean*. See the previous chapter for recommendations on how to clean your stones.

or planetary healing. If we want to work on ourselves, our clients, or our environment, it is first necessary to have tools that are uncontaminated by outside frequencies, much like we expect a surgeon to use sterilized instruments. At a deeper level, the act of cleansing crystals deepens our relationship with them and helps us tidy our own interior landscapes. Just like the principle of correspondence, which states "As above, so below," when we cleanse our crystals, we are also cleansing ourselves. The result is a sense of clarity that enables us to do our work more effectively and authentically.

Do All Stones Need to Be Cleansed?

There is a popular idea that certain crystals never need to be cleansed. This notion began with the publication of the Love Is in the Earth series by Melody. Initially her list of crystals that never need to be cleansed consisted only of citrine and kyanite, but it has grown to include nearly thirty different crystals. In the wake of this, popular lore in the crystal community insists that some commonly available tools like selenite and hematite do not need to be cleansed either.

It's not often that I consider something to be black-or-white, but I make an exception when it comes to cleansing crystals. Either *all* crystals need to be cleansed, or *no* crystals need to be cleansed; however, the truth is that both are true depending on how you look at the situation. Remembering that there is a consciousness inherent in each member of the mineral kingdom, we can liken their need to be cleansed as being similar to metabolizing the energy that they ingest, in the same way we metabolize our food. Rocks and minerals can clear their energy on their own, but they frequently do this on the scale of geological time—a pace that is much slower than our lifetime. Thus virtually any stone can be said to never need cleansing or clearing, provided that we are patient enough.

However, if we are seeing clients back-to-back (or even more than once a year), we will need to cleanse our crystals of the energetic memories left by the last treatment we gave. Otherwise it would be a lot like a surgeon using the same scalpel for different patients without sterilizing it between use. Some crystals will surely burn off discordant energy faster than others, and they may not need thorough cleansing between uses, but others will hold on to those patterns of disharmonious energy for much longer. Cleansing your crystals often will solve this problem. As well, be aware that disharmonious energies can be released in a crystal healing session, and so care should be taken to attend to spiritual hygiene and protection practices, a subject we'll take up in greater detail in chapter 10.

Methods of Cleansing

Searching online or in books, you'll soon discover that there are a multitude of ways to cleanse your crystals; however, sometimes these methods are confusing or downright contradictory. The more common methods for cleansing crystals include:

- ▶ Sunlight and moonlight
- ▶ Salt
- ▶ Rinsing with running water
- ▶ Smoke from cleansing herbs like sage, cedar, or palo santo
- ▶ Sound
- ▶ Breath
- ▶ Burying in the earth
- ▶ Rain, snow, or wind
- ▶ Immersing in flower petals, cleansing herbs, or brown rice
- ▶ Storing inside a pyramid or other sacred geometry formation
- ▶ Placing atop other crystals, such as selenite or an amethyst cluster
- ▶ Using flower and gemstone essences
- ▶ Visualization and prayer

Most cleansing methods fall into the category of either physics-based or faith-based. The former cleansing methods are based on a scientific model that describes why and how they work; the latter works because of our inherent belief in it. Sunlight, sacred smoke, and prayer are examples of faith-based methods of cleansing. Sound and alternating currents of warm and cool water both impact the crystal lattice, thereby invoking the laws of physics to describe how and why they work. Each of these methods has its pros and cons. Furthermore, some stones can be damaged by salt, water, soil, and even sunlight. Other methods, such as cleansing or charging under the full moon, are inconvenient most nights of the lunar cycle. Let's explore some of these methods in greater detail.

Sunlight

Light from the sun has been revered as sacred since the beginning of time, and many crystals—quartz in particular—have enjoyed a special relationship with the sun throughout human history. However prolonged exposure to sunlight can cause many of your favorite stones to bleach over time. Some of the most photosensitive minerals include calcite, fluorite, aquamarine, amethyst, rose quartz, citrine, kunzite, hiddenite, morganite, and many others. As a rule of thumb, I avoid direct sunlight for most transparent or translucent-colored gemstones, and I limit sun exposure to not more than fifteen minutes unless a stone is opaque or otherwise colorfast. Sun exposure requires some additional caution, as it can cause stones to heat and cool rapidly, which in turn causes internal fissures that weaken stones. As well, a convex, polished piece of a transparent stone can act as a lens that could start a fire if not attended to. All in all, sunlight should be reserved for cleansing opaque or low-quality stones.

Moonlight

One of the most persistent and popular methods of cleansing crystals involves placing them under the light of the full moon. From a physics-based perspective, there isn't anything especially effective about using moonlight—it's no more special than sunlight or even fluorescent lighting insofar as how it interacts with a crystal's lattice. However the moon has been held sacred by the world's cultures for millennia, and the lunar cycle has a demonstrable effect on the human psyche and on the subtle, immeasurable energies of the spiritual world. Though we cannot measure the moon's effects on crystals, moonlight can indeed be employed for cleansing your crystals. It is safer than sunlight, as it will not cause delicate stones to fade, but be wary of leaving soft, porous, or water-sensitive stones outdoors to soak up the moonlight if nighttime moisture and rain pose a threat. Direct, prolonged moonlight is most effective, although it is not necessary to use only the light of the full moon. It may be inconvenient to round up your entire crystal collection and place it on windowsills to moon bathe, so I prefer to save moonlight cleansing for those special stones with a particular affinity for the moon.

Salt

When I was first introduced to the world of crystals, salt and water were the ubiquitous methods of cleansing one's stones. Crystals can be buried in salt or placed atop a layer of salt in a dish or bowl. For best results, use noniodized natural salt such as sea salt, rock salt, or kosher salt. A simple and effective way to use salt for cleansing your stones is with a slab or block of Himalayan rock salt. These are often sold for use in the kitchen, but they can be repurposed for cleansing crystals. For delicate stones, place a thin, natural-fiber cloth between the salt and your stones to prevent scratching. Nowadays I like to use a dish

Salt can be an effective cleansing tool.

filled with large chunks of Himalayan rock salt for a gentle daily cleanse of my tools; as soon as I walk in the door, I slip out of my shoes and place my pocket stones and crystal jewelry on the salt to neutralize disharmonious or unhealthy energies. The length of time required for cleansing is at least an hour or two; I often leave my crystals to cleanse overnight. Salt should be disposed of and replaced frequently, depending on the frequency of use.

Be mindful that salt can cause irreversible damage to some stones. It is a dessicant, so be extra careful with minerals that have a high water content, such as opals. Soft stones are easily scratched by salt too, so always check the hardness of your crystals before immersing them in salt. Avoid using salt to cleanse minerals with a hardness less than 4 or 5 on the Mohs scale.

Water

Water is regarded as a universal solvent and the elixir of life. Water symbolizes renewal, change, and release, and this is why it is so often recommended for cleansing crystals. Cleansing with water is probably a prehistoric practice, one that stems from the visceral, automatic desire to wash away both physical and psychic dirt. Today there are several variations on cleansing with water. Some employ natural bodies of water, such as streams, lakes, and oceans. Others combine salt—preferably from the sea—with water to rinse or soak crystals and gemstones.

In some ways, water is a physics-based cleansing method. Rinsing in water will often cause a temperature change in the crystal lattice, albeit a minute one, which may initiate the piezoelectric effect, thus discharging some of the stored energy in your stones. Marcel Vogel, however, found that using saltwater actually impeded the effects of crystals that he employed in his healing work, a fact that I have interpreted to mean that cleansing with water-based methods may be rooted more in faith than science.

There are several caveats when using water to cleanse your crystals. The first is to ensure that the stone is durable enough to withstand exposure to water. Some minerals such as hanksite, chalcanthite, or halite will dissolve in water outright. Other minerals, usually fibrous or earthy ones, are friable and will splinter or break apart when exposed to water. Some examples of these include satin spar selenite, chrysotile, sandstone, and chalk. Some crystal clusters and mineral specimens can also be loosened from their matrix when saturated with water. Many other stones are susceptible to the dissolved mineral solids and the pH of water; their surfaces may be marred by these substances, causing their luster to dull over time. Generally speaking, avoid using water-cleansing methods for minerals softer than 4 on the Mohs scale of hardness. It's also a good idea to check that your stone isn't soluble or won't react with water in any other way. Always be sure to dry your stones thoroughly after cleansing and before storing them.

◆ Cleansing with Water

I learned one of my most beloved and practical methods of cleansing crystals from my study of gemstone therapy, a specialized modality of crystal healing that employs high-quality gemstone spheres and strands of beads in its methodology. Gratefully this method is suited to cleansing any water-stable crystal or healing stone. All you'll need is running water from your tap and the stone or stones that you'd like to cleanse. If you'd like to cleanse several at once, they can be placed in a plastic colander.

Set your intention to cleanse your stone, and invite the consciousness of the stone to participate in your cleansing process. Turn the faucet to a warm setting and place the crystal you want to cleanse under the running water. Gradually

Water is a powerful cleanser but should be used with caution on certain stones.

adjust the water temperature so it becomes cooler as the stone is showered by the water. Repeat the process, changing the water from warm to cool and back again several times. Be sure to *never* make the water too hot or cold, or to change the temperature too rapidly, as this can cause damage to your beloved stone.

By using alternating warm and cool water, the crystal lattice of your healing tools will gently expand and contract. This tiny movement is akin to wringing out a sponge, and it sweeps away any old energy or information that your stone is carrying. The running water will direct the energy that is being discharged down the drain. Once your crystal is cleansed, allow it to dry adequately before storing or using.

Sound

Sound is a form of physical energy in that it is a vibrating column of air molecules that we translate into sensory information. Because it is a measurable force, sound is perfect for cleansing crystals as it relies on principles of physics. Waves of sound cause nearly imperceptible deformations in the crystal lattice. Much like using alternating warm and cool water for cleansing, this method invokes quartz's piezoelectric property and releases energy stored within it. Conscious, intentional sound is the best way to go, as opposed to recordings. Bells, chimes, singing bowls, wind instruments, drums, and the human voice can all be used to cleanse your crystals. In high school I experimented with keyboards, piano, and the French horn; each worked surprisingly well.

Sound is one of the safest and most effective ways
to cleanse your crystals.

Sound is by far one of the simplest and safest ways to cleanse your stones. It won't bleach gems with delicate colors the way sunlight does. You won't risk damage to your stones the way you would with water, salt, or other crystals either.

◆ Vocal Cleansing

Using the voice to cleanse your crystals is practical and effective. It requires no additional props, making it ideal for when you're on the go or need to cleanse a crystal quickly. Select the crystal that you would like to cleanse. Set the intention to cleanse your stone and hold it in front of your face in one or both hands, depending on the size and shape. Breathe deeply from the diaphragm, and begin to tone any note or sound, such as an extended *ahhh* as you exhale. It doesn't have to be a beautiful sound—any sound will do.

I use my intuition to select the sound I make to cleanse my stone, but you could combine this method with your favorite mantra or sacred chant. A simple *om* will do, but you might also like to try *om mani padme hum* (the six-syllable mantra of the Buddha of Compassion) or *IAO* (pronounced *ee-ah-oh*, a sacred formula representing the divine used in several occult and spiritual practices). Trust your intuition to find the right pitch, duration, and number of times to repeat your toning.

Smoke

Cleansing with smoke is generally safe for all your crystal healing tools. Herbs and incense with a cleansing energy such as sage, palo santo, cedar, mugwort, frankincense, copal, juniper, lavender, bay, and hyssop (among others) are

The smoke from sacred herbs such as sage, cedar, and palo santo can be used to cleanse your crystals.

effective for clearing stagnant energies and transforming disharmony. Many of these are available as smudging bundles, loose herbs and resins, and as incense sticks and cones. Consider finding herbs that grow in your region so as not to contribute to the overharvesting of plants like white sage and palo santo, two herbs that have gained in popularity in recent years.

With sacred smoke it is easy to cleanse many crystals at once without having to rearrange or transport your entire collection. Smoke shouldn't damage the crystals in your collection (if something is fragile enough to be damaged by smoke, it definitely shouldn't be used in healing directly), and it is also relatively easy to employ. Many people have allergies or sensitivities to the smoke of some of these plants, so use with caution and in well-ventilated areas.

Cleansing with Other Crystals

Using one crystal to cleanse another has become more popular in recent years. The very first iterations of this concept I ever saw made use of either a quartz crystal cluster or a ring of quartz crystals around the stone being cleansed with the quartz points facing away from the central stone to be cleansed. Since then a number of other stones have made their way into the cleansing milieu, chief among them selenite. Slabs and polished plates of satin spar selenite are often used to cleanse and charge other crystals. However, since this variety of selenite in particular is more porous and friable than other varieties, it too needs frequent cleansing. Many people who use selenite (or other stones) to cleanse their crystals often neglect to ensure that their selenite is energetically clean and clear itself. This is a bit like never scrubbing your shower or bathtub—just because you use the tub to clean yourself doesn't mean that it should be left to its own devices.

In addition to selenite, several other stones can be used to cleanse and recharge your crystals. Hematite, shungite, and granite are particularly effective, provided they are cleansed frequently themselves. These stones can be found in slabs or tiles, a shape that's perfect for which to place your stones to be cleansed. A dish or bowl filled with small tumbled pieces of hematite or shungite is also very effective, a method of cleansing that helps to discharge the energies of the crystals that you place inside the the bowl. Remember to be careful when using one stone to cleanse another, as some stones will scratch others if one is soft and the other is hard. If you place unpolished specimens on a polished slab of selenite, you run the risk of scratching or gouging the selenite, depending on the hardness of the other stone. Similarly, soft stones left on quartz or amethyst

Slabs of selenite and granite are popular
crystal-cleansing stones.

crystal clusters can be damaged by the sharp points, whereas stones harder than
quartz can damage the cluster. Always be sure to check the hardness of your
crystals and be careful when using these cleansing methods.

Visualization, Breath, and Prayer

It's no secret that visualizaton, breath, and prayer are my favorite method of
cleansing. If you've read my previous books *The Seven Archetypal Stones* or
Crystals for Karmic Healing, you'll find variations on a technique employed
by renowned scientist-turned-healer Marcel Vogel. Broadly speaking, using the
mind to cleanse one's crystals is faith-based, although when coupled with breath
or other tools there can also be a physical model of how and why cleansing
works this way. From a practical perspective, these methods will not damage
your stones, and they require no tools; thus they are safe for any crystal and can
be employed in virtually every circumstance.

The simplest variations on using the mind use visualization and prayer. In my early days as a student of crystal healing I learned a technique that involves tuning in to the crystal's energy and visualizing a gauge or meter numbered 0 to 100, depicting how saturated in energy it was. To clear the crystal, you simply have to connect to the stone and allow it to show you where its energy level is. Wherever the needle appears on the meter, that represents the stone's current energetic state. Simply will the needle all the way down to zero, intending for all the old energy to dissipate. Then picture the crystal being filled with any intention you may have for healing as the needle moves all the way up to 100.

Other methods for clearing your crystals with the mind include surrounding your stone with the image of water, white light, violet fire, or any other image or energy that represents purification to you. You can also pray, recite an affirmation, or invoke the help of angels, deities, or ascended masters to assist you. A simple way to ask for help from the higher realms to cleanse your crystals is to visualize an ethereal, golden-white light entering your crown chakra and flowing down your arms and into your hands. As you hold the crystal in your hands, bathe it with this cleansing energy. Generally speaking, I find most of these cleansing methods adequate for gentle, daily cleansing, but I prefer more potent cleansing methods when working on more intense issues or when I am using crystals with clients.

◆ *Cleansing with Breath*

Select the stone that you'd like to cleanse and spend a moment or two setting your intention to purify it. As your mind focuses on this, grasp the stone between the thumb and index finger of your dominant hand (or if it is too large or heavy, hold it in the palm of one or both hands). Breathe deeply and rhythmically while making a conscious connection to the stone. Visualize white light or any other symbol of purification flowing into your body with the breath as you inhale, and as you exhale release any stagnant or disharmonious energy. When you feel totally saturated with this cleansing force, you are ready to cleanse your stone. Take a deep breath, filling your whole being with this energy; exhale with a powerful pulse of air through the nose. Imagine this pulse of air carrying white light into your chosen stone and sweeping away any old or unneeded energy, leaving behind a clear slate.

Essences, Sprays, and Elixirs

One of the fastest ways to cleanse your crystals is with the assistance of essences and elixirs. These can be made from flowers, herbs, or gemstones and administered as a spray. Naturally, since essences are water- and alcohol-based, some care should be taken not to dampen sensitive stones, especially soluble ones. However essence sprays are fairly safe to use on many other stones that cannot otherwise be immersed in water.

There are many products available commercially that can be used to cleanse your crystals. My favorites are the cleansing sprays made by GEMFormulas; they are imprinted with therapeutic-quality gemstones and diamonds and work wonderfully. Crab-apple flower essence is adept at clearing harmful or toxic energy, and it makes a great crystal-cleansing spray. There are also many smokeless smudge sprays that use essential oils made from purifying herbs such as sage or palo santo that can be used to cleanse your crystals. You can also make your own gemstone essences to cleanse your stones; see chapter 7 for more details.

How Often Should I Cleanse?

The question I am asked most frequently when it comes to cleansing crystals is "How often?" While there is no hard-and-fast rule, invariably the answer is that we are not cleansing them often enough.

By way of analogy, I like to compare cleansing your crystals to laundering your sheets. There is no single rule of thumb for how often you should wash them, and we each have a different level of comfort with this. However, if you stop to think about it, you sweat every night that you're in bed, and if you really wanted the most hygienic option you would change your sheets every single day. The same is true of your crystals. If you wear the same pendant every day, it will naturally absorb energy from your inner and outer environment; some of that energy is aligned with your goals, and some of it is not. Thus daily cleansing is ideal for stones that get used every day.

That said, daily cleansing may not be viable in every situation. For stones that I wear daily, I place them in a dish of Himalayan salt overnight so that they are refreshed and ready to wear the next day. I do deeper cleansing once a week or twice a month, depending on the situation. If I am wearing crystals for a specific scenario, like fighting off a cold or flu, I may do a deep cleansing several times a day to ensure that my crystals are in tip-top shape for healing. The bottom line when it comes to cleansing is that more frequent cleansing can't hurt, provided that you use safe and effective cleansing methods.

DEDICATING

A step that seems to be missing from the preparatory practices of most crystal books today is that of dedicating your stones and crystals. This simple practice involves setting your intention so that your healing tools will be used only for the highest good of all. It's akin to the rites of consecration found in many mystical traditions. Dedication can be as simple has holding a stone and reciting a prayer or affirmation of intent, or it can be a more complex ritual.

In dedicating your crystals, you are beginning to build a more conscious relationship with the indwelling consciousness or deva within your sacred stones. Not only does it serve to affirm that your crystals will be used only for the benefit of yourself and others, but it also allows the crystals themselves to see that you are devoted to the well-being of all. This generally encourages them to be more willing to participate in healing processes.

◆ Dedication Ritual

For a simple dedication rite, all that is required is having the crystal (or crystals) being dedicated at hand. Before dedicating, ensure that the stone is thoroughly cleansed. As well, cleanse your living space, perhaps by burning a cleansing herb such as sage. If you have a sacred space such as a meditation altar or a home shrine, I suggest performing your dedication there. You can light a candle and burn some incense if you wish.

Hold the crystal between your hands (or in your hand if it's small) and gaze at it or into it. Mentally invite the consciousness of the stone to join you in your sacred space for the dedication ritual. When you feel as though you have connected to the crystal, recite your dedication prayer or affirmation, such as "May this crystal (or gemstone, rock, mineral, etc.) be used only in the name of all that is good and sacred, harming none. May this crystal be a tool of healing, transformation, and love, and may it always serve the highest purpose of all beings."

Hold the crystal to your heart center and visualize it being filled with the energies of unconditional love and trust. You can picture this energy as a prismatic white light (like a diamond), or perhaps as a golden-white or violet light. When finished, thank the stone for joining your healing toolbox and return your awareness to the room.

GETTING TO KNOW
YOUR CRYSTALS

Before beginning any of the deeper, more conscious work with crystals, it is necessary to develop a rapport with them. On the one hand, this helps you familiarize yourself with the energies and influences of individual stones in your collection, which in turn makes you a more sensitive and capable crystal healer. On the other hand, taking the time to get to know your crystals allows you to develop a relationship with the indwelling consciousness of the crystal. This is an essential step in co-creating with crystals for transformation and spiritual growth.

When counseling clients as well as customers at metaphysical stores, people who are new to crystals often stop me to ask what I mean when I encourage them to "work" with their new stones. Truth be told, I rarely have a clear and concise answer for them, as the process looks different for each of us. Sure there are well-defined therapeutic applications for crystals and tried-and-true ways to incorporate crystal energy into your life. However the first steps into the world of crystal healing should be personal and tailored to your own lifestyle and experience.

I suggest starting with one stone at a time when you are beginning to work with crystals. In fact, if you are already well versed in crystal lore and healing, it's still a good idea to strip it down to working with a single stone at a time every once in a while. This affords you the opportunity to make a deeper connection with your crystalline tool. When you acquire a new stone, spend time contemplating it from all angles. Look at it in bright light and compare this view to when it is strongly backlit. If it is translucent or transparent, what does the interior of the stone look like? How does it feel in your hand—rough or smooth, light or heavy, warm or cool? What sensations, images, or other information do you receive when you hold, carry, or wear your chosen stone?

Try keeping a journal of your experiences with your crystals. You can compare meditating with them, a more active function, to working with them passively by wearing or carrying them throughout the day or taking them to bed. In the beginning of forming a relationship with a new stone, keep track of how you feel and what you think about if you wear or carry it, as well as what your dreams are like if you take it to bed. All of these impressions and experiences will provide insight into the specific healing gifts or spiritual tools your stones offer, and you will understand them much more deeply than by merely reading a description in a book.

◆ *Crystal Contemplation*

Here is a simple way to connect with your crystals so that you can get to know them better. You can use this for natural specimens, polished and tumbled stones, gemstone carvings, and jewelry of all varieties. Keep a notebook handy so that you can record your experiences. Start with a freshly cleansed crystal that has also been dedicated, and find a comfortable place to sit where you will be undisturbed, preferably some place with natural light.

Gaze at your crystal as you hold it in your hands. Turn it in every direction and get to know every surface, every pattern, every way that it plays with light. Hold it against a bright light and look into its interior if it is translucent or transparent. Allow yourself to be completely mesmerized as you get to know this crystal optically. Feel yourself relaxing while you contemplate the way your crystal looks.

Now move to your other senses. Assess its density by comparing its weight to other stones of comparable size. Close your eyes and trace your fingers over it to get a better sense of its texture (but be sure to exercise caution with rough, sharp, or fragile crystals). As you move your fingers across it, does the stone produce any noise? Some crystals may have a faint ringing sound, and they can be gently struck like a tiny chime. If you are working with a nontoxic, raw stone, see if it has a scent.

With eyes closed, relax and contemplate the crystal's energy. Where do you feel this energy in your body? Though you might feel the energy in your hands where you hold it, it could also present itself in another body part, chakra center, or in the aura around you. If this energy had a color, a pattern, or a symbol, how would it look? You might be surprised to find that its energy appears to you in a color different from that of the stone's visible color. If this energy produced an audible vibration, what would it sound like? You may experience it as a single note, or perhaps as music; take note of the voices or instruments that it resembles. How does the energy of the stone feel: warm, cool, tingling, pulsing, electric, static, dynamic? If the energy had a scent and a taste, what would that be?

Record your impressions in your crystal notebook and compare your notes as you repeat this with the same and different crystals. Soon you'll be able to discern the crystals' energy from your own energy, as well as that of your environment. Repetition is the key, and it helps us forge deeper relationships with our stones. This crystal contemplation exercise is fun to try with crystals we know nothing about. After jotting down your experiences, compare these notes with what you find in books. More often than not you'll find parallels between what you sense and observe and what is written in crystal books.

PROGRAMMING CRYSTALS

There are several different schools of thought on crystal programming. I have several colleagues whose work has had a huge influence on me and who strongly feel that we should *not* program our stones. There are others who feel that it is a necessary and often overlooked part of our co-creative work with the mineral kingdom. Personally I fall into the latter camp, and I find programming to be a helpful part of my practice with crystals.

Let's start with a deeper look at what programming means. To program (or alternately, to charge) a crystal is to imbue it with an intention so that we can attain a desired outcome. Although on the surface it may resemble the act of dedicating, programming is focused on achieving a specific outcome for one particular application of the stone, whereas dedicating a crystal is a preliminary act of consecration meant to carry over to *any* use of the crystal. Programming is a bit like installing an app on your phone. Your phone has nearly limitless potential, but a specific application is required to look up directions, read your email, or video chat with your best friend. Crystals are similarly multidimensional tools, and programming them permits you to home in on a specific talent that it possesses. If amethyst boosts intuition, enhances our divine connection, supports the health of the nervous system, and breaks bad habits, which of those skills will it exercise while you wear it throughout the day?

Another reason why we program our crystals is because doing so simultaneously programs us. If I spend a few moments consciously connecting to my crystal and charging it with my intention, then I am honing my objective and aiming it toward the specific goal I have in mind. This helps me tend the garden of my mind so that I can cultivate the belief that my goal is possible and that I am deserving of it. Even if all we do is program our stones and then leave them behind, it would still be a powerful act.

It is important to note that programming is best accomplished when we consciously evoke the *feeling* of the goal we want to accomplish. The more you can bring forth these feelings, the more successful your programming will be. For example, if you want to program a crystal for love, imagine what it feels like to be truly loved. Reflect on experiences of love that you have known in your life, focusing only on positive associations. Do the same for any other intention, whether it is perfect health, prosperity, protection, or a new car.

The arguments against programming are varied. Many early authors on crystals used very mechanical analogies for working with stones, treating them much like computers, which strips away the sense that they are sentient beings with an inner spark of consciousness. From this perspective, programming seems more like a command, and many people find that the consciousness within crystals can object to being ordered around in this way. Instead I view programming as an *invitation* to the indwelling consciousness of the stone. It is a co-creative act, not a one-sided, authoritative one.

Some people believe that only clear quartz is programmable because all other stones carry their own inherent programs. If we look at the basic functions that all crystals share (see chapter 1), then you can imagine that this is an all-or-nothing scenario. Since quartz crystals can be programmed, because they all have the ability to store, cohere, amplify, translate, and transmit information, I believe that *all* crystals can be effectively programmed for the same reasons.

A final critique of programming is that it can be too narrow, thereby limiting the scope of what a crystal can offer us. I acknowledge that this is a potential hazard, but it can be overcome with a simple shift of perspective. Instead of focusing solely on a single, specific outcome, we can reframe our program to include the goal *or anything greater.* Another way to do this is to use affirmations, which grants your crystals the liberty to conspire with the universe to find the best outcome for you.

Ultimately any tool that empowers us to work more consciously with our crystals is a good one. By programming our crystals with a clear and focused intention, we are preparing ourselves for success, and we are inviting our crystals to co-create with us. This is a proactive approach to crystal healing, and it makes even passive applications like carrying a stone in your pocket or wearing crystal jewelry much more effective.

◆ Programming with the Breath

My favorite way to program crystals is inspired by the work of Marcel Vogel. Vogel experimented to find the most effective way to work with crystals, and he devised a technique for programming them that incorporates the breath that is not unlike his cleansing method. Vogel's classic program consisted of projecting peace, well-being, and love into his crystals, using the method outlined in the following paragraph. Although Vogel used these three intentions, you can select your own when programming your crystals.

Start with a cleansed crystal and select the intention with which you'd like to charge your crystal. I recommend distilling your intention to a single word or a short phrase. Relax and breathe deeply and rhythmically, focusing on your desired intention. As you breathe, imagine that you are inhaling not only air but also the energy of your goal; visualize any colors or symbols that you associate with your goal coming in with the breath and filling your body and aura. Once you are saturated with this intention, hold your crystal between the thumb and forefinger of your dominant hand, or in one or both palms if this is not comfortable or possible. Breathe in deeply and consciously connect with your crystal. Release your breath in a short, sharp pulse through the nose, and picture the breath carrying your intention into the crystal. I typically use one breath for each intention for which I am programming my crystal. Once finished, spend a moment in gratitude to the crystal and return to your normal awareness.

◆ *Programming with Affirmations*

One of the most effective ways to program your crystal is to compose one or more affirmations, mentally projecting them into the stone. Writing out your affirmation on paper is a good exercise as it engages more of your brain and allows you to make a deeper connection to your intention. Always phrase your intention in the present tense, such as with statements that begin "I am . . ." or "I have . . ." (For example, "I am prosperous" or "I have perfect health.")

Once your affirmation is ready, choose a freshly cleansed crystal and spend a moment calming the mind. Next hold the crystal to your heart or third eye chakra and begin to recite your affirmation like a mantra, either silently or aloud. Mentally project the affirmation into the stone, visualizing it as colored light (the choice of color is yours; consider selecting a color with symbolism corresponding to your goal) emanating from your heart or third eye chakra, which fills the crystal. After a few moments, thank the crystal for co-creating with you and return your consciousness to the room.

How Many Programs Can One Crystal Hold?

You may have several goals that you'd like to work on simultaneously, and the temptation to program one crystal for everything you want may arise. Vogel himself used a three-part intention for programming his crystals, and I often stack more than one goal into the stones with which I'm working. However, this begs the question of how many programs or goals we can instill in a single crystal.

Usually I advise my students to limit themselves to no more than three intentions at a time. Having those intentions aligned around a common theme is also helpful, so that we don't spread our focus—or the crystal's—too thinly. Choosing three unrelated goals, such as manifesting a new car, healing a broken wrist, and attracting a new lover, will pull your energies in too many directions at once. This amounts to the same effect as opening too many tabs in your internet browser. Some of them might load, though most won't, and you run the risk of not getting any of them to work properly.

Instead streamline your intentions so that they work together toward a similar outcome. If you want a new car, you can program your crystal for the car itself and for the money needed to buy it. However don't limit yourself to a single avenue for manifesting your desired outcome; the universe takes the path of least resistance, so it may surprise you in finding creative solutions to your everyday problems. Programming your crystals intelligently helps you achieve your results faster and with greater ease.

ACTIVATING CRYSTALS TO THEIR HIGHEST POTENTIAL

Activating a crystal attunes its energy to its highest potential. Essentially it is like plugging the crystal into your higher consciousness and all the energy reserves available on that plane of existence. Much like programming, this is less a mandate for your crystal and more of an invitation; it relies on your own consciousness to make the connection. An activated crystal is ideal for cord-cutting, weaving a cocoon of light, combing the aura, extracting thoughtforms, and other healing activities. I use an activated crystal to charge grids and layouts, and I often use this technique on my pendulum before using it to dowse the human energy field, such as described in chapter 3.

Be mindful of the termination point of a crystal wand when not in use, as an activated wand emits a potent beam of energy. Although this isn't likely to harm anyone, it may feel intrusive if not contained. To do so, keep your index finger over the tip of the crystal when you are not actively projecting energy or using it for healing. Simply slide your finger back to reveal the apex when you are ready to use it. When finished working with your activated crystal, follow the instructions below to release the activation and return it to its normal state.

◆ *Activating and Deactivating*

After cleansing and programming the crystal you've selected, hold it in your dominant hand and proceed as follows:

Start by stepping outside your normal state of consciousness. I do this by closing my eyes and picturing my conscious mind taking a step back, moving deeper into the realm of the subconscious mind and into the role of the observer or witness. This helps me bypass the ego mind and facilitates a deeper connection with my higher self.

Next move into a higher state of consciousness. Feel yourself rising upward with the breath, as though you are riding an elevator to the next highest floor in the mansion of your mind. Once there you will see yourself surrounded by radiant, prismatic white light. When you are in this higher state of consciousness, project your intention to activate the crystal. Like the exercise Programming with the Breath on page 115, fill yourself with your intention to activate your crystal as you inhale, holding the crystal before you. Release this energy with a single breath via a short, sharp pulse of air through the nostrils. Now bring your awareness back to the room. Your crystal is now activated.

To deactivate the crystal, hold it firmly in your dominant hand and shake it out once while pulsing the breath as above. As you do so, hold the intention to release the state of activation.

6

Crystal Meditations

MEDITATION IS THE BASIS OF MANY successful healing modalities and spiritual practices. Regular meditation provides real results on both our physical and psychological well-being; it reduces stress, counteracts anxiety, improves sleep, boosts concentration and memory, and leads to greater peace and contentment. Before we can really engage in crystal healing we need to build a rapport with the crystals and gemstones in our toolbox. Meditation fosters that deeper relationship so that we can build the skill set necessary to be sensitive and proficient crystal healers. Meditation also trains the mind and teaches us how to be more present, a necessity when working on ourselves and on our clients.

Throughout this chapter we will explore some of my favorite ways to include crystals in a meditation practice. The meditations that follow build on the Crystal Contemplation exercise in chapter 5. Although the only tools required are your stones, you may find that dimming the lights, lighting a candle, burning incense, playing soft music, or diffusing essential oils may facilitate a deeper state of meditation. Make time so that you are free from interruptions when you meditate; put your cell phone on airplane mode and power down the computer or tablet. I recommend keeping a notebook and pen nearby so that you can record your experiences and track your progress over time.

GETTING STARTED

Meditation can be a scary word to those who are just starting out on the spiritual path. In pop culture it has at times conjured images of contorting oneself into an uncomfortable position, chanting unintelligible mantras, and emptying the mind of all thought. Truthfully, meditation only requires that we be willing to relax and focus the mind so that we can cut through all the mental chatter that normally accompanies waking consciousness. All we need is fifteen minutes at a time to meditate, and there are no complicated protocols involved that would prevent anyone from trying.

When we meditate we are making time and space to reset the body, mind, and spirit. By committing to a regular meditation practice, we are also giving our higher consciousness permission to take over. Start with just a few minutes when you first set out to build a regular meditation practice, perhaps only five or ten minutes a day, two or three days a week. Over time you can increase the duration and frequency, and you'll be able to incorporate new techniques during your meditations.

Posture and breathing are paramount to successful meditation. We can meditate in virtually any position, but being upright, either in a chair or on the floor, discourages us from falling asleep in meditation. It helps to start off seated until you are comfortable with staying focused and alert; after that, if you wish, you can try meditating in a reclined position, such as you might do during a crystal healing session. Full, regular breathing supplies your body with sufficient oxygen and helps you relax; be sure to breathe from the diaphragm. Aim to make your inhalation and exhalation about the same in length.

Even experienced meditators rarely arrive at a state of no thoughts. Thoughts are not the enemy of meditation. Instead it's the desire to *pursue* the thoughts that arise that makes meditation challenging. When thoughts arise simply observe them without judgment. Like ships passing on the horizon, just let them pass. If you have trouble letting go, just ask yourself *What will I think of next?* Often you'll find that the mind goes blank when we put it on the spot. Otherwise, return your awareness back to your breath.

When meditating with crystals, always cleanse them prior to use; it's often a good idea to cleanse them afterward too.

The following three exercises are excellent ways to start your meditation practice. I always use a grounding and centering technique each day before my meditation practice. In addition, basic visualization is an excellent skill to hone, so I'm offering a way to do so with your favorite crystals.

◆ *Grounding and Centering*

Among the most important techniques I have learned are grounding and centering practices. *Grounding* consists of linking your energy field to the earth's. This creates a complete circuit of energy, allowing us to discharge and release whatever energy doesn't support our well-being and to receive spiritual nourishment from the earth herself. *Centering,* on the other hand, helps us collect our awareness and create a sense of focus. It gathers in our personal power so that we no longer feel off-kilter or scattered. Grounding and centering should be the very first steps in your own meditation and healing practice, as they provide the energetic support needed for spiritual development and pave the way to a more successful meditation practice.

Start preparing your environment by eliminating distractions, dimming the lights, and, if you wish, lighting any incense or candles that you deem appropriate. Sit comfortably with good posture and begin to breathe rhythmically and easily. I suggest closing your eyes for this meditation, although you may find success with eyes slightly open and cast downward. As you breathe imagine that your roots of light are growing from the soles of your feet and/or base of your spine. They wind their way through the ground below you, coursing through soil, bedrock, mantle, and core—all the way to the heart of Mother Earth.

Exhale any worry, tension, stress, or other source of disharmony into the earth. Picture these vibrations being carried by your roots into the molten core of the planet, where they are broken down and repurposed into positive energy. Reverse the direction of the flow and inhale these positive vibrations up through your roots of light and into your body as you inhale. Allow them to circulate through both your physical and energetic bodies, nourishing body, mind, and spirit.

Next make a mental assessment of your spiritual center. Are you off-balance in any way? You may see this as your chakras or layers of your aura off-center or otherwise out of balance. As you drink in the healing energy of Mother Earth, visualize all the parts of yourself realigning and returning to center. When you feel completely grounded and centered, thank Mother Earth and draw your awareness back to the room around you. Open your eyes and pause before engaging in mundane activities.

◆ *Crystal Visualization*

Basic visualization supports our spiritual practice in so many ways. It's also an excellent support for our work with crystals. We can improve our ability to program crystals by visualizing the outcomes we seek, and as we sharpen our ability to see images in the mind, we will also notice that our psychic vision is improving.

To try this, select a stone for this meditation. Start with one that is not too complex—a tumbled stone may be an easy way to begin. As you gain proficiency with this exercise, you can move on to more challenging specimens, such as crystal clusters or mixtures of minerals, both raw and polished.

Cleanse your stone and prepare the environment for meditation. As with the Crystal Contemplation in chapter 5, sit in a well-lit place and explore your stone from every angle. Note the precise color and texture and the way it plays with the light. Record every visual aspect of the stone in your memory. When you feel totally familiar with the stone, set it down and continue the meditation without holding it. Close your eyes and relax. Ground and center yourself and call forth the image of the stone on the screen of your mind.

Picture the stone before you. Imagine yourself reaching out and touching the stone. Feel its weight and texture. Turn it over in your mind's eye and recall how it interacts with the light. Inspect it from every angle as you re-create its image in your mind. Now ask yourself where you feel the stone's energy—perhaps in your physical body or in the chakras or the aura. Just as in the Crystal Contemplation exercise, use all five senses to assess the stone's energy. When you are finished, release the image of the stone and ground and center yourself once more. Return to the room and record your experiences.

With practice you will be able to call on your crystals even when they are not present. When you are going about your day and have need of a specific crystal, this exercise will permit you to have access to the energy of your crystal as the need arises, such as invoking the calming energy of lepidolite or rhodonite if you are upset or stressed. As you train your visualization skills, you can re-create specimens that you have seen in photos in your mind's eye and connect to their energy. This allows you to connect more deeply to a crystal's energy remotely, and it proves helpful when shopping for crystals online.

◆ Crystal Gazing

One of the simplest and most profound meditations I know of is the act of crystal gazing. This is also referred to as *scrying,* and it has been employed as a meditative focus and a form of divination since antiquity. Traditionally obsidian, beryl, and quartz have been used as tools for crystal gazing, but virtually any stone will do. For our purposes a transparent or translucent stone is best, especially when you are starting out. Polished stones such as spheres or palm stones, with a variety of inclusions and flaws, are ideal, as they grant the eye an interior landscape to explore.

Start with a cleansed crystal, and prepare the space for meditation. I like to hold my stone for scrying, but you may be more comfortable with it propped on a stand or a pillow in front of you. Traditionally firelight or moonlight is used to illumine the crystal, though you may adjust the lighting—natural or artificial—to your liking. Ground and center yourself, and visualize yourself bathed in a protective atmosphere of crystalline, prismatic light.

Scrying can be used to answer specific questions, or it can be left open-ended and used for inspiration and guidance. If you have one, ask your question and gaze into the crystal with a relaxed gaze. Stare into the heart of the stone and allow your gaze to soften and unfocus. Still your mind and observe any images, symbols, or thoughts that emerge as you gaze into the crystal. These may appear within the stone, or you may see them in your mind's eye. Bear in mind that the subconscious mind speaks in symbols that require interpretation, therefore it is helpful to take notes as you scry. When you have asked all your questions or want to end the crystal-gazing session, close your eyes and express your gratitude to the crystal. Ground and center and return your awareness to the room.

Like many skills, crystal gazing requires practice to achieve consistent and accurate results. Don't fret if few or no images appear, or if these symbols seem to initially lack meaning. Stick with your practice, and you will improve over time. What you see is not written in stone, as our futures are mutable and influenced by free will, so use the information you obtain via scrying to help inform the best decisions to make in life.

ADVANCED MEDITATIONS

Once you have mastered the basic meditations described above, the following exercises will expand your practice and prepare you for healing with crystals. These simple exercises are merely the tip of the iceberg when it comes to meditating with crystals; allow your creativity to guide you as you explore these meditations and create your own.

◆ Crystal Breathing

Several of the exercises in my books *The Seven Archetypal Stones* and *Crystal Healing for the Heart* were developed from this simple meditation that follows. In this Crystal Breathing exercise you will saturate your body and energy field with the energy of a specific stone, thereby reaping its healing benefits. Select a stone to use in this meditation, either intuitively or based on the qualities it confers. Cleanse the stone and prepare your space for meditation. Ground and center yourself; hold the crystal in your nondominant hand as you begin your meditation.

Initially allow yourself to visualize the stone in your mind's eye as you did in the earlier Crystal Visualization exercise. Place the stone on your body; hold it in place if you are sitting up, or lay it on your body if you are reclining. Select the spot intuitively or based on the results you want to achieve, such as a corresponding chakra or part of the body.

Wherever you have placed the stone, begin to picture yourself breathing through the stone, as if it is a substitute for your nose or mouth. As you inhale you are filled not only with oxygen but also with the crystal's energy. Visualize this energy as liquid light. I usually see it as the same color or combination of colors as the stone itself, though there are often exceptions to this. Observe how the stone's energy flows through your body and your aura. Watch for areas where the energy is weak or does not flow at all. Consciously breathe crystal energy into these places, picturing them saturated with the light of your stone. Note how you feel as the crystal energy circulates through your entire being. Be aware of any changes in mood, thoughts, or energy. When you are finished, thank the stone and ground and center to release and discharge any excess or uncomfortable energy.

Experiment with this exercise and compare your results. Try the same stone in different locations, as well as different stones in the same location. Compare and contrast using programmed versus unprogrammed crystals. Not every crystal will feel comfortable, and this often indicates the crystals that can highlight or transform your own imbalances. Be sure to cleanse your crystals after meditating, as they can store any disharmony that is released during the exercise.

◆ Journeying within Your Crystal

I began my meditation practice as an adolescent, and one of the first crystal meditation techniques I learned was to project my consciousness into a crystal to explore its interior landscape. Over the years I have incorporated some version of this meditation into most of the workshops I've taught, and it has always been one of my favorite ways to get to know a new stone. I suggest working with a crystal with which you've already familiarized yourself through any of the previous exercises, at least while you are just beginning your crystal practice.

Before beginning select the crystal that you'd like to use for this exercise and cleanse it thoroughly. If it is small enough, hold the crystal in whichever hand feels most comfortable. Prepare your space by silencing your phone and other distractions. Sit comfortably, close your eyes, and breathe deeply and easily. Start your meditation by grounding and centering yourself. Next, in your mind's eye picture your crystal before you. Imagine that it is growing larger and larger, until it is as big as a house. See yourself walking up to the side of the stone, peering within it if it is transparent. Silently ask for permission to enter the crystal, and a doorway, gate, or other opening appears before you.

Step through the opening and envision yourself in a hallway that leads to the center of the crystal. As you walk along this corridor, use all your senses to attune more deeply to the crystal. What do you see in the stone; is it clear or cloudy, dark or light? What sounds, if any, do you hear within your crystal? If you breathe deeply, do you detect a scent? Trace your fingers along the walls as you walk and ask yourself how it feels: warm or cold, smooth or rough, soft or hard. Finally, if you feel called to, you can energetically taste the crystal (this is done only in your mind, as many minerals are toxic if ingested in real life). Is it salty, sweet, bitter, spicy, or earthy? By the time you arrive at the end of the hallway, feel yourself vibrating in harmony with the crystal.

At the end of the hallway is a large central room. Many different doorways, stairwells, and labyrinthine corridors extend in all directions. A spiral staircase leads to the apex of your crystal. Most of the rooms are marked with their purpose, such as signs that read "healing," "manifestation," "library," and "meditation." Others may have symbolic representations posted above or on the doorways; these symbols will have personal significance to you. While within the crystal you may ask to be guided to whichever room(s) from which you can benefit the most or ask to be directed to a specific room. Each room is furnished with tools and symbols that support the intention posted outside. The contents of these rooms will change to reflect your needs with each visit.

When you are ready to end your journey within the crystal, ask to be guided back to the outside of the stone. You may feel a magnetic pull to return to the central room and back down the hallway to the exterior. As you exit the crystal, offer it your gratitude for permitting you to enter the sacred spaces within its heart. Visualize the crystal shrinking until it returns to its normal size. Allow the image of the crystal to fade away, then ground and center yourself before returning to normal consciousness.

You may find that some crystals and gemstones have inner worlds that resemble buildings and man-made structures, while others may seem to be re-creations of natural settings, real or imagined. Still others may be abstractions of light and energy, constantly in motion. However the crystal's inner world appears to you, accept this without judgment and observe how it makes you feel. With regular practice you will be able to revisit the sacred spaces within your stones to receive healing, insight, and wisdom from the consciousness of the mineral kingdom.

◈ *Meeting the Crystal Devas*

The more we work with crystals for healing and spiritual support, the more we see that there is something beyond their physical structure and chemical makeup. There is consciousness within all of creation. This inner essence is sometimes referred to as the *spirit, deva,* or *soul* of the stone. Because this spark of conscious energy is unique—just like our own individual human consciousness is unique—each crystal will seemingly exhibit its own personality. By regularly partnering with our crystals in meditation and healing, we can slowly develop a relationship with the deva that guides the stone and get a sense of its personality. To jump-start this process, let's meet the deva in this exercise.

Prepare as you did in the previous exercise, Journeying within Your Crystal. It is better not to charge or program your crystal for anything specific before meeting the deva within it. This signals to the indwelling consciousness of the stone that you are willing to show up to listen when you first meet. When you are ready to begin the meditation, ground and center yourself, close your eyes, and breathe deeply and comfortably. Consciously affirm your intention to connect to the deva of your stone, as if you are extending an invitation to the consciousness that resides within.

Picture the crystal growing in size until it is as large as a house. Ask permission to enter the crystal for the express purpose of meeting the deva of the stone. If the deva grants you permission, a doorway will appear, as in the previous exercise; if not, thank the crystal regardless and end your meditation. If the doorway opens, step into the crystal and attune yourself to the stone as before, using all five senses. When you reach the room at the end of the corridor, the spiral staircase at the center seems to glow. You begin to ascend the staircase effortlessly, climbing to the very top.

When you reach the top of the staircase, you find yourself in a sacred chamber in the apex of the crystal. This room is full of light, and it contains comfortable furniture and an altar adorned with tools of healing and ceremony. Beside the altar is the deva of the crystal. This being may appear to you as a person who is either male or female (or perhaps both or neither), or it may present itself to you as an animal, mythical creature, angel, spirit, or simply as pure energy. However you per-ceive the deva, bow your head in gratitude and introduce yourself. Give the deva an opportunity to introduce itself, and allow it to share whatever wisdom it has for you. You may sit and listen to whatever the deva has to share, or you may ask questions. Whatever you do, do it with respect. Though most of the conversation may be related to the specific applications of the crystal you are within, you may also receive wisdom related to other areas of your life.

When you and the deva have finished your conversation, thank it for sharing its time, teachings, and space with you. As you say farewell, you may be embraced by the deva and offered a gift from the altar in the room. This may be a natural object, such as a stone, shell, or feather, or it may be a more abstract gift. Stow it away for safekeeping. Begin your descent down the spiral staircase and exit the crystal via the same route you entered.

Once outside the stone, visualize it returning to its normal size and let the image fade from view. Ground and center yourself before returning your awareness to your surroundings. Record your experiences with the crystal deva in your journal.

PRACTICE, PRACTICE, PRACTICE

Like all skills, meditation requires practice to build confidence and achieve proficiency. Commit to a regular meditation practice, even if for only fifteen minutes a day several times a week. Meditation helps us forge bonds with our healing tools—and with the consciousness within them—while simultaneously exploring our own subconscious world.

One important consideration when meditating with your crystals is to challenge yourself to perceive more and project less. *Projection* is a function of the ego-mind, and it means that we are filtering or creating our experience according to our expectations. Projection can steer our meditative journeying inside the crystal as well as influence what we see when we close our eyes. *Perception,* on the other hand, is merely the pure observation of our experience. Perception hinges on a well-trained mind and heightened intuition.

Sometimes what feels like perception can really be our ego or subconscious projecting a hope, dream, fear, or other pattern onto our spiritual experience. We've all heard that quiet voice in our head or seen a beautiful image in the mind's eye and wondered if we created it or simply observed it. The goal in our spiritual practice is to improve the ratio between these two processes. Pare back the projection so that you can increase your perceptive ability.

Ultimately crystal meditation should be an enjoyable and helpful part of your journey. It will help you further integrate the healing benefits of your crystals and gemstones, and it will prepare you for authentic spiritual growth.

7

Crystal Elixirs

AFTER CARRYING OR WEARING YOUR CRYSTALS, one of the simplest ways to use crystal energy in your life is with gem-infused waters. These are sometimes called *essences, elixirs,* or simply *gem waters.* There is a bit of a difference in how gem waters and crystal elixirs are prepared, yet when made correctly, both are simple and effective ways to use crystal energy to transform your life.

- ▶ Gem water (or crystal water) is water that has been imprinted with crystal energy; these infusions do not receive a preservative, as they are made for immediate use.
- ▶ A crystal elixir or crystal essence requires a preservative such as brandy or glycerin, and they usually require a longer infusion time than gem waters. Crystal elixirs carry a more concentrated energy than gem waters, and they are often administered with dropper bottles or as sprays. Crystal elixirs work because water has memory, and this memory retains an imprint of the energy field with which it comes into contact. Because crystals have highly ordered, coherent energy fields, they encourage water molecules— and therefore the water's energy—to be similarly coherent. When we ingest, spray, or come into contact with a crystal elixir, its energy trains our human energy field the same way that a crystal does. Crystal elixirs can provide safe and economical alternatives to working with stones that are difficult to obtain or challenging to work with.

MAKING CRYSTAL ELIXIRS

Generally speaking, there is no single method for producing gemstone elixirs that is better than the rest. You'll find that this is true as you begin to develop your own protocol, your own ritual, as you practice making them. Provided that you follow the proper safety guidelines (see box below, "Crystal Cautions"), you are welcome to experiment to find the ways that work best for you.

Crystal Cautions

Before discussing how to make and use crystal elixirs, it is vital to understand that not every crystal is suitable for use in this way. Stones like those listed below should only be used to make elixirs via *indirect* methods, and they should never be placed directly into your drinking water.

Some stones can be damaged by water, while others can be potentially hazardous to your health. Always exercise caution when making crystal elixirs. Be sure to double-check the composition, hardness, and other physical and chemical properties of your stones before putting them directly into water.

Following is a general list of cautions when considering stones for use in elixirs; specifically, those with any of the following characteristics should *not* be used to make elixirs via the direct method described in this chapter.

- Stones with toxic components—like lead, arsenic, mercury, antimony, copper, uranium, and the like—such as azurite, galena, vanadinite, and wulfenite
- Stones that are soluble, such as chalcanthite, halite, and hanksite*
- Stones that are fragile, friable, or may be damaged in water, including selenite, some varieties of serpentine and tourmaline, and pyrite (which breaks down and produces sulfuric acid when wet)
- Stones attached to an unknown matrix
- Stones that have been dyed, irradiated, stabilized, varnished, or otherwise treated
- Stones that have a hardness of 4 or less, such as angelite, barite, calcite, celestite, fluorite, and rhodochrosite

Most cautionary lists of stones that you'll find online do not take into account all of the crystals' properties; composition alone is not a sufficient indicator of whether a specimen is safe to put in water. For example, aluminum can be poisonous, but sapphire and ruby,

---

*Although none of the minerals in chapter 11 are soluble outright, always exercise caution. Some can dissolve under special conditions, including changes in temperature, pressure, and pH.

which are aluminum oxide (Al_2O_3), are perfectly safe for your drinking water. This is because exposure to water does not leach out any of the ingredients in these stones, as they are hard enough to hold their own in elixir-making. Some softer stones, such as calcite, aragonite, and fluorite, are generally safe for exposure to water but their finish may be dulled over time, and dissolved solids or slightly acidic water may mar their surfaces.

Use water that is as neutral as possible, and stick to tumbled or polished specimens. Water that has been purified in some way, such as via distillation or filtration is preferable to water that contains a high amount of dissolved minerals. Always be sure to check for the presence of inclusions and accessory minerals, as some of these can be toxic. For example, although your favorite piece of calcite might not be toxic, it may have pieces of galena or pyrite attached, which are toxic.

The bottom line when infusing gem energy into your water is to always err on the side of caution. Stones that are unsafe for direct-infusion methods can be made into elixirs safely by using the indirect methods described in this chapter. Never use a stone directly in your water that you haven't researched. When in doubt, leave it out!

To make gem water you'll need relatively little equipment—basically just clear, colorless glass containers. For elixirs and essences you'll need clear glass containers to make them in and containers to store them in. I like to recycle glass jars and bottles and repurpose them for storing crystal elixirs. Dropper bottles, spray bottles, funnels, and a pair of tongs are also helpful when making elixirs, and you'll need a preservative of your choice, either an alcohol like brandy or vodka, or a nonalcoholic substance like glycerin. Use good-quality filtered, distilled, or purified water to produce effective elixirs.

Before making your elixir, clean your stone(s) and vessels physically and spiritually. The former is especially important if you are making an elixir via the direct method, as you do not want any contaminants in your water. A mild, natural soap can be used provided that this will not damage the stone. Once your crystals have been appropriately cleaned, program them to support your intention in making the elixir. I also like to say a prayer or blessing over my water and my tools before proceeding.

There are two ways to prepare crystal elixirs: the direct method and the indirect method. In the direct method, as the name implies, the crystals are placed directly in the water, and in the indirect method they are separated from the water. The direct method should only ever be used when you are certain of a crystal's safety; for all other stones, use the indirect method.

Direct Method

To make an essence or gem water via the direct method, place your cleaned, cleansed, and programmed stones into a clean glass container. Gently pour water into the bowl, taking care not to disturb the crystals. Place the bowl in a safe location, perhaps in sunlight or moonlight, to infuse (see "Infusion Guidelines" on page 133). I hold my hands over the water and ask that the crystals' energy will transfer to the water and that the water will lovingly receive this energy.

Crystals that are safe and stable for water exposure
can be used to make gem water via the direct method.

After infusing for the desired amount of time (see "Infusion Guidelines" on page 133), carefully remove the stones from the water (I use silicone tongs for this). The resulting essence can be consumed immediately as gem water or as an elixir for longer use if you add a preservative. If you see traces of your stones or other contaminants in the water, filter the water before using or consider gifting this batch to the earth and try again using the indirect method.

Indirect Method

In making an elixir via the indirect method your crystals will not come into contact with the water. The simplest way to accomplish this is by placing your stones in a small glass jar, bowl, or cup; set this inside a larger bowl; and add the water to the larger bowl. The glass container in which your stones are placed will serve as a physical barrier, protecting the water from being contaminated by toxic or hazardous minerals contained in the crystal, yet allowing the crystal's energy to transfer into the water.

Use an indirect method for making elixirs if you have
any doubts about the safety of your crystals.

Another way to make an elixir by indirect means is to place your vessel of water inside a grid made from the stones (see chapter 8 for more information on crystal grids). I usually use six or twelve stones around my glass container of water when employing a crystal grid for indirect infusion, but you may vary this to suit your needs.

If you are making an elixir from a blend of gemstones, you can also use a hybrid of direct and indirect methods as circumstances permit. For example, if you want to make an essence of galena and quartz, the galena should be left out of the water because of its lead content. However the quartz can go directly into the water, provided that it is free of inclusions and accessory minerals that would be unsafe to consume.

Infusion Guidelines

Generally speaking, the longer a crystal elixir infuses, the more potent it is. Gem waters can be infused for fifteen minutes up to several hours. Crystal elixirs, on the other hand, should ideally infuse for a minimum of one hour and may be left to infuse for up to thirty days. The amount of time that elixirs are left to infuse may be determined by the potency desired as well as astrological timing.

Care should be taken when deciding where to place your elixir while it is infusing. Elixirs benefit from receiving natural light while they infuse, but some gemstones will lose their color when exposed to sunlight. Delicate-colored stones may be infused overnight under the light of the moon or during the day but out of direct sunlight. Sunlight has a projective, brightening, uplifting, and energizing effect on elixirs, whereas moonlight infusions are receptive, cooling, introspective, and boost psychic talents. Both sun and moon can be used together to achieve a balance of the two energies.

Be conscious of contamination from your environment when making crystal elixirs. Dirt, dust, and other particles can fall into the water, and outdoor infusions may attract the attention of insects and wildlife. While these foreign materials may not be toxic, they can encourage the growth of mold and microorganisms in your finished product. Be sure to strain your gem-infused waters as needed, and consider covering your bowl if infusing in a dusty location.

Preserving Your Elixir

Gem waters are usually used immediately and require no preservative. However if you choose not to use your gemstone-imprinted water right away, you'll want to make a preserved elixir to make it last longer and to prevent the growth of mold, bacteria, and other organisms. Common preservatives include the following:

▶ Alcohol such as brandy or vodka
▶ Vegetable glycerin
▶ Apple cider vinegar
▶ Salt (sea, kosher, or rock)

The first three preservatives are helpful long-term, while salt can be used to extend an elixir's life by a few hours to a few days. Generally speaking, elixirs should be bottled with anywhere from 25 percent to 50 percent preservative (either alcohol, glycerin, or apple cider vinegar) to effectively deter contamination. I generally use alcohol as my preservative, but nonalcoholic preservatives may be used in roughly the same ratios, though you'll need to aim for about 50 percent if using glycerin. The resulting mixture is called the *mother elixir,* and it may be taken directly or further diluted for use. Like homeopathic remedies, crystal elixirs are made more potent through the principle of dilution; 4 drops of a mother elixir are added to a 1-ounce dropper bottle filled with a mixture of water and preservative (75 percent and 25 percent, respectively). Shake vigorously afterward, and your elixir is ready to use.

Single Gems versus Blends

When making crystal elixirs you'll have the option to make them from single stones or from combinations of crystals chosen to reflect a common theme. There are pros and cons to both approaches.

With single gemstones the finished elixir usually has a laserlike focus; it perfectly exemplifies the energy of the stone you've chosen. However, with crystals that work multidimensionally, the effects of these elixirs can sometimes be a little more diffuse, as they are spreading their efforts to more than one level of our makeup.

Gemstone blends can be chosen to support your intention. Effective blends tend to work faster and reach the core issue faster than single stones. However the key word here is *effective.* If you want to create an elixir for creativity, you can't throw every stone with a creative energy into your drinking water. Less is more when it comes to crystal elixirs; I usually keep my blends to five or fewer types of crystals in an elixir. The best blends are usually those that are chosen for the way they complement one another. Additionally, rocks and minerals with related compositions or crystal structures are usually more compatible in elixir form. Though there are exceptions to this rule, it can be helpful when paring down all the available options.

USING CRYSTAL ELIXIRS

There are virtually no limits to the ways you can use crystal elixirs. Small dropper bottles or sprays can be carried with you to refresh yourself during the day, or they can be added to your morning and evening routine. Following are some of my favorite ways to use crystal elixirs.

- ▸ Take several drops under the tongue.
- ▸ Add them to food and beverages.
- ▸ Spray them in your aura and around your home, office, or car.
- ▸ Add them to the bath.
- ▸ Add several drops to an essential oil diffuser to infuse the scent with crystal energy.
- ▸ Place 1 or more drops on the chakras or pulse points.
- ▸ Massage them into the skin.
- ▸ Add to liquid soap, shampoo, and cleaning products.
- ▸ Place several drops on clear quartz to program with the elixir's energy and wear or carry to receive its benefits all day.

CRYSTAL ELIXIR RECIPES

Stress-Relief Essence
Crystals: citrine, blue chalcedony, lepidolite
Method: indirect

The gemstones in this stress-relief essence each work to help us unwind tension and find greater peace. Citrine relieves tension in the body and aura, strengthening the ability to let go of unneeded energies like stress. It also invites optimism and happiness. Blue chalcedony is one of the most relaxing stones for the mind, and it carries the energy of tranquillity and peace. Lepidolite is a stone of acceptance, helping us face transitions and challenges with grace; its lithium content is very relaxing. Blue lace agate may be substituted for blue chalcedony.

Avoid direct sunlight in making this essence, as citrine's color is sensitive to sunlight. Try assembling the ingredients in the morning so that it will be ready to drink, or add them to the bath after a long day of work. Combine with relaxing fragrances like lemon, lavender, or jasmine for optimal effects in the bath.

Protection Elixir

Crystals: amber, black tourmaline, labradorite, obsidian, pink tourmaline
Method: direct*

Each of the stones in this protection elixir work to support our energetic defenses in different ways. Amber is a helpful stone for sensitive people; it averts psychic attack and has been used as a protective amulet for millennia. Black tourmaline is stabilizing, and it transmutes harmful and foreign energies. Labradorite brightens and strengthens the aura, thereby making it less susceptible to intrusion by outside sources. Obsidian is highly reflective, and it can be used to understand the source of negativity and deflect it altogether. Pink tourmaline strengthens the emotional body, helps one feel safe, and protects against harmful energies in the environment.

This stone combination can be used as a gem water and consumed immediately, or it can be bottled with a preservative and used as a spray in the aura or environment. As a spray, consider adding a pinch of sea salt with your preservative and a few drops each of protective essential oils, such as cedar, juniper, and pine.

Physical Regeneration Essence

Crystals: emerald, green tourmaline, hematite, ocean jasper, rhodonite
Method: direct

This regeneration essence is nourishing to the physical body and stimulates the body's ability to repair itself. Emerald is a master healer of the physical body, and green tourmaline is adept at tissue repair. Hematite grounds and strengthens the physical body and is ideal for recovery after injury, illness, or surgery. Ocean jasper is revitalizing and rejuvenating at the cellular level, carrying the energies of the other stones to our most basic level of organization. Rhodonite accelerates the healing of open wounds and clears emotional trauma left by physical injury.

This essence can be made via the direct method, in sunlight. I recommend using it as a gem water and consuming it immediately after infusing for one to two hours.

---

*Some specimens of black tourmaline may be fragile, or friable, and it may be necessary to use an indirect method unless you are working with a polished, tumbled, or otherwise safe piece of black tourmaline.

Immune Boost Elixir
Crystals: carnelian, bloodstone, clear quartz, green aventurine, red calcite
Method: direct

Carnelian, bloodstone, and red calcite all work to strengthen and mobilize the immune system. Green aventurine soothes and detoxifies the body. Clear quartz is a master healer, and it amplifies the other stones in this mixture. This mixture helps kick the immune system into action and is helpful for treating allergies, cold, and flu. Blue-green apatite can be added to combat viral infections, or moldavite may be used for fungal conditions.

Use a direct method to infuse this elixir, preferably in full sunlight. As a gem water, it can be infused for one to six hours and consumed immediately. If infused for several days (up to a week) and properly preserved, several drops can be taken under the tongue or in your favorite tea or juice.

Vitality Essence
Crystals: carnelian, quartz, ruby, serpentine
Method: indirect

When you need a quick boost of energy, this combination of gemstones supplies it. Carnelian is a fast-acting gemstone that revitalizes your entire being—body, mind, and spirit. It brings enthusiasm and optimism, and it can jump-start your metabolism. Quartz supplies nourishing energies to every chakra and augments your energy level, while ruby strengthens your life force. Serpentine gently grounds and uplifts the mood and gradually awakens your hidden reserves of vital energy.

Make this elixir via the indirect method if you are using a fibrous variety of serpentine, although polished specimens of compact, massive stones are generally safe for direct infusions. Leave this blend in direct sunlight for several minutes to make a gently energizing gem water, or for one to three hours for a preserved essence. In addition to the usual methods of use, this vitality essence can also be rubbed into tired or sore muscles for a quick energy boost, or it can be placed on the temples to provide focus and stamina.

Mental Magic Elixir
Crystals: fluorite, optical calcite, pyrite, sodalite, tanzanite
Method: indirect

The combination of fluorite, calcite, pyrite, sodalite, and tanzanite has a strong effect on the mind and the mental body. The first three encourage order and support memory. Fluorite also breaks down barriers to learning. Calcite enables us to be more present, and optical varieties invite us to see things from a new perspective. Pyrite catalyzes quick thinking and helps us take action on our thoughts. Sodalite purifies the mind and integrates the conscious mind with the intuition. Tanzanite expands consciousness and strengthens the imagination, thereby empowering creative problem-solving skills.

Avoid direct sunlight when making this elixir, as it will cause fluorite to fade. Allow the mental magic elixir to infuse for up to one week, then bottle and preserve it. It can be used internally (under the tongue or in beverages) or as a spray to boost mental function and support memory. This elixir is a great tool for students of all ages.

Communication Blend

Crystals: amazonite, chrysocolla, rutilated quartz
Method: indirect

This simple blend facilitates clear and sincere communication. Amazonite is a stone of personal truth, and it helps us resolve conflict—inner and outer—for better communication on all levels. Chrysocolla empowers us to use our voices creatively. It stirs the cauldron of inspiration so that every word we speak is brimming with creativity and sincerity. Rutilated quartz works to boost the signal of our communication; it forms an energetic bridge between the speaker and the audience to convey the message beyond the verbal level. Rutilated quartz also boosts our ability to listen actively, making us more empathetic and effective communicators all around.

Because of chrysocolla's composition, this elixir should be made via indirect method. I prefer to use both sunlight and moonlight to represent both the active and passive aspects of communication. Leave it in a place that will receive the light from both luminaries for a full twenty-four hours, and use it as a mist, in the bath, or sublingually.

Self-Confidence Essence

Crystals: blue lace agate, mahogany obsidian, rhodochrosite, sunstone, topaz
Method: direct*

---

*Many specimens of rhodochrosite contain inclusions of minerals such as pyrite, thereby rendering them unsafe for direct infusion.

This self-confidence essence works holistically to give you a confidence boost from the inside out. For starters, blue lace agate sifts through every layer of the aura to help highlight and release foreign energies. As it does this we become more truly who we are meant to be and develop resilience and inner strength. Mahogany obsidian raises self-esteem and helps us feel confident and charismatic. Rhodochrosite invites us to cultivate confidence, releases emotional and karmic baggage, and teaches us how to cultivate inner freedom. Sunstone is a stone of leadership, as it helps us lead by example and allows us to thrive in the spotlight. Lastly, topaz (preferably golden or imperial topaz) is a great stone for aligning our intention with our higher will; it boosts empathy while also improving willpower, thereby simultaneously making us more confident and more sensitive to the needs of others.

This essence is best made in full sunlight. Since rhodochrosite is fairly soft, be sure not to let it infuse for more than one to two hours. It may be consumed right away as a gem-infused water, or it can be bottled with the preservative of your choice. Use it on pulse points or as a mist to help you step into your personal power and reveal a more confident you.

Energy-Cleansing Elixir
Crystals: aquamarine, black tourmaline, Herkimer diamond, selenite, shungite
Method: indirect

This energy-cleansing elixir clears out stagnant and harmful energies. Aquamarine and black tourmaline work together to release and transmute stagnant or discordant energy. Shungite absorbs and neutralizes harmful energies. Herkimer diamond promotes clarity and invokes a purifying energy while amplifying and cohering the other stones in the blend. Selenite has a brilliant, angelic vibration that inundates your aura with white light.

This blend can be sprayed in the aura, around the room, or on crystals to clear their energy. Although an indirect method is suggested, all of the stones except selenite can be placed directly in the water, with several pieces of selenite (ideally six or twelve) gridded around the container. This elixir is best made on the full moon. The stones can be left to infuse for two weeks during the waning moon, but take care not to leave the infusion in direct sunlight, as aquamarine bleaches in sunlight. After the stones are removed, add a pinch of sea salt and preserve with alcohol.

Psychic Awakening Elixir
Crystals: amethyst, azurite, lapis lazuli, moonstone, purple fluorite
Method: indirect

These five stones are each powerful awakeners of psychic talents in their own right, and they work synergistically to enhance one another's gifts. Amethyst strengthens our connection to divinity and reminds us of the inner ocean of wisdom that lies within each of us. Azurite fosters greater insight and is stimulating to the third eye chakra. Lapis lazuli unites the heart and mind, promoting self-mastery; this gemstone also stimulates the psychic senses and awakens the intelligence centers of the body and mind. Moonstone parts the veil between the worlds and provides psychic protection, thereby preventing us from being too sensitive to harmful energies. Finally, purple fluorite breaks down barriers to using our intuitive faculties and helps us become more disciplined for honing the psychic senses.

   This crystal elixir is best made under the light of the moon, preferably while full. It should be infused overnight and bottled with a preservative. To use, take 3 or 4 drops under the tongue or in a beverage and anoint the brow. It can also be used as a spray to prepare the space before any psychic or intuitive work.

Dreamtime Essence
Crystals: jade, Herkimer diamond, prehnite, sugilite
Method: direct

The combination of these four stones supports restful sleep and enlivens the dream state. Jade is a classic dream stone, and it opens the psychic door for dreamtime travels. Herkimer diamond is a brilliant form of quartz that clarifies the dream state and promotes relaxation for better, more restful sleep. Prehnite supports the action of jade and promotes sharper recall of one's dreams. Sugilite awakens the psychic senses and provides gentle protection for your dreamtime travels; this gemstone also intensifies the dream state. Together these stones can invite more vivid, prophetic dreams and encourage astral travel in the sleep state.

   Make this essence overnight during the new moon under the light of the stars. In the morning bottle it and add a preservative before the sun gets too bright. Take 7 drops before bedtime to enhance your dreams and get more restful sleep.

8

Crystal Grids

THE IMPETUS TO ARRANGE STONES in specific geometric forms is an ancient one—our ancestors have made stone circles, medicine wheels, and giant monuments out of rocks for eons. These are the prototypes of the crystal grids we use in healing today. I think the single most popular crystal application today is making crystal grids; grids have been covered in books, podcasts, and posts on social media. These eye-catching arrangements of crystals and gemstones (sometimes adorned with candles, flowers, or other objects) are an effective and fun way to bring crystal energy into your life.

So what exactly is a crystal grid? I define it as an intentional placement of crystals or gemstones arranged geometrically to manifest a specific intention or outcome. One of the key words in this definition is *intentional;* merely emptying your pockets on your counter does not a grid make! Sometimes crystal grids go by the names *crystal arrangements, crystal arrays, crystal mandalas, crystal wheels,* and *crystal nets*. Some of these terms may have specific connotations in different forms of crystal healing, while in other forms of practice they are synonymous.

Crystal grids owe their remarkable effects to the law of synergy and the principles of sacred geometry. The law of synergy illustrates that in creating something the end result is greater than the sum of its parts. The energy of crystal grids is not additive—we are not simply combining the influence of each stone in the grid in a linear fashion. Instead the energies coalesce in a greater whole, something bigger and better than can be achieved by a single stone. Sacred geometry is the application of symbol and meaning to form and proportion; it is a powerful catalyst for healing, spiritual growth, and planetary evolution.

MAKING GRIDS

Crystal grids can be made in a number of ways. They can be precise, geometric patterns, or they can be free-form arrangements co-created spontaneously. Grids can be large enough to fit around a building or small enough to fit in the palm of your hand. Above all else, your intention (as well as your focus, feelings, and follow through) should be aligned with your purpose in building a grid.

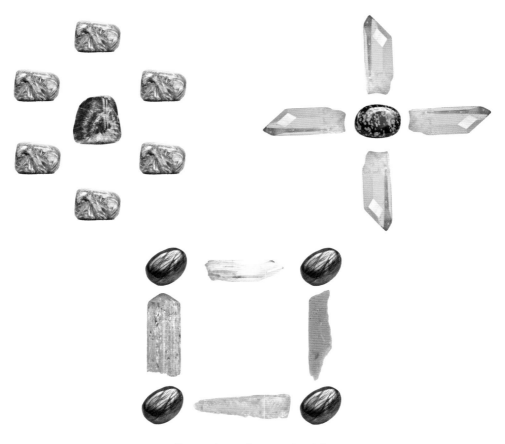

Examples of crystal grids

There are some practical considerations when making grids. Although they can be as large and complex as we can dream, we are limited by our space and the contents of our toolboxes. If we only have one piece of smoky quartz, we obviously cannot build a grid that requires four pieces without either making a substitution or obtaining more smoky quartz. Likewise a crystal grid that fills your entire living room is an amazing experience, but leaving it intact may pose a danger to both your stones and to the inhabitants of your house.

When selecting the stones to put into your grid, choose those that relate to your underlying theme or intention as well as some stones that serve as a secondary support to this theme. For example, a single piece of fire agate can represent love and passion, and it can be surrounded by a ring of rose quartz to make a simple grid for a loving, passionate relationship. We can choose multiples of the same stone, or make all the stones unique according to our needs and the tools available to us.

For size and location, always consider the practicality of your crystal grid installation. If you have a separate room devoted to your healing or spiritual practice, it may be feasible to make a large grid consisting of many crystals to be left up for weeks at a time. For most of us, however, we will have to find another means of maintaining our crystal grids. They can be placed on an altar, end table, shelf, dresser, or other safe place off the floor. Always be sure that sharp, fragile, and toxic stones remain out of reach of children, animals, and anyone else. You can also choose the location of your grid based on the symbolism of the four directions or the *ba gua* map used in feng shui.

Once you have an intention, location, and size in mind, it is time to select your stones and begin building your crystal grid.

Steps in Building a Grid

The actual construction of your crystal grid can be as elaborate or as simple as you like. I have colleagues who create sacred space (complete with candles, incense, sacred music, etc.) and charge or program every single crystal, and even call on assistance to access the higher realms, every time they prepare to build a crystal grid. I also know many people who prefer to keep it simple and just dive right into the process of setting up. My own process varies between these two, as I adjust the process to the circumstances.

I don't believe in rigid rules when it comes to the art of crafting a crystal grid. Some of my most powerful grids have been made spontaneously, with no intention other than to merely follow the lead provided by the crystals themselves. Other times I have co-created grids that catalyzed unimaginable healing processes by carefully selecting stones and designing a grid according to the conventions outlined in this chapter. That said, there are a few basic steps involved in creating a crystal grid:

1. State your intention.
2. Identify and cleanse the stones that support this intention.

3. Choose the style of grid: either a free-form, intuitive grid, or a planned-out geometric grid.
4. Build your grid in an appropriate location according to the style you have selected.
5. Test for the soundness of energy when finished, and adjust as needed.
6. Activate your crystal grid.
7. Enjoy the effects and reenergize as needed.

As you construct your grid, do so as mindfully and intentionally as possible. You may want to invite your higher self, spiritual guides, crystal devas, or any other beings from the higher realms to join you in this co-creative process. After the entire grid has been laid out, you can check its energy by either tuning in intuitively, feeling the energy with your hands, or dowsing with a pendulum or dowsing rods. Make whatever adjustments are needed to ensure a consistent and stable flow of energy. You might need to reposition, add, subtract, or substitute one or more stones to achieve optimum results. Once the grid is completed, it can be activated as described later in this chapter. Check in with the energy of your grid to reenergize it and reactivate it as needed.

The Keystone

The *keystone* is the crystal or stone that serves as the energetic focus of your grid. It may be the largest crystal in the grid, and it may be in the very center of the arrangement of stones. However the design and intention of your grid may require that the keystone be placed somewhere else. Conversely, some grids will have no keystone in them at all.

The keystone is the unifier of the grid's energy. It may also be the antenna of your grid, broadcasting the unified energy of the entire grid out into the cosmos. Natural points, crystal clusters, and polished shapes such as obelisks, spheres, and pyramids are all excellent keystones, as they receive and transmit energy very well.

Choose the keystone to embody the most basic intention of your grid. For physical healing it might be a piece of clear quartz, aventurine, malachite, or emerald. For emotional healing you might select a specimen of rose quartz or lepidolite. The simplest grids will require only a keystone and several crystal points or pieces of tumbled quartz placed around it; you can select the number and arrangement of these outer crystals based on numerology and the geometry

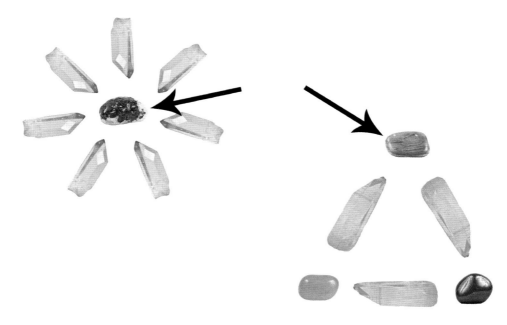

The arrow indicates the keystone in these grids.

of your grid, as described later in this chapter (in the section "Numerology and Geometry of Crystal Grids" on page 147).

For grids that make use of a keystone, you'll typically place them at the focal point. This is often the center of a grid that exhibits radial symmetry, such as a star, a circle, or a square. Other designs might require that the keystone be placed at the top or bottom of the formation, or even off-center, to create the desired flow of energy. The keystone of any grid should generally be programmed to support the specific intentions of your grid (please refer to chapter 5 to review the instructions on programming crystals). If you've already created your grid and it needs to be re-energized, the keystone can be removed, cleansed, and reprogrammed before being returned to its place in the grid. Afterward be sure to activate the grid again.

Activating Your Crystal Grid

One of the most overlooked aspects of grid-making is activating it. Once the entire grid has been built, activation serves to gel the different energies and coordinate the disparate parts of the grid so that all parts of the grid contribute to a single intention. Activating a grid makes a huge difference in terms of its impact. A grid in its nonactivated state is beautiful and provides energy that can be harnessed. However, once activated, the energy of the grid becomes more coherent and radiates more brilliantly. It's a bit like appreciating a stained-glass window: it is beautiful always, but its colors are best revealed when lit from behind. Activating a grid is like looking out through the stained-glass window when the sun is behind it.

To activate your grid you'll only need a terminated crystal or wand. It may be polished or natural, as long as it is large enough to comfortably hold in your hand. I usually use large wands when activating larger grids, but I try to listen to the essence of the grid to find the right tool to activate it. I suggest cleansing your wand and programming it with the same intention that you used to build the grid. The wand will then be used to connect to each of the stones in the grid and to unify their energies. Repeat this activation daily, weekly, or as often as needed to maintain the energy of your crystal grid to support your intention for healing, manifestation, and personal growth.

◆ Crystal Grid Activation

Once you've built your crystal grid, select the crystal wand you'd like to use to activate it. Cleanse and program your wand. Ground and center yourself, and enter a light meditative state while reflecting on the purpose of the grid.

While holding your crystal wand in your dominant hand, direct its point toward the grid. Trace the shape of the grid, and imagine that you are creating threads of light that connect each of the stones in the grid to one another. Pay special attention to the keystone, if there is one, linking each of the other stones to it. For complex grids that might be difficult to connect in this way, trace a spiral over the entire grid, starting at the perimeter and coiling in toward the center of the grid; once I've done this I like to reverse the spiral and work my way from the center out.

Once finished with connecting the individual stones, hold your crystal wand over the center of the grid (or wherever the keystone is located). Visualize a stream of light flowing from the universe into your crown chakra, down your arm, and through the crystal wand. Direct this energy into the grid, and visualize it coursing through all the crystals and expanding from the entire grid, as if you are increasing the aura or energy field generated by the grid itself. Intend that this field of light is carrying your energy out into the universe as it expands.

When the grid feels sufficiently charged, release your attention from the grid itself and relax your body. Ground any excess energy and offer your gratitude to your wand and to all the stones in the grid. Return your awareness to the room. This exercise can be repeated as often as necessary to re-energize your crystal grid.

NUMEROLOGY AND GEOMETRY OF CRYSTAL GRIDS

Although you can trust your intuition and allow a grid to reveal itself through divine inspiration, you can also select the number of stones and the shape of your crystal grid according to the meanings attributed to numbers and forms, thus aligning the shape and number of stones with your intention for building the grid. Use the descriptions of the numbers and forms in this chapter as a springboard for your own creativity. These descriptions are my own, and they draw from a variety of sources. As you work with crystal grids, you'll find that you will develop your own symbolic language of numbers and forms that is woven into each of your crystal grids.

Numerology

Numbers are powerful catalysts for healing, each one encoded with many layers of meaning. Numerology is an ancient practice of decoding the inherent symbolism and energy of numbers, and it has been practiced across the globe. When creating crystal grids, understanding the secret meaning of numbers can help you select your stones and arrange them in meaningful patterns. Use the information in the section below, "The Meaning of Numbers," to help you choose which numerological values to incorporate into your crystal grids.

The Meaning of Numbers

1 represents unity, oneness, anchoring. It is the energy of new beginnings, of solidarity, and the self. It becomes the focus, or keystone, of the grid.

2 creates balance, polarity, duality, and supports healthy choices. It can be used to invite compassion and equality. It is the number of reciprocal exchange and healthy relationships.

3 balances the positive, negative, and neutral forces. It supports change and represents body/mind/spirit balance. It is expansive and relates to the Holy Trinity, and instills serenity and simplicity. It is a very mental number and is related to the fire element.

4 represents all-around support, stability, and grounding. It connects to the four directions and the four elements (earth, air, fire, water). It affirms strength and is a stabilizing or slowing force. It can mean completion, and it helps find direction. This number symbolizes the home and foundation; it is also used for protection and banishing.

5 invokes, balances, and strengthens feminine energy. It connects to the five elements of Chinese medicine (earth, metal, water, wood, and fire) and the four material elements plus the quintessence from other traditions (earth, air, fire, water, and spirit/ether/akasha/mind) and brings the material plane into balance with the spiritual plane. The number 5 is protective; it represents building and empowerment (like the five fingers of the hand), and it improves memory. It is the number of cyclic change, and it governs the family.

6 is the number of harmony and mastery. It represents three-dimensional space and is excellent in all forms of manifestation. Spirituality, perfection, love, and self-improvement fall under the domain of 6. This number also represents the synthesis of the four classical elements and the forces of alchemy. It rules efficiency, passion, and movement.

7 prepares us for significant shifts or release. This number is ideal for creativity, and it is considered lucky, sacred, and full of mystery. It supports your life vision coming into fruition, and it actualizes your true will. This number can help you tap into the realm of dreams and ancestors.

8 is grounding, opening, and expansive. This number represents evolution, wisdom, and abundance. It rules eternity, achievement, strength, and movement.

9 is the number of endings, of terminal points and destinations. It is the threshold of change, reminding us that where there is an end, there is a new beginning. This number also invites self-reflection.

There are many ways to incorporate numerology into your crystal grids. Let's look at an example of a square grid for healing, made of two hematite and two aventurine stones, with a clear quartz in the center.

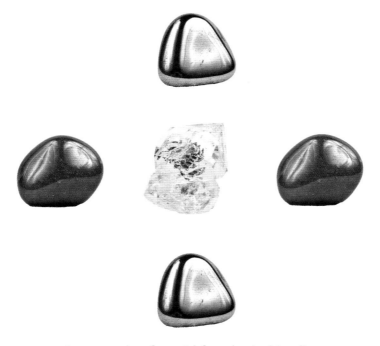

An example of a grid for physical healing
made of hematite, aventurine, and clear quartz

The numbers 1, 2, and 4 are immediately apparent in this grid; the number 3 is hidden in the three different types of stones used. In this grid, 4 is found in the four points of the square; it represents the material plane, directing the energy of the grid into the physical body. The vibration of 4 also stabilizes and anchors the healing energies sent out by the grid. The vibration of 2 can be found in the two types of stones that compose the square, as well as in the two specimens each of aventurine and hematite. The number 2 moderates between extremes and supports healthy choices; this grid can help us make good decisions that will bring our health back into balance. The vibration of 3 promotes positive changes; it gets us out of a pattern of disease or disharmony. The number 1, at the center of this grid, represents the concept of oneness and integrates the overall energies of the grid.

In the grid on the previous page, all of the numbers relate to the fundamental theme of physical healing. However it's possible that you will create a grid that unavoidably incorporates numbers that are irrelevant to your goal. In this case simply choose not to interpret them as part of your grid's makeup. Because we are the co-creators of our grids, we can choose which symbols, including numbers and shapes, contribute to each grid's energy.

Geometry

Sacred geometry inspires the different shapes of many crystal grids. A full exploration of the relationship between spirit and form is beyond the scope of this book, but a few examples provide a worthwhile consideration for dedicated crystal grid creators.

The Meaning of Form

Circle: The circle has no beginning or end. It represents unity, wholeness, cycles, completion, and potential. Circles are sacred containers, and they become wheels (symbolizing change and movement) when spokes are added. Circles also symbolize protection and healing.

Triangle: Built around the number 3, triangles represent change, the trinity, and serenity. Upright triangles resemble mountains, arrowheads, and teeth, so the triangle helps us overcome obstacles and feel secure. It is the shape of manifestation, creation, and integration.

Square: The square relates to the element of earth; it is protective and grounding. Squares help with regeneration and renewal and consolidate and stabilize energy.

Cross: Crosses confer stability, balance, and protection. The equal-armed cross is a symbol of solar energy, and it represents the crossroads, thereby helping us navigate life. The cross can be rotated to become an X, a symbol of discovery, banishing, loyalty, and increase.

Pentagon and pentagram: These are five-sided figures that balance elemental energies, provide protection, and clear old karmic patterns. Both pentagons and pentagrams are shielding, and the latter can represent the head and limbs of a human being.

Hexagon and hexagram: These six-sided figures engender harmony, balance, and unity. Hexagons are often found in nature, largely because of the ratio of their perimeter to area, making them masters of efficiency. The hexagram embodies the esoteric axiom "As above, so below," and it is probably the most universally used shape for simple crystal grids.

Lemniscate: Also known as the infinity symbol or the figure 8, the lemniscate links disparate energies and provides steady momentum. This figure invites abundance, balances polarities, and can be used to heal relationships between two people or parties.

Heart: The heart is a symbol of love, emotional healing, and compassion. Heart-shaped crystal grids are effective tools for attracting love, romance, friendship, and psychological well-being. Other key words associated with the heart include *loyalty, happiness, romance,* and *relationship.*

Spiral: Spirals are found worldwide as symbols of change, evolution, movement, and the Divine Feminine. Spiral grids can be used to overcome stagnant energy in your environment, either by drawing energy in or out. Grids with this shape can also propel us along our spiritual path, helping us draw from the well of inspiration and manifest rapid change.

Flower of life: The flower of life is a pattern used in sacred geometry to represent the spiritual blueprint of creation. It can be used as a template for building grids of virtually any shape, as crystals can be placed anywhere along its overlapping circles to create other geometric forms. The flower of life is used for manifestation, activation, and healing on a personal and a planetary level.

In addition to these shapes, polygons and other geometric shapes often share their meaning with the numbers on which they are based; pentagons and pentagrams will innately resonate with the energy of the number 5, described on page 148.

The shapes of your grids are endless. You can create grids based on abstract, geometric designs or use other symbols, including eyes, crescents, symbols representing the planets, and the signs of the zodiac. Animals, plants, objects, and people can also be made into crystal grids. The best and most reliable way to find the right shapes for your crystal grids is to experiment. Try them out and find out which forms produce the energies most conducive to the goals you seek to manifest.

CRYSTAL GRID TEMPLATES

The following crystal grid templates are intended to provide inspiration for your own creations. Treat these templates as recipes—feel free to add, subtract, substitute, and otherwise customize when making your own grids. Suggestions for programming stones, empowering keystones, and activating grids are just that—suggestions.

Love and Romance Grid
Crystals: rose quartz, jade, ruby

Ruby symbolizes emotional strength and the power of love to transform our lives. Rose quartz invites love to transform old hurts and reminds us to love ourselves. Green jade harmonizes the heart and anchors peace in all that we do. Jade attracts faithful, committed love.

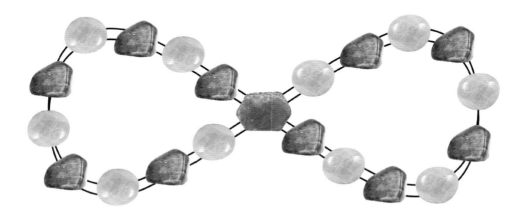

Collect enough jade and rose quartz to form either a figure 8 (shown above) or a heart shape. Alternate the rose quartz and the jade throughout the grid. Empower your ruby to be the keystone, and place it in the center of the grid.

Prosperity Grid

Crystals: citrine, garnet, pyrite

Citrine is the quintessential stone of abundance; it helps us fulfill our potential on every level and eliminates obstacles. Pyrite is often carried or worn to attract abundance. It catalyzes action, helping us work toward attaining prosperity, and it also reminds us of the true worth of our efforts. Garnet is traditionally associated with wealth and prosperity, and because it belongs to the cubic crystal system it will anchor the energies of the grid on the material plane.

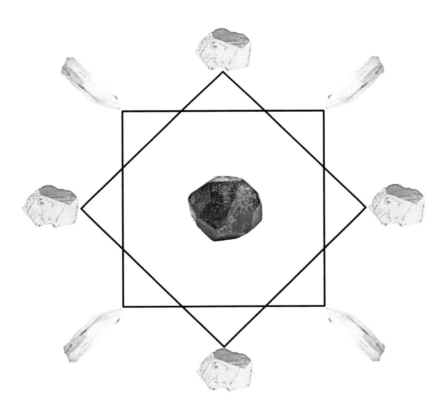

To build the prosperity grid, arrange four pieces of citrine in a square, and make another square of four pyrite pieces rotated at 90 degrees to the citrine square. This makes a ring of eight stones (two sets of four) to expand and grow your wealth, while simultaneously anchoring your intention. Use the garnet as your keystone, and place it in the center of the grid.

Creativity Grid

Crystals: aquamarine, carnelian, chrysocolla

Carnelian is a classic stone of creativity; it is revitalizing and encourages us to take action. Aquamarine is one of my favorite stones for inspiration; whenever I feel stuck it is one of the first stones I reach for. Chrysocolla helps us listen to our heart and allows us to channel our inner muse. This combination of stones empowers us to take risks with our self-expression, thereby helping us channel our creativity into fulfilling projects.

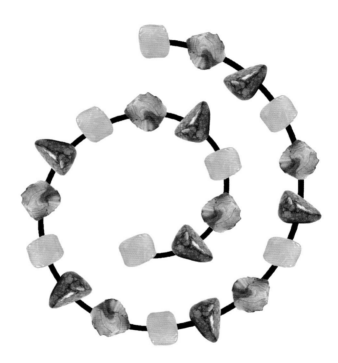

Create a spiral from these crystals, repeating them in the same sequence from start to finish. Numerologically this draws from the number 3 to promote positive change, while it helps you overcome whatever is blocking your creativity. When activating the grid, trace the spiral from the outside toward the center to symbolize drawing inspiration from the universe to yourself, and then trace the spiral from the center back out again to represent the return of your creative energy as you channel that energy into your life.

Home Protection Grid
Crystals: amethyst, black tourmaline, selenite

Amethyst is a stone of protection, serenity, and spirituality. It has an uplifting and purifying effect on our personal space. Black tourmaline is strongly grounding, and it transmutes negativity. Selenite bathes us in radiant white light, and it dissolves and releases harmful energies.

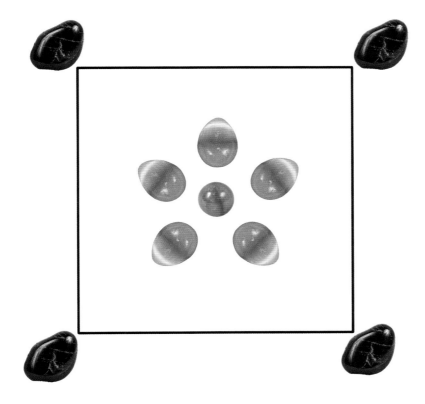

One version of the home protection grid is made by placing black tourmaline in the four corners of your home or room and selenite along each wall. A cluster of amethyst (or a bowl full of rough or tumbled amethyst) is placed as close to the center of your home or room as possible. Another version is a grid that is small enough to place on a shelf or table, as shown above. Make a square of black tourmaline; within that arrange five pieces of selenite and a piece of amethyst in the center of the grid as the keystone.

Healing Grid
Crystals: clear quartz, emerald, malachite, bloodstone

Clear quartz is a master healing stone, supporting our well-being on every level. Emerald nourishes and transforms the physical body, while malachite purges old patterns and releases pain. Bloodstone kicks the immune system into action and strengthens the physical body.

Place the emerald, malachite, and bloodstone in a triangle. Arrange three quartz crystals in another triangular shape, placing them between the first three stones to form a six-pointed star. In the center you can place a piece of quartz such as a sphere, obelisk, or cluster to transmit the healing energies of the grid to the intended recipient. Try placing a photograph or a notecard with the recipient's name written on it beneath the keystone in the middle of the grid.

Positivity Grid
Crystals: blue lace agate, carnelian, golden calcite, lepidolite, rhodochrosite, and yellow fluorite

This combination of crystals fosters a positive outlook and a can-do attitude. Blue lace agate calms the mind and boosts confidence. Carnelian fills us with enthusiasm and creativity. Golden calcite helps us be more present, and it shifts our perspective in positive ways. Lepidolite is a stone of acceptance, and it provides a sense of emotional buoyancy that ultimately leads to joy. Rhodochrosite feeds the inner child and instills a sense of inner freedom. Yellow fluorite cultivates a positive outlook and helps us stay the course even when it's challenging to remain positive.

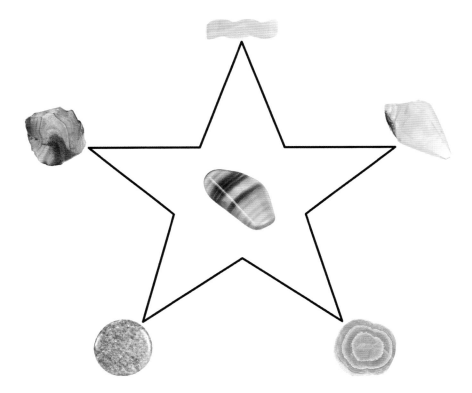

Make a five-pointed star with blue lace agate, carnelian, golden calcite, lepidolite, and rhodochrosite; follow your intuition to decide their exact placement. Place the yellow fluorite in the center of the grid. Rearrange the crystals at the points and reactivate the grid whenever you need a boost in your positivity.

9
Crystal Layouts for Healing

THE ART OF ARRANGING CRYSTALS and gemstones on and around the body of a person is often referred to as the *laying-on-of-stones*. Crystal layouts, sometimes called *crystal arrangements, crystal arrays, crystal placements,* and *crystal nets,* work much like crystal grids. The energy of these intentional arrangements of crystals is synergistic, creating effects that are greater than the sum of their parts. A crystal layout is an easy way to make a lasting change because it infuses all of the bodies of a person—physical and subtle—with crystal energy in a relatively short amount of time.

These layouts are essentially crystal grids that can be placed directly on or around the body of your client, and their application is therefore very similar to that of making crystal grids. The layouts can be chosen in advance or created intuitively based on the needs of the situation at hand. Both approaches have their strengths, but it is generally good to temper all techniques and suggestions with your own intuition.

USING CRYSTAL LAYOUTS

The basic steps involved in constructing a layout are more or less identical to those for making a crystal grid: the intention is set, the crystals are selected and cleansed, the style and structure of the layout is determined, the layout itself is built, and then the person is left to relax within the arrangement of crystals. Afterward the crystals are removed, the person is gently brought back to waking consciousness, and the tools are thoroughly cleansed. Different styles of crystal healing will employ their own methodology, but the general format is usually the same. Before using layouts on your clients, be sure to try them out on yourself.

Selecting Stones
There are different approaches to selecting the stones used for customized layouts. When I first learned about the art of laying-on-of-stones, I was

taught that the practitioner selected the necessary stones according to the needs of the person. I learned both simple arrangements that could be placed around the person's body as well as more complex arrangements that were placed on the body, especially focusing on the chakras. It was emphasized that these templates could be amended or changed on a case-by-case basis.

Later on I learned a technique taught by my late friend JaneAnn Dow in which the person selects their own stones intuitively. These stones are then supplemented by the practitioner so as to make a safe and well-rounded layout. Each of us has our own intuitive sense (even though we may not exercise it in daily life). Therefore we are likely to be drawn to exactly the stones we need if we approach them with an open heart and mind.

In my own practice I combine these approaches. When my client and I begin a session we discuss why the person has come in for a crystal healing session. I then choose stones based on their words, body language, and subtle energy. I usually also invite the person to select some crystals on their own; some people will feel drawn to certain stones immediately. I've even had clients inform me that they brought some of their own stones without knowing why. I do my best to incorporate these into the layout, one way or another.

One last point to consider when selecting the stones for your layouts is size. Larger crystals may have profound effects, but they may be impractical—if not harmful—to place directly on the person's body. Oversized stones can, however, be used in grids and layouts placed *around* the body rather than on it.

Building the Layout

The overall size and shape of the layout will be influenced by the space available, the mobility of your client, the issues on which you are working, and the crystals that you have available. If you are working on the floor, it is very easy to lay stones directly on the body as well as place them in geometric patterns all around it. If the person is lying on a massage table you will be limited to placing stones on the body only, although you could construct a crystal grid on the floor beneath the table to supplement this. If the person is unable to lie on the floor or on a table, a layout can be placed around a chair instead.

If you are planning a layout for yourself, it can be challenging to put all the stones in place on your own body. In this case it can be helpful to lay them out ahead of time in the pattern you'll be creating; place this within arm's reach so that you can access and arrange the stones as easily as possible once you are lying down.

The Importance of Being Present

As the facilitator, the crystal healer should remain present with the client for the duration of the treatment. If we are performing crystal layouts on ourselves, this is easy enough to do. If we offer crystal layouts to friends, family, or clients, then we need to ensure that they feel comfortable during the entire session. Strong emotions, flashbacks, and palpable transmissions of energy frequently occur when inside a crystal layout, and having a practiced and empathetic witness can make it easier to handle these situations. If the person in the layout is having any sort of difficulty, remind them to bring their awareness back to the present moment; focusing on the breath, the smooth inhalation and exhalation, is very helpful in this respect.

While the person is lying in the crystal layout, you may employ other crystal healing methods as needed, such as those described in chapter 10. While the person is lying in the layout you can also dowse their aura and chakras or apply other healing modalities, such as color therapy, Reiki, aromatherapy, flower essences, singing bowls, or whatever else you practice. Check in with the person from time to time and note any intuitive impressions that arise during the session.

Treatment Length

With crystal layouts longer sessions do not necessarily mean better treatments. I have witnessed powerful changes take place within a quarter of an hour; other times it can take an hour of dedicated work inside an arrangement of crystals and gemstones to initiate profound healing.

For the most part shorter increments of time are more practical because they are more easily achieved. If we needed to spend an hour or more every day inside a crystal layout for healing to take place, then we probably wouldn't bother. I usually recommended starting with fifteen to thirty minutes for most layouts, depending on the issue being worked on and the crystals chosen for the job. High-energy, intensive healing stones should be used for shorter durations, while gentler stones can be used for longer amounts of time. You can also dowse or use applied kinesiology (i.e., muscle testing) to help determine the treatment length.

People who are sensitive to subtle energies may feel overwhelmed after a short amount of time, especially if there are not enough grounding stones in the arrangement. Always check in with the person inside the crystal layout to determine the correct amount of time and add more grounding stones if needed.

After a Layout

Once you've finished administering a crystal layout, whether on yourself or another person, it's helpful to signal that the session has ended and remind the recipient to consciously ground and return their awareness to the room. Otherwise, simply removing crystals from the person's body may disturb them or bring them back to waking consciousness too abruptly. I like to use a gentle signal at the close of a session, such as sweeping the aura with selenite or playing a singing bowl to help the person integrate the positive changes and sweep away the energies that have been released during the treatment inside the layout.

At the conclusion, after you've removed the stones, give the person a chance to lie still and integrate. Once they have opened their eyes and are capable of a coherent conversation, I ask them about their experience with the layout, taking careful note of their impressions, as well as any images or internal experiences they wish to share. Once they have left I cleanse the stones that were in the layout very thoroughly. I tend to employ deeper cleansing methods after a treatment than before it, as old energy patterns have been released and disharmonious energies may still be hanging around the room and imprinted on the stones.

BASIC LAYOUTS

The crystal layouts covered in this section are among the most universally helpful, and they can be adapted to most of the scenarios that your clients will experience. Many good books on crystal healing will also include a variety of basic layouts that can be incorporated into your practice; consult the bibliography for recommended reading. Books such as Katrina Raphaell's *Crystal Healing,* Ashley Leavy's *Crystals for Energy Healing,* and Simon Lilly's *The Crystal Healing Guide* have a variety of layouts available for reference.

Seal of Solomon

Crystals: six quartz crystal points

In this layout six crystals are arranged in a hexagonal pattern, often called the Star of David or Seal of Solomon. This is the very first crystal layout I learned. In the crystal books of the 1980s and 1990s, this was the basic layout used in crystal healing. The shape and name of this technique is derived from the hexagram used in magical traditions that is often ascribed to King Solomon. This

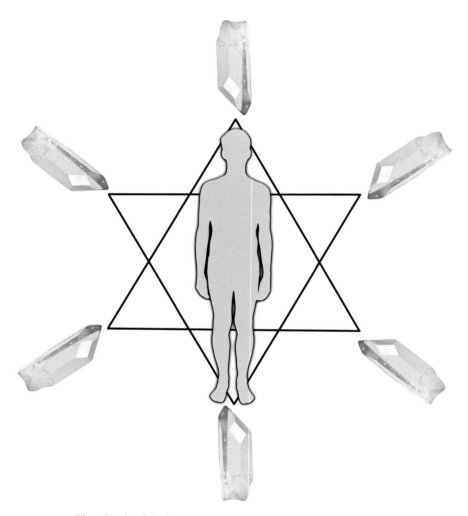

The Seal of Solomon is a crystal layout constructed
of six crystals arranged in a hexagram around the body.

pattern unites the energies of heaven and earth, and the layout can help calm body, mind, and spirit. It is a versatile arrangement of crystals, and it can be applied to virtually any scenario.

To create the Seal of Solomon layout, select six quartz crystals of roughly equal size. Although clear quartz is suggested, you could use any other variety of quartz, such as amethyst, citrine, or smoky quartz, provided they are all the same variety and roughly the same size and shape. Ensure that the

crystals are thoroughly cleansed; they may be programmed for a general purpose (such as healing, peace, etc.) or for a specific purpose customized to the
person. Lay the crystals in the pattern pictured above, with one point above
the crown, two level with the shoulders, two more at the knees, and one below
the feet.

Start with the points directed outward to discharge and release energy;
reverse their direction halfway through the treatment to nourish and reenergize the person in the layout. After arranging the stones around the person I
like to activate the layout using the same method described in chapter 8 (see
"Activating Your Crystal Grid" on page 145), as this will deepen the healing
effects of this layout. Smaller, localized versions of the Seal of Solomon can be
placed around individual chakras or over parts of the body that require additional healing in lieu of or in addition to the full-size layout.

The Three Tanden
Crystals: three pieces of the same stone

This method is based on the energy centers used in Japanese and Chinese
traditions. The Japanese word *tanden* (or *dantien* in Chinese) means "crimson
field." It refers to the vital energy assimilated and processed in these three
parts of our energetic anatomy. The tanden are categorized as the upper (in
the head), the middle (at the heart), and the lower (at the *hara,* an area just
below the navel). These three tanden are excellent for assimilating the energy
of crystals, and placing the same stone on each of the tanden floods your
energy field and body with the healing energy of the crystals you use. This
is a simple and effective way to receive the healing benefits of one type of
crystal or gemstone. Even a short treatment of the three tanden can produce
significant results.

Cleanse the three stones of similar type, such as three pieces of quartz,
three amethyst, or three celestites. Place them on the three tanden, starting
with the lower, then the middle, and finally the upper tanden. Leave the crystals in place for ten to twenty minutes. When complete, remove the crystals
and cleanse them thoroughly. If you do not have three specimens of the same
type of stone, you can perform this therapy one tanden at a time, spending
approximately five minutes at each, starting from the lower tanden and working your way up.

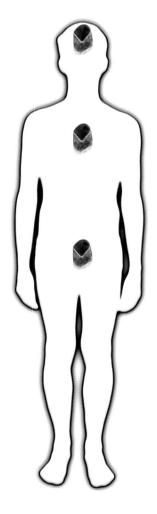

Place the stones of your choice on the three tanden for balance and healing.

Chakra Balance

Crystals: Select one stone for each of the seven major chakras, plus two quartz crystals, one piece of selenite, and one black tourmaline

Although the popular approach for balancing the chakras is not the mainstay of my practice, I wanted to include a simple means of performing an easy layout that targets the chakra system itself. For many practitioners a seven-color chakra layout is their first foray into the world of hands-on crystal healing. To perform this layout, select one stone that corresponds with each of the seven main chakras; you may select them intuitively or refer to the crystal directory in part 2 of this book. Note that it is not imperative that these stones match the colors associated with the Western chakra system; they can be chosen for

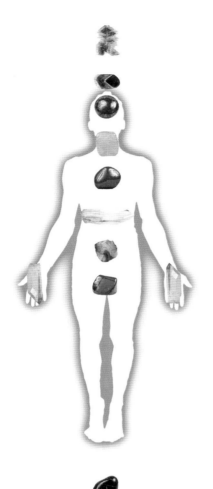

A sample chakra-balancing layout using (from the bottom to the top) black tourmaline, red jasper, carnelian, citrine, aventurine, aquamarine, lapis lazuli, amethyst, selenite, and quartz

their spiritual qualities even if their colors do not correspond to the commonly accepted model. Cleanse all the crystals prior to use; program them only if working on a specific condition.

Begin by placing the black tourmaline on the earth star chakra; if this is not possible, place it between the feet. Starting with the root chakra, proceed by placing a stone on each of the chakra centers. Place the selenite on the soul star chakra and one quartz crystal in each hand as depicted. Leave the layout in place for up to twenty minutes. Remove the stones from the top down: soul star, crown, third eye, throat, heart, solar plexus, sacral, and root chakras; leave the remaining quartz crystals and black tourmaline in place for five to ten minutes to help circulate and integrate the positive effects of this chakra-balancing layout.

Transforming Trauma

Crystals: six pieces of carnelian

One of simplest and most effective layouts you can add to your toolbox makes use of carnelian, and it is often called the *carnelian net* or the *etheric body net*. Crystal experts Sue and Simon Lilly have worked with this layout extensively, and it was through their work that I was first introduced to it.*

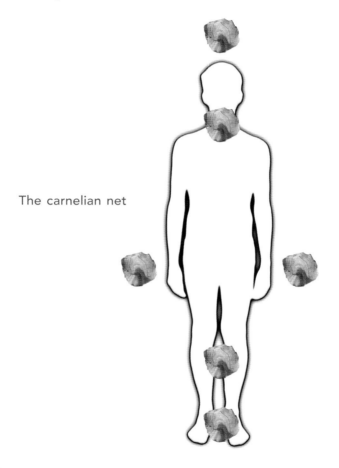

The carnelian net

Before creating the layout ensure that the carnelians are thoroughly cleansed. Then place one stone just above the head and another at the base of

---

*The Lillys' student Nick Edgell originally created the carnelian net, and he has graciously given permission to use it and publish it. More information about this layout can be found in Simon Lilly's *The Crystal Healing Guide* (p. 154); it is also available as a free PDF download on the Lillys' Mandala Complementary Studies (MCS) website.

the throat. Next place one on each side of the body, just outside the hands. The next carnelian is placed between the legs, slightly below the knees, and the final stone goes below that, level with the ankles. Leave the stones in place for ten to thirty minutes. Remove the stones in the same order in which they were placed and cleanse them thoroughly afterward.

ADDITIONAL LAYOUTS

The layouts described above are all multipurpose tools that can be used in many different scenarios. The layouts described in this section are designed with specific goals in mind. Each of the stones and patterns has been chosen with purpose, but substitutions can be made according to the needs of your client and the tools available in your collection.

Restful Sleep

Crystals: four amethysts, plus one each of sodalite, jade, jet, and hematite

Today's world places so many demands on us that many people have difficulty relaxing properly and getting a full night's sleep. This layout can be used to enhance the quality of sleep, either by meditating inside it briefly before retiring or by gridding your bed with these stones. It is designed so that it is easy to place beneath your bed or between the mattress and boxspring to help you sleep soundly every night.

After cleansing your crystals and programming them to help you rest, create a rectangular array of amethyst. Amethyst is a stone of tranquillity, and it confers a gently protective influence while simultaneously uplifting the atmosphere to help you drift into dreamland. The number 4 and shape of the amethyst configuration is subtly grounding and stabilizing, thereby keeping you grounded and centered as you prepare for bed.

A piece of hematite is placed below the feet to settle the entire energy field and nourish the earth star chakra. Sodalite is placed above the head to shut off repetitive thoughts and quiet an overactive mind. On one side of the grid place a piece of jet, and on the other a specimen of jade (which side is unimportant). Jet has been touted for protecting against nightmares for centuries, and it removes unwanted and foreign thoughtforms from the aura. Jade is a dreamtime ally that shuts down the ego mind and ensures peaceful and meaningful dreams.

If you use this layout to meditate before bed, give it no more than fifteen

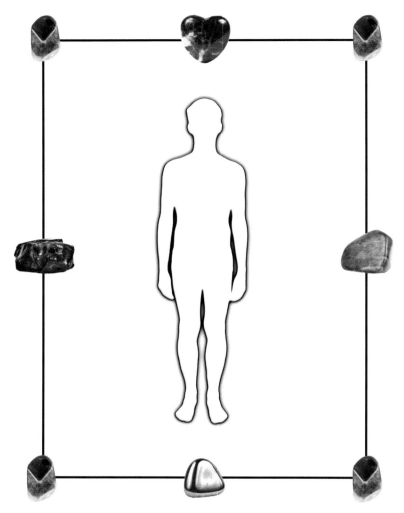

This simple layout invites restful sleep.

minutes, lest you fall asleep inside it. If you choose to construct this in your bedroom instead, be sure to cleanse the crystals and reactivate your grid once a week.

Releasing Pain

Crystals: two pieces of copper, one hematite, one malachite, plus clear quartz (optional)

The goal of the releasing pain layout isn't to produce overnight results; rather, it is to gently ease physical pain while simultaneously coaxing the memory of pain

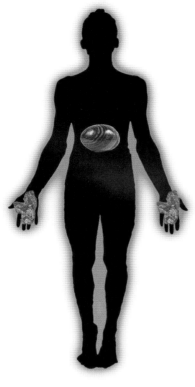

Crystal layout for
treating pain

from afflicted cells. Although this layout works well for widespread, chronic pain, clear quartz can be applied to a specific location to treat a localized illness or injury.

Copper plays an important role in this therapy. In its pure form it is placed in each of the hands, while a copper carbonate, malachite, is positioned at the solar plexus. Copper is a popular remedy for chronic pain. It gently energizes and revitalizes the entire being, especially when placed in each hand.

Malachite is a powerful healing stone, and its familiar bands create a bull's-eye effect, thereby allowing it to target the source of pain. The gentle waves of energy produced by this green gem ripple through our whole being, seeking out the origin of our symptoms, no matter how deeply seated they are. It purges and releases these stored energy patterns, thereby freeing our physical body from the pain we carry around.

Hematite is another mineral often recommended for treating pain. Hematite is grounding, balancing, shielding, and strengthening. It draws out pain and illness, and its action complements the effects of malachite. Hematite directs the energy being released into the earth.

As always, cleanse and program the stones being used. Place the copper pieces in the hands of the person. Place a large piece of hematite at the earth star chakra, or use two smaller pieces below the soles of each foot. Gently place the malachite on the solar plexus.

Hold the intention of the stones reaching deep into all the bodies of the person, the physical body and the subtle bodies, so that they seek out and empty the person of any stored pain. Optionally, place a quartz compress or poultice on a target site. This can be made with a natural-fiber pouch filled with tumbled quartz or with a strand of polished quartz beads.

After approximately thirty minutes (or less if the person becomes uncomfortable), remove the malachite first, followed by the copper. Direct the person to breathe deeply through the soles of his or her feet as the hematite remains in place for several breaths, then remove the hematite. Finally, if you are using a quartz compress, remove that. Afterward cleanse all the stones. This treatment will produce the best results when repeated several times a week. From there, follow up with at least one treatment a week until conditions improve or resolve.

Protection

Crystals: one each of labradorite and obsidian, four or more black tourmaline, and four or more shungite

Sometimes the world around us gets the better of us, and when our boundaries falter we may feel ourselves becoming depleted physically, emotionally, and spiritually. The protection layout is designed to help restore and reinforce our natural defenses.

Cleanse the crystals you've selected and program them for protection. Begin the layout by placing labradorite over the thymus (the location of the higher heart chakra). Labradorite amplifies the light of the aura, thereby making it harder for external forces to negatively affect us. By placing this stone over the thymus, it acts as an energetic filter; it trains the entire aura to discern when to allow the energy field to be receptive and when to stay on guard.

Next place the obsidian over the solar plexus chakra. The combination of this stone sitting on this location amplifies your personal power and prevents a drain on your spiritual essence, such as through psychic vampires and energetic

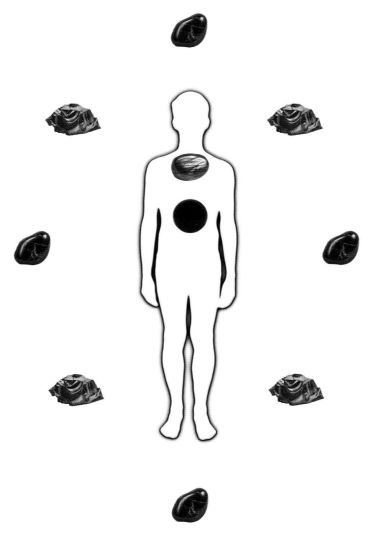

This crystal layout can boost your energetic defenses.

cords. Obsidian helps to deflect other people's negative emotions too, thereby preventing you from taking them on.

Finally, encircle the body with alternating shungite and black tourmaline. Start below the feet with black tourmaline and move clockwise around the person. Although there are four of these stones pictured in the figure above, feel free to use as many as you have available. Connect and activate the outer ring of tourmaline and shungite as described in chapter 8. Allow the person to remain in the grid for ten to thirty minutes, as needed. Remove the labradorite and obsidian first; then remove the ring of tourmaline and shungite, starting below the feet and moving in a counterclockwise direction.

Forgiveness

Crystals: six rose quartz, and one each blue lace agate, lepidolite, aquamarine, and green calcite

Forgiveness is a necessary part of our healing journey. Throughout life we are faced with unmet expectations, heartbreak, abuse (both intentional and not), and other scenarios that lead to our harboring resentment, bitterness, anger,

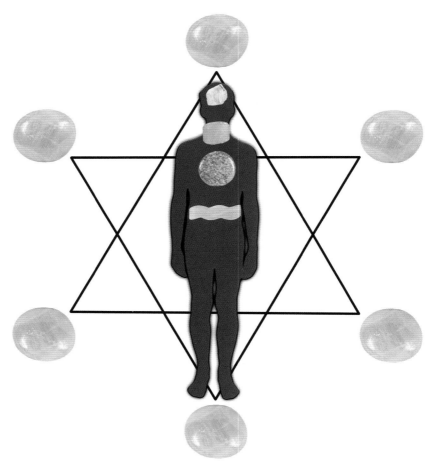

Use this layout for cultivating forgiveness.

sadness, guilt, shame, and other unhealthy patterns. The imbalances created by these emotional patterns can lead to pain and disease in the body, mind, and spirit. Forgiveness is the key that releases us from the bonds of these harmful patterns. Each of the stones in this layout helps us find and express forgiveness for ourself and for others.

Start by cleansing all the stones required for this layout. They can be programmed for forgiveness if desired. Place the six rose quartz stones in the Seal of Solomon layout around the person. Rose quartz restores fluidity to emotional patterns and directs our focus to more loving experiences. In the Seal of Solomon pattern it works to restore balance to the entire being, especially focusing on the emotional body, where patterns in need of forgiveness may dwell.

Next place the blue lace agate on the solar plexus chakra. This gemstone is supremely calming. It soothes anger, fear, worry, and depression, and it helps us develop confidence and self-awareness. Blue lace agate also sifts through the layers of baggage and pain that envelop past traumas. Doing so enables us to find the inherent lessons that these experiences provide.

Place the lepidolite on the heart. Lepidolite acts like a balm to an unquiet heart and mind. Thanks to its lithium content, this mineral has a warm and comforting presence that uplifts the psyche. This gemstone instills acceptance and nonattachment, thereby leading us toward forgiveness.

Aquamarine is placed on or near the throat to help initiate emotional release and encourage expression. In many cases forgiveness is best achieved when we communicate our forgiveness. Aquamarine is a stone of courage and flux; it emboldens us to speak our mind and opens us to the transformational power of our voice.

The green calcite is placed on the brow (or above the head if you have a larger piece). Green calcite is one of the premier stones for healing the mind. It breaks down old and outdated beliefs, fears, and conditioned behaviors. By placing the green calcite on the brow, it carries the energy of the forgiveness layout deep into both the conscious and subconscious mind. It combats stubbornness and helps the mind surrender to the heart and spirit as we seek forgiveness.

Leave the layout in place for up to thirty minutes. Remove the stones from the person's body first, and then dismantle the hexagram of rose quartz encircling them. Cleanse the crystals afterward.

Grounding

Crystals: two pieces of petrified wood, one ruby, two smoky quartz or black tour-maline, and one fluorite

We all need additional support to remain grounded from time to time. Grounding allows us to complete the circuit of energy between the human energy field and that of the planet, thereby giving us an outlet to discharge unwanted or disharmonious patterns and replenish our energy reserves with the earth's nourishing energy. Whether you or your client needs additional support with grounding or just a gentle pick-me-up, consider using this layout.

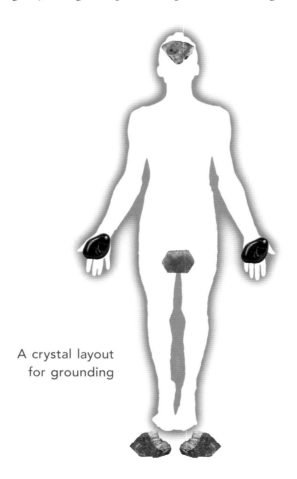

A crystal layout
for grounding

The petrified wood is placed below the feet first. This stone helps us connect to the earth and strengthens the earth star chakra, as well as the minor chakras in the souls of the feet, all of which support our ability to stay grounded. Petrified wood also confers strength and resilience during times of transition.

Next place the ruby on or near the pubic bone (alternatively, two rubies can be used, each placed on the hips, to either side of the root chakra). Ruby is dynamic, energizing, and revitalizing. It opens and activates the root chakra and helps our reserves of life force to circulate through the body.

Place the fluorite on the brow chakra to ground and stabilize the mind. Fluorite's cubic crystal structure brings order and structure to the mental body while it anchors the awareness in the physical body, thereby supporting the underlying need to ground from the psychological level.

Finally, place the two smoky quartz crystals or black tourmaline pieces in the hands. I prefer to use unpolished, terminated crystals for this. The crystal in the left hand should be directed inward, and the crystal in the right hand should be directed outward. This will help complete the circuit of energy between the person's field and that of the earth.

Leave the stones in place for ten to fifteen minutes as needed. Remove them in reverse order and cleanse them thoroughly.

CREATING YOUR OWN LAYOUTS

There will be many times when the standard layouts you find in books don't quite fit the situation you face. Once you've built a relationship with the crystals in your toolbox, you can rely on your intuition to guide you in crafting your own layouts. You can involve your clients in this process by encouraging them to help choose stones, and together you can decide how to incorporate shapes, numbers, and patterns into the layout. Consult the guidelines for numbers and shapes in chapter 8 as needed. Before closing this chapter, here are some helpful tips for creating your own layouts.

▶ **Balance is key:** Always aim to create some sense of balance in your layouts. Balanced shapes create balanced energies. There are times when asymmetry is both desired and required in a crystal grid or layout; in these cases, ensure that the overall energy is balanced and appropriate. Layouts placed on the body usually exhibit some degree of bilateral symmetry, although the distribution and arrangement of crystals is highly variable.

▸ **Bigger isn't always better:** Size isn't everything when it comes to crystals. Bigger stones and bigger layouts are not necessarily better. However, since the mass of a crystal affects the amplitude (volume) of its energy field, bigger *is* louder. Sometimes we need to shout to be heard, other times we don't; the same goes for the amplitude of the energies with which we work. Big shifts may require bigger and more complex tools, but sometimes simple gets the job done just as well. The overall number of stones you use and the complexity of your crystal layouts is subject to the same guidelines too.

▸ **Remember to stay grounded:** Both the practitioner and the client benefit from being adequately grounded. When creating your own layouts, double-check to ensure that there are sufficient stones for grounding. If you are using high-consciousness stones such as selenite, moldavite, and danburite, make a point of balancing them with earthier energies, such as those embodied in jasper, black tourmaline, or hematite. We all have different responses to energies, so it's helpful to have several grounding stones on hand to provide the best tool for each layout.

▸ **Activate your layouts:** As a general rule I always activate crystal layouts that are placed around my clients, just like I do with my crystal grids. For layouts that rest on the body, I typically only use the activation procedure occasionally, as it can feel too intense for many people, whether or not they consider themselves sensitive to energy.

▸ **Adjust in the moment:** Crystal layouts do not have to remain static. In longer healing sessions I will often retouch the arrangement of crystals as I go, adding, subtracting, or substituting crystals as the energy shifts during the session. There is one caveat: less is more, as constantly moving crystals (especially those that lie on the body of the person you are treating) is disruptive, and it can distract from an otherwise relaxing experience. If significant changes to the layout are needed, consider building two entirely separate layouts rather than fiddling with one throughout the session.

▸ **Be creative:** Making crystal layouts should be enjoyable and effective. It's a great way to unleash your inner child, and this helps to engage your whole being in the healing process. Beautiful arrays of healing stones can be as simple or as complex as you like—you are limited only by the tools you have available. Consider snapping a photo of the layout and sending it to the person to reflect on whenever they need a spiritual pick-me-up after the treatment has ended.

◆ *Intuitive Crystal Layout*

As in the above layouts, begin with freshly cleansed crystals. If you are less sensitive to energies, I recommend dowsing the person's energy field to glean some inspiration on which areas might need to be targeted in your layout as well as which stones correspond with those areas. If you are so inclined or sensitive enough, you can scan the energy field intuitively via other means.

Once you've assessed the person's energetic state of being, select the stones that will target these areas. You can mentally connect to your crystals and ask which stones will volunteer to join the layout; even if you don't consider yourself psychic, you'd be surprised at how you'll be drawn to specific stones after asking. Sometimes you'll see where they should be placed in your mind's eye, and other times it will feel as if they are leading your hand to where they need to be placed.

Next begin the process of laying the stones on or around the person's body. Ensure that you have included sufficient grounding stones, and check the soundness of the energy field of the layout as a whole. You may add, subtract, move, or substitute stones until they feel right. Feel free to ask the recipient of the layout how they feel; their feedback may help you identify ways to improve the layout.

Allow the layout to remain in place for an appropriate amount of time (refer to time guidelines discussed earlier in this chapter). Afterward gently direct the person's awareness back to the present moment; let them know that the treatment is drawing to a close. Remove the stones and allow the person to return to normal consciousness. Once completed, cleanse your crystals thoroughly and record the layout and your experiences with it.

10
Spiritual Hygiene
and Protection

ANY BOOK ON CRYSTAL HEALING would not be complete without a discussion of how to responsibly handle the energies being released and transformed during a crystal healing session. As a practitioner you should be aware that some of the patterns of energy that are released during a session can be harmful to your own well-being. During our healing work we naturally become more open and sensitive to subtle energies. When we attune to the devic and mineral kingdoms' pure energies, we can be susceptible to other outside energies too *unless* we exercise good spiritual hygiene and maintain healthy psychic boundaries. Preparing yourself and your healing space can prevent unhealthy energies and malignant entities from sticking around. Although we might want to believe that crystal healing is nothing but love and light, we will encounter people (including ourselves) who will release some painful or even dark energies, whether karmic in nature or the result of past traumas in this life. Some of these energy patterns may even result from nonphysical entities that attach themselves to a host, just as parasites do.

The techniques in this chapter offer the tools you need to proactively handle the more challenging energies you may encounter. These practices consist of preparing your space, protecting yourself, and removing harmful energies from the aura of your client and yourself. These techniques are built on the foundation of grounding and centering, as discussed in chapter 6. Psychic protection works to protect the subtle anatomy and consciousness much in the same way that our physical body protects itself from pathogens with the immune system. Psychic protection fortifies the aura and eliminates harmful energies and entities, thereby preventing harm from taking place on a spiritual level. A healthy aura generally offers sufficient protection from external energies, but during healing sessions we may need additional support. Work with the techniques in this chapter to offer psychic protection and maintain a healthy environment for healing.

CLEANSING YOUR SPACE

When practicing any healing art or spiritual/energetic method, clearing out old, stale, unhealthy energies paves the way for a more successful practice. Additionally, by claiming your space and marking it as sacred, you can keep negativity at bay and attract more of the good that you want for both yourself and your clients into your environment. You can enhance your practice by incorporating some basic space-clearing methods, such as any of the following:

- ▶ Burning cleansing herbs and incense
- ▶ Lighting candles
- ▶ Visualizing white, violet, or golden light filling your space
- ▶ Playing bells, chimes, singing bowls, and other sacred instruments
- ▶ Spraying crystal elixirs, flower essences, and essential oils
- ▶ Tracing in the air or visualizing sacred symbols on the walls, ceiling, and floor
- ▶ Reciting mantras, prayers, and incantations
- ▶ Carrying representations of the four elements around your space to clear it

You can be as creative as you like when cleansing your working space. This is the act of creating sacred space. By creating sacred space, your working space becomes distinguished from your everyday, mundane life, whether that space is just an end table with a crystal grid on it or an entire room devoted to crystal healing and meditation. The above list is just a starting point for how to create sacred space, and you are likely to find many other ways, some involving the use of certain crystals, that will allow you to consecrate your working area.

◆ Energy Clearing with Crystals

If you or your clients are sensitive to candles, smoke, or scents, it may be necessary to find an alternative to some of the more popular spiritual cleansing methods. For this technique select a crystal that is comfortable to hold in your hand and large enough to use as a wand. Selenite and quartz (especially a laser wand or a Lemurian seed crystal) are ideal choices. Cleanse, program, and activate your wand before proceeding.

Begin by standing in the center of the room. Hold your crystal wand to your heart with both hands and ask for protection, guidance, and assistance from Source. Invite any other guides, angels, masters, or deities that are appropriate.

Transfer the wand to your dominant hand. As you breathe in imagine that the universe fills you not only with air but also with a prismatic white light, the energy of cleansing and purification. On an exhalation direct this energy down your arm and through the crystal; visualize it emitting a powerful stream of cleansing energy through its termination. You will use this energy to cleanse and clear your space.

Moving counterclockwise, direct the crystal around the room, guiding its energy across each wall, and into every corner. Pay special attention to any windows and doors in the room; you can trace their outline with the crystal's energy to clear away any disharmony that may squeeze through them. If you can psychically sense any pockets of disharmonious energy, spend extra time flooding them with the white light of purification, and visualize them being transmuted by the crystal's energy.

Once the energy of the room has been cleared, choose a color that complements the room and the work you will do in it. Examples of appropriate colors of light include blue to bring peace, green for regeneration, and violet for spiritual healing; refer to the discussion of color in chapter 2 for more ideas. Breathe your chosen color into yourself and direct it through the crystal as you did with the white light. Point the crystal at the center of the floor or ceiling and trace a clockwise spiral that reaches to the walls of the room. Move the crystal clockwise to fill every nook and cranny of the room with the colored light.

When finished hold the crystal to your heart again and ask that the room be cleansed and protected from all external and internal sources of harm, and visualize it gleaming with colored light. Deactivate the crystal and proceed with your meditation, healing, or other work within the room.

◆ Creating Sacred Space

Before beginning any meditation or crystal healing activity, set aside some time to create sacred space. If you have an altar or other area devoted to your spiritual practice, start by gathering items that represent the four classic natural elements: a candle for fire, incense or herbs for air, a container of water, and some salt for earth. Next light a candle and incense to remain on the altar if you like. Mentally connect to the Divine in whatever terms are comfortable for you, calling on God, Goddess, Source, and others, to guide and protect you during your practice. You can also call on the consciousness of the mineral kingdom to support you in the act of creating sacred space.

Meditate on the light emanating from the candle's flame, and visualize it traveling throughout the room and filling your body, mind, and spirit. Pick up the candle and carefully carry it around your space in a clockwise fashion. Imagine the candle's warmth and light burning away negative and disharmonious energies, leaving positivity in its wake.

Next light a cleansing herb or incense such as sage, palo santo, mugwort, cedar, or lavender. Once the bundle of herbs or incense is smoking adequately, carry it around your space clockwise. Reflect on the qualities of air and smoke, and visualize them blowing away any energies that do not serve you.

Move on to your container of water. Carry it around the room clockwise, sprinkling a little as you go. Visualize a cool stream of water or the ocean's tides washing away any energies that need to be released, refreshing your body, mind, and soul.

Holding your dish of salt, start walking in a clockwise direction around your space. Sprinkle a small amount of salt as you go, and visualize any disharmony being neutralized by the salt and discharged into the earth itself. Feel your space becoming more grounded and protected as you complete your cleansing with the earth element.

Now sit or stand before your altar or in the center of your sacred space. Offer gratitude to the elements and to Source for assisting you in consecrating your sacred space. Extinguish the candles and incense if you wish and proceed to your meditation or other work.

PSYCHIC PROTECTION

A key element in practicing good spiritual hygiene is preventive care. Although it is vital to cleanse your space, your crystals, and yourself both before and after a crystal healing session, regularly practicing psychic protection will prevent you from taking on any patterns or disharmonious energies that are released during a healing session.

Psychic protection comes in many forms, from visualizing a protective sphere of light around your aura to invoking angels, guardians, or other beneficent beings. In crystal healing one of the simplest ways to guard against unwanted energies or entities is to wear or carry crystals that have an apotropaic function. Some of the more traditional protective crystals include amber, black tourmaline, bloodstone, carnelian, emerald, jasper, jet, lapis lazuli, obsidian, onyx, smoky quartz, tiger's eye, and turquoise. Other powerful stones for clearing and protecting your energy field include clear quartz, fluorite, labradorite, pietersite, selenite, shungite, and sugilite, among others. These stones can be programmed specifically for protection before being worn or carried.

In addition to wearing or carrying protective stones, you can use crystal elixirs made of protective stones and take them internally or spray into your aura. Creating a protective crystal grid in your healing room and using exercises such as the Cocoon of Light and the Aura Clearing that appear below will help you maintain the health and integrity of your energy field.

I'd like to voice one final thought on protection before moving on. For some people protection becomes a means of closing themselves off from the rest of the world in an effort to prevent harmful influences from making their way in. One of the most fundamental spiritual truths is that *we are all one*. If we seek to barricade our energy from that of others, we are buying into the illusion that we are separate beings, thereby challenging the truth of our unity. Rather than taking this approach, I choose to view protection through the lens of qualifying the energy that I both receive and give to the world. This means that the protective tools I use aren't walls to keep the world out but rather filters that allow only loving, healing energy to be exchanged between myself and the universe. When practicing self-protection, choosing this paradigm will help shift your awareness from fear into love, thus increasing the amplitude of your energy field overall.

◆ Cocoon of Light

One of my favorite ways to preserve the integrity of my energy field and prevent unwanted attachments or intrusions is the cocoon of light. A single crystal point or wand is used to weave a layer of light around your aura, thus creating a semipermeable membrane that allows you to receive positive energy and release anything that doesn't serve a higher purpose. The cocoon itself filters the energies we both send and receive, thereby preventing us from inadvertently taking on negative energy and sending that negativity out into the world. I enjoy doing this exercise because it does not feel as though I am separated or walled off from the world around me when I build the cocoon around my energy field. In addition to employing the coccoon of light on yourself, it may also be used on your clients to offer them support after a healing session and help them integrate the healing energy that they have received during a crystal healing treatment.

Select a crystal point or polished wand to use for your cocoon of light. Selenite, a laser wand, or a polished crystal like a Vogel-cut wand are all perfect for this task, but any crystal with a termination will do. Be sure to choose one that matches the needs of your circumstances. Cleanse your tool and program it with the intention

Visualize light emerging from the crystal point as you weave it through your energy field.

of helping you generate additional support and protection. The crystal should be activated, as described in chapter 5. Begin weaving the cocoon of light, beginning at your crown. Hold the crystal in your dominant hand and draw lines, spirals, zigzags, or any other patterns around your body. Visualize a thread or cord of golden-white light being emitted by the crystal and placed around your aura, as if you are weaving a layer of mesh or gauze around the aura itself.

Loosely surround the aura, working from one end to the other. Allow your intuition to guide the patterns you choose. Use any combination of circles, waves, zigzags, spirals, and straight lines. Allow them to overlap with one another as you build your cocoon. If you cannot reach all sides of your body, visualize the threads of light weaving their way around the areas you cannot reach to complete the cocoon. You can imagine that the thread harmlessly and gracefully passes through your physical body to reach the opposite side of your aura. Ensure that you make the cocoon large enough so as not to restrict the movement of the aura.

When finished bring the crystal in front of your chest, level with your heart. Tie off the threads of light by weaving a lemniscate pattern (a figure 8 or infinity symbol) several times. Cut the loose end of the thread of energy by flicking or rapidly tugging the crystal down. Your cocoon of light is now complete.

MORE PRACTICES FOR
ENERGETIC CLARITY AND INTEGRITY

As you actively clarify and raise your personal frequencies and increase the quotient of light you hold while working with the mineral kingdom, it becomes increasingly important that you adopt regular, effective routines to ensure that your own energy body and your environs are kept clear, cleansed, and charged with the right energies. Adopting a daily protocol demonstrates to Source and to the mineral kingdom that you are discerning and responsible in your approach to energy work. It helps keep your energy bodies clear and shows your commitment to your own growth as you open to higher realities, and it encourages self-discipline, which is essential as you progress as a crystal healer.

The remaining exercises in this chapter are meant to round out your crystal healing practice and provide additional means of supporting yourself and your clients and loved ones with the mineral kingdom. Try these exercises on yourself first, and experiment with different tools. As you grow more comfortable and confident with these techniques, you can incorporate them into your daily spiritual hygiene.

◆ *Personal Recharge*

This is a simple technique taught in many schools of crystal healing. To perform it you'll need two single-terminated quartz crystals of similar size. Traditionally, clear quartz is used, but you could also use two pieces of amethyst, citrine, or smoky quartz, provided that they are terminated. The placement of the two crystals in your hands helps to recharge and refresh your entire being. Use it when you feel low energy, mental fog, or minor pain or discomfort. A few minutes of the personal recharge may feel as refreshing as a nap. The crystals can be programmed with a specific intention before beginning to fine-tune the process. Try programming your crystal to relieve pain or anxiety, boost your vital energy, clear your mind, or simply for peace.

Ensure that your crystals are adequately cleansed and programmed before beginning. Place the first crystal in your nondominant hand with the termination directed inward, toward the wrist. In your dominant hand, place the other crystal with its termination facing out, toward the fingertips. As you breathe in imagine that the inward-pointing crystal is filling your body with healing energy. On the outgoing breath visualize the outward-pointing crystal releasing any energies that do not serve you.

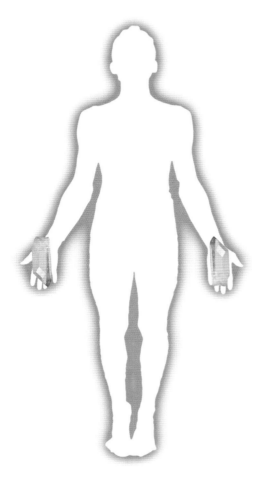

This simple crystal placement will recharge and revitalize your energy.

Continue this visualization for several minutes. When finished bring your awareness back to the room and cleanse your crystals. This is such an easy and safe procedure that you can repeat it as often as desired or combine it with other healing techniques, such as the layouts discussed in chapter 9.

◆ Aura Clearing with Selenite

Aura clearing helps sweep away unwanted or unhealthy patterns of energy from the human energy field. It can be used as a stand-alone treatment on yourself or clients for a simple pick-me-up, at the beginning of a treatment to open your client to deeper healing, or at the end of a treament on yourself or the person you are treating to clear out the energies released and to integrate healing on a deeper level.

This technique employs selenite, perhaps one of the most popular healing stones available today. Though gem-quality, terminated crystals of good size can be pricey, the fibrous variety known as satin spar is affordable, accessible, and available in a multitude of sizes and shapes. Selenite's energy is vibrant and refreshing. It moves through the aura like a waterfall of white light, clearing away disharmonious vibes and old thoughtforms. Because it crystallizes out of water, it is adept at returning stagnant energy to a healthy state of flux, and it especially helps to realign the emotional body with the entire human energy field. For this exercise choose a relatively large piece of selenite, preferably a wand (polished or natural), slab, or palmstone. Cleanse and program the selenite before proceeding.

Aura clearing can be performed with your client seated, lying down, or standing according to whatever is easiest, as well as on yourself. I'll describe the exercise here for a person who is reclined, such as on a massage table, but you can adapt it according to the needs of your scenario. Begin by holding the selenite approximately twelve inches above the crown chakra, where the soul star chakra is located. Visualize the stone clearing and aligning this energy center; when it has saturated the soul star, picture it spilling out into the entire human energy field.

Gently sweep the selenite downward through the aura from the soul star chakra to the earth star chakra. Start slowly and work along the middle of the body first. Make several passes on each side of the midline, covering the entire body. As you sweep, the selenite will help to dislodge unhealthy or outdated energy patterns and realign the subtle bodies of the aura.

Reverse the direction of the sweeping movements, starting below the feet at the earth star chakra and moving to the soul star above the head. Imagine that as you move you are uplifting the entire energy field and smoothing over any patterns of disharmony, as if you are polishing the aura itself.

To finish, hold the selenite over the person's heart (or your own heart if you are working on yourself) and move it gently in a clockwise spiral. Allow the stone to pick up momentum as it moves. Finish by encompassing the entire body in one continuous, circular (or ovoid) movement two to three times, or more if it feels necessary. Afterward cleanse the selenite.

◆ Combing the Aura

The energy of a quartz crystal cluster is emitted in an array of directions, and it tends to be more diffuse and broad-spectrum than the energy of individual crystal points. This makes it a helpful tool for clearing the aura and uplifting the energy of a room. When a crystal cluster is held in the hand with the points directed inward, it can be used like an energetic comb on yourself, or it can be used with the points directed toward the person to comb him or her. I like to use this method to loosen old patterns at the beginning of a treatment as well as at the end of a treatment, to sweep away any vestiges of the energies that were released.

A crystal cluster can be used to clear the aura
by combing it through the energy field.

Use gentle, broad, slow motions when combing the aura. Sweeping in a consistent pattern can loosen the hold of attachments such as negative thoughtforms, energetic cords, and stagnant energy. Since quartz is nourishing and revitalizing on many levels, this technique not only cleanses the aura but also rejuvenates it, especially after other healing methods have been employed. It is also an effective way to combat stress and restore balance and harmony to the nonphysical, subtle bodies. Smaller, tighter movements can be applied to individual areas, such as the chakras or other energy centers, as a means of treating more localized concerns. Aura combing can release stubborn energies that seem otherwise resistant to other energetic methods.

Stick to a cluster that fits comfortably in your hand. Palm-size specimens are affordable and effective. If the stone is too large it can be tiresome to hold for longer periods of time (as well as posing a danger if dropped on a client). Examples that are too small may not penetrate the aura deeply enough for more serious use. In addition to size it is also important to consider the composition and solidity of the cluster. A specimen with a fragile matrix or overly delicate crystals would be inappropriate because of potential breakage.

Start with a freshly cleansed (and programmed, if you like) cluster of quartz. Hold the cluster firmly in your preferred hand with points facing yourself if you are sweeping yourself or toward the person you are treating. Begin above the crown of the head and sweep downward. If working on a client, maintain a safe distance from his or her body. The downward motion is grounding and relaxing.

If at any point you feel resistance, as though the cluster feels stuck at a certain point, focus your attention and efforts on that area. This sensation is usually indicative of an attached thoughtform, entity, or cord. Try moving the cluster in different directions to comb out the energies; imagine that you are untangling a knot. Be diligent, but gentle.

To open and energize the entire system, an upward motion is used. You can also add small circular motions over each chakra to scrub them clean. Be mindful that not all chakras spin in the same direction, so try to go with the flow of the chakra's energy, and note that chakras can sometimes change the direction of their spin. You can dowse the chakras beforehand (see chapter 3) to ensure that you are following the direction of each chakra's spin.

Finish with broader, gentle sweeps. Circular motions that encircle the entire body are an excellent way to finish because they encourage a healthy flow in the aura. When complete, cleanse your crystal cluster.

◆ Cord Cutting

Your energy field can host many kinds of harmful patterns, including negative thoughtforms of your own making, blockages, psychic energies that have attached themselves, and energetic cords that tie you to other people, places, and events. These cords feed unhealthy patterns and may cause you to replay harmful situations in your life. They nearly always have a karmic element to them, and so releasing these cords can help you transform and transmute your karma. Cords are the easiest auric attachments to remove, and crystals can facilitate the process of cutting and releasing them. To perform a cord cutting you'll need a crystal that is sharply terminated or otherwise bladelike in its structure. A laser wand, naturally terminated crystal, polished crystal wand, or raw stones such as selenite, kyanite, obsidian, and flint are all excellent tools for cord cutting. Although the directions that follow are framed as if you are working on a client, you can perform cord cutting on yourself just as easily.

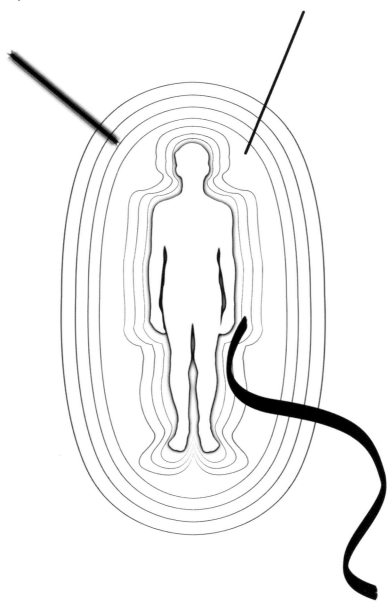

Energy cords in the aura

To begin, cleanse, program, and activate your crystal. Set the intention to locate and remove any harmful cords in your client's energy field; call on Source or any other guides whom you would like to assist you. To locate the cord scan the aura with the crystal or stone as described in chapter 3. Hold the tool in your dominant hand, with the point and base of the crystal between your fingers, if it fits comfortably. Hold the crystal so that its flattest side is facing the person's body and sweep it gently through the aura to locate any cords. When you sense resistance or changes in temperature or energy, this is where a cord is located.

Once located, reposition the crystal so the sharp or terminated end is facing the cord. Use a cutting, chopping, slicing, or sawing motion to sever the energetic connection. Repeat as needed, and call on spiritual help for persistent cords. Once the cord is severed, visualize it being disposed of in a receptacle of violet or golden-white light. Repeat the process of locating and removing cords until there are no more that can be detected.

Once finished clear and smooth the aura by sweeping through it, perhaps with selenite as in the Aura Clearing exercise described earlier in this chapter. Express gratitude for the karmic lessons that the cords represent, and send love to whomever or whatever is connected to the other end of each cord. If you have persistent attachments that resist cutting, you can loosen them with the Aura Scrubbing exercise in this chapter. After the cord cutting is complete, thoroughly cleanse all of your tools, your space, and yourself.

◆ *Extracting Thoughtforms*

Sometimes certain energy patterns get stuck or trapped in the body and energy field. These may be thoughts, beliefs, emotions, and behaviors that create or are created by pain and trauma. When we choose not to consciously process these patterns, they become enveloped by a dense cloud of energy that obscures them from our conscious awareness. This results in a harmful form of energy that gets trapped in the human energy field, one that cannot be easily expressed or released. In these cases a crystal wand can be used to extract and release the thoughtform or pattern of energy to facilitate healing. This exercise can be done on oneself or on the person you are treating.

Of all the exercises in this chapter, this one is more advanced than the others and will require practice and sensitivity to master. Although my method is an amalgam of several techniques I have learned and honed over the years, it is heavily influenced by the work of pioneers in the crystal world, including Katrina Raphaell,

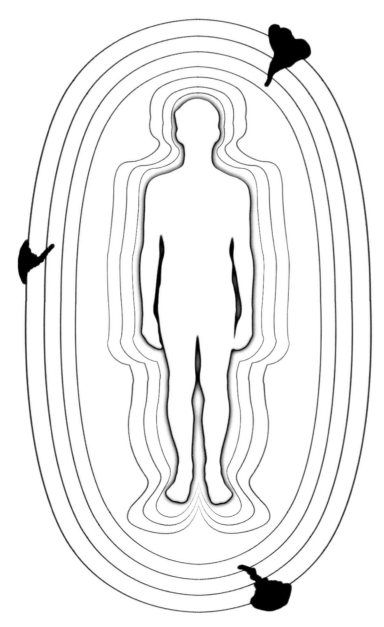

Harmful thoughtforms in the aura

JaneAnn Dow, and Marcel Vogel. To perform this technique you'll need a terminated quartz crystal that fits comfortably in the palm of your hand. I prefer to use
a natural laser wand or an authentic Vogel-cut crystal, but you can experiment to

find what works best for you. As always, ensure that your crystal is cleansed and programmed prior to use.

The root thoughtform may be something of which your client is aware, or it may be something that is suppressed, below their ability to identify. In either case you may need to find this pattern of energy by some other means. Perhaps it is tied to a physical injury or illness, or the person may already know where these dense energies are located. If you are clairvoyantly inclined, you may psychically see it in the body, aura, chakras, or other part of the human energy field. Sometimes you can feel it by moving your palms through the aura, noting changes in the sensations of the energy field itself. Otherwise you can dowse for the thoughtform, similar to the way the chakras are dowsed, as described in chapter 3.

Once you have found the location of the thoughtform, hold your wand in your dominant hand, approximately one to two feet away from the point on the person's body or in their energy field. Aim the crystal at the target location and move it in a clockwise, circular pattern. Start with a wide circle, twelve to eighteen inches in diameter. Gradually move the crystal toward the target; as you approach the person, make smaller circles with the crystal point. As you do so the crystal will trace a conical shape that narrows just above the target area.

While holding the crystal above the location of the thoughtform, trace a small, counterclockwise circle (one to two inches in diameter). Trace this circle several times and hold the intention that the crystal will lock in on the thoughtform and loosen its hold over the person's energy field and body. When this happens you will intuitively sense it; for me it feels as if something clicks into place energetically, like a key in a lock. After the crystal has locked onto the thoughtform, remove it by pulling the crystal away from the person's body and energy field; visualize the thoughtform being pulled out by the tip of the crystal. Flick the end of the crystal away from the person's (and your own) body and intend that the unhealthy energy being removed is directed into the earth, to be grounded and transformed. Repeat the removal sequence as needed until you no longer sense the thoughtform's presence.

Since removing a pattern of energy from the human energy field produces an empty space, it is necessary to fill this void with healing energy to prevent some other unhealthy energy or pattern from taking its place. Bring the crystal point over the target location and trace a clockwise circle several times, visualizing a brilliant white light (or another color, as appropriate) filling the vacancy in the person's energy field. Gradually widen the circle to seamlessly integrate this new energy into their aura.

Once finished, encourage the person to ground and center. There may be an emotional release during this therapy, accompanied by tears or physical and emotional discomfort. Reassure him or her and offer any support they may need. A gentle, nourishing gemstone such as aventurine, rose quartz, or pink tourmaline may be placed over the target location after the treatment to provide comfort and closure to the healing procedure. Cleanse your tools thoroughly once the treatment is complete.

PART TWO

▲▲▲

A Directory of Crystals and Stones

11

Two Hundred Gemstones for Healing

THE MINERAL KINGDOM INCLUDES an unimaginable assortment of rocks and minerals, each one an expression of geometric perfection and spiritual brilliance. This directory of crystals includes two hundred varieties of rocks, minerals, fossils, and gemstones that you can incorporate into your healing practice. I have chosen this assortment of stones to reflect a wide array of tools to support healing on all levels—body, mind, and spirit. Most of these are commonly available, and the rest may be obtained without much difficulty.

Use this directory as a starting point for getting acquainted with the crystals in your toolbox. The properties of each stone are sorted into their physical, psychological, and spiritual attributes. You'll also find some basic geological information about each stone, including its chemical formula, hardness, crystal system, and formation process. You can cross-reference these attributes with the information in chapter 2 to find further properties for each stone.

Generally speaking, you'll find varieties of a family of stones listed under a general heading, such as with garnet, quartz, and tourmaline. Some stones, such as amethyst and agate, are listed separately from their parent mineral (quartz in both cases); the general attributes of their mineral group still apply. You'll also find that many stones have more than one possible formation type listed; formation can vary by location and environment, so it may take further research to determine which process is responsible for the individual specimens in your collection.

My hope is that this crystal directory will be both a reference guide and a bridge to help you forge your own relationships with your beloved crystals. The entries are brief so as to leave room for personal experience rather than to be a prescriptive guide to crystal healing. May this directory offer inspiration and support as you deepen your connection to the mineral kingdom.

Agate (General)

Formula: SiO_2

Hardness: 6.5–7

Crystal system: trigonal

Formation process: igneous or sedimentary

Chakra: various (see the chakra listings under specific agate types below)

Tumbled agate

Physical healing: Generally speaking, agates of all varieties promote overall health and well-being. The fine-grained structure refines, stabilizes, and protects the body. Agates are often employed for tissue regeneration and for healing the internal organs. This gemstone stimulates the digestive system too. Agates of all varieties address the lymphatic system, the skin, and the eyes. Agate can also promote more restful sleep.

Psychological healing: Agate is often associated with protection and luck, and it confers these qualities by stimulating our inner psychological processes responsible for self-awareness, analysis, and pragmatism. Agates also promote grace, peace, and good fortune.

Spiritual healing: Agate has a refining effect on spiritual development. Most often found with pronounced bands of color, agate reveals the core cause of discontent and disharmony in one's life, peeling away the scenario layer by layer. Agate can strengthen the aura's boundaries, making it less susceptible to intrusions from outside influences. Virtually all varieties of agate provide support during times of change and transition, as they are gently grounding and protective.

Blue Lace Agate

Formula: SiO_2

Hardness: 7

Crystal system: trigonal

Formation process: igneous

Chakra: solar plexus, heart, throat

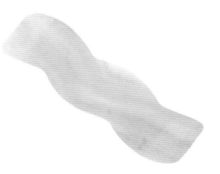

Polished pendant
of blue lace agate

Physical healing: Blue lace agate works on the respiratory system, adrenal glands, eyes, and skin. It breaks up congestion and strengthens the lungs. It soothes strained eyes and improves coordination. Blue lace agate alleviates rashes, acne, and other skin conditions. It can be used to strengthen the bones and nails, assuage dizziness, and overcome impotence.

Psychological healing: A deeply calming gemstone, blue lace agate provides peace and lightheartedness. This stone promotes self-forgiveness, gently wiping away the weight of past choices so that one can move forward with grace. It eases family tensions and brings peace into the home; it is an excellent tool for harmonious relationships on all levels. As it works to bring the psyche into balance, it supports confidence, self-esteem, and a better awareness of one's identity.

Spiritual healing: This stone encourages acceptance of life experiences, both good and bad, as lessons that the soul is graciously learning. It eliminates foreign energies from body, mind, and spirit and enables you to be more truly yourself. Blue lace agate promotes understanding, and it instills inner and outer strength.

Botswana Agate

Formula: SiO_2

Hardness: 6.5–7

Crystal system: trigonal

Formation process: igneous

Chakra: crown

Tumbled Botswana agate

Physical healing: Botswana agate supports the health of the brain and nervous system, and it is often used to help quit smoking.

Psychological healing: Working with Botswana agate can help eliminate repressed guilt related to sexuality, self-image, and eroticism. It cuts through old programming, particularly from the family, and it encourages harmony. Botswana agate steers one toward creative endeavors and self-expression, making it an ideal stone for artists working in any medium.

Spiritual healing: Botswana agate is protective and cleansing to the aura, and it can facilitate astral travel.

Crazy Lace Agate

Formula: SiO_2

Hardness: 6.5–7

Crystal system: trigonal

Formation process: igneous

Chakra: solar plexus, crown

Mexican crazy lace agate

Physical healing: Crazy lace agate promotes healthy metabolism, and it fights off infections and disorders of the blood vessels. It can also relieve the symptoms of sciatica.

Psychological healing: This type of agate encourages out-of-the-box thinking and increases mental flexibility. It invites action, helping people who are perennial planners put their plans in motion.

Spiritual healing: Crazy lace agate invites elegance and grace, and it increases one's personal magnetism. It is an excellent stone for adapting to rapid change and maintaining a positive outlook in fast-paced environments.

Fancy Agate (Earth-Tone Agate, Fancy Jasper)

Formula: SiO_2

Hardness: 6.5–7

Crystal system: trigonal

Formation process: igneous

Chakra: all, especially root

Fancy agate beads

Physical healing: Fancy agate's composition lies somewhere between that of agate and jasper, which are both classified as chalcedony by gemologists. This stone occurs in a wide range of earthy browns, reds, greens, yellows, oranges, and sometimes purples. It is deeply nourishing to the physical body, and it helps coordinate the body's efforts and resources for healing. Wearing or meditating with fancy agate can reduce or prevent jet lag. This stone reduces tension held in the neck, shoulders, and upper back. It also treats insomnia.

Psychological healing: Fancy agate invites greater peace of mind, especially by reducing background chatter in the mind itself. It encourages organization and better communication and soothes excessive worry. Fancy agate marries logic with instinct.

Spiritual healing: Fancy agate fosters a deeper connection with nature. It can act as a doorway to experiencing past-life memories. Wearing this gemstone helps one attune to the devic kingdom, and it is effective for adjusting to new surroundings.

Fire Agate

Formula: SiO_2 with limonite [$FeO(OH) \cdot nH_2O$]

Hardness: 6.5–7

Crystal system: trigonal

Formation process: igneous

Chakra: sacral, solar plexus

Tumbled fire agate

Physical healing: Fire agate is warming and energizing to the physical body. It stimulates digestion and relieves conditions affecting the intestines (diarrhea, constipation, flatulence, bloating), and it can raise the metabolism. Fire agate supports fertility and boosts libido. This stone also has a stimulating and rejuvenating effect on the body as a whole; it is a wonderful all-around healing stone.

Psychological healing: This gemstone fosters inspiration, creativity, and problem-solving skills. It eliminates fear and doubt, allowing one to become more decisive and confident. Fire agate boosts passion in all areas of life, both personal and professional. It brightens the disposition, and it also eases fears of commitment. This stone helps one feel safe.

Spiritual healing: Fire agate is gently grounding and protective; it also activates the inner fire. Use it to encourage success and ambition in all endeavors, as well as to kindle ecstatic states in meditation.

Flower Agate

Formula: SiO_2

Hardness: 6.5–7

Crystal system: trigonal

Formation process: igneous

Chakra: sacral, heart

Polished flower agate
from Madagascar

Physical healing: Flower agate's energy helps with nutrient absorption and promotes the overall health of the digestive system. Work with this gemstone to treat conditions of the urinary tract and reproductive system.

Psychological healing: This newly discovered agate from Madagascar helps you pursue beauty in myriad ways. Carry it or meditate with it for inspiration in creative pursuits and to cultivate awareness of your own beauty, both inner and outer. It is a stone of sacred sexuality, as it links the heart and the sacral chakras. This makes it ideal for conditions related to self-esteem and sexual expression. Flower agate is a soothing balm to old emotional patterns that are ready for release.

Spiritual healing: Flower agate supports manifestation, abundance, and following your bliss. This gemstone realigns the energy field with the physical body, thereby fostering radiant health while helping you adapt to the changing energies of our world. It is a stone of joy with a fairylike presence that connects to

the devic kingdom and the natural world. It teaches the importance of tolerance, trust, and harmony, thereby making it an ideal stone for fitting into your
community and for supporting the health and well-being of ecosystems, both
in the physical and the spiritual realms.

Moss Agate

Formula: SiO_2 with hornblende
$(Ca,Na)_{2-3}(Mg,Fe,Al)_5(Al,Si)_8O_{22}(OH,F)_2$

Hardness: 6.5–7

Crystal system: trigonal

Formation process: igneous

Chakra: root, heart

Tumbled moss agate

Physical healing: Moss agate is soothing to the physical body. It eliminates
excess mucus, reduces inflammation, and gently initiates detoxification. This
gemstone boosts the immune system and supports lymphatic health. Used as
an elixir it is antifungal. Moss agate can be used to manage diabetes.

Psychological healing: Moss agate is nourishing and balancing to the mind and
emotions. It curbs mood swings and assuages worry.

Spiritual healing: Moss agate can help when you feel disconnected from the
natural world. It builds ties to the devic kingdom and supports healthy plant
growth. Moss agate supports manifestation by anchoring your intention from
the higher realms into the material plane.

Pink Agate

Formula: SiO_2

Hardness: 6.5–7

Crystal system: trigonal

Formation process: igneous or
sedimentary

Chakra: heart

Tumbled pink agate

Physical healing: Pink agate soothes inflammation, and it is helpful for treating conditions of the eyes, digestive system, skin, and pancreas. Pink agate stimulates the metabolism, and it is sometimes used to promote the health of the female reproductive system.

Psychological healing: This gentle pink stone alleviates fear and emotional pain, especially that which originates in early childhood. It bolsters self-esteem and helps to lovingly transform psychological traumas.

Spiritual healing: Pink agate initiates a state of unconditional love and compassion, thereby promoting tolerance and acceptance of all.

Snakeskin Agate

Formula: SiO_2

Hardness: 6.5–7

Crystal system: trigonal

Formation process: sedimentary

Chakra: root, sacral

Snakeskin agate from Oregon

Physical healing: Snakeskin agate is touted as a stone for healing conditions of the skin, including dryness, itching, blemishes, and wrinkles. It relieves congestion and can reduce irritation of the mucous membranes. Snakeskin agate also calms an upset stomach.

Psychological healing: Snakeskin agate fosters rationality and pragmatism and strengthens problem-solving skills. This stone also boosts confidence and self-esteem. Use it to promote more direct communication.

Spiritual healing: The serpentine symbolism of this stone connotes transformation and rebirth. Snakeskin agate assists in shamanic travel, soul retrieval, and kundalini activation.

Tree Agate

Formula: SiO$_2$ with manganese oxide (Mn$_x$O$_y$) or iron oxide (Fe$_2$O$_3$)

Hardness: 6.5–7

Crystal system: trigonal

Formation process: igneous

Chakra: root, heart

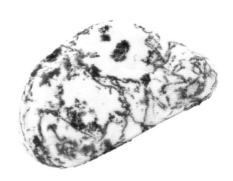

Tumbled tree agate

Physical healing: Tree agate balances the microbiome, supporting and maintaining beneficial microorganisms in the digestive tract as well as inhibiting the growth of harmful pathogens. It supports the health of the skin, liver, and digestive system. Tree agate can also lessen the intensity of seasonal allergies.

Psychological healing: Tree agate's stabilizing and harmonizing qualities can treat shock and resolve emotional trauma. It counteracts anxiety, anger, and sudden mood swings.

Spiritual healing: Much like its effect on the ecology of the human body, this mineral balances ecosystems on a larger scale too. It promotes harmony and balance among members of a group or environment. Working with this stone facilitates contact with the intelligent forces of the natural world, such as devas, fairies, and spirits. Tree agate is gently grounding.

Turritella Agate

Formula: SiO$_2$

Hardness: 6.5–7

Crystal system: trigonal

Formation process: sedimentary

Chakra: earth star, root

Tumbled turritella agate

Physical healing: Turritella agate is not a true agate but rather a chalcedony filled with fossil shells. It can detoxify the body and protect against pathogens, allergens, and toxins in the environment. Turritella agate also supports the eliminatory and digestive systems and facilitates nutrient absorption. This stone combats fatigue and overactive adrenals.

Psychological healing: Turritella agate helps us set and pursue goals. It is an excellent stone for contending with guilt. This gem can help when we feel homesick or are separated from family.

Spiritual healing: This fossiliferous chalcedony combats egotism. It also keeps us protected and grounded, nourished by the energy of the land. It has an elemental energy that enables communication with devas, spirits, and guides. As a fossil-bearing stone, turritella agate is helpful for karmic healing and past-life recall. It can be used in planetary healing, especially for polluted land.

Amazonite

Formula: $KAlSi_3O_8$ with traces of lead (Pb)

Hardness: 6–6.5

Crystal system: triclinic

Formation process: igneous

Chakra: heart, throat

Tumbled amazonite from Madagascar

Physical healing: Amazonite can alleviate cramps, liver imbalances, and seasonal allergies. It supports the health of the skeletal system, including the assimilation of calcium, strengthening and aligning joints and preventing tooth decay. Amazonite has traditionally been used for the female reproductive system, as in relieving menstrual cramps and facilitating childbirth.

Psychological healing: Amazonite works on the cause of psychosomatic conditions, especially those that are stress related. It strengthens the throat chakra and encourages communication. Amazonite helps resolve conflict, and it can release one from the mind-set of victimhood.

Spiritual healing: Amazonite helps us develop the freedom necessary to express our personal truth. It resolves feelings of unfulfillment from striving for societal or familial expectations rather than seeking personal freedom. It helps us live outside the box and encourages harmony among different people, groups, and cultures.

Amber

Formula: C, H, O, S, and trace inorganic compounds

Hardness: 2–2.5

Crystal system: amorphous

Formation process: organic (sedimentary)

Chakra: root, solar plexus

Rough amber from
Indonesia

Physical healing: Amber is a fossilized tree resin that promotes physical vitality. It has traditionally been used to treat childhood conditions, especially colic and pain from teething. Amber is gently detoxifying, and it reduces swelling. It can treat infections and promote healthy digestion. A stone can be carried or worn to ward off the symptoms of seasonal affective disorder.

Psychological healing: Like solidified sunlight, amber brings warmth, illumination, and comfort to its bearer. It brightens the disposition and breaks through timidity and doubt. Amber is a confidence-boosting gem, and it promotes creativity, flexibility, and joy. Working with amber allows us to clear emotional baggage, and it stills the mind to bring greater awareness to one's mental processes.

Spiritual healing: Amber exerts a protective influence on the aura; psychically sensitive and empathic people can wear or carry amber to prevent the feeling of being overwhelmed by other people's energies. Amber also prevents psychic attack, and it helps in recovering from the same. It grounds and centers scattered energies in the etheric body and brings greater awareness to one's karma, particularly ancestral or genealogical karma. It is a stone of ancient wisdom, and it helps one connect with the energy of the natural world.

Amethyst

Formula: SiO_2 with traces of iron (Fe)

Hardness: 7

Crystal system: trigonal

Formation process: igneous

Chakra: third eye, crown

Amethyst crystal from
California

Physical healing: Amethyst is a violet variety of quartz, and it can be used to treat headache, imbalanced hormones, indigestion, tumors, broken bones, acne, and tissue degeneration. This gemstone is sometimes used to regulate blood sugar levels, and it bolsters the health of the nervous system. It supports well-being on all levels and is a helpful adjunct to many other healing stones.

Psychological healing: This violet gemstone helps one overcome anxiety, stress, and other conditions. It conquers bad habits and addictions, and it promotes equanimity. Amethyst bridges the mental and spiritual realms, helping us culti-vate trust in our inner guidance.

Spiritual healing: Amethyst is famous for its spiritual properties, including enhanced meditation and dreaming, psychic development, spiritual cleansing, and connecting to higher realms. It is a stone of wisdom and serenity, and it facilitates spiritual alchemy. Amethyst highlights our most limiting conditions so that we can release them. Amethyst can be used to transmute the energy of one's environment.

Chevron Amethyst

Formula: SiO_2 with iron (Fe)

Hardness: 6.5–7

Crystal system: trigonal

Formation process: igneous

Chakra: all, especially third eye

Tumbled chevron amethyst

Physical healing: Chevron amethyst exhibits the same physical healing properties as other varieties of amethyst, with the added benefit of treating the lungs, pancreas, liver, intestines, and skin. Some practitioners employ chevron amethyst for stimulating the thymus gland and supporting immune function. It harmonizes the organ systems of the body and promotes overall health by encouraging cooperation and balance on the physical level. Additionally, chevron amethyst can repair damaged DNA.

Psychological healing: Chevron amethyst reaches into the many layers of the psyche to release long-held beliefs and patterns, especially those linked to issues of self-worth. This gemstone helps us locate reserves of inner strength when we are faced with challenges. It is perfect for setting and attaining goals. It relieves anxiety and combats bad behavior and addiction.

Spiritual healing: Chevron amethyst is a helpful tool for manifestation, protection, meditation, and psychic development. It shields and strengthens the aura and helps prevent and recover from psychic attack. Chevron amethyst also fosters a state of unity, deepening our connection to others. It facilitates empathy, compassion, and intuition.

Lavender Quartz (Cape Amethyst)

Formula: SiO_2 with iron (Fe)

Hardness: 6.5–7

Crystal system: trigonal

Formation process: igneous

Chakra: all, especially third eye

Lavender quartz sphere

Physical healing: Technically a variety of amethyst, itself a form of quartz, this stone is better known as *lavender quartz** or simply *lavender* in gemstone therapy. It heals on all levels and improves the alignment of the body; use it to address conditions of the joints, particularly the spine, sacrum, skull, and jaw. This gemstone reduces pain, addresses lethargy, and reduces blood pressure. It can expedite recovery from surgery and supports the body during times of extreme stress and transition. Work with lavender quartz when faced with confusing or contradictory symptoms.

Psychological healing: Lavender quartz provides relief from loss, grief, and emotional turmoil. It improves one's negotiation skills and helps one release old wounds and emotional baggage.

Spiritual healing: Lavender quartz puts one in touch with higher wisdom. It aligns and integrates body, mind, and spirit. This gem invites peace, cultivates stillness, and instills a greater sense of justice. Working with lavender quartz can help you feel more in touch with your sense of purpose.

---

*Several varieties of quartz are sold under the moniker *lavender quartz*, including purplish quartzite rock, lavender rose quartz, and pale, transparent amethyst. The lavender quartz described here is distinct from these varieties.

Ametrine

Formula: SiO$_2$ with iron (Fe)

Hardness: 7

Crystal system: trigonal

Formation process: igneous, sedimentary, or metamorphic

Chakra: solar plexus, third eye, crown

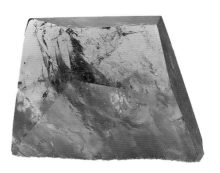

Faceted free-form ametrine from Bolivia

Physical healing: Ametrine promotes greater balance of the brain and nervous system. It is often used for treating indigestion and headache. It supports memory and can treat dementia and stroke. Ametrine supports healthy metabolism and is thus a useful tool for weight loss. Additionally, it exhibits the properties of both amethyst and citrine.

Psychological healing: This bicolored stone is empowering and encouraging; it incites optimism, joy, and action. Ametrine enhances perception and critical thinking; it is a helpful tool for people crippled by introversion and indecision. Ametrine also helps release deeply held fears.

Spiritual healing: Ametrine promotes greater clarity and assurance on one's spiritual path. It deepens intuition and facilitates channeling information from the higher realms. This stone enhances one's receptivity to Divine guidance, and it fosters greater inspiration. It can be used to remove obstacles from one's life path so as to make spiritual progress. Ametrine initiates greater equilibrium between spiritual and worldly pursuits, especially by balancing the rational and intuitive aspects of the mind. It can help reconcile the ideas of wealth and success with spiritual teachings, reminding us that poverty is not inherently more spiritual than abundance.

Angelite
(Blue Anhydrite)

Formula: $CaSO_4$

Hardness: 3.5

Crystal system: orthorhombic

Formation process: sedimentary

Chakra: heart, throat, third eye, crown

Tumbled angelite
from Peru

Physical healing: Angelite readily absorbs water and thus is used to control the water balance and fluid levels of the physical body. It treats water retention and swelling and is thus helpful in alleviating conditions of the kidneys. Angelite is also used in the treatment of arthritis, poor appetite, and cold extremities, and it promotes the health of the liver and uterus.

Psychological healing: Angelite gently bolsters confidence and communication as it eases insecurity. It imparts tact and is helpful in cases of obsession, phobia, and self-harm. This stone is very soothing and eases heartache and a troubled mind.

Spiritual healing: Also known as *blue anhydrite,* angelite is highly regarded as a stone for initiating contact with the angelic realm. This gemstone awakens the third eye chakra and deepens one's intuitive and psychic faculties, such as clairvoyance. Angelite can help you cultivate a greater sense of belonging.

Apatite (Blue Apatite)

Formula: $Ca_{10}(PO_4)_6(OH,F,Cl)_2$

Hardness: 5

Crystal system: hexagonal

Formation process: igneous, sedimentary, or metamorphic

Chakra: third eye

Tumbled blue apatite

Physical healing: Blue apatite is a premier stone for healing the skeletal system. It nourishes bones and cartilage and treats conditions of the bone marrow. Blue apatite counters body pH that is too acidic, and it has been used to treat conditions of the gums and mouth. This gemstone is also helpful in treating viral infections but should be used with caution by persons with HIV or latent viral conditions, as it can occasionally exacerbate symptoms. Blue apatite provides balance and well-being to children with autism.

Psychological healing: Blue apatite is helpful when you are experiencing restlessness, irritability, or aloofness. It fosters independence, and it has been used as an adjunct in treating eating disorders.

Spiritual healing: This blue gemstone imparts humanitarianism, encouraging a sense of service to humankind. Blue apatite also deepens meditation and increases telekinetic abilities. Placed at the base of the spine and the crown chakra simultaneously, this gemstone can also facilitate kundalini awakening.

Golden Apatite

Formula: $Ca_{10}(PO_4)_6(OH,F,Cl)_2$

Hardness: 5

Crystal system: hexagonal

Formation process: igneous or metamorphic

Chakra: solar plexus

Natural golden apatite

Physical healing: Like all apatite, the golden variety is nourishing to the skeletal system. It alleviates pain in the joints, promotes healthy eating habits, and realigns one's posture. This gemstone facilitates cellular regeneration and catalyzes the body's ability to repair broken bones. Gold apatite helps when you feel physically depleted or have a low sperm count or poor digestion. It balances and harmonizes the endocrine system and metabolism, thereby facilitating weight loss.

Psychological healing: This form of apatite is adept at releasing apathy, sorrow, anger, guilt, and mania. It overcomes laziness and inactivity by revealing motivation and mental clarity. It improves self-esteem, strengthens willpower, and invites hope.

Spiritual healing: Golden apatite clears blockages in the solar plexus chakra and helps you process and integrate life lessons and mental patterns. This gemstone stimulates underactive chakras, especially those having difficulty assimilating energy from your own aura or environment. It is often recommended for improving your manifestation skills and to draw abundance.

Green Apatite

Formula: $Ca_{10}(PO_4)_6(OH,F,Cl)_2$

Hardness: 5

Crystal system: hexagonal

Formation process: igneous or metamorphic

Chakra: solar plexus, heart

Natural crystal
of green apatite

Physical healing: Green apatite, like other colors of this mineral, works strongest on the skeletal system. Of all colors of apatite, the green variety is the most nourishing to the cartilage and bone marrow, and it promotes the health of the bones and teeth. This gemstone can help overcome infection of the bones and bone marrow, as well as promote the overall health of the kidneys and spleen. Green apatite neutralizes the effects of radiation, including X-rays and radiation therapy. It increases physical strength and stamina while also improving coordination. It can be used in the treatment of cardiac illness.

Psychological healing: Green apatite brings peace and contentment. It is helpful when you are mentally, emotionally, or physically depleted. It is a stone of hope, and it invites emotional balance and harmony.

Spiritual healing: Green apatite can help heal your relationship with abundance and material wealth. It can also reveal the karmic underpinnings of physical illness and injury.

Red Apatite (Hematoid Apatite)

Formula: $Ca_{10}(PO_4)_6(OH,F,Cl)_2$
with hematite (Fe_2O_3)

Hardness: 5

Crystal system: hexagonal

Formation process: igneous

Chakra: root, third eye

Tumbled red apatite
from Madagascar

Physical healing: Upon close inspection, this new find of apatite is actually a blue apatite carrying enough hematite to make it appear red. It is extremely nourishing to the circulatory system and supports the production of red blood cells in the bone marrow. Red apatite can promote the health of the eyes, bones, and teeth. It also promotes nutrient absorption and a healthy metabolism. Wearing red apatite can help one cope with chronic illness and viral infections. It can also treat conditions of the male reproductive system, including impotence. This gemstone supports the health of muscle tissue and cartilage.

Psychological healing: Red apatite quells anger, restlessness, irritability, despondency, and anxiety. It helps you believe in yourself and find motivation and follow-through for healing, personal development, and spiritual growth.

Spiritual healing: The dynamic combination of apatite with hematite results in a tool that accelerates spiritual growth, manifestation, and healing on all levels. Red apatite opens the psychic doorways and provides tangible psychic sensations in the body. Red apatite is an excellent tool for opening the third eye chakra, and it helps us act on psychic information.

Apophyllite

Formula: $(K,Na)Ca_4Si_8O_{20}(F,OH)\cdot 8H_2O$

Hardness: 4.5–5

Crystal system: tetragonal

Formation process: sedimentary or metamorphic

Chakra: third eye, crown

Apophyllite crystal

Physical healing: Apophyllite is soothing to the eyes and skin. Placed on the eyes, it has a cooling effect; it alleviates itchiness and puffiness from allergies or lack of sleep. Apophyllite also soothes dry and wrinkled skin and reduces irritation of the mucous membranes. It relieves irritation of the respiratory system, including allergies and asthma. It lowers blood pressure, promotes better sleep, and assists in quitting smoking.

Psychological healing: Apophyllite fosters clarity and insight. It helps you relinquish patterns of insecurity, anxiety, and nervousness. This gemstone cuts through extravagant desires and excess, promoting self-control.

Spiritual healing: Apophyllite encourages you to see the big picture. It fortifies the etheric body and provides stability and regularity to spiritual practice. Apophyllite is one of the preeminent stones for astral travel; it facilitates contact with the Akashic records, reveals past-life information, and links the spiritual and mental bodies. This mineral enhances psychic development and intensifies the dream state. Working with apophyllite illuminates the soul's blueprint and enables you to understand and integrate the underlying lessons of karma. It instills harmony in the family and helps resolve ancestral karma.

Aquamarine

Formula: $Be_3Al_2(SiO_3)_6$ with
traces of iron (Fe)
Hardness: 7.5–8
Crystal system: hexagonal
Formation process: igneous
Chakra: heart, throat, crown

Tumbled aquamarine

Physical healing: Aquamarine is among the most versatile of healing tools. It resolves pain, swelling, and inflexibility. This gemstone is helpful for calcifications, water retention, and healthy skin and complexion. It helps initiate detoxification and promotes youthfulness.

Psychological healing: Aquamarine invites a sense of flexibility, awareness, and illumination. It clarifies emotions and mental patterns and releases stale psychological patterns. This gemstone is a powerful tool for relaxation; it can help you overcome grief and other emotional traumas. Aquamarine invites courage, clear communication, and a sense of peace.

Spiritual healing: This blue-green beryl awakens latent information from your spiritual blueprint. It invites lightheartedness and promotes greater awareness. Aquamarine ultimately enables you to better understand and act on spiritual guidance. This stone facilitates spiritual growth via release and detachment, and it helps you to more truly become who you are meant to be.

Aragonite (General)

Formula: $CaCO_3$

Hardness: 3.5–4

Crystal system: orthorhombic

Formation process: sedimentary

Chakra: heart, throat, third eye

A natural twinned crystal
of aragonite

Physical healing: Overall, aragonite's effects are stabilizing and centering. This mineral can be used to balance processes of growth and decay, thus it treats conditions such as cancer and necrosis. Aragonite is beneficial to muscle tissue, and it has a cooling effect on the body. Work with aragonite to regulate the blood pressure, support the skeletal system, stimulate the immune system, and relieve conditions affecting digestion.

Psychological healing: Overall, aragonite combats nervousness, restlessness, and indecision. It boosts cognitive function and helps remove bias. Aragonite is calming and soothes emotional imbalances.

Spiritual healing: Aragonite exerts a protective influence and provides relief from geopathic stress; that is, distorted or disrupted electromagnetic fields. This stone is gently grounding, and it infuses the body, mind, and spirit with nourishing energy from nature. Aragonite can spark new interest in personal growth, and it helps you stay committed to your spiritual path.

Blue Aragonite

Formula: $CaCO_3$ with traces of iron (Fe)

Hardness: 3.5–4

Crystal system: orthorhombic

Formation process: sedimentary

Chakra: heart, throat,
third eye

Tumbled blue aragonite

Physical healing: Blue aragonite has a cooling effect on the body. It flushes out toxins, balances the brain and nervous system, and treats conditions of the respiratory system. It can be used to promote better sleep, especially by preventing nightmares.

Psychological healing: Blue aragonite is calming to both mind and heart, and it helps you find centered stillness. Meditating with this stone encourages greater awareness of the emotions, both your own and those of others. This greater emotional awareness facilitates authentic communication and connection. It soothes anger and helps you navigate in times of high stress.

Spiritual healing: Blue aragonite gently stimulates the intuition and encourages you to use psychic pursuits in service to others. This stone also assists in interpreting dreams.

Brown Aragonite

Formula: $CaCO_3$

Hardness: 3.5–4

Crystal system: orthorhombic

Formation process: sedimentary

Chakra: sacral

Tumbled brown aragonite

Physical healing: Brown aragonite offers balance and support to the digestive system, in particular the stomach and small intestine. It also ameliorates conditions affecting the joints, especially the spine and knees.

Psychological healing: Brown aragonite is a stone of patience and resilience. This gemstone is grounding, calming, and motivating all at once. It helps you release old emotional burdens that have resulted in repressed guilt and shame. Brown aragonite allows you to remain level-headed in crisis situations.

Spiritual healing: Brown aragonite offers stability along the spiritual path, allowing you to develop at an appropriate pace—neither too fast nor too slow. It encourages greater presence and awareness of the present moment, making it a great stone for meditation.

Green Aragonite

Formula: $CaCO_3$

Hardness: 3.5–4

Crystal system: orthorhombic

Formation process: sedimentary

Chakra: solar plexus, heart

Tumbled green aragonite

Physical healing: Green aragonite can treat conditions of the skin, scalp, and hair. It rejuvenates dry skin and helps prevent or slow down hair loss. Green aragonite can calm an upset stomach.

Psychological healing: Green aragonite promotes discernment, and it invites deep emotional healing. It can help you organize your emotions so that you can process and release old emotional wounds.

Spiritual healing: Green aragonite helps you communicate with the devic consciousnesses of the natural world. It has a softening effect on your spiritual burdens and teaches you to surrender to the present moment rather than perpetually feeling like a salmon swimming upstream.

Aragonite Sputnik (Aragonite Starburst)

Formula: $CaCO_3$

Hardness: 3.5–4

Crystal system: orthorhombic

Formation process: sedimentary

Chakra: all, especially solar plexus

Starburst-shaped aragonite from Morocco

Physical healing: Radial aggregates of yellowish brown aragonite are often called "starbursts" or "sputniks" for their cosmic appearance. These clusters support the health of the skeletal and nervous systems and promote wound healing. They also stimulate the immune system.

Psychological healing: Aragonite starbursts support the ability to let go and surrender. This formation counteracts hypercritical tendencies and softens moodi-
ness. Working with this form of aragonite boosts confidence and promotes your
ability to communicate with tact and sensitivity, while preventing you from
being oversensitive to others' criticisms.

Spiritual healing: This gemstone clears, aligns, and strengthens the aura and
all the subtle bodies of which it is composed. This aragonite formation facilitates shamanic journeying, meditation, dreaming, and communication with
the angelic realm. It can clear blocked or stagnant chakras and integrate lost or
broken fragments of the soul. This stone promotes group harmony and initiates
greater cohesiveness within families and communities.

White Aragonite

Formula: $CaCO_3$

Hardness: 3.5–4

Crystal system: orthorhombic

Formation process: sedimentary

Chakra: crown

Natural white aragonite
from Mexico

Physical healing: White aragonite supports the health of the skeletal and digestive
systems. It can also ease pain from pinched nerves and misaligned vertebrae.

Psychological healing: White aragonite helps you overcome self-doubt and
inconstancy. It is the ideal stone for those who feel like they don't fit in, especially people who are dreamers or who feel unable to express themselves adequately. It assists in finding balance between emotional extremes by helping
you to better articulate your emotions and thoughts.

Spiritual healing: White aragonite encourages steady spiritual growth. It teaches
the importance of pragmatism in spiritual development, and it helps you integrate spiritual and psychic abilities without distracting from the deeper lessons
offered by your spiritual practice.

Aventurine (Green Aventurine)

Tumbled
green aventurine

Formula: SiO_2 with fuchsite [$K(Al,Cr)_3Si_3O_{10}(OH)_2$] and other minerals

Hardness: 6.5–7

Crystal system: trigonal

Formation process: igneous, sedimentary, or metamorphic

Chakra: heart

Physical healing: Green aventurine is soothing to the physical body. Lighter shades of green aventurine help eliminate pain, while dark green aventurine is more strongly detoxifying to the physical body. Aventurine helps the body combat infection and can help regulate blood pressure.

Psychological healing: Aventurine is equally soothing to the mind as it is to the body. It nurtures self-love and encourages adequate self-care. This gemstone can be used to treat irritability and aggression.

Spiritual healing: Aventurine is considered a stone of luck, abundance, and love. It symbolizes growth and helps new projects blossom.

Blue Aventurine

Tumbled
blue aventurine

Formula: SiO_2 with dumortierite [$Al_7BO_3(SiO_4)_3O_3$], nitrogen (N), copper silicates (variable composition including Cu, Si, O), or other minerals

Hardness: 6.5–7

Crystal system: trigonal

Formation process: metamorphic

Chakra: third eye

Physical healing: Blue aventurine has a cooling effect on the body, and it is therefore used to reduce fever and inflammation. It regulates the body's hormones and can treat disorders of the nervous system.

Psychological healing: Blue aventurine, especially varieties containing dumortierite, fosters patience and calm awareness. It promotes a sense of clinical detachment in your studies, and it helps you stay disciplined. Blue aventurine banishes bad habits and helps you cultivate newer, healthier habits to replace them.

Spiritual healing: Blue aventurine cultivates lasting peace, like the imperturbable peace of the Buddha. It deepens your psychic abilities and enhances meditation.

Peach Aventurine

Formula: SiO_2 with iron oxide (Fe_2O_3) and other minerals

Hardness: 6.5–7

Crystal system: trigonal

Formation process: igneous, sedimentary, or metamorphic

Chakra: solar plexus, heart

Tumbled
peach aventurine

Physical healing: Peach aventurine positively affects the circulatory system and promotes production of new blood cells in the marrow. It initiates liver detoxification and regeneration, and it can treat pain and numbness in the extremities.

Psychological healing: Peach aventurine calms the heart and mind, silencing the inner saboteur, the critical voice that we have within us. This is an ideal stone for overcoming shyness and soothing anxiety. It instills dignity, patience, and a calming presence.

Spiritual healing: Peach aventurine encourages hope; it helps you strive for your goals and cultivate self-improvement along the way.

Azurite

Formula: $Cu_3(CO_3)_2(OH)_2$

Hardness: 3.5–4

Crystal system: monoclinic

Formation process: sedimentary

Chakra: third eye

Raw azurite from Arizona

Physical healing: Azurite supports the health of the liver and nervous system. It also balances the thyroid.

Psychological healing: Azurite pinpoints and releases limiting beliefs and mental habits, especially those that affect self-perception, worldview, and one's ability to grow. It invites honest and critical self-reflection to bring greater understanding of one's mental-emotional makeup. It can reveal the emotions to the conscious mind. It is also helpful for students, as it helps the mind accept new information.

Spiritual healing: A stone of insight, azurite initiates deep states of reflection. It enhances intuition and develops clairvoyance and other psychic senses.

Barite

Formula: BaSO$_4$

Hardness: 3–3.5

Crystal system: orthorhombic

Formation process: igneous, sedimentary, or metamorphic

Chakra: earth star, throat, third eye, crown

Blue barite
from Morocco

Physical healing: Barite's composition makes it warming, anchoring, and detoxifying. It is used in the treatment of a variety of infections, including parasites, fungal infections (like candidiasis), and acute viral infections. Barite has a drying effect, and it is helpful in treating conditions of the skin such as dermatitis, acne, eczema, cysts, and pustules. Work with barite to treat sore throats, upset stomach, gas, and bloating. Barite helps erase muscle memory and correct poor posture. Barite is one of the most effective stones for balancing the hemispheres of the brain, and it can restore cognitive function after illness or injury. Wear barite or use an indirectly made elixir to protect against harmful radiation.

Psychological healing: Barite boosts mental function, cuts through confusion, and enhances memory. Working with this stone can also alleviate social anxiety and shyness. It helps you enforce healthy boundaries and develop sincere friendships. Barite teaches us about the nature of our fears and insecurities, and it reminds us to cultivate happiness by following our purpose. This mineral helps us stay grounded and aware of our responsibilities to ourselves and to others.

Spiritual healing: Barite is a dynamic stone that facilitates spiritual growth and psychic development in many ways. It facilitates astral travel, dream recall, and contact with beings in other dimensions or planes. Barite is both insulative and conductive; it protects against harmful or disruptive energies and entities while serving as a beacon of light and higher consciousness. This stone rapidly expands our capacity to carry higher frequencies and anchors these changes in our physical body and everyday life. Barite encourages clear vision and precise communication of our psychic impressions, thereby making it an ideal stone for channeling and psychic readers. Work with barite to unveil your higher purpose and to reveal your deepest spiritual truths.

Black Onyx

Formula: SiO$_2$ with traces of carbon (C) and/or iron (Fe)

Hardness: 7

Crystal system: trigonal

Formation process: igneous or sedimentary

Chakra: root

Raw black onyx

Physical healing: Black onyx treats the structural components of the body, especially the bones and teeth. It can be helpful in fungal infections such as candidiasis. It helps you feel more secure and present in your physical body.

Psychological healing: Black onyx is chief among stones for overcoming bad habits. It helps you face your fears by surrendering them to the unconditional love of the universe. It promotes self-discovery and reminds you to set healthy boundaries.

Spiritual healing: Black onyx is grounding and protective. This gemstone helps when you feel overwhelmed or unfocused. It highlights where you are in conflict with your higher self so that positive changes can be made.

Bloodstone

Formula: SiO_2 with hematite (Fe_2O_3)

Hardness: 7

Crystal system: trigonal

Formation process: igneous

Chakra: root

Tumbled bloodstone

Physical healing: Bloodstone is grounding, strengthening, and stabilizing to the physical body. It is one of the best stones for mobilizing the immune system, and it helps combat allergies, colds, and infection. Bloodstone is considered detoxifying and purifying to the physical body and has been used to cleanse the blood. This gem also supports nutrient absorption. Applied topically it can stanch the flow of blood and facilitate recovery after illness, injury, and surgery.

Psychological healing: Bloodstone helps fight fear. It bolsters courage and alleviates anxiety and irritability. Wear or carry bloodstone to remain level-headed when faced with life's challenges. It counters disappointment and discouragement.

Spiritual healing: This gemstone engenders sincere courage, allowing you to invest your whole heart in the task at hand despite feeling fearful or vulnerable. For this reason it is a helpful stone when branching out into new endeavors. Bloodstone has been carried and worn for protection for centuries.

Calcite (General)

Formula: $CaCO_3$

Hardness: 3

Crystal system: trigonal

Formation process: igneous or sedimentary

Chakra: all

Calcite cluster
from Mexico

Physical healing: Calcite is a popular healing stone, one that promotes health of the bones, teeth, skin, and endocrine system. In Chinese medicine calcite is revered for its cooling effect on the body and has been employed for centuries to rid the body of parasites. Calcite lessens the intensity of acute symptoms associated with chronic conditions, and it has a diuretic effect.

Psychological healing: Calcite generally supports the mind and the emotions. Since it typically crystallizes out of aqueous solutions, it is associated with clarity in the emotional body. It supports the memory and helps you think outside the box. Calcite promotes adaptation and helps you integrate changes in your thoughts and emotions.

Spiritual healing: Calcite of all colors supports spiritual growth. It links parallel realities to support the manifestation process. It clarifies your sense of purpose, enhances the right use of will, and encourages spontaneity. Calcite gently erodes blockages in the aura and chakras.

Blue Calcite

Formula: $CaCO_3$ with traces of iron (Fe)

Hardness: 3

Crystal system: trigonal

Formation process: sedimentary

Chakra: throat

Rhombohedral blue calcite

Physical healing: In addition to possessing the general properties of calcite listed above, blue calcite is an excellent choice for treating sore throat, tonsillitis, and swollen lymph nodes. It reduces headaches and treats neurological conditions. Blue calcite clears the lymph, supports liver detox, and reduces high blood pressure.

Psychological healing: Of all the calcites, blue is probably the most calming and serene. It counteracts anxiety and nervous tension and improves confidence. Blue calcite is a stone for healthy expression and helps one overcome creative blocks. For this reason it is a great stone for writers. Blue calcite helps those who feel unable to fulfill their ambitions.

Spiritual healing: Blue calcite dismantles ingrained judgments while promoting discernment and clarity. It improves psychic and intuitive skills, especially clairvoyance.

Golden Calcite

Formula: $CaCO_3$ with traces of iron (Fe)

Hardness: 3

Crystal system: trigonal

Formation process: igneous or sedimentary

Chakra: solar plexus, crown

Golden calcite crystal from Ohio

Physical healing: Golden calcite supports the health of the endocrine system and balances blood sugar levels. It also helps the physical body respond to changes in the nonphysical anatomy with greater ease.

Psychological healing: Golden calcite promotes confidence, persistence, and resilience. It is a stone of mental clarity, promoting both insight and action. Golden calcite stimulates intellectual pursuits and strongly increases memory.

Spiritual healing: This variety of calcite strengthens the manifestation process by aligning one's individual will with Divine Will. It is a stone of higher consciousness and links personal willpower with spiritual truth. Golden calcite is a stone of spiritual initiation and evolution.

Green Calcite

Formula: $CaCO_3$ with traces of iron (Fe), copper (Cu), or chromium (Cr)

Hardness: 3

Crystal system: trigonal

Formation process: sedimentary

Chakra: heart

Green calcite from Mexico

Physical healing: Green calcite is a gentle and reliable healing stone. It is among the best stones for bone health. It also soothes conditions related to the heart and chest; work with green calcite for heartburn, high blood pressure, shortness of breath, and congestion in the lungs. It reduces inflammation and stimulates the body's natural detoxification processes. Green calcite also promotes the health of the reproductive organs, particularly in providing relief and recovery from STDs. This stone also reduces the symptoms of PMS.

Psychological healing: Green calcite is decidedly more mental than emotional in its psychological influence. It promotes forgiveness, often by enabling one to better understand the situation. Green calcite is an important stone for letting go; it resolves bitterness, anger, and rage.

Spiritual healing: Green calcite is an imaginative stone that increases love, compassion, and peace. It initiates a state of renewal and promotes balance on all levels.

Mangano Calcite

Formula: $(Ca,Mn)CO_3$

Hardness: 3

Crystal system: trigonal

Formation process: sedimentary

Chakra: solar plexus, heart

Polished mangano calcite

Physical healing: Mangano calcite is one of my favorite stones for healthy digestion and elimination. It can be used as an adjunct to medical treatments for cancer and other diseases that eat away at the physical body. This soothing pink stone also supports the health of the heart by regulating blood pressure, heart rate, and rhythm and by strengthening the blood vessels. It alleviates shortness of breath.

Psychological healing: Mangano calcite is as soothing to the emotional body as it is to the physical. It promotes relaxation and forgiveness by eliminating painful and distracting thoughts and feelings that gnaw at the subconscious mind. This stone helps overcome bitterness, fear, anxiety, and other states of emotional balance. It encourages a friendly, open-minded attitude.

Spiritual healing: Mangano calcite promotes a greater sense of freedom and confidence. It reminds you to stay centered in the present moment, and it strengthens the flow of life force in the physical and emotional bodies. Mangano calcite helps you view and understand love (as well as other emotions) from the soul's perspective.

Optical Calcite (Iceland Spar)

Formula: $CaCO_3$

Hardness: 3

Crystal system: trigonal

Formation process: sedimentary

Chakra: all

Raw optical calcite

Physical healing: By bringing light into the physical body, optical calcite releases blockages throughout the body. It stimulates absorption of water, promotes a healthy metabolism, and reduces pain. Like other calcites, it is an excellent choice for the bones and teeth. Optical calcite also heals conditions related to the mucous membranes and connective tissues.

Psychological healing: Optical calcite promotes mental clarity and brings insight. This stone can help you see through another person's eyes, and it is thus a wonderful stone for improving relationships, both platonic and romantic. It also quells an excessive sex drive.

Spiritual healing: Optical calcite clears and activates all of the chakras, particularly the crown. It infuses one's entire being with brilliant light and clears blockages from the physical and nonphysical bodies. Optical calcite accelerates manifestation and draws prosperity. Work with this stone to enhance meditation and psychic development and to deepen your spiritual practice.

Orange Calcite

Formula: $CaCO_3$ with traces of iron (Fe)

Hardness: 3

Crystal system: trigonal

Formation process: sedimentary

Chakra: sacral

Tumbled orange calcite

Physical healing: Orange calcite promotes healthy digestion, skin, and bones. It also increases the metabolism, thus making it effective at promoting weight loss. Orange calcite also increases energy.

Psychological healing: Orange calcite boosts creativity and confidence. It instills self-respect, enthusiasm, and motivation. This stone enables you to remain realistic without losing sight of your goals. Orange calcite overcomes shyness and dissolves guilt and shame, especially regarding sex and intimacy. It encourages open and honest communication with your romantic or sexual partner(s).

Spiritual healing: Orange calcite helps translate willpower and creativity into action. It can lend stamina to pursuing your spiritual path.

Red Calcite

Formula: $CaCO_3$ with iron (Fe) or hematite (Fe_2O_3)

Hardness: 3

Crystal system: trigonal

Formation process: sedimentary

Chakra: root, heart

Raw red calcite

Physical healing: Red calcite stimulates the immune system, heals wounds, and supports the overall health of the blood. This stone strengthens bones and nourishes the marrow, and it is sometimes used as an adjunct to medical treatment for HIV. Red calcite promotes fertility and the overall health of the reproductive system. Taking red calcite to bed can help with insomnia, though some people find it too stimulating.

Psychological healing: Red calcite is a great confidence booster. It is stabilizing and grounding, helping to curb laziness and channel an overactive mind into concrete activity. Red calcite also helps break addictions to food, and it can help in settling disagreements with others.

Spiritual healing: Red calcite is a dynamic grounding stone that circulates energy throughout the entire chakra system. It strengthens one's abilities to manifest through action, and it overcomes feelings of discomfort associated with being poorly grounded. Red calcite is a wonderful tool for people who feel uncomfortable in their bodies.

Yellow Calcite

Formula: $CaCO_3$ with iron (Fe)

Hardness: 3

Crystal system: trigonal

Formation process: sedimentary

Chakra: sacral, solar plexus

Tumbled yellow calcite
from Mexico

Physical healing: Yellow calcite soothes an upset stomach, improves digestion, and regulates the endocrine system. Its effects are similar to orange calcite.

Psychological healing: Yellow calcite bolsters self-esteem. It encourages expression, and it improves memory. This stone also helps dissolve emotional blockages.

Spiritual healing: Yellow calcite promotes happiness, joy, and contentment. It reminds you to stay in the present, and it empowers creativity and originality in your spiritual practice.

Zebra Calcite (Phantom Calcite, Bumblebee Calcite)

Formula: $CaCO_3$ with hematite (Fe_2O_3)

Hardness: 3

Crystal system: trigonal

Formation process: sedimentary

Chakra: root, sacral, solar plexus

Raw zebra calcite

Physical healing: Zebra calcite consists of bands of yellow, black, and white calcite. It exhibits all the properties of yellow calcite, plus the additional ones outlined here. Zebra calcite is an ideal stone for conditions that affect the liver, digestive system, and metabolism. It also supports the immune system.

Psychological healing: Zebra calcite helps us reconcile our shadow with our light. This stone assists us in processing the emotional baggage that we push deep into the subconscious and initiates a state of self-forgiveness so that we can gently integrate the long-forgotten lessons offered by our repressed emotional pain and trauma. It invites us to feel more optimistic and hopeful, and it boosts self-esteem and self-confidence. Zebra calcite can help with conditions affecting self-image.

Spiritual healing: Zebra calcite enhances the aura's natural boundaries, thus conferring protection and preventing psychic attack. It is strongly cleansing, and it helps release foreign energies, etheric cords, and attached entities from the aura and chakras.

Carnelian

Formula: SiO_2 with hematite (Fe_2O_3)

Hardness: 7

Crystal system: trigonal

Formation process: igneous or sedimentary

Chakra: root, sacral

Raw carnelian from Madagascar

Physical healing: Carnelian is one of my most well-used gemstones for physical conditions. It treats low energy, pain, inflammation, and infection. This gemstone is strengthening, and its iron content is grounding. Carnelian supports the well-being of the immune system, especially the lymph nodes, and it increases hemoglobin production. Carnelian is a trusted stone for sexual dysfunction, ameliorating impotence, frigidity, irregular menstrual cycles, and infertility. It also helps with detoxifying the physical body.

Psychological healing: Carnelian inspires the psyche with enthusiasm, optimism, and charisma. It is a great stone for curbing procrastination because it invites swift, though rational, action. Carnelian clears the mind and supports concentration and memory. It helps to release deeply held trauma such as PTSD.

Spiritual healing: Carnelian mediates between the extremes in life. It uplifts the soul and helps you find both resolve and enjoyment in spiritual practice. Carnelian can help you free yourself from karmic ruts, and it has long been touted as a stone of protection and kundalini activation.

Cavansite

Formula: $Ca(VO)Si_4O_{10} \cdot 4(H_2O)$

Hardness: 3–4

Crystal system: orthorhombic

Formation process: igneous

Chakra: heart, higher heart (thymus), throat

Cavansite on stilbite matrix

Physical healing: Cavansite promotes the health of the skeletal system, especially by preventing or treating bone loss such as from osteoporosis or tooth decay. It is often used in the treatment of conditions related to the eyes and ears, as it ameliorates irritation and improves vision and hearing. Cavansite is also effective at treating conditions affecting the blood.

Psychological healing: Cavansite provides profound emotional support and healing. As a stone of expression, this brilliant blue mineral enables us to express our emotions with ease and clarity. It is especially helpful at teaching us to express love of all varieties (romantic, familial, platonic) through more creative means. It is a deeply nurturing stone that helps us learn to better nurture ourselves and those around us—in that order. It opens the mind to accepting new ideas and allows us to think more creatively.

Spiritual healing: Cavansite is a stone of beauty and truth; it helps us recognize these energies within and all around us. This mineral promotes sincere compassion and empathy. Like the ocean whose color it resembles, cavansite is expansive and cleansing; it aligns and clears the aura and chakras as a whole. Cavansite steers us toward our soul's path and encourages us to seek spiritual fulfillment amid everyday life. This gemstone allows us to feel comfortable expressing our spirituality, even when those around us cannot understand or accept it. It boosts psychic abilities and leads us to the beauty of stillness in meditation. Cavansite inspires joy and helps us find our inner genius.

Celestite

Formula: SrSO$_4$

Hardness: 3–3.5

Crystal system: orthorhombic

Formation process: sedimentary

Chakra: throat, third eye, crown

Celestite cluster from
Madagascar

Physical healing: Celestite is better suited to emotional and spiritual healing, although it supports the health of bones and teeth. It is used for clearing infection and regulating the metabolism.

Psychological healing: Celestite invites peace, hope, and stillness. It overcomes fear, especially that of illness and injury, and it can counteract hypochondria and psychosomatic disorders. There is a hidden fire in celestite that fuels creativity and inspires artistic endeavors.

Spiritual healing: This gemstone is strongly cleansing, and it releases attachments from the aura and chakras. Celestite's hopeful vibration engenders grace, and this stone facilitates angelic contact and communication with the spiritual realm. It balances the throat chakra and opens the crown and third eye chakras.

Chalcedony (General)

Formula: SiO_2

Hardness: 7

Crystal system: trigonal

Formation process: igneous or sedimentary

Chakra: various (see chakra listings under specific chalcedony types below)

Raw chalcedony rosette

Physical healing: Chalcedony is soothing to the physical body. It is traditionally used to treat conditions of the female reproductive system. It also clears toxins and reduces heat in the body. Chalcedony is helpful in treating cold, flu, and seasonal allergies.

Psychological healing: Virtually all varieties of chalcedony induce peace and tranquillity. It is comforting in times of stress, and it provides relief from anxiety, nervousness, fear, and worry.

Spiritual healing: Chalcedony is a stone of service and charity. It is a stone of the Divine Feminine, and it can be used to help restore balance to the masculine and feminine polarities of the world at large. It promotes positive change, planetary healing, and compassion. Chalcedony is often worn for safe travel, as it is a gentle protector.

Black Chalcedony (Doctor Stone)

Formula: SiO_2 with iron (Fe)

Hardness: 7

Crystal system: trigonal

Formation process: sedimentary

Chakra: all

Botryoidal black chalcedony from Medicine Bow, Wyoming

Physical healing: Black chalcedony is a versatile healing stone that offers support to every aspect of one's physical body. For this reason it is sometimes known as the "doctor stone," as it identifies and treats a wide variety of physical conditions, especially pain and chronic illness. It can be used in cases of dizziness, sciatica, and thyroid conditions.

Psychological healing: Black chalcedony invites the deep sense of peace and grace that comes with all varieties of chalcedony into the realm of the subconscious. Although it lacks the ability to reflect the shadow self like obsidian or black onyx, it can be partnered with these stones to achieve greater psychological balance. Work with this stone for better communication and to raise self-esteem.

Spiritual healing: Black chalcedony is more grounding than other chalcedonies. It anchors positive changes on the material plane. This stone helps us explore and transmute karma and past-life baggage.

Blue Chalcedony

Formula: SiO_2

Hardness: 7

Crystal system: trigonal

Formation process: igneous or sedimentary

Chakra: heart, throat, third eye

Turkish blue chalcedony

Physical healing: Blue chalcedony releases tension. It has a cooling effect, thereby ameliorating fever and inflammation. It treats conditions of the ears, eyes, and sinuses. Blue chalcedony treats conditions of the respiratory system, including asthma, coughing, and congestion. It is also used in the treatment of sore throat, thyroid conditions, and conditions affecting speech.

Psychological healing: Blue chalcedony represents renewal, and it invites deep peace and hope. It assists communication and soothes frazzled nerves. It is a wonderful stress-relieving stone.

Spiritual healing: This gentle blue gem brings inspiration. It relaxes the mind and the mental body in the aura. Blue chalcedony also facilitates meditation, insight, and channeling. This gem assists in the pursuit of truth.

Grape Chalcedony (Grape Agate)

Formula: SiO_2

Hardness: 6.5–7

Crystal system: trigonal

Formation process: igneous

Chakra: sacral, third eye

Botryoidal grape chalcedony
from Indonesia

Physical healing: Grape chalcedony supports neurological health. It can treat conditions that affect the eyes, brain, and nervous system. This gemstone also restores balance to neurotransmitters. It flushes toxins from the lymph nodes and can relieve ulcers and upset stomach.

Psychological healing: This variety of chalcedony gently erases old emotional programming and invites deeper serenity amid everyday life. Grape chalcedony is adept at removing fear, and it helps empty the mind of unnecessary thoughts while catalyzing emotional growth. Grape chalcedony is a stone of pure joy and wonder, and it feeds the inner child.

Spiritual healing: Grape chalcedony facilitates deep meditative states and initiates ecstatic gnosis and transmissions from the higher planes. This stone supports spiritual healing on all levels, and it boosts the efficacy of other healing modalities. Grape chalcedony breaks karmic cycles and helps heal divisions at the community, national, and global levels.

Pink Chalcedony

Formula: SiO_2 with manganese (Mn)

Hardness: 7

Crystal system: trigonal

Formation process: igneous or sedimentary

Chakra: heart

Tumbled pink chalcedony

Physical healing: Pink chalcedony treats conditions of the circulatory system such as diabetes, poor circulation, and heart disease. It promotes health of the spleen and stimulates lactation in mothers.

Psychological healing: Pink chalcedony is nurturing to the emotional body; it brings clarity and calm to the emotions in the same way that blue chalcedony influences the mind. This gemstone boosts self-confidence by helping you get in touch with your inner and outer beauty. It cultivates love and romance.

Spiritual healing: Pink chalcedony carries the energy of innocence. It heals the inner child and initiates lighthearted joy. Pink chalcedony reminds us of the divine love that is available to us at all times.

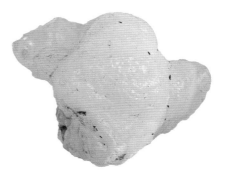

White Chalcedony

Formula: SiO_2

Hardness: 7

Crystal system: trigonal

Formation process: igneous or sedimentary

Chakra: heart

Botryoidal white chalcedony

Physical healing: White chalcedony is traditionally worn to promote lactation in new mothers in several parts of the world. It can be taken as an elixir to remove mucous buildup and placed topically to treat conditions of the skin.

Psychological healing: White chalcedony helps you to remain neutral and impartial; it reconciles disparities between the emotions and the intellect. It is a nurturing stone with a motherly energy.

Spiritual healing: White chalcedony is an important stone for attaining grace and peace. It promotes restful sleep and insightful dreams. It is a stone of stillness, and through that stillness it helps you cultivate a relationship with the Divine.

Chalcopyrite

Formula: CuFeS$_2$
Hardness: 3.5–4
Crystal system: tetragonal
Formation process: igneous, sedimentary, or metamorphic
Chakra: solar plexus

Raw chalcopyrite

Physical healing: Chalcopyrite, often called *peacock ore,* has been used to treat inflammation, neurological conditions, and weakened immune function. It relieves pain, stimulates hair growth, and is cleansing to the liver, kidneys, and colon. Crystal healers often use chalcopyrite when treating certain forms of cancer (as an adjunct to medical treatment); it is especially helpful in counteracting the side effects of radiation treatment and chemotherapy.

Psychological healing: Chalcopyrite reveals the psychological causes of some forms of illness; it reminds us that the mind is a powerful creator that needs to be monitored and at times redirected. This mineral empowers one to make changes in life to course-correct. It helps us learn from our mistakes and promotes versatility in all aspects of life. Chalcopyrite supports both the conventional intellect and the emotional intelligence, enhancing analytic and meditative states.

Spiritual healing: Working with chalcopyrite balances masculine and feminine energies. It breaks up energy blockages and balances opposing forces. It inspires curiosity and can lead overly rational and intellectual people toward spiritual exploration.

Charoite

Polished
charoite

Formula: $K(Ca,Na)_2Si_4O_{10}(OH,F)\cdot H_2O$ with manganese (Mn)

Hardness: 5–6

Crystal system: monoclinic

Formation process: metamorphic

Chakra: solar plexus, heart, third eye, crown, soul star

Physical healing: Charoite works more readily at the psychological and spiritual levels than at the physical level. However it can help to rebuild and repair cellular structures such as the DNA in accordance with shifts in our spiritual path. It also clears fluid retention and can support skeletal health. Taken as an elixir, charoite speeds recovery from sunburn as well as damage from ultraviolet light and electromagnetic pollution.

Psychological healing: Charoite empowers us to confront long-held issues preventing growth. It instills psychological stamina and enables us to release resistance to positive change. The manganese content of this stone is gently grounding to the emotional body and stabilizing to the heart chakra. This allows charoite to invite objectivity and transmute fear and help us identify and release limiting behaviors.

Spiritual healing: Charoite stirs the psychic senses and intensifies the dream state. Because it promotes objectivity, it allows us to process intuitive and psychic information without emotional bias. Charoite is a stone of spiritual purpose, enabling us to create joy through service so as to manifest our full potential and live our true purpose. Charoite purges causal patterns by releasing and transmuting karma.

Chrome Diopside

Formula: $CaMgSi_2O_6$ with traces of chromium (Cr)

Hardness: 5.5–6.5

Crystal system: monoclinic

Formation process: igneous

Chakra: heart, third eye, earth star

Polished
chrome diopside

Physical healing: Chrome diopside is adept at facilitating healing overall. It stimulates regeneration and repair on all levels while offering nourishing energy from the earth herself. It can be helpful for conditions of the bones, gallbladder, kidneys, and heart. This brilliant green gem can be used as an adjunct to medical treatment for bone cancer. It is helpful for conditions affecting the intestines and eliminatory system. Chrome diopside helps resolve psychosomatic conditions too.

Psychological healing: One of the greatest gifts of chrome diopside is inspiration. It elevates the mind to think creatively for solving problems and overcoming obstacles. Diopside is generally good for analytical pursuits too. This gemstone is great for writer's block, as it encourages artistic expression. Chrome diopside instills motivation and resiliency, thereby allowing one to overcome fear, regret, and indecision. It opens the heart and releases stress, tension, and anxiety.

Spiritual healing: Working with chrome diopside helps distribute life force throughout the entire body and aura. It balances yin and yang energies, encourages spiritual development, and helps you attune to your spiritual guides. The brilliance of this gemstone lights the spiritual flame within that cultivates wisdom, understanding, and a sense of the interconnectedness of everyone—and everything—on earth. This gemstone is both protective of your personal energy and inspires a sense of stewardship and guardianship, thereby inviting you to protect and care for the earth. Chrome diopside promotes a deeper connection to the mineral kingdom in particular, thereby enhancing an understanding of how gemstones can be used for healing and personal development. Connect to this gemstone for planetary healing and for learning how to communicate with guides, animals, gemstones, and the intelligences of the natural world.

Chrysocolla

Formula: $(Cu,Al)_2H_2Si_2O_5(OH)_4 \cdot nH_2O$

Hardness: 2.5–3.5

Crystal system: orthorhombic

Formation process: igneous or sedimentary

Chakra: throat

Tumbled chrysocolla

Physical healing: Chrysocolla's physical benefits are mostly relegated to the domain of the throat chakra. It soothes sore throat, balances the thyroid, and offers relief from tonsillitis. This gemstone can be applied to treat fever, muscle spasms, asthma, and stress-related illness (especially of the respiratory and digestive systems).

Psychological healing: This stone is nurturing and soothing; it eases states of emotional imbalance and facilitates heartfelt expression. Chrysocolla empowers the voice, making it an ideal stone for public speakers, singers, actors, writers, and other people engaged in creative pursuits.

Spiritual healing: Chrysocolla is the muse stone. It floods the mind and spirit with inspiration and helps one perceive and pursue beauty in all moments. It can be held or worn in meditation to experience a deeper connection to Source, as well as for connecting to the current of the Divine Feminine.

Chrysoprase

Formula: SiO_2 with nickel (Ni)

Hardness: 7

Crystal system: trigonal

Formation process: igneous

Chakra: heart

Raw Australian chrysoprase

Physical healing: Chrysoprase is a variety of chalcedony. Traditionally it has been used to strengthen eyesight and soothe the eyes. It also treats conditions of the skin, urinary tract infections, and fungal and bacterial infections. As an elixir chrysoprase can help detoxify the physical body, removing pathogens and heavy metals.

Psychological healing: Chrysoprase releases codependency, jealousy, and despair. It is the ideal stone for healing a broken heart, and it fosters trust, security, and hope. Chrysoprase rebuilds self-esteem after loss and rejection. This gemstone promotes forgiveness and helps us break free from abusive relationships.

Spiritual healing: This green gem was once thought to confer invisibility; in reality this points to its gift of helping us see the unseen world through the lens of the heart. It opens us to wonder and instills hope and imagination. Chrysoprase can provide a sense of security during times of deep transition and upheaval, and it encourages us to trust the process by reminding us that challenging circumstances are opportunity for spiritual growth.

Citrine

Formula: SiO$_2$ with traces of lithium (Li) and aluminum (Al)

Hardness: 7

Crystal system: trigonal

Formation process: igneous

Chakra: solar plexus

Natural citrine from Zambia

Physical healing: Citrine is the most effective stone for vitalizing the eliminatory organs and processes in the physical body, including the kidneys, bladder, liver, lungs, skin, and large intestine. It unwinds tension in the spine, muscles, and fascia. Citrine can boost the metabolism, and it supports the health of the stomach.

Psychological healing: *Letting go* and *empowerment* are two of citrine's key themes. It helps us let go of old beliefs and feelings, such as those projected onto us by friends and family, so that we can step into our personal power. Citrine works to increase self-esteem, and it boosts productivity.

Spiritual healing: The primary mission of citrine is to help us fulfill our purpose. It brings optimism and aligns our life path with a deeper sense of purpose. Citrine encourages us to be fully actualized human beings, thereby helping us claim success in all areas of life. For this reason it is often used for prosperity and abundance.

Creedite

Formula: $Ca_3Al_2SO_4(F,OH)_{10}\cdot 2(H_2O)$

Hardness: 3.5–4

Crystal system: monoclinic

Formation process: metamorphic

Chakra: sacral, brow, crown, soul star

Creedite cluster

Physical healing: Creedite's composition lends itself to healing disorders of the muscles and skeletal system. Employ it for recovery from injury, to help assimilate vitamins, and to promote the health of the liver. Creedite is one of the premier stones for healing conditions of the reproductive system, particularly those resulting from the psyche. This mineral also addresses the etheric counterparts of physical illness, thereby speeding up healing of any physical condition.

Psychological healing: Creedite boosts mental faculties that facilitate learning and personal development. This stone seeks to mediate conflict, especially by sweeping away drama from our lives. It is a stone of creativity, expression, and motivation; work with it to overcome obstacles of any sort. Creedite is also helpful in cases of sexual trauma or shame; it invites us to embrace sexuality as a sacred and healthy part of life.

Spiritual healing: Creedite is expansive, enlightening, and evolutionary. This stone promotes the balance of masculine and feminine energies. It helps us seek wisdom through internal work such as meditation and journeying, as well as through the study of sacred texts and ancient teachings. Creedite can facilitate ancestral healing and helps us access the Akashic records. Through conscious meditation, creedite can support the activation of kundalini. It refines intuition and psychic development, raises consciousness, and helps ground higher energies into the physical body.

Danburite

Formula: $CaB_2Si_2O_8$

Hardness: 7–7.5

Crystal system: orthorhombic

Formation process: igneous, sedimentary, or metamorphic

Chakra: heart, crown

Danburite crystal

Physical healing: Danburite brings light into the physical body. It vitalizes the respiratory system, especially the lungs and sinuses. This gemstone also mitigates the effects of stress and stress-related illness.

Psychological healing: The structure of danburite makes it extremely balancing; it can mediate between extremes of emotion and soothe antagonistic relationships.

Spiritual healing: Danburite dissolves dualistic worldviews, helping one see the inherent interconnection and oneness of all things. It unites the heart and the crown chakras and supports a heart-centered approach to life. Danburite strengthens psychic senses, enabling us to perceive the messages of the spiritual world all around us. By aligning our physical body with our etheric body, this stone allows us to be perfect channels for the higher realms.

Dioptase

Formula: $CuSiO_3 \cdot H_2O$

Hardness: 5

Crystal system: trigonal

Formation process: igneous or sedimentary

Chakra: heart, higher heart

Polished dioptase in calcite matrix

Physical healing: Dioptase is traditionally recommended for the health of the eyes. This gemstone can help regenerate damaged tissue, especially the liver. Both the color and the copper content suggest that this stone is related to the heart; place it over the sternum to ensure cardiac health and to support the immune system.

Psychological healing: The greatest gift offered by dioptase is that of forgiveness. It teaches self-love and opens the heart chakra. Dioptase reveals the heart's desires and encourages us to follow them.

Spiritual healing: Dioptase activates the higher heart chakra and is a stone of unconditional love. It reminds us that the very nature of love is alchemical and transformative. It fosters spiritual freedom and awakens us to the higher truth.

Dumortierite

Formula: $Al_7BO_3(SiO_4)_3O_3$

Hardness: 7

Crystal system: orthorhombic

Formation process: igneous

Chakra: throat, third eye

Tumbled dumortierite

Physical healing: Dumortierite is used in the treatment of pain such as headaches and cramps. This stone alleviates disorders affecting the digestive system, including nausea.

Psychological healing: Dumortierite can offer resolve, commitment, and responsibility when treating addiction and obsession. It boosts confidence, assuages fear and anxiety, and invites greater organization. This stone can help you enforce healthy boundaries as well as release toxic people and circumstances from your life. It is a powerful mental healer and brings clarity, focus, and discipline.

Spiritual healing: Dumortierite is the premier stone of patience. This gem helps you learn to embrace stillness, thereby facilitating meditation. Dumortierite can also stimulate psychic development and past-life recall. It is a helpful stone for karmic healing.

Emerald

Formula: $Be_3Al_2SiO_6$ with trace chromium (Cr)

Hardness: 7.5–8

Crystal system: hexagonal

Formation process: igneous or metamorphic

Chakra: heart

Tumbled emerald

Physical healing: Emerald is a master physical healer, a soothing balm for the overall health of the physical body. It is rejuvenating, soothes the eyes, supports cardiac health, and heals imbalances of the reproductive system.

Psychological healing: Emerald is famed for instilling virtue, attracting love and fidelity, and nourishing the emotional and mental levels of one's makeup. It overrides the patterns responsible for unhappiness, despondency, and disconnection and is helpful for depression and isolation. It promotes forgiveness.

Spiritual healing: Emerald awakens the intelligence of the heart chakra and helps one surrender to the transformational power of unconditional love. Emerald cleanses the body, mind, and soul of guilt, blame, shame, and family karma, helping one atone for previous errors. This gem illuminates truth and seeks justice.

Epidote

Formula: $Ca_2Al_2(Fe^{3+};Al)(SiO_4)(Si_2O_7)O(OH)$

Hardness: 6–7

Crystal system: monoclinic

Formation process: metamorphic

Chakra: heart

Epidote crystals

Physical healing: Epidote is an excellent stone for overall physical healing. It targets the health of the thyroid, adrenals, liver, gallbladder, and digestive system. This mineral treats damaged and diseased organs and is used to enhance recovery from long-term illness. It dissipates blockages in the physical and energetic bodies and breaks down tumors, fatty lumps, cysts, and fibroids. Epidote can help regenerate physical tissues and encourages the recovery of the liver from cirrhosis.

Psychological healing: Epidote brings clarity and focus to one's intentions. It instills patience and releases anxiety, self-pity, hopelessness, and negative attitudes. This stone softens overly sarcastic and rude personalities, revealing and soothing the cause of these emotional defenses. It is the stone of the silver lining, instilling hope and patience in the midst of adversity.

Spiritual healing: Epidote raises your vibration. It alleviates the symptoms of ascension/spiritual growth by clearing the physical body and better integrating the spiritual into the physical. It boosts the manifestation process by prompting you to "act as if," thereby attracting the end goal through your actions. It draws prosperity and ensures that your physical, emotional, and spiritual needs are being met.

Fluorite (General)

Formula: CaF_2

Hardness: 4

Crystal system: cubic

Formation process: igneous or sedimentary

Chakra: all, especially third eye, crown

A polished fluorite skull

Physical healing: Fluorite relates to order and structure. In the physical body this translates to supporting the health and well-being of the skeletal system. Fluorite nourishes bones, ligaments, and cartilage, and it promotes healthy joints and spinal alignment. This gem relieves joint pain and is especially effective at treating conditions affecting the jaw. Fluorite is a quintessential stone for the brain, promoting balanced brain hormones and healthy tissue in the nervous system. It breaks down barriers to healing and is a potent tool for chronic, persistent physical (and psychological) conditions that resist other forms of treatment. Fluorite is antiparasitic, improves coordination, and regenerates mucous membranes.

Psychological healing: Mentally, fluorite is stabilizing and balancing. It improves concentration and fortifies self-discipline, making it an ideal stone for canceling out distractions. Fluorite is also helpful for drawing suppressed or latent emotions to the surface for expression and resolution. It is among the best stones for learning; wearing or holding a piece boosts memory and encourages critical-thinking skills. Fluorite is the gateway to the subconscious realm; it promotes authenticity and expands awareness. Working with this gemstone overcomes narrow-minded thinking and helps you move outside the comfort zone.

Spiritual healing: Fluorite facilitates meditation. It helps you stay focused and opens the mind to spiritual experiences. This gemstone encourages psychic development, as it helps sense and interpret the energy of people, objects, events, and places. Fluorite can facilitate change at the global level too, as it breaks down old patterns of injustice and oppression so that newer and more stable systems can be built in their place. Its cubic structure is grounding, and it anchors positive changes and spiritual development.

Blue Fluorite

Formula: CaF_2 with iron (Fe)

Hardness: 4

Crystal system: cubic

Formation process: igneous or sedimentary

Chakra: all, especially throat, third eye

Raw blue fluorite from China

Physical healing: Blue fluorite helps release longstanding tension from the body, especially when it results from the mind. It supports the health of the eyes, nose, throat, and ears; blue fluorite also relieves pain, particularly in the joints. This gemstone can be used for the health of the respiratory system, brain, spine, and skeletal system. It can eliminate parasites and prevent or repair damage to the DNA. Bluish-green fluorite is especially helpful for the urinary tract.

Psychological healing: Of all fluorites, blue is the most calming to the mind. It reduces worry and fear, thereby instilling deep-seated peace. Blue fluorite directs mental energy away from frustration, disappointment, and obsession, channeling this energy toward a healthier focus, such as developing new hobbies and interests. It facilitates clear and concise communication, favoring one's intellect over emotion.

Spiritual healing: Working with blue fluorite deepens one's commitment to truth and justice. It is a stone of peace, thereby facilitating meditation. Blue fluorite integrates fragmented pieces of the soul and encourages greater understanding of the karmic cycles at play in life.

Blue John Fluorite

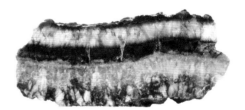

Formula: CaF_2 with petroleum (chiefly C and H)

Hardness: 4

Crystal system: cubic

Formation process: igneous or sedimentary

Chakra: all, especially throat, third eye

Polished Blue John flourite from Derbyshire, England

Physical healing: Blue John fluorite is sometimes used in the treatment of fatigue, fever, and chills, as well as conditions of the respiratory system. It is helpful in cases of chronic illness, and it can improve nutrient absorption.

Psychological healing: Like all forms of fluorite, Blue John works mainly on the mind. It is a stone of mental and manual dexterity. It inspires creativity and innovation and helps the mind adapt to changes in technology, language, and culture.

Spiritual healing: This gemstone is especially helpful for empaths, as it allows you to recognize others' emotions and detach from them rather than feel swept away by them. Blue John fluorite is a stone of support and clarity that allows us to be of service to others. It can be used to help heal the planet, especially by reducing atmospheric and environmental toxins, both physical and spiritual. This stone encourages altruism, generosity, and service. Blue John brings luck (especially with regard to legal troubles), and it promotes astral travel and psychic development.

Green Fluorite

Formula: CaF_2 with chromium (Cr)
Hardness: 4
Crystal system: cubic
Formation process: igneous or sedimentary
Chakra: all

Octahedral green fluorite

Physical healing: Green fluorite is an excellent stone for physical healing. It targets all manner of infections, including viral infections like influenza, shingles, and the common cold. It is also used to treat conditions affecting the eyes, ears, tear ducts, sinuses, nose, and throat. Green fluorite can be taken as an elixir for fungal infections. Use this gemstone to quell vomiting and diarrhea. This member of the fluorite family is detoxifying, and it remedies psychosomatic conditions.

Psychological healing: Green fluorite builds a bridge between the mind and the heart. It intensifies emotional states to facilitate conscious awareness and the understanding of them. This stone expands the mind, opening it to new possibilities, and it is helpful in treating addictions.

Spiritual healing: Generally speaking, green fluorite helps remove blocks to your overall well-being and growth. It is cleansing to all the chakras but works most intensively on clearing the heart chakra. Green fluorite helps you find direction in life, and it can help you become a more efficient and sensitive healer.

Purple Fluorite

Formula: CaF_2

Hardness: 4

Crystal system: cubic

Formation process: igneous or sedimentary

Chakra: all, especially third eye

Purple fluorite from Morocco

Physical healing: Purple and violet shades of fluorite alleviate headaches and insomnia, and it promotes the overall health of the skeletal system, including bones, teeth, cartilage, ligaments, and joints. Purple fluorite is used to treat the brain and nervous system, the DNA, and infections. It can be used to treat female infertility and to reduce the growth of tumors. Purple fluorite can also decrease some of the secondary symptoms of diabetes.

Psychological healing: Of all forms of fluorite, this variety is perhaps the most adept at breaking through barriers to growth and healing, especially mentally and spiritually. This gemstone helps break unwanted habits, and it addresses depression, bipolar disorder, and grief. Purple and violet fluorite are purifying to the mind, providing emotional stability and boosting memory.

Spiritual healing: Just as green fluorite bridges the mind and the emotions, purple/violet fluorite bridges the mind and the spirit. It expands consciousness, enhances intuition, and makes our dreams more vivid. This is a stone for the spiritual seeker, promoting liberation and determination on the path. Purple fluorite helps when we feel we have too many responsibilities weighing on our shoulders, especially if they relate to the welfare of others. It is a great stone for healers, therapists, counselors, teachers, and members of the medical profession.

Rainbow Fluorite

Formula: CaF_2

Hardness: 4

Crystal system: cubic

Formation process: igneous

Chakra: all, especially third eye and crown

Polished rainbow fluorite from China

Physical healing: Rainbow fluorite exhibits more than one color (and often many) in its makeup. It is the most versatile of the fluorite family for physical healing, as it can exhibit all the traits of the various colors it contains. Rainbow fluorite is noted for treating the skin, mucous membranes, nerves, and skeletal system. It can be taken as an elixir or placed on the chest for persistent, dry cough and acute respiratory conditions. Rainbow fluorite also promotes flexibility in the joints and aids in recovery after injury.

Psychological healing: Rainbow fluorite is expansive to the mind. It helps you explore the full range of human emotion and opens you to the possibilities of new ideas, thoughts, and dreams. This gemstone promotes creativity and innovation.

Spiritual healing: Rainbow fluorite boosts intuition, promotes freedom, and enhances meditation. It helps in the assimilation of new energies, such as during and after a healing session (regardless of the modality), and it is cleansing and restorative to the human energy field. Use it to repair leaks or tears in the aura and to seal the energy field after releasing attachments or cords.

Yellow Fluorite

Formula: CaF_2

Hardness: 4

Crystal system: cubic

Formation process: igneous or sedimentary

Chakra: all, especially solar plexus

Yellow fluorite cluster from Spain

Physical healing: Yellow fluorite, like other varieties, promotes the health of the skeletal system. It can also be used in the treatment of the thyroid, liver, and digestive system. This stone can be used as part of a balanced treatment for eating disorders, and it helps maintain healthy blood pressure and cholesterol levels.

Psychological healing: Yellow fluorite promotes learning, helping you understand and assimilate new information easily and quickly and process new experiences in life. Use this stone when you have trouble letting down your boundaries and allowing others to get close to you. It boosts the intellect, quiets worries, and helps you cultivate a positive outlook.

Spiritual healing: Yellow fluorite's key theme is *understanding.* It is extremely centering, and it facilitates the integration of new information, energies, and experiences. It supports growth and expansion in the pursuit of spiritual truth, and it bolsters cooperative efforts within your community. Yellow fluorite translates information derived from personal gnosis into practical, experiential wisdom.

Fuchsite

Formula: $K(Al,Cr)_2(AlSi_3O_{10})(OH)_2$

Hardness: 2.5

Crystal system: monoclinic

Formation process: metamorphic

Chakra: heart

Raw fuchsite

Physical healing: Fuchsite is a chrome-bearing mica that imparts flexibility to the body. It supports the health of the metabolism, circulatory system, and skin. This green mineral can be used to treat itchiness, rashes, cough, allergies, and hemorrhoids.

Psychological healing: Fuchsite confers the same flexibility and resilience to the psyche that it does to the body. Its energy is playful, and it inspires joy. Working with this stone decreases mental chatter and opens the floodgates to creativity, innovation, and freedom. It can enhance expression and encourage healthy boundaries.

Spiritual healing: This green mica aligns the mental and physical bodies. It encourages us to see the big picture, and it serves as a reminder that when we resonate with unconditional love we leave an indelible mark on all that we touch. Fuchsite helps us accept and adapt to changes in life, helping us see setbacks as spiritual lessons.

Galena

Formula: PbS

Hardness: 2.5

Crystal system: cubic

Formation process: igneous, sedimentary, or metamorphic

Chakra: root

Natural galena crystal

Physical healing: Galena is used in the treatment of infection and systemic toxicity. It neutralizes radiation and promotes regeneration on the cellular level. It alleviates stiffness and pain in the joints and combats inflammation.

Psychological healing: Galena is used to ward off melancholy, depression, and seriousness, each one a saturnine quality that points to the lead in this mineral's makeup. It teaches responsibility, patience, and independence.

Spiritual healing: Galena's lead content is alchemical and transformational. It helps us understand cycles that repeat in our lives, including those of a karmic nature. It stimulates past-life recall, and it is a potent tool for grounding. As we work with galena, it reveals the big picture, thereby empowering us to make improvements in our lives based on this expanded awareness.

Note: Galena is toxic; handle with care.

Garnet (General)

Formula: $X_3Y_2(SiO_4)_3$

Hardness: 6.5–7.5

Crystal system: cubic

Formation process: igneous or metamorphic

Chakra: root

Cluster of garnet crystals

Physical healing: Garnets represent a diverse group of closely related mineral species, including almandine, andradite, grossular, spessartite, and uvarovite, each with variations in color. These stones are grounding and fortifying to the body. Red garnet is especially enlivening physically, enhancing vitality and stamina. Generally speaking, garnet helps to regulate the homeostatic mechanisms of the body, as well as their nonphysical counterparts in the aura and chakras. This gemstone strengthens the muscles and skeleton and provides greater balance to the endocrine system. Work with garnet to resolve hormonal imbalances and stimulate the metabolism.

Psychological healing: Garnet counteracts feelings of isolation by providing stamina, resolve, and motivation. It enhances mental acuity and efficiency. Garnet invokes passion, creativity, sensuality, and physical attraction, making it an excellent stone for love and romance.

Spiritual healing: Garnets of all varieties are symbols of abundance, unconditional love, and awareness of one's innate connection to the Divine. Red garnet in particular stabilizes the root chakra and cultivates kundalini energy. Garnet's cubic crystal structure anchors our thoughts and awareness on the physical plane, thereby facilitating manifestation.

Almandine Garnet (Red Garnet)

Formula: $Fe_3Al_2(SiO_4)_3$

Hardness: 7–7.5

Crystal system: cubic

Formation process: igneous or metamorphic

Chakra: root

Almandine garnet from Pakistan

Physical healing: Almandine is one of the most common species of garnet, and it is the most abundant of the red varieties. It is revitalizing, strengthening, and protective to the body. Work with almandine to recuperate after illness or injury. The aluminum content makes this stone helpful for conditions of the nervous system, while the iron helps keep the physical body grounded and protected. It nourishes the heart, blood, and blood vessels, supporting the overall health and well-being of the circulatory system.

Psychological healing: Because almandine, like other garnets, is so grounding, it grants us greater peace and serenity by connecting to the present moment. Almandine helps us overcome worry, stress, anxiety, and fear; it is a stone that stimulates positive thinking. The cubic crystal structure supports organization, memory, and mental clarity.

Spiritual healing: Almandine is protective and empowering. It can initiate the rise of kundalini, though it does so more slowly and safely than other gemstones. Almandine is usually an earthy red color, and it can help us maintain a grounded state without being too stimulating. For this reason it is an excellent meditation stone.

Black Garnet (Melanite)

Formula: $Ca_3Fe_2Si_3O_{12}$ with titanium (Ti)
Hardness: 6.5–7
Crystal system: cubic
Formation process: metamorphic
Chakra: earth star, root

Cluster of black garnet

Physical healing: Melanite garnet is a black, titanium-bearing variety of andradite garnet. It fortifies the skeletal system and encourages absorption and assimilation of calcium to strengthen the bones. It stimulates growth and helps elongate and straighten the spine. Black garnet also promotes kidney health.

Psychological healing: Black garnet encourages reliability and trustworthiness. This gem helps you hone your skills and talents as well as cultivate trust in yourself as you develop these skills. It is strongly supportive of your willpower and can enable you to break bad habits and develop healthy behaviors in their place. Highly empowering, black garnet provides the impetus necessary to overcome depression and anxiety and lends the courage needed to break free from patterns of abuse.

Spiritual healing: Black garnet is both grounding and protective. It is an ideal stone for psychic development and shamanic journeying. An ally to highly sensitive people, black garnet can help empaths learn to identify and separate foreign energies and emotions from their own.

Green Garnet

Formula: $Ca_3Al_2(SiO_4)_3$ or $Ca_3Fe_2Si_3O_{12}$ with chromium (Cr) and/or iron (Fe)

Hardness: 6.5–7.5

Crystal system: cubic

Formation process: igneous or metamorphic

Chakra: root, heart

Green andradite from Madagascar

Physical healing: Green garnet, typically a variety of either grossular or andradite, promotes regeneration of the body and stimulates the growth and repair of tissues damaged by illness and injury. Green garnet can help expel mucus and break down congestion. It supports the health of the respiratory system, kidneys, liver, and pancreas. Placed topically, green garnet also softens tight muscles and rigid joints and can help shrink fatty deposits such as lipomas.

Psychological healing: Green garnet releases paranoia, assuages anxiety, and promotes emotional stability. Work with this stone to invite feelings of gratitude and peace.

Spiritual healing: Green garnet evokes the energies of growth and expansion. It enhances manifestation, especially with regard to material wealth and abundance. It is among the premier stones for abundance and prosperity. Green grossular garnet, in particular, instills zeal, benevolence, and joy.

Hessonite Garnet

Formula: $Ca_3Al_2(SiO_4)_3$ with manganese (Mn) and/or iron (Fe)

Hardness: 7–7.5

Crystal system: cubic

Formation process: metamorphic

Chakra: root, sacral, heart

Raw hessonite

Physical healing: Hessonite, sometimes known as *cinnamon stone,* is a form of grossular garnet. It strengthens the circulatory system and helps the body eliminate wastes. This gemstone nourishes and fortifies the kidneys, liver, and endocrine system. It regulates the hormonal balance of the body and can reduce the symptoms of menopause. Hessonite treats infertility and sexual dysfunction in women and men alike.

Psychological healing: Hessonite cultivates self-esteem and a healthy body image. It encourages self-respect, appreciation, and healthy communication. This form of garnet can help you confront bullies and others who deride or mock you. It gently increases confidence by helping you know your strengths and weaknesses, allowing you to stay centered and maintain composure when faced with aggravation and difficulties.

Spiritual healing: This soothing stone brings clarity to life, helping you to better see the big picture. It is restorative and promotes spiritual growth. It allows you to grow and transform, not only for your own benefit but also so that you can bring your skills to the world. Hessonite increases self-love, which also attracts love from the world around us. It can be used to help you dream and strive toward your dreams.

Rainbow Garnet

Formula: $Ca_3Fe_2Si_3O_{12}$

Hardness: 6.5–7

Crystal system: cubic

Formation process: metamorphic

Chakra: all, especially earth star, root, crown

Japanese rainbow garnet

Physical healing: Rainbow garnet, a variety of andradite, supports the health of the liver, regulates the production of blood cells, and imparts vitality. It is purifying, protective, and uplifting to the physical body. This stone restores mobility after injury, and it can regulate menstrual cycles.

Psychological healing: This form of garnet enhances creativity, sharpens the intellect, and increases mental flexibility. It instills shrewdness and can help you be more discerning—qualities that make it an excellent stone for facing your shadow self.

Spiritual healing: Rainbow andradite draws out the mystical within the mundane world. It increases your willpower by aligning the personal will with Divine Will. Wearing or carrying this gemstone purifies the aura, stimulates creativity, and balances masculine and feminine energies. It helps you orient yourself within the cosmos by dynamically grounding you while opening your crown to the heavens above, thus creating a bridge between heaven and earth. It feeds the inner child and encourages a state of playful awe throughout all of life.

Rhodolite Garnet (Pink Garnet)

Rhodolite from Mexico

Formula: $(Mg,Fe)_3Al_2(SiO_4)_3$

Hardness: 7–7.5

Crystal system: cubic

Formation process: igneous or metamorphic

Chakra: root, heart

Physical healing: Rhodolite is a member of the pyrope-almandine series of garnets displaying a pinkish or purplish shade of red. It enhances circulation and metabolism, drawing warmth to cold extremities. This gemstone counteracts frigidity and infertility in women, and it is also an excellent stone for addressing conditions affecting male impotence.

Psychological healing: Rhodolite is an uplifting member of the garnet family. It promotes optimism, self-worth, trust, and love. It helps us be more loving—first toward oneself before directing that love outward. It grounds the heart and mind into the physical body, thereby facilitating expressions of love, romance, and sexuality. It incites loving and passionate connection while simultaneously releasing inhibitions impeding erotic expression.

Spiritual healing: Rhodolite increases zeal and joy. It maintains stability during times of spiritual and emotional transformation and acts as a reminder of the unconditional love that surrounds and supports us at all times. Rhodolite promotes awareness of the here and now, and it is a gemstone of abundance, love, and satisfaction. It protects and uplifts the home, making it a perfect stone to maintain positivity, love, and health in your personal environment.

Heliodor

Formula: $Be_3Al_2(SiO_3)_6$ with iron (Fe)

Hardness: 7.5–8

Crystal system: hexagonal

Formation process: igneous

Chakra: solar plexus, crown, soul star

Natural heliodor

Physical healing: Heliodor, also called *golden beryl,* is traditionally used for treating conditions of the digestive system and vision disorders and for strengthening the immune system. It improves vitality and can be used to stave off cravings for unhealthy food.

Psychological healing: Heliodor elevates the mood and helps you remain calm and positive under stress. This gemstone reduces aggressive tendencies and helps channel anger and frustration into healthy outlets. Heliodor is an important gemstone for building self-worth, as it improves your view of yourself. It is a stone of courage, commitment, and joy.

Spiritual healing: Golden beryl is the most nourishing gemstone for the causal body. It stimulates past-life recall, helps in overcoming karmic patterns from previous incarnations, and aligns our personal power with the Divine. This gem can increase focus during meditation and encourage perseverance, thus leading us closer to enlightenment.

Hematite

Formula: Fe_2O_3

Hardness: 5.5–6.5

Crystal system: trigonal

Formation process: igneous or sedimentary

Chakra: earth star, root

Tumbled hematite

Physical healing: Hematite is tonifying and strengthening to the body. It assists regenerative processes and is especially effective for promoting the health of the blood and circulatory system. It draws out pain, stanches bleeding, and reduces inflammation. Use hematite to reduce headaches and increase iron absorption. It is an ideal stone to work with when recovering from surgery. Hematite can counteract insomnia and provide a good night's rest, though some people find its iron content too stimulating.

Psychological healing: The iron content in hematite encourages drive, ambition, and resolve. It confers a deeply rooted calm and induces greater mastery over the mind. Wearing hematite enhances memory and brings discipline to the mind, especially in meditation or during study.

Spiritual healing: Hematite is a master grounding tool, promoting better awareness, no matter the circumstance. This stone grounds us in the present moment and provides the strength necessary to review old experiences, habits, and situations to understand our role in them. It highlights our inner strengths and weaknesses so that we can leverage them for our growth on all levels.

Hiddenite

Formula: LiAl(SiO₃)₂ with traces
of chromium (Cr) or iron (Fe)

Hardness: 6.5–7

Crystal system: monoclinic

Formation process: igneous

Chakra: heart, higher heart, third eye

Rough hiddenite

Physical healing: Hiddenite, a green variety of spodumene, is cooling and sooth-ing to the body. It reduces inflammation and pain and is thus used in the treat-ment of arthritis, neurological disorders, and toothache. Hiddenite promotes the health of the liver, nervous system, heart, and thymus. It can boost the immune system and is effective in treating childhood illnesses.

Psychological healing: As a lithium-bearing mineral, hiddenite is adept at transforming psychological imbalances. It releases anger, anxiety, irritabil-ity, melancholy, fear, and feelings of unworthiness. Hiddenite supplants these negative patterns with joy and gratitude. Working with hiddenite improves decision-making skills and helps those who feel that they are burdened with too much responsibility. This stone can also be used as an adjunct in treating addiction.

Spiritual healing: By filling us with gratitude, hiddenite makes us more receptive to prosperity and abundance. It is a stone of new beginnings, bringing serenity and devotion to the heart, mind, and spirit. Hiddenite dissolves the ego's hold over the conscious mind, boosts intuition, and promotes blissful, ecstatic states during meditation.

Howlite

Formula: $Ca_2B_5SiO_9(OH)_5$

Hardness: 3.5

Crystal system: monoclinic

Formation process: sedimentary

Chakra: third eye, crown

Tumbled howlite

Physical healing: Howlite breaks up stagnant energy and toxicity in the body. It is helpful for counteracting dehydration, especially when used as a crystal elixir. Howlite corrects irregularities in the DNA and helps us assimilate spiritual or psychological information and energy on the physical plane.

Psychological healing: Howlite is one of the preeminent stones for treating stress. It induces deep relaxation and filters anxious, nervous thoughts from the mind. This stone improves concentration and is an important mental healing tool. Howlite strengthens reasoning skills as well.

Spiritual healing: Howlite empowers our ability to co-create with the universe through our reasoning skills. It tempers our daydreams with the actionable steps required to bring them to fruition.

Iolite

Formula: $(Mg,Fe)_2Al_4Si_5O_{18}$

Hardness: 7–7.5

Crystal system: orthorhombic

Formation process: metamorphic

Chakra: third eye

Tumbled iolite

Physical healing: Iolite targets the nervous system and sensory organs and alleviates nerve pain, numbness, and paralysis. This stone also prevents memory loss and can help retrieve lost memory following illness or injury. It is strongly detoxifying and breaks up calcification and fatty deposits. Use it to clear the arteries, reduce fatty lumps (especially in the breasts or along the spine), drain fluids, reduce swelling, and control high fevers. Iolite also works on the eyes and can help with sinus pressure and other symptoms of environmental or seasonal allergies.

Psychological healing: Iolite invites hope in the face of adversity. It promotes mental-emotional endurance and taking responsibility, which further encourages us to take the steps necessary to create positive changes in life. Iolite offers reassurance to people who fear the unknown, helping them view life circumstances with a healthy amount of detachment and objectivity. It softens spite and eases the need for control.

Spiritual healing: Iolite pushes us to look past the material plane to see the many layers of reality all around us. It is a visionary stone that supports meditation, dreaming, and visualization. It stimulates an upward flow of energy through the aura and chakra system and facilitates astral travel and shamanic journeying. Iolite helps us recognize fractured pieces of the soul in the process of soul retrieval. This stone facilitates past-life recall and helps us embrace ordinary consciousness and psychic awareness simultaneously.

Jade (Nephrite)

Formula: $Ca_2(Mg,Fe)_5Si_8O_{22}(OH)_2$

Hardness: 6–6.5

Crystal system: monoclinic

Formation process: metamorphic

Chakra: sacral, heart

Tumbled green jade
from Canada

Physical healing: *Jade* refers to two different stones: nephrite and jadeite. While both exhibit similar properties, the jade discussed in this entry is the more common and less precious of the two, nephrite. Nephrite jade promotes healthy kidney function. It can be used for urinary tract infections, allergies, hearing loss, and to boost fertility. Nephrite strengthens the connective tissues and restores collagen. It promotes healthy skin and encourages longevity. Jade also invites restful sleep.

Psychological healing: Jade induces deep peace and harmony and promotes marital bliss and fidelity. This stone helps us break free from limiting beliefs about money so that we can overcome the poverty mentality and attract true abundance.

Spiritual healing: Jade releases karmic patterns, stimulates past-life recall, and enhances shamanic healing. It facilitates out-of-body experiences, lucid dreaming, and astral travel. Jade cultivates refinement of the spirit and helps us aim toward enlightenment.

Jasper (General)

Formula: SiO_2

Hardness: 7

Crystal system: trigonal

Formation process: sedimentary or igneous

Chakra: root, sacral (varies by type)

Tumbled jasper

Physical healing: Jasper fortifies and nourishes the physical body. It promotes overall health and healing and is both grounding and energizing. Jasper can relieve conditions that affect the intestines and sex organs. This stone supports our connection to the earth and to the abundance of energy available to us in the natural world.

Psychological healing: Jasper is a stone for idealists, escapists, and procrastinators, as it eliminates distraction and strengthens one's focus. This gemstone also curbs anxiety and reduces insecurity. Jasper is carried or worn to heighten courage and determination. It makes us more emotionally resilient, allowing us to recover from rejection and failure.

Spiritual healing: Jasper has an ancient tradition of being a protective stone. It is used to confer success, especially in business endeavors, and it assists in attaining wealth, health, and happiness. Jasper is a wonderful grounding stone that facilitates a connection to the world around you.

Dragon's Blood Jasper

Formula: SiO_2 with epidote $[Ca_2Al_2(Fe^{3+};Al)(SiO_4)(Si_2O_7)O(OH)]$ and piemontite $[Ca_2(Al,Mn^{3+},Fe^{3+})_3(SiO_4)(Si_2O_7)O(OH)]$

Hardness: 6–7

Crystal system: trigonal and monoclinic

Formation process: igneous

Chakra: all, especially earth star, heart

Tumbled dragon's blood jasper from South Africa

Physical healing: Dragon's blood jasper has an affinity for the immune system and assists in physical regeneration and detoxification. This stone promotes the health of the brain and nervous system as well as that of the liver, gallbladder, thyroid, and intestines. Work with dragon's blood jasper to strengthen hair and nails as well.

Psychological healing: Dragon's blood jasper imparts strength, courage, and resiliency. It is especially helpful when we experience doubt and self-pity. This stone invites greater discernment and patience, and it improves our reasoning skills even when we are under pressure. Carry or wear it to enhance your studies.

Spiritual healing: This member of the jasper family is closely linked to earth energies and the natural world. It is grounding and protective and fosters the attainment of wisdom when meditated with or worn. This gem can initiate the rise of kundalini energy, and it also nourishes the inner child. Dragon's blood jasper removes obstacles along the path of self-discovery, and it helps us get in touch with our sense of purpose.

Green Jasper

Formula: SiO_2 with actinolite $[Ca_2(Mg,Fe)_5Si_8O_{22}(OH)_2]$, chlorite $[(Mg,Fe)_3(Si,Al)_4O_{10}(OH)_2\cdot(Mg,Fe)_3(OH)_6]$, or iron (Fe)

Hardness: 7

Crystal system: trigonal

Formation process: igneous or sedimentary

Chakra: root, heart

Rough green jasper

Physical healing: Green jasper is strengthening and rejuvenating to the tissues. It reduces inflammation, regulates body temperature, and promotes weight loss. Green jasper stimulates liver function and alleviates spasms and pain in the joints.

Psychological healing: Green jasper teaches you how to look out for yourself by promoting independence and awareness of any needs not being met. It confers business acumen and stimulates critical thinking.

Spiritual healing: Holding or meditating with green jasper invites greater balance and harmony. It is cleansing to the aura and softens internal resistance to change. Green jasper attunes one to nature.

Leopardskin Jasper (Orbicular Rhyolite)

Formula: quartz (SiO_2), feldspar [$K(AlSi_3O_8)$], biotite [$K(Mg,Fe)_3AlSi_3O_{10}(F,OH)_2$], and hornblende [$(Ca,Na)_{2-3}(Mg,Fe,Al)_5(Al,Si)_8O_{22}(OH,F)_2$]

Hardness: 6–7

Crystal system: trigonal, monoclinic, triclinic

Formation process: igneous

Chakra: root, solar plexus

Tumbled leopardskin jasper

Physical healing: Leopardskin jasper supports the metabolism and any rhythmic processes in the body. It can help reduce the effects of aging and counteract stress-related illness. It is especially effective for the skin, as it balances both moisture and dryness. It can reduce the formation of scar tissue and support digestion and elimination. This stone can be applied to the wrist to treat carpal tunnel syndrome.

Psychological healing: Leopardskin jasper offers clear thinking, flexibility, and understanding. It is a stone of adaptation, and it strengthens the memory. This gemstone is ideal for people who feel stuck or are unable or unwilling to change; it helps them reset their sense of timing and rhythm in life.

Spiritual healing: Leopardskin jasper has a tonifying effect on the causal body. It appears as though it attracts positive influences, though in reality it is resetting our own inner timing and rhythm to match that of the universe. This allows us to become centered in the flow of unlimited abundance that the universe offers. This stone aligns us with our spiritual blueprint and keeps us grounded, protected, and present in everyday reality.

Mookaite

Formula: SiO_2 with amorphous silica (SiO_2)

Hardness: 7

Crystal system: trigonal and amorphous

Formation process: sedimentary

Chakra: root, sacral, solar plexus, third eye

Polished mookaite

Physical healing: Mookaite jasper regulates blood pressure, reduces scar tissue, and knits together open wounds. Mookaite also has an antiaging effect on the skin; made into an elixir it can be used as a face wash to brighten and hydrate the skin while eliminating fine lines and wrinkles. This stone also strengthens hair and nails.

Psychological healing: Mookaite stimulates memory and recall. It promotes emotional flexibility, creativity, and motivation. This stone fosters emotional warmth, and it is adept at mitigating loneliness and grief.

Spiritual healing: Mookaite's earth energies nourish and help us sift through karmic patterns to resolve ancestral or genealogical karma.

Ocean Jasper (Spherulitic Chalcedony)

Formula: SiO_2

Hardness: 7

Crystal system: trigonal

Formation process: igneous

Chakra: root, solar plexus, heart, throat

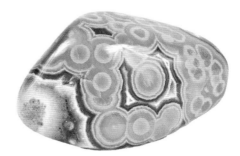

Tumbled ocean jasper

Physical healing: Ocean jasper's appearance resembles cellular structures, and so not unsurprisingly this stone promotes regeneration at the cellular level. It supports the health of the thyroid and adrenals and can synchronize the natural rhythms of the body's processes.

Psychological healing: Ocean jasper helps us examine the inner tides of the emotions. Working with this stone soothes turbulent emotions and leads you to stillness and peace. It also helps you express repressed emotions and promotes understanding, cooperation, empathy, and kindness.

Spiritual healing: Ocean jasper encourages a state of surrender. It facilitates meditation and provides deep attunement to the tides and rhythms of life. This gemstone connects to the Divine Feminine and helps heal and provide balance at the community level.

Picture Jasper

Formula: SiO_2

Hardness: 7

Crystal system: trigonal

Formation process: igneous or sedimentary

Chakra: root

Tumbled
picture jasper

Physical healing: Picture jasper combats fatigue and provides strength during chronic illness. This stone can be used to stimulate bone growth, promote healthy digestion, and alleviate the symptoms of allergies. Picture jasper also promotes the health of the connective tissue.

Psychological healing: This mineral inspires resilience, helping you cope with rejection and encouraging creative problem-solving skills. Picture jasper encourages you to keep a level head in the midst of stress and offers emotional renewal.

Spiritual healing: Picture jasper helps you stay the course. It teaches you to make adjustments along the way to ensure that your life purpose is being fulfilled each step of the way. It initiates communion with the planet and may be used to tap into the energy of sacred sites around the world. It sifts through the soul's memory and stimulates past-life recall.

Polychrome Jasper (Desert Jasper)

Formula: SiO_2

Hardness: 7

Crystal system: trigonal

Formation process: sedimentary

Chakra: all, especially root

Polished polychrome jasper from Madagascar

Physical healing: Polychrome jasper stimulates the metabolism and promotes the health of the feet and ankles. This gemstone is gently detoxifying and supports the function of the immune system. It can also be used to lessen the symptoms of seasonal allergies.

Psychological healing: Wearing or meditating with polychrome jasper stimulates creativity and passion. It helps us see the richness of all of life's experiences— whether pleasant or not—so that we can integrate each of the lessons offered to us. This stone births new ideas and fresh attitudes. It improves organizational skills and confers determination and courage. It helps curb feelings of jealousy and resentment and protects us from the envy of others.

Spiritual healing: Polychrome jasper helps us find joy in everyday activities. It is deeply grounding, connecting us with the energy of the Earth Mother. This stone is very adaptable and teaches us versatility and authenticity.

Poppy Jasper

Formula: SiO_2 with hematite (Fe_2O_3)

Hardness: 6.5–7

Crystal system: trigonal

Formation process: sedimentary

Chakra: root

Tumbled poppy jasper

Physical healing: Poppy jasper is uplifting, energizing, and stimulating; in fact, many people find that wearing this gemstone is as effective as drinking a cup of coffee in the morning. It overcomes low energy, stimulates the metabolism, and can be placed over sluggish or inactive organs to restore their vitality. Poppy jasper can be worn to increase strength and endurance and is a helpful aid during labor and childbirth.

Psychological healing: Carrying or wearing this gemstone invites greater joy and creativity. It combats limiting beliefs, ameliorates depression, and addresses any tendencies toward procrastination. Poppy jasper enlivens body and mind, all the while infusing you with optimism and cheer. It fosters a can-do attitude and helps you break through creative blockages.

Spiritual healing: Poppy jasper helps us take action to better ourselves and the world around us. When you feel overwhelmed at the state of the world, this gemstone helps you find solace in doing, such as through volunteer work, helping friends, or actively participating in healing the planet through spiritual means. This form of jasper deepens our connection to the planet and all life on it, thus facilitating compassionate action.

Red Jasper

Formula: SiO_2 with hematite (Fe_2O_3) or iron (Fe)

Hardness: 7

Crystal system: trigonal

Formation process: sedimentary

Chakra: root

Rough red jasper

Physical healing: Red jasper lends strength and energy to the physical body. It breaks up stagnation, promotes a healthy heart, and regulates blood pressure. This mineral improves virility and sexual performance.

Psychological healing: Red jasper is an ideal stone for improving concentration and developing greater willpower. People drawn to this gemstone often have a need for a new creative outlet. It reduces irritability and increases passion.

Spiritual healing: The rich color and iron content of red jasper make it highly activating to the root chakra. In meditation and therapeutic layouts this stone awakens the slumbering kundalini energy coiled at the base of the spine. Red jasper is considered strongly protective; it has long been used to drive away nightmares and unwelcome entities.

Silver Leaf Jasper

Formula: SiO_2

Hardness: 7

Crystal system: trigonal

Formation process: sedimentary

Chakra: root, solar plexus, third eye

Tumbled
silver leaf jasper

Physical healing: At the physical level silver leaf jasper is used in the treatment of conditions affecting the sensory organs. It can also improve liver function. Overall this mineral is very healing and grounding and can be used as a general tonic for physical well-being.

Psychological healing: This variety of jasper instills confidence and clarity and is especially adroit at combatting uncertainty, doubt, and despair. It works by inviting self-reflection so that we can assess our inner state and release what doesn't serve us. Silver leaf jasper imparts serenity and fosters independence. Work with this stone to encourage discipline and follow-through.

Spiritual healing: Silver leaf jasper helps you trust your instincts and intuition. It makes spiritual truths more tangible via meditation and contemplation. This gemstone can be used to resolve ancestral patterns and karmic cycles that are playing out in the present. Work with it to invite new beginnings.

Yellow Jasper

Formula: SiO_2 with limonite
$[FeO(OH) \cdot nH_2O]$
Hardness: 7
Crystal system: trigonal
Formation process: sedimentary
Chakra: root, solar plexus

Tumbled
yellow jasper

Physical healing: Yellow jasper balances conditions that affect the skin and connective tissues. It alleviates the symptoms of fibromyalgia and helps expel phlegm. Yellow jasper is also used for maintaining the health of the immune system, spleen, liver, kidneys, and intestines. It can support endeavors for weight loss as well. This gemstone promotes healthy digestion and can be used to reduce irritable bowel syndrome and flatulence.

Psychological healing: Yellow jasper inspires endurance, tenacity, and resilience. Similar to the way it aids physical digestion, it helps us digest experiences, emotions, and old programming; afterward it helps us eliminate the patterns that no longer serve us.

Spiritual healing: Yellow jasper is protective during all modes of travel and helps you fulfill your purpose in life. It promotes the necessary discipline and pragmatism needed to experience continuous spiritual development.

Jet

Formula: complex and variable;
rich in carbon (C)

Hardness: 2.5–4

Crystal system: amorphous

Formation process: organic (sedimentary)

Chakra: root

Raw jet

Physical healing: Though not a proper mineral, jet's use, together with various other gemstones and crystals, dates back to antiquity. This black gem is principally used to draw out physical pain; it alleviates headaches and inflamed joints. Jet treats conditions that affect epithelial tissues, such as diseases that impact the mouth and gums. It can be placed on the abdomen or made into an elixir to quell digestive complaints, especially conditions of the intestines, and can initiate detoxification of the physical body.

Psychological healing: Jet is famed as a stone of mourning, as it helps draw out pent-up grief and sadness so that we can process and release it. Jet ensures a restful night's sleep and has traditionally been employed as an amulet against nightmares. It is affirming, grounding, and centering—a soothing balm when we feel a loss of willpower or are undergoing oppression and abuse. Jet can motivate us to make healthy changes that support our spiritual identity.

Spiritual healing: Jet is considered strongly protective and gently grounding. Much like the way it is used to draw out pain, this stone draws out impure or unwanted energies from the aura and chakras and removes attached thought-forms, cords, and entities. It can be used to access past-life memories and may boost the ability to communicate with discarnate beings, such as spirit guides and deceased loved ones. Jet can motivate us to make healthy changes in life that support our spiritual identity.

Kunzite

Formula: LiAlSi$_2$O$_6$ with manganese (Mn)

Hardness: 6–7

Crystal system: monoclinic

Formation process: igneous

Chakra: heart, higher heart

Raw kunzite

Physical healing: Kunzite offers soothing energy for the health of the heart and nervous system. It alleviates hypertension and soothes aching joints. Additionally, kunzite supports the immune system.

Psychological healing: This gemstone brings joy and peace to the heart center. Its lithium content enables it to be profoundly relaxing, making it an ally in healing anxiety, nervousness, and other psychological conditions. It promotes growth and forward momentum in healthy relationships. Kunzite also encourages forgiveness, thereby healing and transforming emotional baggage from past relationships.

Spiritual healing: Kunzite opens our awareness to the currents of divine love coursing through the universe. It channels our love into a higher expression, guiding us toward a greater understanding and expression of unconditional love. Kunzite promotes tolerance.

Kyanite
(Blue Kyanite)

Formula: Al_2SiO_5

Hardness: 4.5–6.5

Crystal system: triclinic

Formation process: metamorphic

Chakra: all, especially third eye

Raw
blue kyanite

Physical healing: Kyanite is a stone of alignment, specifically addressing the spine as well as providing overall balance to the nervous system, including the brain and cerebrospinal fluid. This stone is also helpful for improving coordination and treating conditions of the sensory organs.

Psychological healing: Blue kyanite facilitates clear thinking and analysis. It awakens the higher mind and helps us develop objectivity and rational thinking. Kyanite expands our perspective and facilitates deep connection between the conscious mind and the subconscious.

Spiritual healing: Blue kyanite gently restores balance to the nonphysical anatomy by bringing the chakras and layers of the aura into alignment. It is a capable stone for examining the how and why of karmic patterns, pointing to the source of recurring patterns in life. Work with kyanite for better meditation and for traveling—both inner-plane journeys and outer-world trips.

Black Kyanite

Formula: Al_2SiO_5 with iron (Fe)

Hardness: 4.5–6.5

Crystal system: triclinic

Formation process: metamorphic

Chakra: all, especially third eye

Fan-shaped formation
of black kyanite

Physical healing: Black kyanite accesses any imbalances of the cellular memory, thus restoring harmony to the physical body on the most fundamental level.

It alleviates pain, lowers blood pressure, increases dexterity, and coordinates all the systems of the body. It is an excellent stone for conditions affecting the throat and voice, as well as for disorders affecting the brain.

Psychological healing: Working with black kyanite improves mental clarity, logic, and memory. It untangles emotional baggage and reveals patterns stored deep within the subconscious mind. This mineral releases victimhood and facilitates positive changes that allow one to feel in control of life. It is calming and stabilizing, and it can help align the subconscious with the conscious mind.

Spiritual healing: Black kyanite is one of my favorite stones for clearing the aura and chakras; it can be combed or raked through the energy field to remove attached energies, entities, and other attachments. It is most effective at removing karmic debris from the causal body. Black kyanite also breaks up and releases blockages in the aura. This stone facilitates past-life recall. It is helpful for planetary healing, empowering humankind to accept responsibility for the material and spiritual well-being of the planet.

Green Kyanite

Formula: Al_2SiO_5 with iron (Fe) and vanadium (V)

Hardness: 4.5–6.5

Crystal system: triclinic

Formation process: metamorphic

Chakra: all, especially heart, throat

Raw green kyanite

Physical healing: Green kyanite nourishes the myelin sheaths around the nerve cells. It alkalizes overly acidic conditions in the body, both local and systemic. This stone improves manual dexterity. It balances the body's ecosystem by maintaining helpful bacteria in the body.

Psychological healing: Green kyanite inspires honesty, truthfulness, and heart-centered communication. It links the higher mind to the heart center, bringing clarity to confusing or conflicting emotional patterns. Green kyanite also addresses feelings of victimhood, especially when you feel resigned to defeat.

Spiritual healing: Green kyanite, like other varieties, aligns all of the chakras and the subtle bodies of the aura, linking these with the heart chakra and providing an even more centering effect than other colors of kyanite. This mineral facilitates connection with the devic intelligence of the natural world. It furthers exploration of one's sense of identity and facilitates karmic healing and shamanic journeying.

Orange Kyanite

Formula: Al_2SiO_5 with manganese (Mn)

Hardness: 4.5–6.5

Crystal system: triclinic

Formation process: metamorphic

Chakra: all, especially sacral

Orange kyanite
from Tanzania

Physical healing: Orange kyanite ameliorates conditions of the lymphatic system and bone marrow, such as leukemia. It rectifies imbalances of the adrenals, helps us overcome eating disorders, regulates blood sugar, and eliminates sciatic pain. This stone also integrates and releases the energetic and karmic patterns underlying physical illness and injury.

Psychological healing: Orange kyanite stimulates the memory. It is mentally energizing and promotes creativity. Working with orange kyanite can help us improve our relationships, both platonic and romantic, as this stone facilitates connection and improves our understanding of the karmic nature of relationships.

Spiritual healing: This variety of kyanite sharpens the intuition and psychic talents by cultivating an instinctive knowing. It initiates a sense of timelessness and helps us break out of karmic ruts. Orange kyanite helps us find pleasure in all areas of life.

Labradorite

Formula: $(Na,Ca)(Al,Si)_4O_8$

Hardness: 6–6.5

Crystal system: triclinic

Formation process: igneous

Chakra: all, especially crown

Polished labradorite

Physical healing: Labradorite is an effective massage tool for pain, as it draws out any imbalance that is responsible for the pain. This gemstone is soothing. It alleviates cold and flu and supports the function of the kidneys. Working with labradorite can provide insight into the root cause of confusing physical symptoms.

Psychological healing: Labradorite strengthens visionary skills and enhances the imagination. It is also helpful for an overactive imagination or excessive daydreaming, as it focuses the imagination on concrete goals and counteracts escapism. It is an effective stone for overcoming extreme introversion and depression. This gemstone supports problem-solving skills.

Spiritual healing: Labradorite's spectral colors, called *labradorescence,* echo its effect in the energy field: it strengthens and brightens the aura, repairing any leaks, tears, and attachments. Labradorite strengthens the boundaries of the auric field, making it a helpful stone for psychic protection. It is also useful for meditation, manifestation, and spiritual development. It helps to maintain a connection to and awareness of our divine purpose, especially through the feedback of our inner guidance and our innate psychic talents.

Lapis Lazuli

Formula: lazurite $(Na,Ca)_8(Al,Si)_{12}O_{24}(S,SO_4)$ with pyrite (FeS_2) and calcite $(CaCO_3)$

Hardness: 5.5

Crystal system: cubic (lazurite, pyrite), trigonal (calcite)

Formation process: metamorphic

Chakra: heart, throat, third eye

Polished lapis lazuli

Physical healing: In the ancient world lapis lazuli was used to treat conditions of the eyes, as this gemstone promotes healthy vision. It also treats inflammation and digestive problems and supports the circulatory system and overall cardiac health. In addition, lapis lazuli can be used to promote healthy bones and teeth.

Psychological healing: Lapis lazuli works primarily to harmonize the heart and the mind. It gently awakens the higher capacity of the mind by removing conflict between the emotions and the intellect, allowing them to work together toward healing and spiritual development. Lapis lazuli promotes clear communication and fosters deep insight. It instills hope, nurtures friendship, and promotes both logical and intuitive reasoning.

Spiritual healing: This gemstone awakens the intuition and encourages self-mastery. It facilitates meditation, enhances psychic perception, and helps us master karmic lessons.

Larimar

Formula: NaCa$_2$Si$_3$O$_8$(OH) with traces of copper (Cu)

Hardness: 4.5–5

Crystal system: triclinic

Formation process: igneous

Chakra: throat, heart

Polished larimar

Physical healing: Larimar clears stagnation, including congestion in the sinus and lungs, poor circulation, or even stagnant energy in the subtle bodies. It can be used to treat urinary tract infections and to alleviate headache and menstrual pain. Larimar is the ideal stone for treating childhood illnesses.

Psychological healing: Larimar's energy is deeply nurturing to the emotional body. It ameliorates the pain of grief, abandonment, loss, and rejection by reminding us of the infinite ocean of unconditional love that flows within and around each of us. It is also recommended for overcoming indecision. Larimar gently stimulates healthy communication. This gemstone teaches us to be more loving.

Spiritual healing: Larimar invites us to release on every level. It brings healing to the inner child, deepens the meditative state, and initiates a state of surrender. It is a stone of profound inner peace.

Lepidolite

Formula: K(Li,Al,Rb)$_2$(Al,Si)$_4$O$_{10}$(F,OH)$_2$

Hardness: 2.5–3

Crystal system: monoclinic

Formation process: igneous

Chakra: heart, higher heart

Polished lepidolite

Physical healing: As a variety of mica, lepidolite imparts flexibility to the joints, being most effective on the hips and shoulders. Lepidolite is also occasionally used as an adjunct to conventional cancer treatments.

Psychological healing: Due to its lithium content, lepidolite is extremely soothing. It induces a state of calm awareness and is one of the most effective stones for treating anxiety, depression, and bipolar disorder. Lepidolite helps us overcome emotional trauma, nervousness, worry, anger, and emotional baggage. It initiates forgiveness and turns the heart toward joy.

Spiritual healing: Lepidolite gently encourages independence while breaking longstanding patterns. It erodes the ego's hold over waking consciousness, releasing us from the accrued beliefs, behaviors, and attitudes that inhibit the perception of love and goodness. It engenders a state of calm acceptance and helps promote surrender to the eternal now.

Magnetite

Formula: Fe_2O_4

Hardness: 5.5–6.5

Crystal system: cubic

Formation process: igneous or metamorphic

Chakra: earth star, root, third eye

Natural octahedron of magnetite

Physical healing: Magnetite has a stabilizing, grounding, and regulating influence on the entire being. It supports the well-being of the brain and stimulates the pineal gland. Magnetite is also used to treat dizziness and alleviate aches and pains. This mineral has long been thought to stop bleeding and strengthen the circulatory system. Work with magnetite to treat conditions of the liver, bone marrow, gallbladder, and endocrine system.

Psychological healing: Magnetite resolves imbalances of the psyche, usually by digging deep into the subconscious. It may stabilize rapid changes in mood. Magnetite can improve our charisma and personal magnetism too.

Spiritual healing: Magnetite works to align us with our higher purpose, helping us find direction in life and teaching us to trust our instincts. At the same time it grounds and aligns the subtle bodies and chakras and balances polar energies, including our inner balance of masculine and feminine energies. It is a protective stone that activates our higher awareness. Working with magnetite improves manifestation and grounds our spiritual work on the material plane.

Malachite

Formula: $Cu_2CO_3(OH)_2$
Hardness: 3.5–4
Crystal system: monoclinic
Formation process: sedimentary
Chakra: solar plexus, heart

Polished malachite

Physical healing: Adept at drawing out pain, malachite is a must-have in every crystal healing toolbox. It harmonizes the visceral organs of the body, promoting cooperation and correct timing of the various organ systems. Malachite's influence on timing helps to counteract irregular cycles of all types, such as heartbeat, menstrual cycles, sleep cycles, and the like. Malachite is used to regulate blood pressure, provide relief from sinus congestion, and encourage regular elimination. As well, this mineral has been used for centuries for ocular health and improving sight.

Psychological healing: Malachite is a master emotional purger. Similar to its ability to draw out physical pain, this gemstone teases out psychological pain and distress. It heals old emotional wounds and is helpful in cases of anxiety and PTSD. Malachite strengthens the willpower. It also enhances love, dedication, and fidelity in our relationships and allows us to grow from the lessons of our relationships.

Spiritual healing: The energy of malachite circumvents the ego and aligns us with Divine Will. Malachite supports inner vision and helps with creative visualization. This gemstone's energy moves in waves through the aura to identify and release foreign energies.

Moldavite

Formula: mostly SiO_2

Hardness: 5–6

Crystal system: amorphous

Formation process: metamorphic

Chakra: heart, third eye, crown

Raw moldavite

Physical healing: Moldavite is generally better suited to spiritual and emotional healing rather than physical. However it can help us attain a better understanding of an illness or injury, thereby initiating the internal changes needed to effect change on the physical level. It is sometimes indicated for fungal infections and parasites. It can accelerate the symptoms of a healing crisis to bring about a resolution of a health issue.

Psychological healing: Moldavite activates the intelligence of the heart, helping it transcend the limitations of the rational intellect. It awakens the presence of long-held emotional and spiritual wounds and helps us embrace the underlying lessons and gifts of this baggage. Moldavite can also initiate new patterns of thought, stirring us to think creatively for better problem solving.

Spiritual healing: Moldavite's chief mechanism is one of transformation. It works at the spiritual level by preparing us for rapid change. This mineraloid activates the heart, third eye, and crown chakras, thereby accelerating the learning of spiritual and karmic lessons and helping us integrate our psychic powers. Work with this stone to develop many spiritual skills, including channeling, clairvoyance, manifestation, astral travel, meditation, and similar practices.

Moonstone

Formula: KAlSi3O8

Hardness: 6–6.5

Crystal system: monoclinic

Formation process: igneous

Chakra: third eye, crown

Polished
white moonstone

Physical healing: Moonstone balances the cycles and rhythms of the physical body. It has a special affinity for the female reproductive system and can treat cases of infertility, painful menstruation, and other conditions. It improves lactation, reduces the symptoms of menopause, and ensures healthy pregnancy and childbirth. This gemstone promotes youthfulness, healthy skin, and deeper sleep.

Psychological healing: Moonstone helps you set healthy boundaries and resolve baggage from childhood. It invites a sense of wonder and imagination while providing a sense of validation and encouragement. It strips you of illusions and helps you break cycles of magical thinking by leading you to take actionable steps toward healing.

Spiritual healing: As a stone of spiritual development, moonstone strengthens the intuition, intensifies dreams, and provides protection.

Rainbow Moonstone

Formula: (Na,Ca)(Al,Si)$_4$O$_8$

Hardness: 6–6.5

Crystal system: triclinic

Formation process: igneous

Chakra: third eye, crown

Rainbow moonstone
cabochon

Physical healing: Rainbow moonstone is closely related to labradorite and exhibits similar properties of physical healing. It energizes the supraphysical aura that contains the blueprint of the physical body, thereby rejuvenating, strengthening, and enhancing the flexibility of physical tissue. It also affects the sinuses and throat, helping to provide clear airways and combating the symptoms of allergies. It can lessen the severity of ulcers, acid reflux, and other conditions of the stomach. Rainbow moonstone can improve hearing too.

Psychological healing: Rainbow moonstone is a peaceful and illuminating stone. Like other forms of moonstone, it enhances emotional well-being and is adept at clearing vestiges of emotional trauma from the the aura. It buoys the heart, inspiring hope and optimism.

Spiritual healing: Rainbow moonstone provides protection for the auric field, sealing off any leaks or tears. It strengthens the intuition and psychic senses, especially clairvoyance and clairaudience. Rainbow moonstone is helpful for tapping into one's inner feminine energy, connecting us to the Divine Feminine. This gemstone brings clarity and purity to the nonphysical anatomy (the aura and chakras), supporting all levels of well-being and spiritual transformation.

Obsidian
(Black Obsidian)

Formula: mostly SiO_2

Hardness: 5–6

Crystal system: amorphous

Formation process: igneous

Chakra: root

Obsidian sphere

Physical healing: Obsidian promotes cardiovascular health and dissolves tightness and blockages in the body. It alleviates pain and constriction of vascular tissues and is used for a healthy digestion and metabolism.

Psychological healing: Obsidian catalyzes self-awareness by reflecting the contents of the subconscious mind. It helps us overcome grief, fear, addiction, and depression. Obsidian can help release trauma, and it leads us to the origin of many out-of-balance emotions.

Spiritual healing: Obsidian is a tool of illumination. It brings light to the darkened recesses of the subconscious, and this act of illumination prepares us for rapid spiritual growth. Obsidian represents death, rebirth, and initiation. Sharpened pieces of this volcanic rock can be used to cut cords and remove negative attachments and energies from the aura. It is strongly protective and can shield sensitive people from negative energies and entities.

Apache Tears

Formula: mostly SiO_2

Hardness: 5–6

Crystal system: amorphous

Formation process: igneous

Chakra: root

Natural Apache
tears in matrix

Physical healing: Apache tears promote the health of the eyes and tear ducts, and they also support the female reproductive system. These obsidian nodules resolve pain and tightness, especially in the lower back. Apache tears can be used to treat nutrient deficiencies and conditions affecting the circulatory and immune systems and to promote growth of the hair and nails.

Psychological healing: The lucency of Apache tears allows them to bring clarity to both the mind and the emotions. This mineral is helpful for emotional release and is adept at helping us let go of conditioning learned during childhood. Apache tears are among the best stones for grief and trauma, as they give us permission to experience these emotions without judgment. These stones lead us to experience joy in each moment of life.

Spiritual healing: Apache tears have long been considered stones of luck and good fortune. Like all obsidian, Apache tears are protective. They enhance communication with devas and other nature spirits and highlight the fact that all beings arise from a common source. Carry one of these stones to cleanse the aura and remain gently grounded in the present moment.

Mahogany Obsidian

Formula: mostly SiO_2 with iron (Fe) and magnesium (Mg)

Hardness: 5–6

Crystal system: amorphous

Formation process: igneous

Chakra: root, sacral, solar plexus

Raw mahogany obsidian

Physical healing: Mahogany obsidian is strengthening to the physical body. It relieves inflammation, enhances circulation, lowers fever, and treats sinus pressure. It is more stabilizing than other forms of obsidian, and it is a good stone for treating both the physical and emotional components of shock, PTSD, and hyperactivity.

Psychological healing: Mahogany obsidian can help you develop a healthy body image; it boosts confidence and refreshes the body and mind. It points toward the core causes of any feelings of inadequacy and shame so that these patterns can be released altogether. It helps you overcome depression, poor concentration, irritability, short temper, and fear of intimacy.

Spiritual healing: Since it is grounding, this gemstone is a helpful tool in meditation. It helps you find motivation and passion for self-development.

Platinum Obsidian

Formula: mostly SiO_2

Hardness: 5–6

Crystal system: amorphous

Formation process: igneous

Chakra: all, especially earth star, root

Polished platinum obsidian

Physical healing: Platinum obsidian vitalizes the entire physical body. This type of obsidian nourishes cartilage and is used for healing the ears and hearing.

Psychological healing: Platinum obsidian primarily works on themes of self-worth and emotional balance. It does this by allowing patterns held in the subconscious mind to surface. Although it does not actually release these mental-emotional patterns, it can be effectively combined with other stones to achieve this result. Platinum obsidian assists in recovery from abuse, transforming grief, and dissolving issues related to self-image. It teaches us how to trust, especially after rejection or betrayal.

Spiritual healing: Like all forms of obsidian, the platinum variety is protective and stabilizing. It assists in identifying the root cause of imbalance and illness on all levels via spiritual means such as shamanic journeying or clairaudience. Platinum obsidian strengthens and purifies the aura and chakras, and it energizes the earth star chakra to promote grounding.

Rainbow Obsidian

Formula: mostly SiO_2

Hardness: 5–6

Crystal system: amorphous

Formation process: igneous

Chakra: root, heart

Polished rainbow obsidian

Physical healing: Rainbow obsidian restores balance to the endocrine and exocrine glands of the body. It can be used to improve circulation and reduce bruising, inflammation, and pain resulting from injury. Rainbow obsidian is occasionally employed in the treatment of certain forms of cancer (including cancer of the breasts, ovaries, testicles, adrenals, and thyroid) and in the healing of broken bones. This gemstone helps us understand the root cause of illness.

Psychological healing: Working with rainbow obsidian helps us break addictions, resolve the underlying cause of depression, and alleviate feelings of sadness and disappointment. This stone helps those who are stuck in the past, especially when plagued by anger and fear; it reveals the underpinnings of these emotions so that we can choose to move beyond them. Rainbow obsidian is also used to release trapped memories that can lead to physical imbalance.

Spiritual healing: Rainbow obsidian leads us to wisdom and transformation. It is a stone of surrender, countering despair and confusion with the light of hope. It reveals the inner workings of the spiritual path, heightens the intuition and psychic senses, and confers protection. Rainbow obsidian is the ideal stone for use in soul retrieval.

Snowflake Obsidian

Formula: mostly SiO_2 with inclusions of cristobalite (SiO_2)*

Hardness: 5–6

Crystal system: amorphous (obsidian), tetragonal (cristobalite)

Formation process: igneous

Chakra: root

Tumbled snowflake obsidian

Physical healing: Snowflake obsidian can treat low blood pressure, poor circulation, and joint pain. This stone can locate hidden pockets of infection in the body; partner it with other stones to eliminate the imbalance.

Psychological healing: Snowflake obsidian reveals hidden fears along with wellsprings of inspiration buried in the subconscious. It is a gemstone of balance, and it can help us move through life harmoniously.

Spiritual healing: Snowflake obsidian represents movement and illumination. It breaks up stagnant energies, providing momentum on one's spiritual path, and it helps us find greater awareness and understanding. It is a wonderful stone for gaining greater insight and clarity, and it protects against negative influences.

---

*Cristobalite is a polymorph of quartz; they share the same chemical formula but belong to different crystal systems.

Opal (General)

Formula: $SiO_2 \cdot nH_2O$

Hardness: 5.5–6

Crystal system: amorphous

Formation process: igneous or sedimentary

Chakra: all

Raw opal

Physical healing: Opals of all varieties tend to affect the skin, respiratory system, and kidneys. Opal is generally rejuvenating and balances the fluid levels of the body. Most forms of opal promote the health of the female reproductive system.

Psychological healing: Opals have a high water content, which enables them to be most effective at healing the emotions. Opals restore balance, usually by magnifying and clarifying emotional patterns and helping you better understand your emotions. This stone clears confusion and doubt while promoting responsibility.

Spiritual healing: Opals are auspicious gemstones that confer faith, luck, love, and hope. These stones transform rigid energy patterns in the physical body, aura, and chakras, allowing these energies to return to a more fluid state. Opal is a tool for higher consciousness—it grants wisdom, helps you embrace change, and facilitates rebirth.

Black Opal

Formula: $SiO_2 \cdot nH_2O$

Hardness: 5.5–6

Crystal system: amorphous

Formation process: igneous or sedimentary

Chakra: all, especially root, crown

Black opal from Honduras

Physical healing: Black opal is the most coveted member of the opal family. It is adept at breaking down blockages in the physical body and can be used to shrink growths such as tumors and cysts. This gemstone stimulates the body's natural cleansing processes.

Psychological healing: Black opal draws light into the subconscious, thereby bringing it into view. It promotes acceptance, transmutes lower emotions, and is a powerful stone for confronting fear.

Spiritual healing: Black opal clears and expands the aura. It magnifies one's intentions for manifestation and magical workings and facilitates psychic development. Black opal initiates out-of-body experiences, such as astral travel and shamanic journeying, and strengthens one's will to live and grow.

Blue Opal (Andean Opal)

Formula: $SiO_2 \cdot nH_2O$ with copper (Cu)

Hardness: 5.5–6

Crystal system: amorphous

Formation process: igneous

Chakra: heart, throat

Andean blue opal

Physical healing: Blue opal is soothing to the respiratory system, reducing irritation and inflammation of the airways. It combats allergies and fatigue and encourages better sleep. This variety of opal lowers blood pressure and supports the function of the lymph nodes and kidneys.

Psychological healing: The copper content in some blue opal enables it to calm the mind and open the heart. Blue opal also encourages communication and quiets the mind. It strengthens the memory too.

Spiritual healing: Blue opal invites a healthy sense of detachment, allowing you to access the role of the observer (therefore bypassing the ego) with greater ease. This enhances perception and deepens your intuition. Blue opal encourages the state of surrender.

Dendritic Opal

Formula: $SiO_2 \cdot nH_2O$ with psilomelane $[(Ba,H_2O)_2Mn_5O_{10}]$ or other manganese-bearing minerals (Mn)

Hardness: 5.5–6

Crystal system: amorphous

Formation process: igneous or sedimentary

Chakra: root, heart, crown

Polished dendritic opal from Madagascar

Physical healing: Dendritic opal cleanses the lymph and supports the immune system. This stone helps the body fight off colds and flu and improves the overall health of the circulatory and nervous systems. Dendritic opal imparts better equilibrium and reduces the symptoms of vertigo.

Psychological healing: Dendritic opal helps maintain the balance between the intellect and the emotions. It reduces stress and boosts the memory. It is a great stone for students and others learning new information.

Spiritual healing: Dendritic opal symbolizes growth and expansion. Most are black and white in appearance, and these stones impart greater spiritual balance and mastery. Dendritic opal encourages quiet contemplation and facilitates meditation.

Ethiopian Opal
(Welo Opal or Crystal Opal)

Formula: $SiO_2 \cdot nH_2O$

Hardness: 5.5–6

Crystal system: amorphous

Formation process: igneous

Chakra: all, especially root, heart, crown

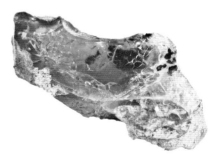

Raw Ethiopian opal

Physical healing: Ethiopian opals are clarifying to the physical body, promoting overall healing and providing balance to the sympathetic and parasympathetic nervous systems. Ethiopian opal has been used to treat eating disorders, and they can help you attain a healthy weight.

Psychological healing: These brilliant gemstones impart joy and elegance. They are helpful in treating mental disorders. Ethiopian opals also show promise in treating psychosomatic illnesses.

Spiritual healing: Ethiopian opals are my favorite gems for karmic healing. They transmute stale energy (especially karma) and promote spiritual expansion and evolution. They facilitate contact with the Divine, opening the consciousness to higher states of awareness. This gemstone accelerates psychic development and shields the aura.

Fire Opal

Formula: $SiO_2 \cdot nH_2O$ with iron (Fe)

Hardness: 5.5–6

Crystal system: amorphous

Formation process: igneous or sedimentary

Chakra: sacral, heart

Raw fire opal from Mexico

Physical healing: Fire opal invigorates the physical body, dispelling the effects of fatigue and overstimulation. It balances the hormones and stimulates the sex drive. Fire opal supports the health of the reproductive system in both men and women and ameliorates conditions affecting the gonads.

Psychological healing: Fire opal is a stone that invokes passion, creativity, and enjoyment. It overcomes shyness and breaks down limiting beliefs; it encourages assertiveness while releasing fear. Fire opal imparts sensuality and helps one find greater fulfillment through sex and intimacy.

Spiritual healing: Fire opal can accelerate one's spiritual growth on all levels. It channels the heart's energy into the lower chakras, unifying and strengthening them. It can activate kundalini energy and inspire ecstatic spiritual practice.

Green Opal

Formula: $SiO_2 \cdot nH_2O$

Hardness: 5.5–6

Crystal system: amorphous

Formation process: igneous

Chakra: solar plexus, heart

Green opal from Madagascar

Physical healing: Green opal is one of my favorite stones for colds, flu, and sinus conditions. It stimulates detoxification at the physical level, especially via the lymph and kidneys. Green opal can be used to provide more nutrients to the cells. It also offers insight into the karmic origins of recurring or chronic illness.

Psychological healing: Green opal invites joy and freshness into one's life. It promotes a state of perpetual gratitude.

Spiritual healing: This gemstone allows you to see with a new perspective and encourages you to explore new directions in life. Green opal invites you to be more grateful for the karmic lessons unfolding in your life.

Pink Opal

Formula: $SiO_2 \cdot nH_2O$ with manganese (Mn)

Hardness: 5.5–6

Crystal system: amorphous

Formation process: igneous

Chakra: heart

Pink opal from Peru

Physical healing: Pink opal works to nourish the heart, skin, and circulatory system. It has been used to regulate blood sugar levels too.

Psychological healing: Emotional healing is pink opal's greatest strength. It eases worry, shame, shyness, and dissatisfaction. This gemstone invites warmth, affection, and compassion.

Spiritual healing: This soothing gemstone releases the memory of old trauma, especially that which is karmic in nature. Pink opal equalizes karmic debts, including those relating to romantic relationships. It promotes contact with the angelic realm and inspires generosity and equanimity.

Purple Opal (Purple Opaline, Violet Flame Opal)

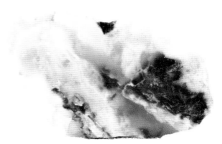

Formula: $SiO_2 \cdot nH_2O$ with traces of manganese (Mn)

Hardness: 5.5–6

Crystal system: amorphous

Formation process: igneous

Chakra: heart, third eye, crown

Raw purple opal
from Mexico

Physical healing: Purple opal treats illnesses and injuries affecting muscle tissue. It enhances the assimilation of nutrients, and it can be used as an adjunct to medical treatment for diabetes. Purple opal supports vision, both literal and metaphorical. Use it to decalcify the pineal gland and to treat disorders affecting the eyes. This gem can improve color vision.

Psychological healing: Purple opal has a transformational effect on the psyche. It transforms and releases old emotional patterns, particularly those associated with grief and sorrow. This gem invites you to let go of old burdens. Purple opal enhances rational thinking, supports objectivity, and boosts the intellect. It instills healthy emotional and intellectual boundaries.

Spiritual healing: This member of the opal family offers insight and enhances psychic abilities. Purple opal is a visionary stone that can improve meditation, open the third eye chakra, and offer clarity in life. It helps you understand the true meaning of wealth, and it reminds you that abundance and prosperity are defined by more than just money. This gemstone connects to the alchemical archetype of the violet flame, and it can therefore transmute negative and disharmonious energies into positive healing energies.

White Opal

Formula: $SiO_2 \cdot nH_2O$

Hardness: 5.5–6

Crystal system: amorphous

Formation process: igneous or sedimentary

Chakra: all

Tumbled white opal

Physical healing: White opal, both precious and common, supports the health of the skin, hair, nails, and lymphatic system. It treats conditions of the respiratory system and facilitates easy breathing. It also heals conditions of the female reproductive system, particularly painful menstruation. Common white opal encourages lactation.

Psychological healing: White opal works mostly to bring one's emotions into conscious awareness. It is an emotional amplifier and facilitates emotional release.

Spiritual healing: Wearing or meditating with white opal clears and protects the aura. It brings movement to the emotional body, thereby releasing stagnant energies. White opal inspires us to seek beauty and embody grace.

Yellow Opal

Formula: $SiO_2 \cdot nH_2O$, probably with traces of iron (Fe)

Hardness: 5.5–6

Crystal system: amorphous

Formation process: igneous or sedimentary

Chakra: solar plexus

Tumbled yellow opal from Kenya

Physical healing: Yellow opal supports the health of the nervous system, circulatory system, and digestive system. It has been used to eliminate calcifications, cysts, and tumors. Yellow opal strengthens the eliminatory system and helps fight infection. It is gently energizing.

Psychological healing: Yellow opal unites our emotions with our will, thereby reducing internal conflict and creating inner and outer strength. It is a stone of joy and happiness, and it strengthens commitment and dedication. Yellow opal eliminates limiting beliefs and behaviors. It also stimulates learning, creativity, and problem-solving skills. It is particularly helpful for overcoming regret, replacing it with joy.

Spiritual healing: Yellow opal inspires freedom and creativity on your spiritual path. It can help you align your will with your higher self and the Divine. It opens and aligns the solar plexus chakra.

Peridot

Formula: $(Mg,Fe)_2SiO_4$

Hardness: 6.5–7

Crystal system: orthorhombic

Formation process: igneous

Chakra: heart

Peridot crystal from Pakistan

Physical healing: Peridot is physically nourishing and detoxifying and accelerates healing processes. This gem is a helpful tool for alleviating the symptoms of colds and flu. It stimulates the appetite, promotes healthy liver and gallbladder function, and can reduce skin blemishes and warts.

Psychological healing: Peridot engenders optimism and warmth and promotes loving thoughts. This stone brings mental clarity, increases self-worth, and helps us receive with grace.

Spiritual healing: Peridot grants wisdom and invites gratitude. It is used to promote prosperity by improving one's relationship with money and removing poverty consciousness. Peridot helps release familial patterns and karmic lessons, especially those relating to finances and achievement. It can also grant prophetic dreams.

Petalite

Formula: $LiAlSi_4O_{10}$

Hardness: 6–6.5

Crystal system: monoclinic

Formation process: igneous

Chakra: higher heart, third eye, crown

Raw petalite from Brazil

Physical healing: Petalite is helpful for dissipating pain, especially chronic pain. This gemstone supports the health of the nervous system and sensory organs and promotes cardiac health.

Psychological healing: Petalite is one of the most soothing and balancing stones for psychological health. It eases anxiety, fear, apathy, depression, and all kinds of trauma. This stone assists in recovering from abuse. It is calming, uplifting, and nourishing.

Spiritual healing: Petalite is considered the stone of mindfulness; it also assists in the dissolution of the ego. It supports meditation, increases intuition, facilitates angelic communication, and supports spiritual growth.

Petrified Wood

Formula: usually SiO_2

Hardness: 6.5–7

Crystal system: triclinic

Formation process: sedimentary

Chakra: earth star, root

Raw petrified wood

Physical healing: Petrified wood stabilizes the metabolism. It is a good general healing stone, one that promotes weight loss.

Psychological healing: Petrified wood points us toward the root of rigidity of one's belief system or behaviors. It can be used as an adjunct to treating bad habits and breaking old patterns. Petrified wood may soften controlling personalities. It helps us handle stress and transition with more grace.

Spiritual healing: This fossil invites us to be more fully present. It both grounds and shifts the perspective away from being entirely focused on the material world. Petrified wood encourages the awareness of spiritual planes and the beings who dwell therein. It helps us surrender to the process of personal development and invites new beginnings. Petrified wood awakens past-life memories and resolves personal and ancestral karma.

Phenakite (Phenacite)

Formula: Be_2SiO_4

Hardness: 7.5–8

Crystal system: trigonal

Formation process: igneous or metamorphic

Chakra: third eye, crown, soul star

Polished Russian phenakite

Physical healing: Phenakite works more strongly at the subtle levels than the physical one. In this way it helps to clear and resolve imbalances of the subtle bodies that are responsible for physical conditions. Phenakite may also be used to facilitate healing of the nervous system (particularly the brain) and to repair damage to the DNA.

Psychological healing: Phenakite offers profound focus and clarity to the mind and the emotions. This mineral bridges higher spiritual consciousness with the level of the waking mind to help promote overall psychological balance and well-being. Phenakite can spark courage and strengthen a sense of resolve. It helps to clear confusion and instills understanding of the extant patterns in the mind and the emotions.

Spiritual healing: Phenakite is best suited to spiritual healing. It clears and activates the body of light as a whole, stimulating and opening all the chakras and energy channels while activating each of the subtle bodies. Phenakite enhances and supports meditation and creative visualization. It is an aid for manifestation and for spiritual development in general. This stone facilitates contact with nonphysical beings such as spirit guides, angels, and ancestors; it also enhances psychic abilities. It is truly an oracular stone, enhancing the vividness and accuracy of your visions, dreams, and premonitions. Phenakite raises the consciousness and links you to the Akashic records. It is a stone of initiation that ushers the soul toward the next stage of its evolution.

Pietersite

Formula: SiO_2 with riebeckite $[Na_2(Fe^{2+}_3Fe^{3+}_2)Si_8O_{22}(OH)_2]$

Hardness: 6.5–7

Crystal system: trigonal

Formation process: sedimentary

Chakra: solar plexus, third eye

Polished pietersite

Physical healing: Pietersite can be used to regulate the endocrine system and treat diabetes. It has a tonifying effect on the nervous system and can be used to stimulate repair and regeneration after suffering nerve damage. Pietersite initiates detoxification of the physical body, particularly when taken as an elixir. It can be used to moderate blood pressure and improve circulation of the blood, lymph, and other bodily fluids. Pietersite also sharpens the senses and combats fatigue.

Psychological healing: Pietersite has a stormy energy that purges old patterns from the body, mind, and spirit. This gemstone imparts insight, bolsters confidence, and helps us embrace change. It also helps us reclaim our willpower. Pietersite wipes away outdated programming that we have accumulated in life, such as the programming derived from family, school, and career. It is adept at confronting fear, especially fear of loss, failure, and vulnerability; in doing so, this gem reminds us that we are powerful beings who can shape our future.

Spiritual healing: Pietersite helps us overcome obstacles to growth, and it facilitates living our personal truth. It strengthens the etheric body, stimulates clairvoyance, and facilitates astral travel and shamanic journeying. Pietersite reminds us of the innate connection between the self and Creator, thereby dispelling the illusion of separation. It can be used to facilitate past-life regression and clear out genealogical karma stored in the DNA, aligning us with our spiritual blueprint. Pietersite helps us weather all manner of storms in life.

Prehnite

Formula: $Ca_2Al(AlSi_3O_{10})(OH)_2$

Hardness: 6–6.5

Crystal system: orthorhombic

Formation process: igneous or metamorphic

Chakra: solar plexus, heart, third eye

Tumbled prehnite

Physical healing: Prehnite is used to treat conditions of the kidneys, bladder, connective tissue, and circulatory system. It clears stagnation on many levels, including digestive, lymphatic, and bruising. Prehnite can also lessen the severity of varicose veins. It promotes detoxification and boosts the metabolism, primarily the metabolism of fats. It has a softening effect on physical tissue, helping us overcome rigidity and replacing it with flexibility and permeability.

Psychological healing: Prehnite is a wonderful stone for sleep and dreams. It makes dreams more vivid and enhances recall of one's dreams. Prehnite also wards off nightmares. This gemstone fosters a healthy connection between the heart and mind, and it is an ideal stone for forgiving oneself. Work with it whenever you find yourself avoiding something; it initiates acceptance.

Spiritual healing: For me prehnite has always been the stone of the wounded healer. It helps you learn to prioritize your own needs so as to be better equipped to help others. This stone helps you integrate the hidden lessons in life, such as those revealed in the dream state, allowing you to feel connected to the universe.

Pyrite

Formula: FeS$_2$

Hardness: 6–6.5

Crystal system: cubic

Formation process: igneous, sedimentary, or metamorphic

Chakra: root, solar plexus

Raw pyrite crystal

Physical healing: Pyrite is strongly grounding and stabilizing. It strengthens the physical body and initiates detoxification, thereby overcoming infection. Pyrite nourishes the male reproductive system and can treat impotence and infertility, especially by revealing any psychological factors underlying these conditions. This stone is also warming and can be used to promote circulation in the extremities.

Psychological healing: Pyrite is an excellent stone for mental order, memory, and recall. It strengthens willpower and combats fear. Working with pyrite improves self-confidence, creativity, and assertiveness, so it is a good choice in treating depression, apathy, and low self-esteem.

Spiritual healing: While pyrite is protective, it also enables quick and easy grounding. This stone increases our ability to anchor higher energies on the material plane, thereby facilitating manifestation and spiritual development. Pyrite inspires action, and it also draws wealth.

Quartz (Clear Quartz, Rock Crystal)

Formula: SiO_2

Hardness: 7

Crystal system: trigonal

Formation process: igneous, sedimentary, or metamorphic

Chakra: all

Quartz
from Hot Springs, Arkansas

Physical healing: Quartz is the most versatile tool offered by the mineral kingdom. It infuses the body with greater life force and can be applied to virtually any condition. Quartz reduces pain, targets infection, balances fever, repairs damaged tissue, and breaks up blockages. Clear quartz has a special affinity for the lungs and improves respiratory health overall; use it to treat congestion, asthma, allergies, bronchitis, and other respiratory conditions.

Psychological healing: Quartz invites mental and emotional clarity, focusing its energy on areas that are out of balance. It directs willpower and promotes personal responsibility. Quartz can sweep away worry, anger, bitterness, fear, grief, detachment, and other emotional states. It has been used to treat depression, anxiety, and other mental-emotional disorders.

Spiritual healing: In spiritual healing quartz is a stone of mastery. It provides clarity and illumination to our spiritual practice. It facilitates meditation, expedites the manifestation process, and strengthens the human energy field. Placed on any chakra, it provides balance to both overactive and stagnant energy centers. Quartz is protective, and it also provides inspiration and discipline on the spiritual path. Quartz can be programmed for virtually any intent for healing body, mind, and spirit.

Amphibole Quartz (Angel Phantom Quartz)

Formula: SiO_2 with amphibole $[AX_2Z_5(Si,Al,Ti)_8O_{22}(OH,F,Cl,O)_2]$, sometimes hematite (Fe_2O_3), limonite $(FeO \cdot nH_2O)$, and kaolinite $[Al_2Si_2O_5(OH)_4]$

Hardness: 6.5–7

Crystal system: trigonal (quartz), monoclinic, or orthorhombic (amphibole)

Formation process: igneous

Chakra: third eye, crown, soul star

Natural amphibole quartz

Physical healing: This crystal repairs the etheric body, thereby assisting recovery from injury and illness. It works more closely with the mind and spirit than the physical body.

Psychological healing: Amphibole quartz can help us process trauma and release the psychological and spiritual causes of imbalance and disease from the body, mind, and spirit. It is an introspective stone that brings a lighthearted sense of peace and joy.

Spiritual healing: The amphibole inside this variety of quartz sometimes resembles feathery angel wings, and indeed this crystal facilitates angelic communication and connection to the spiritual planes. Amphibole quartz purifies the causal body by burning off stale karma, especially when the quartz is colored red by traces of hematite. It can be used for cutting cords, aligning the subtle energy bodies, and reminding us to be of service to one another and to Source.

Elestial Quartz

Formula: SiO_2

Hardness: 6.5–7

Crystal system: trigonal

Formation process: igneous

Chakra: all, especially earth star, solar plexus

Brazilian elestial quartz crystal

Physical healing: Elestial quartz is a master healing stone. It retrieves information from the blueprint to shed light on why physical (and psychological and spiritual) imbalances occur. This crystal can lend grounding and strength to both the healer and the recipient, augmenting any healing session. It is sometimes used for treating conditions of the skeletal system and as an adjunct to medical treatment for cancer.

Psychological healing: This special crystal formation purges emotional and mental patterns that are repressed or stagnant. Placed on the solar plexus, it brings disharmony to the surface so that it can be released. The complexity of this quartz formation reminds us of the complexity of the subconscious mind; it allows you to safely explore what lies beneath the surface of your psyche.

Spiritual healing: Elestial crystals are transformational, alchemical, and evolutionary. This gemstone provides deeper insight into the trajectory of the soul's path, often revealing past-life information in doing so. Elestials are said to be gifts of the angels, and they can help us communicate with beings on the higher planes. This crystal can restructure the aura and chakras, updating them to reflect changes on our path and helping us integrate new frequencies that we receive from the higher planes. Elestials are soul-level healers that help us express the perfection of our spiritual blueprint.

Garden Quartz (Shaman Quartz, Dream Stone, Lodolite)

Formula: SiO_2 with various mineral inclusions, such as chlorite $[(Mg,Fe)_3(Si,Al)_4O_{10}(OH)_2 \cdot (Mg,Fe)_3(OH)_6]$, actinolite $[Ca_2(Mg,Fe)_5Si_8O_{22}(OH)_2]$, limonite $(FeO \cdot nH_2O)$, and rutile (TiO_2)

Hardness: 6.5–7

Crystal system: trigonal

Formation process: igneous

Chakra: all

A polished garden quartz crystal

Physical healing: The inclusions in garden quartz are cleansing, empowering, and tonifying to the physical body. This crystal supports the health of the thymus gland and overall immune function. It alleviates congestion and allergies too.

Psychological healing: Garden quartz magnifies the power of the imagination. This crystal formation helps us overcome boredom, promotes relaxation, and refreshes the mind. Garden quartz can also quell the pain of rejection, disappointment, and heartbreak; it allows us to be openhearted and vulnerable without fear or worry.

Spiritual healing: Garden quartz is both grounding and centering. It facilitates shamanic travel, dreamwork, visualization, and past-life recall. It eliminates negative energy and toxins from the environment and initiates contact with the spirits of the land. Work with it for karmic and ancestral healing, planetary healing, and extracting negative entities, cords, and foreign energies from the environment and the human energy field.

Herkimer Diamond Quartz

Formula: SiO_2, often contains carbon (C) and clay

Hardness: 7–7.5

Crystal system: trigonal

Formation process: sedimentary

Chakra: all, especially crown, soul star

Herkimer diamond quartz
from New York

Physical healing: Herkimer diamonds are excellent healing tools. They heal on all levels—body, mind, and soul. Working with this crystal formation provides pain relief, eases headaches, and promotes healing on the cellular level. This stone is detoxifying; it alleviates inflammation in the airways and provides better sleep. Herkimer diamond protects against radiation and is sometimes used to diminish the side effects of radiation therapy. It is a powerful regulator of the rhythm of the body and supports the homeostatic mechanisms within us.

Psychological healing: Herkimer diamond provides clarity, discernment, and focus. It also relieves stress.

Spiritual healing: This crystal is strongly activating to the aura and chakras. Herkimer diamond promotes spiritual awareness, enhances one's inner vision, and hastens the development of spiritual and psychic pursuits. It is an excellent dream stone, intensifying imagery in the dream state and fostering better remembrance of the content of one's dreams. Herkimer diamond engenders a sense of spiritual responsibility and is a wonderful stone to use in grids for planetary healing. Work with this crystal for shamanic journeying, astral travel, soul retrieval, and connecting to your spirit guides or angels. Herkimer diamond can be used to enhance and harmonize other crystals, thereby improving the results of your healing sessions.

Lemurian Seed Crystal

Formula: SiO_2

Hardness: 6.5–7

Crystal system: trigonal

Formation process: igneous

Chakra: all, especially heart, higher heart, crown, soul star

Lemurian seed crystal from Serro do Cabral, Brazil

Physical healing: In treating the physical body, Lemurian seed crystal tends to behave much like other quartz crystals (see the general entry for quartz above). It has a special affinity for the brain, nervous system, and heart.

Psychological healing: This crystal counteracts feelings of isolation and separation; it reminds us of the support of our families, both literal and spiritual. This variety of quartz strengthens ties to one's community and helps us feel more nurtured and loved.

Spiritual healing: Lemurian seed crystals are beacons of light, healing, and ancient wisdom in the modern world. They enable us to feel more connected to the natural world, and through this connection we find clearer communication with the higher self, spirit guides, and angelic beings. These stones promote karmic healing, especially concerning patterns that stem from lifetimes in Lemuria. They are excellent tools for psychic surgery, acting as wands or scalpels to cut cords, remove attachments, seal the aura, and create sacred space for healing.

Lithium Quartz

Formula: SiO_2 with traces of lithium (Li) and other minerals

Hardness: 6.5–7

Crystal system: trigonal

Formation process: igneous

Chakra: all, especially higher heart

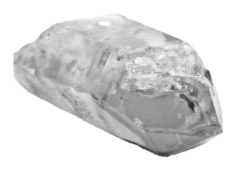

Natural lithium quartz

Physical healing: Although this quartz contains very little lithium, it has similar (albeit subtler) effects as other lithium-bearing minerals; the quartz simply amplifies the effects of the lithium inclusions. This stone is a master healer, acting as a restorative tool on all levels of the body, mind, and spirit. It is adept at pain relief, especially radiating pain such as sciatica. It diffuses tension and eases stress-related illness. Lithium quartz can help ease end-of-life transitions.

Psychological healing: Lithium quartz addresses mental and emotional imbalances, including depression, bipolar disorder, anxiety and panic disorders, nervousness, anger, shyness, unrest, grief, and abandonment. It relieves interpersonal tension and helps heal relationships.

Spiritual healing: Lithium quartz is supremely balancing. It moderates the yin-yang, masculine-feminine polarities within each of us. This formation also helps tease out deeply hidden past-life information and can help release our attachments to outcomes. Lithium quartz is purifying to the aura, balances all the chakras, and clears out the central channel of the spiritual anatomy. It enhances meditation, induces surrender, and helps us attune to higher consciousness.

Phantom Quartz

Formula: SiO_2 with various minerals

Hardness: 6.5–7

Crystal system: trigonal

Formation process: igneous, sedimentary, or metamorphic

Chakra: all (varies by mineral content)

Natural phantom quartz
from Arizona

Physical healing: Phantom quartz crystal supports the overall growth and development of the body. It is helpful for gaining insight into developmental disorders or chronic conditions that have their roots in childhood. This crystal formation can treat congestion in the lungs as well as seizures. Phantom crystals will exhibit the properties of the mineral(s) contained within them.

Psychological healing: Phantom crystals are excellent tools for sifting through the subconscious. These crystals facilitate exploring the shadow self and the inner child; they often point toward aspects of the self that need more love and support. Phantom crystals can also help enforce healthy boundaries.

Spiritual healing: Phantom quartz facilitates past-life recall, enhances karmic healing, and grants access to the Akashic records. It supports meditation, psychic development, and spiritual growth.

Rose Quartz

Formula: SiO_2 with with trace minerals

Hardness: 7

Crystal system: trigonal

Formation process: igneous

Chakra: heart

Polished rose quartz

Physical healing: Rose quartz addresses conditions of the skin and heart. It promotes a healthy complexion, slows a rapid pulse, and releases tightness in the muscles and joints. Rose quartz promotes healthy circulation, heals conditions of the reproductive organs, and restores fertility. This gemstone clears away emotional patterns that collect in the physical body.

Psychological healing: Rose quartz is nourishing to the heart chakra and emotional body. It teaches self-love, forgiveness, compassion, and tenderness. It is ideal for people who repress or have difficulty expressing emotions. It promotes sensitivity and empathy but can also help us enforce healthy boundaries. When needed, rose quartz helps us stand firm and offer tough love to those who might take advantage of our generosity and kindness.

Spiritual healing: Rose quartz reminds us that we are the product of love. It invites more love and appreciation into our lives and can also attract romance.

It instills strength through service and initiates cleansing of the emotional body in the aura. Use rose quartz to sort emotional patterns out of the physical body and back into the emotional body.

Rutilated Quartz

Formula: SiO_2 with rutile (TiO_2)

Hardness: 7

Crystal system: trigonal (quartz), tetragonal (rutile)

Formation process: igneous

Chakra: all

Tumbled
rutilated quartz

Physical healing: Rutilated quartz occurs when needles of rutile penetrate quartz. This mineral is an effective tool for achieving breakthrough healing and is considered to be generally energizing, restorative, and regenerative. Rutilated quartz stimulates hair growth, encourages the healing of wounds, and counteracts the side effects of radiation therapy. This stone can also treat numbness, pain, and carpal tunnel syndrome.

Psychological healing: Working with rutilated quartz enhances communication, as each needle of rutile works like an antenna to boost the signals being sent and received, whether they are verbal, psychic, or otherwise related to communication. It encourages better listening skills, thereby deepening all kinds of relationships.

Spiritual healing: Rutilated quartz enhances personal magnetism, expands the aura, and supports manifestation and healing on all levels. It is a strongly creative stone, as it is a beacon for receiving inspiration from the higher realms.

Scepter Quartz

Formula: SiO_2

Hardness: 6.5–7

Crystal system: trigonal

Formation process: igneous, sedimentary, or metamorphic

Chakra: all, especially solar plexus, heart

Natural scepter crystal

Physical healing: Scepter crystal can break up blockages, stagnation, and inflammation in the physical body as well as the nonphysical bodies. Additionally, it can regulate the hormonal balance of the body and is helpful for treating sexual dysfunction, particularly in men.

Psychological healing: This quartz formation helps us stand firm, boosting confidence and empowering us to take responsibility for and ownership of life. These stones inspire good leadership skills and ignite action. They are helpful for addressing the misalignment of the will. These stones plant the seeds of respect and wisdom and help us engage these skills in all our actions.

Spiritual healing: Scepter crystals point toward the root of a condition, whether physical, psychological, or spiritual, even when the origin is unknown. Because of this they are sensitive tools that can help the healer connect to the client and direct healing into the heart of the matter at hand.

Smoky Quartz

Formula: SiO_2 with traces of aluminum (Al), lithium (Li), and/or sodium (Na)

Hardness: 7

Crystal system: trigonal

Formation process: igneous

Chakra: root

Natural smoky quartz from Montana

Physical healing: Smoky quartz is grounding and helpful in the overall healing of the physical body. Specifically, it promotes better sleep, lowers high blood pressure, alleviates pain (especially carpal tunnel syndrome), and soothes sunburn. Smoky quartz offers protection from electromagnetic radiation, such as from electronics and appliances, and it promotes clear airways, making it effective for treating asthma. Smoky quartz also encourages the health of the male reproductive system.

Psychological healing: This form of quartz provides focus and clarity and supports intelligence. It is a capable antistress stone and is helpful for people who often feel too spacy and ungrounded. Smoky quartz imparts diplomacy and empowers one to take control of life.

Spiritual healing: Smoky quartz is an ideal tool during times of transition and transformation, both personal and planetary. It consolidates energy and resources and promotes the overall health of the aura and chakras by releasing foreign entities and transmuting disharmony. Smoky quartz catalyzes the manifestation process by anchoring higher consciousness on the material plane.

Spirit Quartz (Cactus Quartz)

Formula: SiO_2 with iron (Fe)

Hardness: 6.5–7

Crystal system: trigonal

Formation process: igneous

Chakra: third eye, crown, soul star

Spirit quartz from South Africa

Physical healing: Spirit quartz generally demonstrates the same physical healing properties as amethyst. Additionally, it may be helpful for conditions affecting the skin as well as for harmonizing the various systems of the body. It promotes the health of the brain and central nervous system.

Psychological healing: Spirit quartz uplifts the mood. It invites cooperation and harmony while simultaneously sweeping away fear and pain. This form of quartz promotes generosity and compassion.

Spiritual healing: Spirit quartz is deeply transformative on the spiritual level. A powerful karmic healer, it transmutes old karma, initiates past-life recall, and highlights your soul family across your many incarnations. It instills group harmony and is ideal for planetary healing. Spirit quartz also draws abundance.

Tangerine Quartz

Formula: SiO_2 with iron compounds (Fe or Fe_2O_3)

Hardness: 6.5–7

Crystal system: trigonal

Formation process: igneous

Chakra: sacral

Tangerine quartz from Brazil

Physical healing: Tangerine quartz is enlivening and stimulating to the endocrine system. This form of quartz also supports the health of the liver and treats conditions of the reproductive system.

Psychological healing: This orange variety of quartz invites optimism and warmth. It is a stone of self-confidence, as it overrides feelings of inadequacy and fear of the unknown. Tangerine quartz also feeds the inner child, thereby inspiring joy, creativity, and playfulness.

Spiritual healing: Tangerine quartz initiates greater alignment among the subtle bodies. It enhances clairvoyance and encourages one to act on information gleaned via psychic and intuitive resources.

Tibetan Quartz (Tibetan Black Quartz)

Formula: SiO_2 with inclusions

Hardness: 6.5–7

Crystal system: trigonal

Formation process: igneous or sedimentary

Chakra: all, especially crown, soul star

Double-terminated quartz from Tibet

Physical healing: Tibetan quartz often exhibits dark inclusions and phantoms of other minerals. It supports the health of the nervous system (particularly the vagus nerve) and helps the body draw on reserves of spiritual energy to repair and regenerate the physical body. It is sometimes used in the treatment of eating disorders.

Psychological healing: Tibetan quartz promotes better relationships; it decreases codependent tendencies while strengthening sympathy, compassion, and generosity. This stone helps one break limiting habits and mental-emotional patterns.

Spiritual healing: Tibetan quartz encourages one to cultivate a healthy sense of detachment, thereby eliminating the suffering that comes from overidentification with the ego. It has a high and clear vibration that accelerates spiritual growth. This stone opens the mind, magnifies psychic and intuitive abilities, and facilitates contact with spiritual beings. Tibetan quartz is both protective and purifying. It strengthens the aura and makes it more resilient. This crystal formation clears and protects all of our nonphysical anatomy: the bodies of the aura, the chakras, the meridians, and the nadis. It enhances meditation, augments chanting or mantra practice, and promotes greater clarity and insight. It facilitates connection to the Akashic records and assists in past-life recall. Working with Tibetan quartz instills a greater sense of justice, social responsibility, and equality; it makes an ideal stone for planetary healing.

Tourmalinated Quartz

Formula: SiO_2 with tourmaline (usually schorl) [$Na(Fe,Mn)_3Al_6B_3Si_6O_{27}(OH)_3(OH,F)$]

Hardness: 6.5–7

Crystal system: trigonal

Formation process: igneous

Chakra: all, especially earth star, soul star

Tumbled quartz with tourmaline inclusions

Physical healing: Tourmalinated quartz reduces pain, lowers blood pressure, and alleviates physical tension. Placing or wearing this stone over the chest can improve respiration, particularly wheezing and coughing from asthma, allergies, and bronchitis. It improves the function of the eliminatory system and offers support during dieting, fasting, and cleanses.

Psychological healing: Tourmalinated quartz has a harmonizing effect on the mind and emotions. It reduces depression and sadness and eases internal conflict. Work with this crystal formation to clear confusion, as it assists in identifying and releasing disharmonious mental and emotional patterns.

Spiritual healing: Tourmalinated quartz is strongly purifying; it's like an etheric vacuum cleaner for the aura and chakras. This stone can be employed to release blockages, stagnant energies, and attachments. It resolves imbalances in yin and yang energies to create longlasting harmony. It can be used to repair defects in the aura such as tears, holes, leaks, and cords.

White Quartz (Snow Quartz, Milky Quartz, Quartzite)

Formula: SiO_2

Hardness: 6.5–7

Crystal system: trigonal

Formation process: igneous, sedimentary, or metamorphic

Chakra: all

Raw white quartz from Wales

Physical healing: White quartz has a slowing and stabilizing effect on the body. It has a long tradition of being used for healing overall, and it helps maintain the effects of other gemstones and healing modalities. White quartz is used to treat conditions affecting the lungs, particularly shortness of breath, as well as for decreasing an overactive metabolism.

Psychological healing: Psychologically, white quartz is cooling, stabilizing, and dampening. It calms the temper and stills an overactive mind. Work with white quartz when faced with lack of discipline, poor endurance, or ADHD. It also enhances the imagination.

Spiritual healing: White quartz anchors and maintains the positive changes we make in all aspects of life. Wear or carry white quartz when it feels as though life is moving too quickly; it helps to slow the rate of our development so that we can catch up.

Rhodochrosite

Formula: $MnCO_3$

Hardness: 3.5–4

Crystal system: trigonal

Formation process: sedimentary

Chakra: solar plexus, heart

Polished cross-section of rhodochrosite stalactite

Physical healing: Rhodochrosite improves the health of the circulatory system, promotes elasticity of the blood vessels, and regulates blood pressure. This gemstone can restore libido, treat acute hearing loss, and address overall weakness and lethargy.

Psychological healing: Rhodochrosite is the quintessential stone of healing the inner child. It encourages forgiveness, spontaneity, and joy. This gemstone clears emotional debris from the chakras and aura, sorting it into the correct layers of the aura itself and thus bringing clarity and understanding to emotional patterns in one's life. It reveals old wounds, often from childhood and past lives, that continue to play out in our current life scenarios. It neutralizes destructive habits and conditioning. This stone also enables expression of feelings, especially erotic and passionate ones.

Spiritual healing: Rhodochrosite is a powerful stone for developing freedom, for it sweeps away old patterns and karmic ties and grants a blank slate. It helps one exercise compassion and creativity, and it renews passion for life itself. Its compassionate energy also resolves longstanding karmic patterns, including ancestral and global karma. It fosters self-confidence and promotes humanitarianism.

Rhodonite

Formula: MnSiO$_3$

Hardness: 5.5–6.5

Crystal system: triclinic

Formation process: metamorphic

Chakra: root, heart

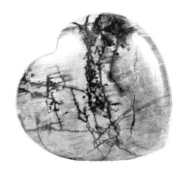

Polished rhodonite heart

Physical healing: Rhodonite's formation process resembles the body's response to cuts, scrapes, and other open wounds, making it a first-aid stone par excellence. It heals wounds, mends broken bones, and reduces bruises and inflammation. Rhodonite can facilitate weight loss, decrease the severity of menopause, dissipate blood clots, and counteract the effects of overexertion. It can be used to alleviate allergies and bronchitis, as well as to promote healthy digestion.

Psychological healing: This gemstone is my favorite tool for emotional balance. It grounds and fortifies the emotional body, lending stability and order to the emotional patterns contained therein. It resolves anxiety, nervousness, mania, and fear. Rhodonite also treats phobias and enhances feelings of self-worth. It promotes healthy romantic relationships and emotional fortitude, lending stamina to the healing of emotional wounds.

Spiritual healing: Because it is so stabilizing for the emotions, rhodonite makes room for greater clarity and understanding of current life scenarios; eventually this leads to a greater understanding of one's life purpose. Rhodonite also encourages altruism and generosity, and it helps draw out one's innate skills and talents so that they can be applied to healing, spiritual growth, and transformation.

Ruby

Formula: Al₂O₃ with traces of chromium (Cr)

Hardness: 9

Crystal system: trigonal

Formation process: metamorphic or igneous

Chakra: root, heart

Natural ruby crystal

Physical healing: Ruby revitalizes, tones, and strengthens the body. It resonates with muscle tissue, fortifies the heart, and promotes cardiovascular health. Use ruby to accelerate the healing of wounds and to recover after the loss of blood. This red stone infuses the physical body with the life force, thereby combatting fatigue and lethargy. Ruby supports the health of the spleen, adrenals, and reproductive organs. It fights infection by initiating a fever to help the body stop the invading pathogens.

Psychological healing: Ruby is as invigorating to the mind as it is to the body. It generates emotional strength, often providing the stamina and resolve needed to face difficult situations. Ruby helps you breathe through pain, whether emotional or physical, thereby clearing the heart of stale emotions. This gemstone fosters decisive action and heightens physical attraction, passion, and sensuality. Ruby counteracts depression and psychosomatic illness.

Spiritual healing: Ruby initiates movement of the life force in the body, mind, and spirit. It strengthens and activates the root chakra and provides protection to the heart chakra. It activates kundalini energy coiled at the base of the spine. Ruby can be used to gain a better understanding of divine love, and it prevents stagnation in the aura.

Ruby in Zoisite (Anyolite)

Formula: Al_2O_3 with traces of chromium (Cr) in green zoisite $[Ca_2Al_3(SiO_4)(Si_2O_7)O(OH)]$ with pargasite $[NaCa_2(Mg_4Al)(Si_6Al_2)O_{22}(OH)_2]$

Hardness: 9

Crystal system: trigonal (ruby), orthorhombic (zoisite), monoclinic (pargasite)

Formation process: metamorphic

Chakra: root, heart

Tumbled ruby in zoisite

Physical healing: Ruby in zoisite is an excellent stone for treating the heart and circulatory system. It has a generally regenerative, fortifying, and energizing effect on the physical body, thereby making it adept at aiding recovery after injury and healing both chronic and acute illnesses. This combination of minerals promotes fertility and may be used to treat conditions of the reproductive system.

Psychological healing: This metamorphic rock brings movement to the emotional body, helping to release stagnant emotions. It instills compassion and empathy, thereby displacing discord and disagreement. Work with this gemstone to release long-held emotional trauma as well as to invite forgiveness and reconciliation. Ruby in zoisite promotes passion and understanding in romantic relationships.

Spiritual healing: Ruby in zoisite's primary mission is to bring complementary energies into harmony. It can balance yin and yang energies while also inspiring us to realize our dreams. This gemstone eliminates roadblocks on the path toward spiritual development. It can be used to promote communication with spiritual guides, release energies rooted in past lives, and promote joy.

Sapphire

Formula: Al_2O_3

Hardness: 9

Crystal system: trigonal

Formation process: igneous or metamorphic

Chakra: throat, third eye

Blue sapphire from Sri Lanka

Physical healing: Sapphire—blue sapphire in particular—supports the health of the nervous system and sense organs, especially the eyes. It can be used to treat conditions affecting the myelin sheaths around the nerves and the walls of blood vessels. Processes in the body involving movement are nourished by this gem; it works on any vessel that carries or moves a substance or message. Blue sapphire is often used to treat headaches, conditions that affect balance, and parasitic infections. It also treats neurological disorders and improves cognitive function and chronic degenerative conditions. Sapphire supports weight loss as well.

Psychological healing: Blue sapphire is perhaps the most nourishing gemstone for the mind and the mental body. It improves mental clarity and focus while also enhancing mental strength and discipline. Sapphire improves self-control and assuages gullibility. It is a great aid to studying and learning any subject.

Spiritual healing: Spiritually, sapphire is expansive and enlightening. It helps you become the empty vessel, releasing attachments and ego in the process. Blue sapphire promotes better communication with the higher realms and supports the pursuit of spiritual power. Meditating with or wearing blue sapphire imparts a sense of inner peace and improves psychic abilities. This gemstone deepens spiritual practice, especially meditation, and helps you act with integrity in all areas of life. Sapphire helps you synthesize wisdom from knowledge and instills a sense of celestial hope.

Scapolite

Formula: varies from $Na_4Al_3Si_9O_{24}Cl$ to $Ca_4Al_6Si_6O_{24}CO_3$

Hardness: 5–6

Crystal system: tetragonal

Formation process: igneous or metamorphic

Chakra: third eye

Brazilian scapolite

Physical healing: Scapolite nourishes the eyes and has been used in the treatment of glaucoma and cataracts. This gemstone supports the function of the urinary tract, especially the kidneys and bladder, and it treats incontinence. Scapolite promotes the alignment of the body and alleviates tension held in the shoulders, neck, and upper back. This stone is also used to treat disorders of the bones. It is an excellent stone for recovery from illness, injury, or surgery. Since scapolite restores flexibility and movement to the body, it is an effective adjunct to physical therapy.

Psychological healing: This stone strengthens the intellect and willpower. It enhances analytical pursuits and fosters self-reflection. Scapolite encourages independence and liberates one from obsession, denial, and fear. It assists in making changes, attaining goals, and breaking bad habits by encouraging self-reflection and follow-through on the goals themselves. Scapolite assists in overcoming self-sabotage, especially stemming from guilt and shame. It is an excellent stone for writers.

Spiritual healing: Scapolite weaves together the gifts of the intellect with the intuition. It fosters spiritual freedom, allowing you to pursue what brings you true happiness. It deepens your awareness of your life path and helps you engage all of your skills to attain your soul's purpose on earth. This mineral encourages trust in the process of self-realization and transformation. Scapolite encourages you to allow life to unfold rather than rushing through it. It facilitates astral travel and communication with other realms. Scapolite permits you to see how you fit in the big picture and how you relate to all other forms of life, including the spiritual beings in your environment.

Selenite (Gypsum)

Formula: $CaSO_4 \cdot 2H_2O$

Hardness: 2

Crystal system: monoclinic

Formation process: sedimentary

Chakra: crown, soul star

Twinned selenite
from Mexico

Physical healing: Selenite (crystalline gypsum) supports the alignment of the spine. It can be used for treating infection or injury of the nerves and spine. It also helps regulate the movement and function of bodily fluids. Selenite is effective at addressing neurological conditions and supports the overall health of the nervous system. It has a clarifying effect on the skin and is used for treating burns, wrinkles, and dry skin in Chinese medicine.

Psychological healing: The water content of selenite initiates emotional release and balance. It clarifies confusing emotions and draws light to the subconscious. Working with selenite improves judgment and encourages insight.

Spiritual healing: Selenite actively opens the crown chakra and aligns it with the higher transpersonal chakras. This facilitates contact with the higher self and encourages you to trust your inner guidance. It is among the most potent tools for clearing the aura; when swiped or brushed through the energy field, selenite dislodges negativity and transforms it with its lofty vibrations. Selenite enhances meditation and catalyzes psychic development.

Desert Rose Selenite

Formula: $CaSO_4 \cdot 2H_2O$ with sand inclusions

Hardness: 2

Crystal system: monoclinic

Formation process: sedimentary

Chakra: solar plexus, heart, crown, earth star

Natural
desert rose crystals

Physical healing: Desert rose selenite is gently detoxifying. It promotes fertility, relieves fatigue, and promotes the health of connective tissues.

Psychological healing: These selenite formations are playful, joyful, and loving. They can attract love, deepen our appreciation for life, and allow us to see more magic in the everyday world. Desert roses can boost mental healing, especially by releasing old patterns of belief and replacing them with healthy ones.

Spiritual healing: Desert rose formations are deeply linked to the spirit world and the energy of Mother Earth. They can be used to provide protection to your home or land, and when added to grids they support the well-being of the whole planet. Desert rose allows unconditional love and compassion to blossom within us.

Golden Selenite

Formula: $CaSO_4 \cdot 2H_2O$

Hardness: 2

Crystal system: monoclinic

Formation process: sedimentary

Chakra: solar plexus, crown, soul star

Golden selenite
from Texas

Physical healing: Golden selenite promotes all-around physical healing, especially healthy hair and nails. It can also be helpful for the urinary tract, particularly the bladder. The bright, luminous energy of this stone alleviates seasonal affective disorder and fatigue.

Psychological healing: Golden selenite is clarifying to the mind, countering doubt, confusion, and indecision. It reduces critical and judgmental tendencies, leading us instead to a more positive outlook that seeks opportunity. Golden selenite is a strong boost to the will.

Spiritual healing: Of all members of the selenite group, golden selenite is the most balancing of the masculine and feminine energies—it feels like the sun and moon in one stone. Golden selenite also helps us remain objective and detached when faced with trauma, transition, or pain; it allows us to choose to grow in all moments. This stone aligns the human will with Divine Will.

Satin Spar Selenite

Formula: $CaSO_4 \cdot 2H_2O$

Hardness: 2

Crystal system: monoclinic

Formation process: sedimentary

Chakra: crown,
soul star

Polished satin spar selenite

Physical healing: In addition to displaying the general properties of selenite, satin spar works mostly to bring light to the physical body, thereby releasing blockages, softening tightness, and alleviating pain.

Psychological healing: This fibrous form of selenite improves clarity, focus, and perception. It can be helpful in healing cases of fear, obsession, and anxiety.

Spiritual healing: Satin spar offers a much gentler energy than transparent, crystalline selenite. Because it is porous and fiber optic, it is adept at drawing out stagnant energies from the aura and chakras. It also helps us learn to relinquish control in life. It is a visionary stone that enhances psychic development and meditation.

Seraphinite
(Clinochlore)

Formula: $(Mg,Fe^{2+})_5Al_2Si_3O_{10}(OH)_8$

Hardness: 2–2.5

Crystal system: monoclinic

Formation process: metamorphic

Chakra: all, especially heart, crown

Tumbled seraphinite

Physical healing: Seraphinite, a variety of the mineral clinochlore, is one of the best overall healing stones for the physical body. It corrects systemic imbalances, promotes regeneration at the cellular level, and strengthens the homeostatic mechanisms of the body. This gemstone can support immune health and is used to treat autoimmune conditions. Among these disorders, seraphinite is most effective at treating allergies, and it can bring relief to sinus pressure and congestion. This stone regulates body temperature and dissipates stiffness and tension. It can be used as an adjunct in cancer treatment to regulate the growth of cancerous cells and assist in recovering from medical treatment.

Psychological healing: Seraphinite treats imbalances of the mind and emotions, including obsessive-compulsive disorder. It dissolves feelings of betrayal and helps mend a broken heart after rejection.

Spiritual healing: Seraphinite strengthens and purifies the spiritual anatomy much the way it does the physical body. It facilitates contact with higher realms, especially angels, devas, and spirit guides. Seraphinite helps us integrate rapid spiritual changes, as it aligns the physical and the nonphysical bodies. This gemstone initiates the rise of kundalini energy and clears and activates each of the chakras. It invites lightness of spirit as it supplants chaos with order. It confers confidence and greater spiritual attunement. Seraphinite supports planetary healing.

Serpentine

Formula: $(Mg,Fe)_3Si_2O_5(OH)_4$

Hardness: 2–5

Crystal system: monoclinic

Formation process: metamorphic

Chakra: root

Tumbled serpentine

Physical healing: Serpentine mobilizes and strengthens the immune system. It promotes healthy digestion and elimination and regulates mineral absorption. Traditionally serpentine has been used to heal the bites and stings of venomous creatures; it also treats infections, parasites, and candidiasis. Serpentine encourages flexibility of the physical body and eases cramps and pain, including menstrual symptoms. This stone promotes the growth and rejuvenation of physical tissue and is sometimes used to treat the symptoms of diabetes.

Psychological healing: Serpentine's initial effects resemble those of jade—it brings clarity and inspiration. This stone encourages compromise and creative problem-solving skills. It also stabilizes mood swings.

Spiritual healing: Serpentine awakens ancient wisdom and attunement to the natural world. It breaks up stagnant energy and is gently protective. The formation process of serpentine has an upward trajectory; similarly, it promotes ascending energy in the body and aura. This makes it an excellent stone to awaken the kundalini energy sleeping at the base of the spine. It is grounding and will gently open any of the chakras. This stone catalyzes spiritual growth and provides insight into karmic and ancestral patterns. It can initiate past-life recall and facilitate connecting with the Akashic records.

Shungite

Formula: mostly elemental carbon (C)
Crystal system: amorphous
Formation process: metamorphic
Chakra: earth star, root

Raw noble shungite

Physical healing: Shungite is a versatile healing tool that can be used to treat conditions of the skin, digestive system, and eliminatory system. It reduces pain and inflammation and promotes healthy cellular division. Shungite protects against harmful energies in the environment, including electromagnetic pollution, and it is gently grounding to the physical body. This mineral also enlivens the electrical processes of the physical body.

Psychological healing: Shungite acts as a sponge, filtering out disharmonious mental and emotional patterns from one's psyche. It draws out overactive emotional patterns and can be used to calm states of worry and panic. Shungite can also encourage planning (and subsequently acting on one's plans).

Spiritual healing: Shungite is a dynamic grounding stone. It helps us learn to organize and give form to our thoughts, feelings, and dreams, thereby facilitating the manifestation process. It is an evolutionary gemstone that can initiate healing on the blueprint level. Shungite catalyzes purification and restores balance and structure to water—use it as an elixir to reap these benefits. This mineral is protective on many levels, and it can be used to prevent disruptions of your life path that come from external sources. It encourages decisions that help you fulfill your purpose on earth.

Smithsonite

Formula: $ZnCO_3$

Hardness: 5

Crystal system: trigonal

Formation process: sedimentary

Chakra: sacral

Botryoidal smithsonite
from New Mexico

Physical healing: Smithsonite balances the endocrine system and regulates hormonal balance. It supports a healthy metabolism and assists in weight loss. This mineral also promotes fertility and healthy skin. It can accelerate the healing of wounds, especially those related to diabetes.

Psychological healing: Smithsonite is sweet, loving, and gentle. It soothes stress and is a balm for grief, heartache, and worry. This stone helps in recovering from abuse, and it can mitigate shyness. It is the preeminent stone for accepting and expressing one's gender identity and sexual orientation because it integrates an understanding of gender from the soul's perspective. Since the soul is neither male nor female and has been in many bodies over many lifetimes, smithsonite can alleviate gender dysphoria. Additionally, its zinc content supports the healthy expression of sexuality and romantic passion; this stone channels sexual urges into appropriate avenues of expression.

Spiritual healing: Smithsonite shifts our awareness away from ego-based love into unconditional love. It nourishes the inner child and facilitates contact with the angelic realm.

Sodalite

Formula: $Na_8Al_6Si_6O_{24}Cl_2$

Hardness: 5.5–6

Crystal system: cubic

Formation process: igneous or metamorphic

Chakra: throat, third eye

Polished sodalite

Physical healing: Sodalite promotes the health of the lymphatic and immune systems and regulates the bodily fluids. This gemstone treats conditions affecting the throat and larynx, such as sore throat or loss of voice. It overcomes sluggishness, depression, and insomnia. Sodalite also promotes skeletal health and can be used to treat broken bones as well as other conditions affecting the bones, teeth, cartilage, and ligaments.

Psychological healing: Sodalite is extremely purifying to the mental body. It encourages the expression of bottled-up emotions that cause confusion and psychological imbalance. It is a window into the subconscious, and it initiates the pursuit and understanding of personal truth. This gemstone enables you to freely express your personality and empowers you to stand up for your beliefs. Sodalite can clarify your goals and bring order and awareness to the mind. It is a stone of perception—it helps you observe dispassionately.

Spiritual healing: Sodalite enhances intuition and psychic development. Clear, gemmy forms of sodalite are among the most nourishing stones for the third eye chakra. This stone shifts your awareness to the present moment, the eternal now, to set the stage for authentic spiritual practice and personal development. It promotes idealism, the pursuit of higher truth, and a state of nonjudgment. It is a gentle and reliable guide on your spiritual journey.

Spinel

Formula: MgAl₂O₄

Hardness: 7.5–8

Crystal system: cubic

Formation process: igneous or metamorphic

Chakra: earth star, root, solar plexus, heart

Vietnamese spinel

Physical healing: Spinel has an invigorating energy that helps tone and regenerate the entire body. This stone is grounding, thereby anchoring the positive changes it facilitates. Spinel strengthens the homeostatic mechanisms of the body and supports functions related to rhythm and timing, including the circulatory and digestive systems. Spinel strengthens muscle tissue and relieves numbness, tingling, and paralysis in the extremities.

Psychological healing: Spinel facilitates the release of deeply seated emotions, especially fear, pain, and anger stemming from childhood. Its rhythmic nature allows it to regulate the emotions and memories being purged, thus preventing you from feeling overwhelmed. It reaches into your memories to draw out the positive ones as a means of offering comfort and relief from the release of old traumas. Spinel boosts self-confidence, eases depression, and helps you find fulfilment. This gemstone invites you to exercise healthy boundaries and learn to delegate effectively.

Spiritual healing: Working with spinel invites optimism and compassion, thereby steering you toward true happiness. It allows you to perceive hope in the midst of uncertainty and helps you cultivate greater balance and stability in your spiritual practice. Spinel also promotes tolerance and acceptance, making it an ideal stone for healing much of the discord, conflict, and oppression facing our world today.

Stilbite

Formula: NaCa$_4$(Si$_{27}$Al$_9$)O$_{72}$·28(H$_2$O)

Hardness: 3.5–4

Crystal system: monoclinic

Formation process: igneous, sedimentary, or metamorphic

Chakra: solar plexus, heart, crown

Polished stilbite

Physical healing: Working with stilbite supports the health of the intestines, nervous system, kidneys, and brain. It balances the hemispheres of the brain, improves cellular metabolism, and enhances the health of the sensory organs, particularly those related to taste and smell. It can be used to treat a sore throat. Make an elixir of stilbite by indirect means to detoxify environmental poisons and toxins in the diet; this elixir may be sprayed in the environment, applied topically, or taken internally. Stilbite is also helpful for people with learning disabilities.

Psychological healing: Stilbite exudes a calming, gentle energy. This mineral promotes self-inquiry, helping you get to the root of fear, anxiety, guilt, and unrest. Its absorptive nature releases bottled-up emotions while clearing confusion and granting you permission to truly feel whatever emotions arise.

Spiritual healing: As a stone of spiritual healing, stilbite invites authentic forgiveness and compassion. It dispels illusion and delusion alike, reminding us of spiritual truth and navigating us toward authenticity and integrity. It wards off separation and isolation by helping us embrace vulnerability as a form of true strength. Stilbite helps us maintain a trajectory of spiritual growth, enabling us to follow our dreams. It invites us to cultivate a healthy amount of detachment from our pain, thereby releasing patterns of suffering and chaos.

Sugilite

Formula: $KNa_2(Fe, Mn, Al)_2Li_3Si_{12}O_{30}$

Hardness: 6–6.5

Crystal system: hexagonal

Formation process: igneous or metamorphic

Chakra: heart, third eye, crown, higher heart

Tumbled
sugilite

Physical healing: Sugilite is an effective stone for neurological conditions. It induces more restful sleep and is thus used to treat insomnia. Sugilite is sometimes recommended for the treatment of cancer, although it is not a substitute for medical treatment. This gemstone alleviates allergies (especially food-based sensitivities) and provides support against environmental toxins. It can also be used for relieving toothache.

Psychological healing: This lithium-rich mineral is soothing and peaceful. It can be used as an adjunct for the treatment of anxiety, depression, and bipolar disorder. It stabilizes the heart chakra, where its peace and hopefulness displace fear and feelings of being overwhelmed. Sugilite can be helpful for learning disorders and for releasing trauma.

Spiritual healing: Sugilite clears out toxic accumulations in the aura and chakras. Wearing sugilite not only clears the energy field, but it also provides additional protection and light, helping one transmute harmful energies, such as negative thoughts and emotions, energy vampires, and other sources of psychic harm. Sugilite augments the dream state; it is a visionary stone that improves intuition and psychic skills.

Sunstone

Formula: (Na,Ca)Al(Si,Al)Si$_2$O$_8$ (oligoclase) or K(AlSi$_3$O$_8$) (microcline) with inclusions of hematite (Fe$_2$O$_3$) or copper (Cu)

Hardness: 6–6.5

Crystal system: triclinic

Formation process: igneous or metamorphic

Chakra: sacral, solar plexus

Tumbled sunstone

Physical healing: This member of the feldspar group supports the health of the nervous and circulatory systems. It warms cold extremities and counteracts low blood pressure. It is beneficial for treating seasonal affective disorder and general physical weakness.

Psychological healing: Sunstone represents the solar archetype; it fosters success, joy, optimism, action, and motivation. This gemstone promotes healthy discrimination; it can help you make healthy decisions for your body, mind, and soul. It raises your self-worth and self-esteem and is the quintessential stone for fostering leadership. Sunstone can also help resolve depression.

Spiritual healing: Sunstone encourages you to stay true to yourself. It awakens the causal body, thereby supporting memory.

Tanzanite

Formula: $Ca_2Al_3(SiO_4)(Si_2O_7)O(OH)$

Hardness: 6–7

Crystal system: orthorhombic

Formation process: metamorphic

Chakra: all, especially heart, third eye, crown, soul star

Raw tanzanite

Physical healing: Tanzanite is effective at treating conditions of the nervous system, kidneys, gallbladder, and endocrine system. It is especially adept at balancing an overactive thyroid and adrenals; it can also be used to promote healthy weight loss or gain. Tanzanite is employed in the treatment of the eyes, ears, nose, and throat.

Psychological healing: Tanzanite is an important stone for synchronizing the heart and mind. It alleviates worry, strengthens memory, and imparts both curiosity and wonder. This mineral is helpful when you are experiencing a combination of an overactive mind and underactive emotions, helping to normalize the balance of these two aspects of the self. Tanzanite can also intensify the imagination and promote restful sleep.

Spiritual healing: This gemstone cultivates compassion, loving-kindness, and commitment to truth. It is a deeply spiritual stone that helps you develop your psychic and intuitive faculties with ease and joy. Connecting to tanzanite offers spiritual purification, deepens meditation, and improves visualization. This gemstone strengthens the structure of the chakra vortexes themselves, thus improving the health of the chakra system as a whole. It helps you find greater meaning in life and assists you in exploring the origin and trajectory of your soul.

Tektite (Indochinite)

Formula: mostly SiO_2

Hardness: 5.5–6.5

Crystal system: amorphous

Formation process: metamorphic

Chakra: all

Polished indochinite tektite

Physical healing: Tektite's amorphous structure allows it to support the health of the circulatory system. Since it is formed as a result of foreign matter—specifically meteorites—hitting the earth, it is helpful in ridding the body and energy field of foreign entities, including infection and parasites. Tektite is strengthening to the physical body. It accelerates all-around physical healing, protects against harmful radiation, and reduces fever.

Psychological healing: One of tektite's principal gifts is fearlessness. It helps us face the unknown and is thus helpful in cases of phobia, anxiety, and panic. It is adept at releasing repressed emotions. Tektite also promotes friendship, helping us bond more deeply over spiritual matters.

Spiritual healing: Tektite leads us to a recognition of our spiritual self. It balances polarities within us, combats materialism and ego, and teaches us the value of surrender. Tektite boosts psychic senses, enhances meditation and visualization, promotes astral travel, and corrects deficiencies in the chakra system. Tektite can be worn to improve communication with spirit guides and angels to augment your ability to channel wisdom.

Tiger's Eye

Formula: SiO_2 with crocidolite
$[Na_2(Fe^{2+}{}_3Fe^{3+}{}_2)Si_8O_{22}(OH)_2]$ and iron (Fe)
Hardness: 7
Crystal system: trigonal
Formation process: sedimentary
Chakra: solar plexus, third eye

Tumbled tiger's eye

Physical healing: Tiger's eye is recommended for pain relief, lethargy, and over-active adrenal glands. It is grounding and tonifying to the physical body and can improve vision and ocular health.

Psychological healing: Tiger's eye is a stone of balance and harmony. It helps us make healthy decisions by weighing the options carefully. This gemstone bolsters courage and assuages doubts. Tiger's eye can help you exercise your personal power.

Spiritual healing: Working with tiger's eye promotes intuition and spiritual awak-ening, especially in overly grounded persons who have difficulty making prog-ress with spiritual practice. It promotes truth and justice and draws prosperity and abundance.

Blue Tiger's Eye (Falcon's Eye)

Formula: SiO_2 with crocidolite
$[Na_2(Fe^{2+}{}_3Fe^{3+}{}_2)Si_8O_{22}(OH)_2]$ and iron (Fe)
Hardness: 7
Crystal system: trigonal
Formation process: sedimentary
Chakra: throat, third eye

Tumbled falcon's eye

Physical healing: Blue tiger's eye supports the health of the kidneys, spleen, musculoskeletal system, and endocrine system. It reduces overactive hormones and alleviates pain. This gemstone is sometimes used to treat numbness and cold in the extremities. Worn on the chest or taken as an elixir, it works as an expectorant to help clear congestion from the lungs.

Psychological healing: Blue tiger's eye is balancing and calming, particularly for an overactive mind. It sharpens decision-making skills and can help you remain calm in times of crisis. It facilitates communicating with tact, and it can make you a more persuasive speaker or salesperson.

Spiritual healing: Falcon's eye is a stone of truth, wisdom, and perspective. It helps you see the big picture, often bringing missing details to your mind intuitively.

Red Tiger's Eye (Dragon's Eye)

Formula: SiO_2 with crocidolite $[Na_2(Fe^{2+}{}_3Fe^{3+}{}_2)Si_8O_{22}(OH)_2]$ and iron (Fe)

Hardness: 7

Crystal system: trigonal

Formation process: sedimentary

Chakra: root, solar plexus

Tumbled red tiger's eye

Physical healing: Red tiger's eye is grounding and invigorating to the body. It nourishes the circulatory system and is sometimes used to treat anemia, inflammation, and poor circulation. Red tiger's eye can also improve digestion, stimulate the metabolism, and overcome fatigue.

Psychological healing: Red tiger's eye enhances one's perception. It stimulates the libido, increases passion, and helps resolve conflict in romantic relationships, especially conflict that arises from pride.

Spiritual healing: This red gemstone stimulates the circulation of energy in the aura and lower chakras. It can clear blocked energy centers as well as provide more effective grounding. This variation of tiger's eye stimulates the quest for self-improvement, helping one pursue personal growth with greater stamina and vigor.

Topaz (White Topaz, Clear Topaz)

Formula: $Al_2SiO_4(OH,F)_2$

Hardness: 8

Crystal system: orthorhombic

Formation process: igneous

Chakra: solar plexus, crown

Natural topaz
from Pakistan

Physical healing: Overall, topaz has a regulating effect on the metabolism. It promotes the health of the digestive system and helps relieve stress-related conditions connected to eating and digestion. This gemstone assists in the assimilation of nutrients. It is a helpful adjunct to medical treatments for many chronic and terminal conditions, as it is a gemstone that is both strengthening and regenerating. Topaz also treats conditions of the nervous system.

Psychological healing: Topaz helps us examine the underlying intentions and beliefs that inform our decisions and behaviors. It promotes honesty and awareness and enables us to see how we influence our environment and the people around us. This gemstone furthers balance, confidence, and success.

Spiritual healing: Traditionally topaz is associated with wealth, wisdom, and healing. It promotes empathy and sensitizes us to the healing needs of our loved ones, colleagues, and clients. Topaz teaches us to set healthy boundaries. It bridges the mind and the soul, helping them to work in unison. Topaz speeds up the manifestation process.

Blue Topaz

Formula: $Al_2SiO_4(OH,F)_2$ with traces of iron (Fe)

Hardness: 8

Crystal system: orthorhombic

Formation process: igneous

Chakra: throat, third eye

River-tumbled blue topaz

Physical healing: Blue topaz is rejuvenating to the entire body. It promotes healthy fluid levels and enables the skin to repair and rehydrate itself. This gem is sometimes touted as the ideal stone for reversing the aging process. It promotes the health of the nervous and digestive systems, and it alleviates sore throat, headache, and thyroid conditions.

Psychological healing: Blue topaz is relaxing and expansive to the mind. It promotes clear, honest communication by instilling integrity and authenticity. Blue topaz encourages us to be reliable and confident too. It relieves anxiety and helps us embrace change. This gem furthers learning and boosts memory.

Spiritual healing: Blue topaz is adept at helping us integrate life lessons. It enables us to be our most authentic selves. A stone of wisdom and dedication, blue topaz facilitates meditation and communication with spirit guides.

Golden Topaz

Formula: $Al_2SiO_4(OH,F)_2$ with traces of chromium (Cr)

Hardness: 8

Crystal system: orthorhombic

Formation process: igneous

Chakra: solar plexus

Golden topaz crystal from Brazil

Physical healing: Like all topaz, golden topaz is a tonic for the nervous system. It strengthens eyesight, boosts metabolism, and improves digestion. Golden topaz promotes the health of the female reproductive system and is helpful for conditions of the urinary tract, especially the kidneys. This stone also treats exhaustion, as it has a regulating effect on the adrenals.

Psychological healing: The energy of golden topaz inspires creativity, action, and right use of willpower. This gemstone helps us embrace our individuality and uniqueness, and it inspires creative self-expression and dynamic communication. Work with golden topaz to enforce healthy boundaries. Golden topaz is supremely balancing and strengthening, thus making it helpful during times of change. It also stabilizes mood swings.

Spiritual healing: Golden topaz helps us clarify our intentions, magnifying and aligning our personal will with Divine Will. This makes for a powerful aid in manifestation, especially in manifesting abundance. Golden topaz is also protective.

Tourmaline (General)

Formula: $X^+Y^{2+}{}_3Z^{3+}{}_6(OH,F)_4(BO_3)_2Si_6O_{18}$

Hardness: 7–7.5

Crystal system: trigonal

Formation process: igneous or metamorphic

Chakra: varies

Natural tourmaline crystal

Physical healing: Tourmaline is a diverse family of minerals. As a whole, tourmaline sparks the metabolism and mobilizes the immune system. All forms of tourmaline defend against environmental sensitivities, including pollutants and allergens. Tourmaline can provide relief from tension in the neck and back and can be used to treat conditions of the urinary tract.

Psychological healing: Tourmaline imparts patience and understanding. Most members of the tourmaline group combat depression and fear and facilitate self-discovery. Tourmaline strengthens problem-solving skills.

Spiritual healing: Tourmaline excels at transforming energy. Its structure permits it to restore movement to stagnant energy in the aura, chakras, meridians, and physical body. It both protects against and transmutes disharmonious energy patterns. Tourmaline supports the manifestation process, especially via the law of attraction, and facilitates the attainment of wisdom.

Black Tourmaline (Schorl)

Formula: $Na(Fe,Mn)_3Al_6B_3Si_6O_{27}(OH)_3(OH,F)$

Hardness: 7–7.5

Crystal system: trigonal

Formation process: igneous or metamorphic

Chakra: earth star, root

Tumbled black tourmaline from Brazil

Physical healing: Black tourmaline is often used for pain and numbness and to protect the physical body against environmental toxins and pathogens. It mobilizes the immune system and corrects autoimmune conditions.

Psychological healing: Black tourmaline is a stone of self-discovery—it breaks down barriers to the subconscious and reveals the shadow self. This mineral helps you find direction, and it confers protection during periods of emotional vulnerability. Black tourmaline neutralizes stress and can be used to moderate OCD and anxiety.

Spiritual healing: Just like the way it protects the physical body, black tourmaline protects the nonphysical bodies. It does this by maintaining a strong link to the earth, which creates a "cosmic drain" effect in which disharmonious or harmful energies are filtered out of your aura. It transmutes these energies, both in your energy field and in the environment around you. Because it is so grounding, black tourmaline replenishes depleted energy with the energy of the earth.

Blue Tourmaline (Indicolite)

Formula: $Na(Li_{1.5}Al_{1.5})Al_6(Si_6O_{18})$ $(BO_3)_3(OH)_3(OH)$

Hardness: 7–7.5

Crystal system: trigonal

Formation process: igneous

Chakra: throat, third eye

Blue tourmaline from Afghanistan

Physical healing: Indicolite, or blue tourmaline, promotes balance and flux within the physical body. It works primarily on any systems that demonstrate movement and flow, including the circulatory, digestive, eliminatory, and nervous systems. It is used to support the overall health of the bladder and kidneys, and it helps alleviate headaches.

Psychological healing: Blue tourmaline is the premier choice for releasing blocked emotions. It facilitates healthy emotional expression, good communication, and self-awareness with respect to one's innermost thoughts and feelings. This gemstone can help us through crises of grief, allowing the grieving process to flow unimpeded by expectations or resistance. Blue tourmaline promotes tolerance, confidence, and freedom. It can quell an overactive mind.

Spiritual healing: Blue tourmaline can hasten our personal growth. It instills a better sense of ethics and greater trust and faith. This stone pushes us to explore and seek the truth in all matters. Indicolite steers the mind toward awareness of the present moment while simultaneously facilitating contact with the higher self and increasing psychic abilities. It offers emptiness and detachment so that spiritual growth happens for its own sake and not as a means to an end. This gem also supports meditation, journaling, and the use of affirmations, and it can be used to facilitate ecstatic spiritual states.

Brown Tourmaline (Dravite)

Formula: $NaMg_3Al_6(BO_3)_3Si_6O_{18}(OH)_3F$

Hardness: 7–7.5

Crystal system: trigonal

Formation process: igneous or metamorphic

Chakra: earth star, root, heart

Dravite from India

Physical healing: Dravite is a stone of strength; it offers fortitude and stamina to the physical body and can support the building of muscle mass. Dravite also aids in the regeneration of tissues, including muscle and skin. This gemstone can reduce the appearance of both cellulite and scar tissue, especially when made into an elixir and applied externally. It promotes healthy digestion and elimination and alleviates conditions such as stomach ulcers, constipation, and irritable bowel syndrome.

Psychological healing: Dravite encourages pragmatism and flexibility. It helps you reprogram your mind and emotions to make positive changes in your outlook and behavior. It is a shielding mineral and can be used to prevent burnout and an emotional response to high-stress environments. Dravite instills self-love and self-acceptance. It inspires creativity, helps cut through and eliminate addiction, and breaks patterns of self-abuse, whether physical or psychological.

Spiritual healing: Brown tourmaline protects each of the chakras, preventing damage such as tears, leaks, or intrusion by foreign energies/entities. It is grounding and stabilizing and helps you feel protected and secure. Dravite moderates between extremes in behavior, thought patterns, and lifestyle; it promotes the middle way, staving off both self-indulgence and self-denial. This gemstone also strengthens healthy bonds within communities.

Green Tourmaline (Elbaite, Verdelite)

Formula: $Na(Li_{1.5}Al_{1.5})Al_6Si_6O_{18}(BO_3)_3(OH)_4$ with traces of iron (Fe)

Hardness: 7–7.5

Crystal system: trigonal

Formation process: igneous

Chakra: heart

Green tourmaline in matrix

Physical healing: For repairing tissue there is no better stone than green tourmaline. It restores muscles, tendons, and ligaments, supporting their overall strength and endurance. For this reason it is used by Olympic athletes. Green tourmaline promotes a healthy liver and is recommended for lowering blood pressure and cholesterol. Work with green tourmaline when treating chronic fatigue syndrome and HIV/AIDS (though never as a substitute for conventional health care). It supports healthy digestion and regulates diabetes and endocrine health. Green tourmaline encourages the health of the male reproductive system.

Psychological healing: The lithium content of green tourmaline soothes anxiety and emotional imbalance. This stone is effective against resentment and bitterness. It also reduces impulsivity and instills patience.

Spiritual healing: Working with green tourmaline strengthens the archetypal masculine energy while combatting toxic masculinity. It balances the inner masculine with the inner feminine. It instills a sense of gratitude, joy, and wonder while simultaneously encouraging generosity and respect. It teaches us to send loving, healing energy out into the world; it can be helpful for those who focus more on receiving than giving love.

Pink Tourmaline (Rubellite)

Formula: $Na(Li_{1.5}Al_{1.5})Al_6Si_6O_{18}(BO_3)_3(OH)_4$ with traces of manganese (Mn)

Hardness: 7–7.5

Crystal system: trigonal

Formation process: igneous

Chakra: heart

Rough pink tourmaline

Physical healing: Pink tourmaline is one of the chief gemstones for the health of the female reproductive system. It can balance irregular menstrual cycles, relieve cramps and bloating associated with menstruation, and improve fertility. It also diminishes the symptoms of menopause. Pink tourmaline protects against environmental radiation, ameliorates varicose veins, and reduces hypertension.

Psychological healing: This gentle gem encourages feelings of safety and security. It helps us feel safe enough to let down emotional walls and embrace our vulnerability. It promotes harmonious relationships and calms anger, worry, stress, bitterness, and fear. Pink tourmaline can release old emotional wounds and dissolve emotional and mental patterns that are not in harmony with unconditional love.

Spiritual healing: Pink tourmaline's loving energy nurtures the feminine aspect of all life, and it helps us balance our inner masculine and feminine energies. It initiates an inward flow of love, embodying receptivity and grace; it is helpful for people who give more than they receive.

Watermelon Tourmaline

Formula: $Na(Li_{1.5}Al_{1.5})Al_6Si_6O_{18}(BO_3)_3(OH)_4$ with traces of manganese (Mn) and iron (Fe)

Hardness: 7–7.5

Crystal system: trigonal

Formation process: igneous

Chakra: heart, higher heart

Polished watermelon tourmaline

Physical healing: Watermelon tourmaline combats burnout, relieves pain, regulates hormones, and helps heal damaged or infected nerve tissue. It exhibits the healing properties (physical, psychological, and spiritual) of both pink and green tourmaline.

Psychological healing: This multicolored stone elevates the mood, soothes frayed nerves, and eases anxiety. Watermelon tourmaline provides comfort for those who are experiencing gender dysphoria or gender identity disorder.

Spiritual healing: Watermelon tourmaline balances the incoming and outgoing flow of love and healing energy. It promotes perfect balance between masculine and feminine energies. This stone encourages sensitivity to one's environment without becoming upset or imbalanced by outside influences.

Turquoise

Formula: $CuAl_6(PO_4)_4(OH)_6 \cdot 4H_2O$
Hardness: 5–6
Crystal system: triclinic
Formation process: sedimentary
Chakra: heart, higher heart, throat, crown

Tumbled turquoise

Physical healing: Turquoise is an excellent all-around healing stone. It promotes the general health and well-being of the physical body, being especially effective in light of its regenerative and pain-relieving properties. Turquoise is anti-inflammatory as well as effective against viral infections. This mineral helps regulate the moisture organs of the body, including the skin, eyes, mouth, and mucous membranes. It protects against physical injury and accidents.

Psychological healing: Turquoise promotes integrity and honesty. It facilitates clear and concise information, and it emphasizes speaking the truth. This gemstone invokes a calm demeanor; emotionally it is a balancing stone. It dissolves apathy and martyrdom as it fosters foresight and proactivity.

Spiritual healing: This sky-blue stone appeals to spiritual seekers the world over. Turquoise is protective and wise; it enables one to see the big picture and strive toward wholeness. Turquoise invites compassion toward oneself and others, and it helps one adapt to change. Turquoise has been worn for luck and protection for centuries.

Unakite

Formula: orthoclase feldspar ($KAlSi_3O_8$), epidote [$Ca_2(Al,Fe)_3(SiO_4)_3(OH)$], and quartz ($SiO_2$)

Hardness: 6.5–7

Crystal system: mixture of monoclinic and trigonal

Formation process: metamorphic

Chakra: heart

Tumbled unakite

Physical healing: Unakite is used in treating conditions of the liver, gallbladder, and heart. It promotes tissue regeneration and helps accelerate the body's natural healing processes. Unakite is sometimes used to treat tumors (as an adjunct to conventional medical treatment).

Psychological healing: This lightly metamorphosed granite is grounding and stabilizing to the emotional body. It harmonizes disparate or conflicting energies, thoughts, and emotions so that we can learn to exist in a more peaceful state of being. It invites compromise and helps us repair and strengthen our interpersonal relationships. Unakite gives us permission to experience emotions, whether positive or negative, and helps us feel safe enough to express the full emotional spectrum. This stone counteracts self-deprecation and the tendency to be overly critical of oneself. It ameliorates anxiety, especially when we fear failure.

Spiritual healing: Unakite promotes renewal, recovery, and regeneration on all levels of one's being. It harmonizes opposing energies and teaches the value of compromise and compassion. This stone helps us achieve union between spirit and matter. It is helpful when exploring one's true identity.

Vanadinite

Formula: $Pb_5(VO_4)_3Cl$

Hardness: 3–4

Crystal system: hexagonal

Formation process: sedimentary

Chakra: root, sacral, solar plexus, third eye

Vanadinite cluster
from Morocco

Physical healing: Vanadinite is stimulating and energizing to the body. It combats fatigue, exhaustion, and low vitality. Vanadinite can be used to draw out latent illness and reduce inflammation. It increases the libido and enhances endurance in all physical activities.

Psychological healing: Though physically stimulating, vanadinite calms the mind by reducing mental chatter. It fosters more organized thinking and helps you see the underlying beauty of the self and the world around you. Vanadinite combats feelings of despair and isolation and boosts self-esteem and creativity. This stone helps you find and pursue your passions with joy.

Spiritual healing: As a lead-based mineral, vanadinite helps resolve old karmic patterns. This mineral promotes a connection to the natural world and the subtle energies that move therein, thus it can help you hear the spirits of the land, sky, and sea. Vanadinite anchors the soul in the body and helps you attain transcendent states of consciousness.

Vesuvianite (Idocrase)

Formula: $Ca_{10}(Mg, Fe)_2Al_4(SiO_4)_5(Si_2O_7)_2(OH,F)_4$

Hardness: 6.5

Crystal system: tetragonal

Formation process: metamorphic

Chakra: all, especially heart, third eye

Vesuvianite crystal

Physical healing: Vesuvianite exerts an anti-inflammatory response. It is regenerative, subtly grounding, and strengthening. This mineral can treat conditions of the liver, blood vessels, nerves, and tooth enamel. It also eases feelings of spaciness and dizziness, helping you feel more grounded and present in your physical body. Vesuvianite, as an elixir, can help in the assimilation of nutrients.

Psychological healing: Vesuvianite ignites your natural curiosity. It fortifies both heart and will, linking these together to invite greater courage and trust. This gemstone displaces persistent negative thoughts, helps to organize the mind, and dissipates fear. Working with this stone encourages you to feel more enthusiastic.

Spiritual healing: Vesuvianite is a stone of authenticity; it removes facades and false personas. It is also helpful for those who experience an out-of-balance ego, shifting the identity toward the spirit or higher self rather than the ego self. This gemstone encourages honest and open discourse, and it helps one recognize that each moment in life is an opportunity for growth—wherever you are, that is your spiritual path.

Wulfenite

Formula: PbMoO$_4$

Hardness: 3

Crystal system: tetragonal

Formation process: sedimentary

Chakra: sacral, solar plexus

Wulfenite crystals on matrix

Physical healing: Wulfenite boosts energy, increases stamina, and improves metabolism. It addresses the underlying causes of rough, dry skin. Working with wulfenite also helps you recover from injury to the muscles, especially in cases involving atrophy. This mineral is best-suited to remediating instances of sexual and reproductive imbalance; it assists in cases of infertility, impotence, low sex drive, and poor stamina. Wulfenite is helpful in physical and emotional healing after miscarriage and childbirth.

Psychological healing: The vibrant hues and interesting composition of wulfenite make it a stone of creativity, willpower, and inspiration. This stone improves one's ability to focus while remaining open to receiving inspiration from the higher planes. It keeps you grounded and determined. This mineral is perfect for artists, writers, and other creative people, as it helps in overcoming pessimism, procrastination, and feelings of self-doubt that often accompany creative work. Wulfenite cultivates generosity and releases compulsive feelings and behaviors. It is sometimes used to treat victims of sexual abuse.

Spiritual healing: The heavy metals in wulfenite (lead and molybdenum) encourage magical and alchemical processes. This mineral bolsters the ability to manifest desires, improve magical talents, and invite greater authenticity. Working with wulfenite can help you recognize and transcend old patterns, karmic cycles, and soul contracts. It facilitates past-life recall, particularly those involving lifetimes with magical or mystical experiences.

Zincite

Formula: ZnO

Hardness: 4

Crystal system: hexagonal

Formation process: igneous or metamorphic

Chakra: root, sacral, solar plexus

Polish zincite

Physical healing: Zincite increases the overall vitality and life force of the physical anatomy. It stimulates the body's self-cleansing processes and can relieve overtaxed adrenals. This mineral also promotes the health and balance of the reproductive system and the sex hormones, especially targeting the genitalia and gonads. Zincite is also occasionally used to treat nerve pain and diabetes.

Psychological healing: Zincite is a popular stone for promoting creativity and inspiration. It breaks down blockages to creative expression, thereby encouraging communication, artistic pursuits, and sexuality. It instills courage and can help in overcoming sexual abuse.

Spiritual healing: Zincite reminds us that we are spiritual beings embodied in a physical form, thus it reminds us to *enjoy being human!* This mineral also balances masculine and feminine polarities and enables a clear and objective interpretation of subconscious patterns and intuitive information.

Zircon

Formula: $ZrSiO_4$

Hardness: 7.5

Crystal system: tetragonal

Formation process: igneous

Chakra: root, sacral

Natural zircon crystal

Physical healing: Zircon is stimulating to the liver, and it relieves pain. Taken as an elixir, it can be used as part of a detox program, and it will lessen the symptoms of withdrawal (such as from caffeine, refined sugar, tobacco, etc.). It can be used to treat addiction, eating disorders, and repetitive movements. Zircon also stimulates the metabolism.

Psychological healing: Zircon is a soothing balm in times of loss and transition. It is a stone of action, helping us take actionable steps toward mental and emotional well-being. It treats depression and helps us move on from the past.

Spiritual healing: Zircon is both grounding and spiritually expansive. It facilitates lucid dreaming and astral travel. This gemstone counteracts attachments and ego, and it is exceptionally potent at cutting through materialistic tendencies. It reminds us to live each day to the fullest.

Conclusion

LIFE PROVIDES EACH OF US with a unique journey. We undergo periods of joy and sadness, health and sickness, pain and ease. Through it all, we are given opportunities to grow and heal, both individually and collectively. For most, if not all, of human history, the mineral kingdom has offered continuous support on this journey to wholeness.

Although this book provides both a theoretical understanding of how crystals work and instructions for implementing them in your life, there is no substitute for experience. For any tool or technique to prove effective, it must be honed through practice. You can start by following the directions to the letter and then adapt them to your own needs. Ultimately, by working with the mineral kingdom in whatever way you can, you will develop a better rapport with the unique essences of rocks and gems. This connection will lead your practice into exciting new territory.

It is my hope that you'll put the ideas in this book to good use. From a tumbled stone carried in the pocket to an elaborate crystal grid, working with crystals can offer respite from many of life's woes; we need only devote ourselves to sincere communion with the mineral kingdom.

Index of Healing Properties

Note: for those stones with multiple varieties, the properties apply to all colors or variations unless otherwise noted.

PHYSICAL HEALING

acne: agate (blue lace, snakeskin), amethyst, quartz (rose)

adrenal glands: agate (blue lace, turritella), epidote, jasper (dragon's blood, ocean), kyanite (orange), pietersite, ruby, tanzanite, tiger's eye (gold), topaz (golden), tourmaline (green), zincite

alkalizing: kyanite (green)

allergies: agate (tree), amazonite, apophyllite, aventurine (green) bloodstone, carnelian, chalcedony, fuchsite, iolite, jade, jasper (picture, polychrome), moonstone (rainbow), opal (blue), quartz (garden, tourmalinated), rhodonite, seraphinite, sugilite, tourmaline

antiaging: agate (snakeskin), aquamarine, jade, jasper (leopardskin, mookaite), moonstone, topaz (blue)

arthritis: angelite, carnelian, fluorite, hiddenite

asthma: apophyllite, chalcedony (blue), chrysocolla, quartz (clear, smoky, tourmalinated)

bladder: citrine, prehnite, scapolite, selenite (golden), topaz (golden), tourmaline (blue)

blockage: calcite (optical), fluorite, jasper (red), obsidian, opal (black), quartz (clear, scepter, tourmalinated), selenite (satin spar), tourmaline (blue)

blood pressure: amethyst (lavender), apophyllite, aragonite, aventurine (green), calcite (blue, green, mangano), fluorite (yellow), jasper (mookaite, red), kunzite, kyanite (black), malachite, obsidian (snowflake), opal (blue), pietersite, quartz (smoky, tourmalinated), rhodochrosite, sunstone, tektite, tourmaline (green, pink, watermelon)

blood sugar: agate (moss), amber, calcite (golden), fluorite (purple), kyanite (orange), opal (pink, purple), pietersite, serpentine, zincite

bone marrow: apatite (green, red), aventurine (peach), calcite (red), cavansite, kyanite (orange), magnetite

brain: agate (Botswana), amethyst, ametrine, aragonite (blue), barite, chalcedony (grape), fluorite, jasper (dragon's blood), kyanite (all, especially black, blue), magnetite, phenakite, quartz (Lemurian, spirit), stilbite

carpal tunnel: amethyst (lavender), jasper (leopardskin), quartz (rutilated, smoky), sodalite

cartilage: apatite (blue, green, red), cavansite, fluorite, obsidian (platinum), sodalite

cancer (as an adjunct to medical treatment): aragonite, calcite (all, especially mangano), chalcopyrite, chrome diospide, fluorite, lepidolite, obsidian (rainbow), quartz (elestial), seraphinite, shungite, sugilite

cellular regeneration: apatite (gold), chalcedony (black), charoite, chrome diopside, fluorite, jasper (dragon's blood, ocean), kyanite (black), moonstone (rainbow), quartz (clear, Herkimer), ruby in zoisite, seraphinite, shungite, tourmaline (brown, green), turquoise

childbirth: amazonite, chalcedony, jasper (poppy), moonstone, wulfenite

childhood illness: amber, chalcedony, hiddenite, larimar, moonstone, quartz (phantom), rhodochrosite

cholesterol: fluorite (yellow), tourmaline (green)

chronic illness: aventurine (green), chalcedony (black), chrome diopside, emerald, epidote, fluorite (all, especially Blue John), jasper (picture), opal (green), quartz (phantom), ruby in zoisite, seraphinite, topaz, tourmaline (green), vanadinite

circulatory system: apatite (red), aventurine (peach), bloodstone, calcite (red), cavansite, chalcedony (pink), fuchsite, garnet (almandine, hessonite, rainbow), hematite, iolite, jasper (dragon's blood, red), lapis lazuli, larimar, magnetite, malachite, obsidian (all, especially mahogany), opal (dendritic, pink), pietersite, prehnite, quartz (rose), rhodochrosite, ruby, sapphire, spinel, sunstone, tektite, tiger's eye (red), tourmaline (blue, pink), vesuvianite

colds and flu: apatite (blue, red), bloodstone, chalcedony, fluorite (green), jasper (dragon's blood), labradorite, opal (dendritic, green), peridot, sunstone, tiger's eye (red)

cold extremities: amber, angelite, chalcedony (pink), fluorite (Blue John), garnet (rhodolite), jasper (green, red), obsidian, pyrite, seraphinite, spinel, sunstone, tiger's eye (blue)

congestion: agate (blue lace, snakeskin), calcite (green, optical), chalcedony (blue, white), garnet (green), jasper (yellow), malachite, opal (green), quartz (clear, phantom), seraphinite, tiger's eye (blue)

magnetite, obsidian (rainbow), pietersite, quartz (tangerine), smithsonite, tanzanite, tiger's eye (blue), tourmaline (green)

energizing: agate (fire), carnelian, garnet, jasper (all, especially poppy), opal (fire), quartz (clear, rutilated), ruby, tourmaline (green), wulfenite

eyes and vision: agate (all, especially blue lace, pink), apatite (red), apophyllite, cavansite, chalcedony (blue, grape), chrysoprase, dioptase, emerald, fluorite (blue, green), heliodor, iolite, jasper (silver leaf), lapis lazuli, malachite, obsidian (Apache tears), opal (purple), sapphire, scapolite, tanzanite, tiger's eye (gold, blue, red), topaz, turquoise

fatigue: agate (turritella), carnelian, calcite (orange, red), aragonite (sputnik), fluorite (Blue John), jasper (picture, poppy), opal (blue, fire), pietersite, quartz (rutilated), rhodochrosite, ruby, selenite (desert rose, golden), tiger's eye (red), topaz (golden), tourmaline (green, watermelon), vanadinite

fertility: agate (fire), calcite (red), carnelian, garnet (rhodolite), jade, moonstone, pyrite, quartz (rose), ruby, selenite (desert rose), smithsonite, tourmaline (green, pink), wulfenite, zincite

fever: apatite (red), aragonite (all, especially blue), aventurine (blue), chalcedony (blue), chrysocolla, fluorite (Blue John), hiddenite, iolite, jasper (green), obsidian (mahogany), quartz, selenite (desert rose), seraphinite, tektite

flexibility: aquamarine, fuchsite, lepidolite, moonstone (rainbow), scapolite, selenite, serpentine, tourmaline (green)

fluids (regulation of): angelite, aquamarine, charoite, iolite, moonstone, opal, pietersite, selenite, sodalite, topaz (blue), turquoise

gallbladder: chrome diopside, epidote, jasper (dragon's blood), magnetite, peridot, petrified wood, tanzanite, unakite

growth (to promote): aragonite, garnet (black), malachite, quartz (phantom), serpentine

hair: aragonite (green), chalcopyrite, jasper (dragon's blood, mookaite), obsidian (Apache tears), opal (white), quartz (rutilated), selenite (golden)

headache: amethyst, ametrine, calcite (blue), fluorite (purple), hematite, jet, larimar, petalite, sapphire, tanzanite, topaz (blue), tourmaline (blue)

health and healing (overall): agate (all, especially fancy, fire), amethyst, aventurine (green), calcite (green), chalcedony (black), chrome diopside, emerald, epidote, fluorite, jasper, moonstone (rainbow), peridot, petrified wood, quartz (all, particularly clear, elestial, garden, Herkimer, lithium, smoky, spirit, white), ruby in zoisite, selenite (golden), seraphinite, serpentine, shungite, spinel, tektite, topaz, tourmaline (all, especially green), turquoise, unakite

heart: apatite (green), calcite (green, mangano), chalcedony (pink), chrome diopside, dioptase, emerald, garnet (almandine), hematite, hiddenite, jasper (red), kunzite, lapis lazuli, malachite, obsidian (platinum), opal (all, especially Ethiopian, green, pink), petalite, quartz (Lemurian, rose), ruby, spinel, tourmaline (watermelon), unakite

homeostasis: fluorite (Blue John), garnet, quartz (clear, Herkimer, spirit), seraphinite, shungite, spinel, tektite, topaz

hormone imbalance: amethyst, apatite (gold), aventurine (blue), fluorite, garnet (all, especially hessonite), opal (fire), quartz (lithium), smithsonite, tiger's eye (blue), wulfenite, zincite

impotence: agate (blue lace), apatite (red), carnelian, garnet (hessonite, rhodolite), jasper (red), obsidian (snowflake), opal (fire), pyrite, quartz (scepter), tourmaline (green), wulfenite

immune system: agate (moss, tree), amethyst (chevron), apatite (red), aragonite (all, especially sputnik), aventurine (green), bloodstone, carnelian, calcite (red, zebra), emerald, bloodstone, carnelian, chalcedony, dioptase, emerald, heliodor, hiddenite, jasper (dragon's blood, green, polychrome, yellow), kunzite, obsidian (Apache tears, snowflake), opal (dendritic), quartz (garden), seraphinite, serpentine, sodalite, tourmaline (all, especially black, green), turquoise

infection: agate (crazy lace), amber, apatite (blue, green, red), aventurine (green), barite, black onyx, bloodstone, calcite (green, red), carnelian, celestite, chrome diopside, emerald, obsidian (snowflake), chrysoprase, fluorite (green), galena, jasper (green), malachite, moldavite, obsidian (snowflake), opal (yellow), pyrite, quartz (all, especially garden), ruby, selenite, serpentine, shungite, tektite, tourmaline (green, watermelon), turquoise

inflammation: agate (all, especially moss, pink), amber, angelite, aquamarine, aventurine (blue), calcite (green), carnelian, chalcedony (blue), chalcopyrite, hematite, hiddenite, galena, jasper (green), jet, lapis lazuli, malachite, obsidian (mahogany, rainbow), quartz (clear, scepter, smoky), rhodonite, shungite, tiger's eye (red), tourmaline (black, green), turquoise, vanadinite, vesuvianite

injury: aventurine (green), chrome diopside, creedite, fluorite (purple), garnet (almandine, green), hematite, iolite, malachite, obsidian (rainbow), opal (purple), quartz, rhodonite, ruby in zoisite, scapolite, sodalite, tourmaline (green), selenite, topaz (blue, white), turquoise, wulfenite

intestines: agate (fire), amethyst (chevron), chalcopyrite, chrome diopside, citrine, jasper (all, especially dragon's blood), jet, stilbite, tourmaline (brown)

jet lag: agate (fancy), jasper (leopardskin), shungite

joints: amazonite, amethyst (lavender), apatite (red), aquamarine, aragonite (brown), fluorite, galena, garnet (green), hiddenite, jasper (green), kunzite, lepidolite, scapolite

kidneys: angelite, apatite (green), chalcopyrite, chrome diopside, chrysoprase, garnet (black, green, hessonite), jade, jasper (yellow), labradorite, moonstone (rainbow), opal (all, especially blue, green), prehnite, scapolite, stilbite, tanzanite, tiger's eye (blue), topaz (golden), tourmaline (blue)

lactation: chalcedony (pink, white), moonstone, opal (white)

lethargy: amethyst (lavender), carnelian, chrome diopside, rhodochrosite, ruby, selenite (golden), sodalite, tiger's eye (gold), topaz (golden)

libido, to increase: agate (fire, flower), calcite (orange, red), carnelian, creedite, garnet, jasper (red), opal (fire), rhodochrosite, ruby, tiger's eye (red), vanadinite, wulfenite, zincite

libido, to decrease: agate (flower), apophyllite, black onyx, calcite (optical), garnet (black)

ligaments: fluorite (all, especially purple), quartz (lavender), sodalite, tourmaline (green)

liver: agate (tree), amazonite, amethyst (chevron), angelite, aventurine (peach), azurite, calcite (blue, zebra), chalcopyrite, citrine, creedite, dioptase, epidote, fluorite (yellow), garnet (green, hessonite, rainbow), hiddenite, jasper (dragon's blood, green, silver leaf, yellow), magnetite, peridot, quartz (tangerine), tourmaline (green), unakite, vesuvianite, zircon

longevity: jade, moonstone, quartz, topaz (blue)

lungs: agate (blue lace), amethyst (chevron), calcite (green), chrysocolla, citrine, danburite, larimar, quartz (clear, white), tiger's eye (blue)

lymphatic system: agate (all, especially moss), calcite (blue), carnelian, chalcedony (grape), kyanite (orange), opal (blue, dendritic, green, white), pietersite, sodalite, tourmaline (blue), turquoise

menstruation: amazonite, carnelian, garnet (rainbow), larimar, malachite, moonstone, opal (white), quartz (rose), serpentine, smithsonite, tourmaline (pink)

metabolism: agate (crazy lace, fire, pink) ametrine, apatite (red), calcite (optical, orange, zebra), celestite, citrine, fuchsite, garnet, jasper (leopardskin, polychrome, poppy), malachite, obsidian, petrified wood, prehnite, quartz (white), smithsonite, tiger's eye (red), topaz (all, especially clear, golden), tourmaline, wulfenite, zircon

mouth and gums: apatite (blue), jet, sugilite, turquoise

mucous membranes: agate (snakeskin), calcite (optical), chalcedony (white), fluorite, opal (yellow), topaz (blue), turquoise

muscles: apatite (red), aragonite, barite, chrysocolla, citrine, creedite, garnet (all, especially green), opal (purple), quartz (rose), ruby, spinel, tiger's eye (blue), tourmaline (brown, green), wulfenite

nails: agate (blue lace), jasper (dragon's blood, mookaite), obsidian (Apache tears), opal (white), selenite (golden), tourmaline (brown)

nausea: agate (snakeskin), fluorite (green), dumortierite

necrosis: aragonite

nervous system: agate (Botswana), amethyst, ametrine, aragonite (blue, white), aventurine (blue), azurite, chalcedony (grape), chalcopyrite, fluorite, garnet (almandine), hiddenite, iolite, jasper (dragon's blood), kunzite, kyanite, opal (dendritic, Ethiopian, yellow), petalite, phenakite, pietersite, quartz (clear, Lemurian, spirit, Tibetan), sapphire, selenite, shungite, stilbite, sugilite, sunstone, tanzanite, topaz, zincite

nose: fluorite (blue), stilbite, tanzanite, tourmaline (blue, watermelon)

numbness: aventurine (peach), quartz (rutilated), spinel, tiger's eye (blue), tourmaline (black)

nutrient absorption: agate (flower, turritella), apatite (red), bloodstone, creedite, fluorite (Blue John), obsidian (Apache tears), opal (purple), serpentine, topaz (white), vesuvianite

pancreas: agate (pink), amethyst (chevron), garnet (green)

pain: amber, amethyst, aquamarine, aventurine (green, peach), calcite (optical), carnelian, chrysocolla, dumortierite, fluorite, galena, hematite, hiddenite, jasper (green, red, yellow), kunzite, kyanite (black), labradorite, magnetite, malachite, moonstone (rainbow), obsidian (Apache tears, rainbow), petalite, quartz (all, particularly clear, Herkimer, lithium, smoky, rutilated, tourmalinated), selenite (satin spar), serpentine, shungite, sugilite, tiger's eye (gold, blue), tourmaline (black), turquoise, zircon

parasites: barite, bloodstone, calcite, fluorite, moldavite, sapphire, serpentine, shungite, tektite

pineal gland: apophyllite, barite, fluorite (all, especially purple), lapis lazuli, magnetite, moldavite, opal (purple), phenakite, sugilite

radiation (to neutralize): agate (turritella), apatite (green), aquamarine, barite, chalcopyrite, galena, quartz (Herkimer, rutilated, smoky), shungite, tektite, tourmaline (pink)

regeneration: agate, amethyst, chalcedony (black), dioptase, emerald, epidote, garnet (green, rainbow), jasper (dragon's blood, ocean), moonstone (rainbow), pietersite, quartz (rutilated, Tibetan), ruby in zoisite, selenite (desert rose), spinel, topaz, tourmaline (brown), unakite, vesuvianite

rejuvenation: agate (fire, moss), garnet (rainbow), jasper (green), opal, serpentine, sunstone, topaz (blue)

reproductive system, female: agate (flower, pink), amazonite, angelite, calcite (green, red), carnelian, chalcedony, creedite, emerald, garnet (hessonite, rainbow), jasper, larimar, malachite, moonstone, obsidian (Apache tears), opal, quartz (rose, tangerine), rhodonite, ruby, serpentine, topaz (golden), tourmaline (pink), vanadinite, wulfenite, zincite

reproductive system, male: apatite (gold, red), calcite (green, red), carnelian, creedite, emerald, garnet (hessonite, rhodolite), jasper, opal (fire), pyrite, quartz (scepter, tangerine), sunstone, tourmaline (blue, green), ruby, quartz (rose, smoky), sunstone, vanadinite, wulfenite, zincite

respiratory system: agate (blue lace), apophyllite, aragonite (blue), calcite (green, mangano), chalcedony (blue), danburite, fluorite (blue, Blue John, rainbow), garnet (green), larimar, opal (blue, white), quartz (clear, Herkimer, smoky, tourmalinated)

seasonal affective disorder: amber, selenite (golden), sunstone

sensory organs: jasper (silver leaf), kyanite (blue), petalite, pietersite, sapphire, stilbite, tanzanite, topaz (blue)

scar tissue: agate (snakeskin), jade, jasper (leopardskin, mookaite), moonstone, rhodonite, tourmaline (brown, green)

sciatica: agate (crazy lace), aragonite (white), chalcedony (black), kyanite (blue, green), quartz (lithium), topaz (blue)

sinus: carnelian, danburite, fluorite (blue, green), iolite, larimar, malachite, moonstone (rainbow), obsidian (mahogany), opal (green), seraphinite

skeletal system: agate (blue lace), amazonite, amethyst (lavender), apatite, aragonite, calcite (all, especially green), cavansite, celestite, charoite, chrome diopside, creedite, fluorite (all, especially purple), garnet (all, especially black), jasper (picture), kyanite (orange), lapis lazuli, obsidian (rainbow), quartz (elestial), rhodonite, scapolite, selenite, sodalite, tiger's eye (blue)

skin: agate (all, especially blue lace, pink, snakeskin, tree), amethyst (chevron), apophyllite, aquamarine, aragonite (green, sputnik), barite, black onyx, calcite, chalcedony (white), chrysoprase, citrine, fluorite (rainbow), fuchsite, jade, jasper (leopardskin, mookaite, yellow), moonstone, opal, peridot, quartz (rose, smoky), selenite, shungite, smithsonite, topaz (blue), tourmaline (brown), turquoise, wulfenite

sleep: agate, apophyllite, aragonite (blue), calcite (red), hematite, jade, jet, lepidolite, malachite, moonstone, opal (blue), prehnite, quartz (Herkimer, smoky), sodalite, sugilite, tanzanite, turquoise

spine: amethyst (lavender), aragonite (brown, white), barite, citrine, fluorite, garnet (black), kyanite, scapolite, selenite, sodalite

spleen: apatite (green), chalcedony (pink), jasper (yellow), ruby, tiger's eye (blue)

stamina: bloodstone, calcite (orange, red), carnelian, chrome diopside, garnet, hematite, jasper, rhodochrosite, rhodonite, ruby, tiger's eye (red), topaz (golden), tourmaline (brown, green), vanadinite, wulfenite

stomach: agate (snakeskin), aragonite (brown, green), barite, calcite (yellow), chalcedony (grape), citrine, moonstone (rainbow), tourmaline (brown)

strength: apatite (green, red), bloodstone, carnelian, garnet, hematite, jasper (picture, red), magnetite, obsidian (all, especially mahogany), petrified wood, quartz (smoky), ruby, sunstone, tektite, topaz, tourmaline (black, brown, green), vesuvianite

teeth: apatite (all, particularly blue), black onyx, calcite, cavansite, celestite, fluorite, hiddenite, lapis lazuli, sodalite, sugilite, vesuvianite

tension: chalcedony (blue), citrine, fluorite (blue), malachite, obsidian (Apache tears), quartz (lithium, rose, tourmalinated), scapolite, selenite (satin spar), seraphinite, tourmaline

throat: barite, calcite (blue), chalcedony (blue), chrysocolla, fluorite (blue, green), kyanite (black), moonstone (rainbow), sodalite, stilbite, tanzanite, topaz (blue)

thyroid: apatite (gold), azurite, chalcedony (black, blue), chrysocolla, epidote, fluorite (yellow), jasper (dragon's blood, ocean), tanzanite, topaz (blue)

thymus: amethyst (chevron), hiddenite, kunzite, lepidolite, quartz (garden, lithium), sugilite

tumor: amethyst, emerald, epidote, fluorite, opal (black, yellow), shungite, unakite

urinary tract: agate (flower), chrysoprase, citrine, fluorite (blue), jade, larimar, opal (yellow), selenite (golden), scapolite, topaz (golden), tourmaline

vitality: amber, apatite (gold), calcite (orange), carnelian, garnet (all, especially rainbow), heliodor, hematite, jasper (dragon's blood, poppy, red), opal (fire, yellow), quartz (clear, rutilated), ruby, spinel, tiger's eye (gold, red), vanadinite, wulfenite, zincite

warming: barite, carnelian, garnet (rhodolite), jasper (red), pyrite, quartz (tangerine), selenite (desert rose), seraphinite, sunstone, vanadinite

water retention: angelite, aquamarine, opal, selenite, topaz (blue)

weight management: ametrine, apatite, calcite (orange), garnet (hessonite), heliodor, jasper (green, poppy, red, yellow), opal (Ethiopian), petrified wood, quartz (Tibetan, tourmalinated), rhodonite, smithsonite, tanzanite, topaz, zircon

wound healing: aragonite (sputnik), bloodstone, calcite (red), hematite, jasper (mookaite), magnetite, obsidian (snowflake), quartz (clear, rutilated), rhodonite, ruby, smithsonite

youthfulness: aquamarine, garnet (rainbow), moonstone, opal, prehnite, topaz (blue)

PSYCHOLOGICAL HEALING

abuse: garnet (black), jet, obsidian (all, especially platinum, rainbow), petalite, smithsonite, tourmaline (brown), wulfenite, zincite

action: agate (crazy lace), amethyst (chevron), apatite (red), calcite (red), carnelian, garnet (all, especially almandine, hessonite), hematite, howlite, iolite, jasper (poppy, silver leaf), pietersite, pyrite, quartz (tangerine), shungite, sunstone, topaz (golden), wulfenite, zircon

addiction: agate (Botswana), amethyst, apophyllite, black onyx, calcite (red), dumortierite, fluorite (green, purple), hiddenite, jasper (poppy), obsidian (all, especially rainbow), tourmaline (brown), zircon

ambition: agate (fire), apatite (gold, red), carnelian, hematite, jasper (dragon's blood), pyrite, sunstone, topaz (golden)

analytical skills: agate, chalcedony (white), chalcopyrite, chrome diopside, fluorite, jasper (dragon's blood), kyanite (blue), pyrite, sapphire, selenite (satin spar)

anger: agate (tree), apatite (blue, gold, red), aragonite (blue), calcite (green), carnelian, heliodor, hiddenite, lepidolite, obsidian (mahogany, rainbow), quartz (clear, lithium, white), spinel, tourmaline (pink)

anxiety: agate (tree), amber, amethyst, apatite (red), apophyllite, aventurine (peach), barite, bloodstone, calcite (mangano), celestite, chalcedony, chrome diopside, epidote, garnet (almandine, green), hiddenite, howlite, jasper, kunzite, larimar, lepidolite, malachite, petalite, quartz (all, especially clear, lithium, rose, smoky), rhodonite, selenite (satin spar), shungite, smithsonite, spinel, stilbite, sugilite, tektite, tourmaline (black, green, pink, watermelon), unakite

larimar, opal (blue), quartz (rutilated, spirit), rhodochrosite, sapphire, scapolite, smithsonite, sodalite, tiger's eye (blue), topaz (blue, golden), tourmaline (blue), zincite

concentration and focus: black onyx, citrine, dumortierite, fluorite, garnet, hematite, jasper (all, especially red), kyanite, obsidian (mahogany), quartz (clear, Herkimer, rutilated), sapphire, scapolite, selenite (satin spar), sodalite, wulfenite

confidence: agate (blue lace, fire, snakeskin), amber, angelite, apatite (gold), aragonite (sputnik, white), calcite (blue, gold, mangano, orange, red, yellow, zebra), carnelian, chalcedony (black, pink), citrine, garnet (hessonite), jasper (dragon's blood, red, silver leaf), obsidian (mahogany), pietersite, pyrite, quartz (rutilated, scepter), quartz (tangerine), rhodochrosite, selenite (golden), spinel, sunstone, topaz, tourmaline (blue), vanadinite

conflict: amazonite, calcite (optical, red, yellow, zebra), celestite, chalcedony (white), garnet (hessonite, rainbow), jasper (ocean), opal (yellow), quartz (spirit, tourmalinated), rhodonite, ruby in zoisite, serpentine, sodalite, tiger's eye (red), tourmaline (watermelon), unakite

confusion: barite, dumortierite, fluorite, kyanite (green), magnetite, obsidian (rainbow), opal, phenakite, pietersite, quartz (tourmalinated), rhodonite, selenite (all, especially golden), sodalite, stilbite

courage: aquamarine, bloodstone, calcite (golden, zebra), heliodor, hematite, jasper (all, especially dragon's blood, polychrome, red), phenakite, pietersite, sunstone, tiger's eye (gold), topaz (golden), vesuvianite, wulfenite, zincite

creativity: agate (Botswana, fire, flower), amazonite, amber, calcite (all, especially blue, orange, yellow), carnelian, cavansite, celestite, chalcopyrite, chrome diopside, chrysocolla, creedite, fluorite (Blue John, rainbow), fuchsite, garnet (all, especially rainbow), jasper (mookaite, polychrome, poppy, red), kyanite (orange), labradorite, opal (all, especially fire, yellow), pyrite, quartz (rutilated), rhodochrosite, smithsonite, sunstone, topaz (golden), tourmaline (brown), vanadinite, wulfenite, zincite

critical thinking: ametrine, calcite, chrome diopside, creedite, fluorite, jasper (dragon's blood, green, picture), kyanite (blue, orange), quartz (Herkimer), sapphire, scapolite, sodalite, stilbite, topaz

curiosity: chalcopyrite, fluorite (Blue John), tanzanite, vesuvianite

depression: apatite (red), emerald, fluorite (purple), galena, garnet, hiddenite, jasper (poppy, silver leaf), kunzite, labradorite, lepidolite, obsidian (all, especially

(green, rainbow), jasper (ocean), kunzite, quartz (rose), sugilite, topaz, tourmaline (pink)

family healing: agate (blue lace, Botswana, turritella), apophyllite, aragonite (sputnik), cavansite, danburite, lepidolite, quartz (Lemurian, spirit)

fear: agate (fire, pink), amber, amethyst (chevron), ametrine, angelite, apatite (red), barite, black onyx, bloodstone, carnelian, celestite, chalcedony (all, especially grape), charoite, fluorite (blue), garnet (almandine), hiddenite, iolite, jasper, lepidolite, moldavite, obsidian, opal (black, fire), pietersite, pyrite, quartz (clear, elestial, lithium, spirit, tangerine), rhodonite, scapolite, selenite (satin spar), spinel, stilbite, tektite, tourmaline (all, especially pink), unakite, vesuvianite

friendship: barite, calcite (mangano, optical), cavansite, danburite, lapis lazuli, quartz (rutilated), tektite, tourmaline (pink), turquoise

forgiveness: agate (blue lace), calcite (green, mangano), chrysoprase, dioptase, emerald, hiddenite, kunzite, larimar, lepidolite, prehnite, quartz (rose), ruby in zoisite, stilbite, tourmaline (pink), unakite

gender identity: smithsonite, tourmaline (green, pink, watermelon)

grief: amethyst (lavender), fluorite (purple), jasper (mookaite), jet, larimar, lepidolite, obsidian, opal (purple), petalite, quartz (clear, lithium), smithsonite, tourmaline (blue), zircon

guilt: agate (Botswana), aragonite (brown), apatite (gold), calcite (orange), emerald, scapolite, stilbite, tourmaline (pink)

happiness: amber, calcite (yellow), citrine, hiddenite, opal (yellow), scapolite, sunstone

harmony: agate (blue lace, Botswana, flower), aquamarine, calcite (blue), quartz (all, especially spirit), sapphire, sugilite

heart-mind balance: angelite, chalcedony (white), chalcopyrite, emerald, fluorite (green), hiddenite, kyanite (green), lapis lazuli, larimar, moldavite, obsidian (snowflake), opal (dendritic), petalite, prehnite, quartz (tourmalinated), ruby in zoisite, seraphinite, smithsonite, stilbite, tanzanite, tiger's eye (blue), topaz, tourmaline (watermelon), turquoise, unakite, vesuvianite, zircon

honesty: calcite (orange), celestite, fluorite (blue, Blue John), kyanite (green), obsidian, topaz (blue), turquoise, vesuvianite

imagination: cavansite, chrysoprase, fluorite, jasper (picture, polychrome), labradorite, moonstone, quartz (garden, white)

inner strength: agate (blue lace), amethyst (chevron), chrome diopside,

love and romance: agate (pink), aventurine (green), calcite (green, mangano), cavansite, chalcedony (pink), danburite, dioptase, emerald, garnet, hiddenite, jade, kunzite, larimar, lepidolite, malachite, moonstone, obsidian (mahogany), opal (all, especially pink), peridot, quartz (rose, rutilated, smoky), rhodochrosite, rhodonite, ruby, ruby in zoisite, selenite (desert rose), smithsonite, spinel, tiger's eye (red), tourmaline (green, pink, watermelon), unakite

loyalty: garnet, emerald, heliodor, jade, malachite, opal (yellow)

memory: calcite (all, especially golden, green, yellow), creedite, fluorite, garnet, hematite, iolite, jasper (leopardskin, mookaite), kyanite (black, blue, orange), opal (blue, dendritic), pyrite, sapphire, spinel, tanzanite, topaz (blue)

mental clarity: ametrine, apatite (gold), apophyllite, aquamarine, azurite, calcite (all, especially blue, gold, optical), carnelian, chalcedony (blue, grape), chalcopyrite, citrine, dumortierite, emerald, fluorite, garnet (almandine), howlite, jasper (leopardskin, silver leaf, yellow), kyanite (black, blue), lapis lazuli, obsidian, opal (purple), peridot, phenakite, quartz (clear, Herkimer, rutilated, smoky), sapphire, selenite, serpentine, shungite, sodalite, sunstone, tanzanite, tiger's eye (blue), topaz, tourmaline (all, especially black, blue), vanadinite, vesuvianite

mental flexibility: agate (crazy lace), amber, aquamarine, carnelian, citrine, dumortierite, fluorite, fuchsite, garnet (rainbow), jasper (leopardskin, yellow), lapis lazuli, moldavite, sapphire, selenite (satin spar), serpentine, sodalite, tanzanite, tourmaline (brown)

mood swings: agate (moss, tree), aragonite (sputnik), calcite (mangano), danburite, fuchsite, jasper (ocean), lepidolite, magnetite, petalite, quartz (lithium, white), rhodonite, serpentine, sodalite, topaz (all, especially golden), unakite

motivation: apatite (red), aragonite (brown), bloodstone, calcite (golden, orange, red), carnelian, chrome diopside, citrine, creedite, garnet, hematite, jasper (mookaite, poppy, red), obsidian (mahogany), opal (yellow), pyrite, ruby, sunstone, tiger's eye, wulfenite

nervousness: apophyllite, aragonite, chalcedony, dumortierite, hiddenite, howlite, kunzite, lepidolite, petalite, quartz (lithium), rhodonite

nightmares: aragonite (blue), jasper (dragon's blood, red), jet, prehnite, quartz (angel)

objectivity: charoite, fluorite (blue), lapis lazuli, opal (purple), quartz (Tibetan, white), selenite (golden), sodalite, stilbite, zincite

(yellow), scapolite, serpentine, sodalite, tourmaline (all, especially blue, green), unakite

procrastination: apatite (red), carnelian, citrine, fluorite, garnet, jasper (all, especially poppy), pyrite, quartz (smoky), tourmaline (blue), pyrite, sunstone, tiger's eye (gold), turquoise, vanadinite

psychosomatic conditions: amazonite, azurite, celestite, chalcopyrite, chrome diopside, creedite, dumortierite, fluorite (green), kyanite, obsidian (platinum, rainbow), opal (Ethiopian), petalite, quartz (amphibole, lithium, rose), rhodonite, ruby, selenite (desert rose), topaz

rejection: chrysoprase, jade, jasper (all, especially picture), larimar, obsidian (platinum), quartz (garden), seraphinite, smithsonite, zircon

relationships: agate (flower), calcite (optical), cavansite, danburite, dumortierite, emerald, kunzite, kyanite (orange), malachite, obsidian (mahogany), quartz (lithium, rose, rutilated, Tibetan), rhodochrosite, ruby in zoisite, smithsonite, tiger's eye (red), tourmaline (green, pink, watermelon), unakite

relaxation: calcite (mangano), chalcedony (all, especially blue), citrine, garnet, howlite, kunzite, lepidolite, petalite, quartz (garden), rhodonite, selenite (satin spar), sugilite

resentment, bitterness: calcite (green, mangano), jasper (polychrome), quartz (clear), ruby in zoisite, tourmaline (green, pink)

resilience: aragonite (brown), calcite (golden), chrome diopside, danburite, jasper (dragon's blood, picture, yellow), lepidolite, rhodonite, smithsonite, stilbite, topaz

respect: calcite (orange), quartz (scepter), sunstone, tourmaline (blue, green)

responsibility: barite, carnelian, dumortierite, fluorite (purple), galena, garnet (all, especially black, hessonite), hiddenite, iolite, kyanite (black), opal, quartz (clear, Herkimer, scepter, smoky), topaz (blue)

restlessness: aragonite, calcite (red), chalcedony (blue), quartz (lithium), stilbite

sadness: jet, lepidolite, obsidian (all, especially rainbow), opal (yellow), quartz (lithium, tourmalinated), smithsonite, sugilite

self-awareness: agate, aquamarine, azurite, black onyx, calcite (optical), fluorite, garnet (hessonite), jasper (polychrome, silver leaf), lepidolite, obsidian, quartz (all, especially amphibole), sapphire, selenite (satin spar), scapolite, tanzanite, topaz, tourmaline (all, especially black, blue, brown)

self-control: apophyllite, calcite (red), dumortierite, fluorite, galena, heliodor, quartz (smoky), sapphire, tourmaline (green)

self-esteem: agate (blue lace, flower, pink, snakeskin), amethyst (chevron),

transition: agate (all, especially crazy lace), amethyst (lavender), aquamarine, lepidolite, calcite (golden), charoite, chrysoprase, fluorite (Blue John), jasper (leopardskin), obsidian, petrified wood, quartz (smoky), selenite (golden), topaz (golden), tourmaline (black), zircon

trauma: agate (tree), calcite (zebra), carnelian, jet, lepidolite, malachite, moonstone (rainbow), obsidian, quartz (amphibole, lithium, smoky), rhodonite, ruby in zoisite, selenite (golden), sugilite

trust: agate (flower), chrysoprase, creedite, fluorite (yellow), garnet (black), larimar, obsidian (platinum), rhodonite, vesuvianite

understanding: agate (blue lace), azurite, calcite (green), chrome diopside, fluorite, jasper (leopardskin), kyanite, sapphire, tourmaline, turquoise

victimhood: amazonite, calcite (zebra), carnelian, dioptase, garnet (rainbow), kyanite (black, green), obsidian, petalite, turquoise

vulnerability: bloodstone, fluorite (yellow), garnet (rainbow), jet, obsidian, pietersite, quartz (garden), rhodonite, stilbite, tourmaline (black, pink)

willpower: apatite (gold), calcite (all, especially gold, zebra), carnelian, citrine, dumortierite, garnet, jasper (poppy), jet, malachite, opal (yellow), pietersite, pyrite, quartz (clear, elestial, scepter), sapphire, scapolite, selenite (golden), topaz (all, especially golden), vesuvianite, wulfenite

worry: agate (fancy), calcite, chalcedony, fluorite (blue), garnet (almandine), jasper (silver leaf), lepidolite, opal (pink), quartz (clear, garden, lithium, smoky), rhodonite, selenite (satin spar), shungite, smithsonite, stilbite, sugilite, tanzanite, tourmaline (pink), unakite

SPIRITUAL HEALING

abundance, prosperity: agate (flower), ametrine, apatite (gold, green), aventurine (green), calcite (golden, optical), citrine, emerald, epidote, garnet (all, especially green), hiddenite, jade, jasper (green, leopardskin), opal (purple), peridot, pyrite, quartz (spirit), ruby, tiger's eye (gold), topaz (all, especially golden)

acceptance: agate (blue lace, pink), fluorite (Blue John), fuchsite, lepidolite, opal (black), prehnite, quartz (Tibetan), spinel, tourmaline (blue)

ascension process: aquamarine, calcite (all, especially golden), epidote, fluorite, kyanite, moldavite, opal (Ethiopian), petalite, phenakite, pietersite, quartz (elestial, lithium, smoky, spirit, Tibetan), selenite, serpentine, shungite, sugilite, tektite

seraphinite, sugilite, topaz, tourmaline (watermelon), unakite, vanadinite, zincite

centering: amber, aragonite (brown, white), calcite (optical), jasper (polychrome), kyanite, lapis lazuli, lepidolite, magnetite, quartz (all, especially garden, lithium), tourmaline, vanadinite, zircon

chakras (blocked or underactive): aragonite (sputnik), apatite (gold), calcite (optical, zebra), cavansite, celestite, chalcedony (black), chalcopyrite, chrome diopside, fluorite (all, especially green, rainbow), garnet, jasper (poppy), kyanite (black, blue), larimar, obsidian (platinum), phenakite, pietersite, quartz (clear, Herkimer, lithium, smoky, Tibetan, tourmalinated), selenite, seraphinite, serpentine, tanzanite, tektite, tiger's eye (red), tourmaline (all, especially brown)

chakras (overactive): chalcedony (black), garnet (rainbow), howlite, kyanite (black), quartz (clear, smoky, tourmalinated, white), seraphinite, tanzanite, tektite

channeling: ametrine, barite, cavansite, celestite, chalcedony (blue, grape), charoite, danburite, fluorite (Blue John, purple), howlite, magnetite, moldavite, moonstone (rainbow), petalite, phenakite, quartz (all, especially amphibole, Herkimer, rutilated, spirit), scapolite, selenite, seraphinite, tanzanite, tektite, tourmaline (blue)

clairaudience: obsidian (platinum), phenakite, sapphire, sodalite, topaz (blue)

clairvoyance: angelite, azurite, barite, calcite (blue), cavansite, lapis lazuli, moldavite, obsidian, phenakite, pietersite, quartz (clear, Herkimer, rutilated, tangerine), selenite, sodalite, tiger's eye

clarity: ametrine, apophyllite, azurite, apatite (gold), cavansite, garnet (hessonite), howlite, lapis lazuli, opal, phenakite, quartz (clear, Herkimer, Tibetan), selenite, sodalite, tiger's eye (blue), topaz (blue, white)

community, group harmony: agate (flower), aragonite (sputnik), chalcedony (grape), chrome diopside, fluorite (yellow), jasper (ocean), malachite, quartz (Lemurian, spirit), scapolite, tourmaline (brown), unakite

compassion: agate (pink), amethyst (chevron), calcite, cavansite, chalcedony, danburite, garnet (green), jasper (poppy), lepidolite, opal (pink), petalite, quartz (rose, spirit, Tibetan), rhodochrosite, ruby in zoisite, selenite (desert rose), spinel, stilbite, tourmaline (watermelon), turquoise

cords (to remove): kyanite, obsidian, quartz (amphibole, garden, Lemurian, rutilated, smoky, tourmalinated), selenite, tourmaline (black)

devas (connecting to): agate (flower, moss, tree, turritella) aragonite (green), chrome diopside, jasper (dragon's blood, picture), kyanite (green), obsidian

freedom: amazonite, calcite (all, especially mangano), cavansite, carnelian, dioptase, fluorite (rainbow), fuchsite, rhodochrosite, scapolite, tourmaline (blue), vanadinite

generosity: apatite (blue), chalcedony, fluorite (Blue John), garnet (green), hiddenite, jasper (poppy), opal (pink), quartz (spirit, Tibetan), rhodonite, tourmaline (green), wulfenite

geopathic stress: agate, aragonite, chrome diopside, fluorite (Blue John), hematite, hiddenite, jasper (all, especially dragon's blood, picture), malachite, quartz (garden, smoky), selenite (desert rose), serpentine, shungite, tourmaline (black, brown)

good luck: agate, aventurine (green), jade, jasper (green), selenite (desert rose), tektite, turquoise

gratitude: hiddenite, opal (green), peridot, selenite (desert rose), tourmaline (green)

grace: agate (crazy lace), celestite, lepidolite, moldavite, opal (all, especially white), peridot, sapphire

grounding: agate (all, especially fancy, fire, moss, tree, turritella), amber, aragonite (all, especially brown), barite, black onyx, calcite (red, zebra), carnelian, chalcedony (black), creedite, galena, garnet, hematite, jasper, jet, magnetite, obsidian, petrified wood, pyrite, quartz (smoky), rhodonite, ruby, serpentine, shungite, spinel, tiger's eye, tourmaline (black, brown), vanadinite, zircon

harmony: agate (flower), amazonite, aragonite, calcite (blue), celestite, chalcedony (grape), galena, garnet, jade, jasper (green), larimar, lepidolite, quartz, ruby in zoisite, sapphire, tiger's eye (gold), tourmaline (pink), turquoise

higher consciousness: barite, calcite (golden), cavansite, chalcedony (grape), creedite, fluorite (all, especially purple), hiddenite, howlite, kyanite (blue), lapis lazuli, moldavite, opal, petalite, phenakite, pietersite, quartz (all, especially amphibole, Herkimer, Lemurian, smoky, spirit, Tibetan), sapphire, selenite, seraphinite, sodalite, tanzanite, tourmaline (blue), zincite

higher self: black onyx, calcite (golden), fluorite (purple), garnet (rainbow), moldavite, opal (yellow), phenakite, pietersite, quartz (all, especially amphibole, rutilated), selenite, tanzanite, topaz (golden), tourmaline (blue), turquoise

hope: ametrine, apatite (gold, green), aventurine (peach), calcite (zebra), celestite, chrysoprase, iolite, lapis lazuli, larimar, moonstone (rainbow), obsidian (rainbow), opal, sapphire, spinel

illumination: aquamarine, barite, chrome diopside, malachite, obsidian, opal, phenakite, quartz, selenite, sugilite

luck: agate, aventurine (green), chalcedony, chrysoprase, fluorite (Blue John), jade, obsidian (Apache tears), opal, tektite

manifestation: agate (flower, moss), amethyst (chevron), apatite (gold, red), calcite (all, especially golden, optical, orange, red), epidote, fluorite (Blue John), garnet (all, especially green), hiddenite, howlite, jasper (leopardskin), labradorite, magnetite, moldavite, petrified wood, pyrite, quartz (all, especially clear, rutilated, smoky), shungite, topaz, tourmaline, wulfenite

mastery: hematite, lapis lazuli, malachite, moldavite, opal (dendritic), phenakite, quartz, tourmaline (watermelon)

materialism: agate (turritella), galena, petrified wood, pyrite, sapphire, tektite, tourmaline (blue), vesuvianite, zircon

meditation: agate (fire), amethyst, ametrine, angelite, apatite (blue), aragonite (brown, sputnik, white), azurite, aventurine (blue), calcite (blue, golden, optical), cavansite, celestite, chalcedony (blue), chrysocolla, creedite, danburite, fluorite, garnet (almandine), heliodor, iolite, jasper (silver leaf), kyanite, labradorite, lapis lazuli, larimar, lepidolite, moldavite, obsidian (mahogany), opal (dendritic, purple), petalite, phenakite, quartz, sapphire, selenite, sodalite, sugilite, tanzanite, topaz (blue), tourmaline (all, especially blue)

mindfulness: agate (flower), amethyst (lavender), aragonite (brown, green), black onyx, calcite, cavansite, dumortierite, garnet (rhodolite), hematite, jasper (leopardskin), lepidolite, obsidian (Apache tears), petalite, petrified wood, tourmaline (black), prehnite, quartz (all, especially clear, lithium), sapphire, scapolite, selenite (golden, satin spar), sodalite, topaz (blue), tourmaline (blue), vesuvianite

nature (connecting to): agate (fancy, flower, moss, tree, turritella), amber, aragonite (all, especially green), chrome diopside, emerald, jade, jasper (all, especially dragon's blood, green, mookaite, picture, polychrome), kyanite (green), obsidian (Apache tears), petrified wood, quartz (garden, Lemurian, smoky), selenite (desert rose), serpentine, vanadinite

new beginnings: agate (snakeskin), hiddenite, jasper (silver leaf), larimar, obsidian, opal (all, especially green), petrified wood, rhodochrosite, selenite (desert rose), tektite, tourmaline (blue, green), zircon

oneness, unity: amethyst (chevron), chrome diopside, danburite, obsidian (Apache tears), pietersite, prehnite, quartz (amphibole, garden, Lemurian, rose, spirit, Tibetan), scapolite, stilbite

past-life recall: agate (fancy, turritella) amber, apophyllite, chalcedony (black), dumortierite, galena, heliodor, iolite, jade, jasper (mookaite, picture), jet, kyanite (black), lapis lazuli, petrified wood, quartz (elestial, garden,

moonstone, opal, ruby in zoisite, selenite (desert rose), seraphinite, topaz (blue), tourmaline (black, blue), turquoise, unakite

serenity: amethyst, celestite, hiddenite, jasper (silver leaf), lepidolite, sapphire, spinel, tanzanite

service: aragonite (blue), chalcedony, charoite, quartz (amphibole, rose, spirit), spinel

shadow self: black onyx, hematite, kyanite (black), obsidian, quartz (phantom, smoky), tektite, tiger's eye (gold, blue), tourmaline (black)

shamanic journeying: agate (snakeskin), aragonite (sputnik), calcite (zebra), chalcedony, charoite, creedite, garnet (black), iolite, jade, jet, kyanite (green), moldavite, obsidian, opal (black), phenakite, pietersite, quartz (all, especially garden, Herkimer, phantom, smoky), tektite, turquoise, zircon

soul retrieval: agate (snakeskin), aragonite (sputnik), fluorite (blue), iolite, obsidian (all, especially rainbow), opal (Ethiopian), quartz (Herkimer, smoky), tektite

spirit guides: agate (tree, turritella), amethyst, chrome diopside, jet, phenakite, quartz (Herkimer, Lemurian, rutilated, Tibetan), ruby in zoisite, sapphire, scapolite, selenite, seraphinite, tektite, topaz (blue), vanadinite

spiritual blueprint: apophyllite, aquamarine, emerald, fluorite, phenakite, pietersite, quartz (elestial, Herkimer), seraphinite, shungite

spiritual cleansing: amethyst, charoite, jet, fluorite, opal, quartz (clear, elestial, smoky, spirit, tourmalinated), selenite, seraphinite, shungite, tanzanite, tektite, tourmaline (all, especially black)

spiritual growth: apatite (red), aragonite (all, especially sputnik, white), aventurine (green), calcite, cavansite, charoite, chrome diopside, chrysoprase, emerald, garnet (green, hessonite), jasper (dragon's blood, yellow), jet, labradorite, lapis lazuli, moldavite, obsidian, opal (dendritic, Ethiopian), petalite, phenakite, pietersite, quartz (all, especially Herkimer, Tibetan), rhodonite, ruby in zoisite, sapphire, scapolite, selenite, shungite, sodalite, stilbite, tektite, tourmaline (blue), turquoise

stability: agate, aragonite (all, especially brown), barite, chalcedony (black), garnet, hematite, zircon

stillness: amethyst (lavender), cavansite, celestite, chalcedony (grape, white), jasper (ocean), opal (blue, dendritic), petalite, sodalite

success: ametrine, carnelian, citrine, jasper (dragon's blood, green, leopardskin), peridot, topaz

surrender: aragonite (green, sputnik), black onyx, chalcedony (white), emerald,

Bibliography

Ahsian, Naisha. *The Crystal Ally Cards: Evolution Edition.* Sedona, Ariz.: Crystalis Institute Press, 2016.

Calverley, Roger. *The Language of Crystals.* Kleinburg, Ont.: Rock of Ages Distributors, Inc., 1987.

Dow, JaneAnn. *Crystal Journey: Travel Guide for the New Shaman.* Santa Fe, N.Mex.: Journey Books, 1994.

Franks, Leslie J. *Stone Medicine: A Chinese Medical Guide to Healing with Gems and Minerals.* Rochester, Vt.: Healing Arts Press, 2016.

Gienger, Michael. *Crystal Power, Crystal Healing: The Complete Handbook.* London: Cassell Illustrated, 1998.

———. *Healing Crystals: The A to Z Guide to 555 Gemstones.* Forres, Scotland: Earthdancer, 2014.

Hall, Judy. *The Crystal Companion: Enhance Your Life with Crystals.* Blue Ash, Ohio: Walking Stick Press, 2018.

———. *The Encyclopedia of Crystals.* Gloucester, Mass.: Fair Winds Press, 2006.

———. *The Ultimate Guide to Crystal Grids: Transform Your Life Using the Power of Crystals and Layouts.* Gloucester, Mass.: Fair Winds Press, 2018.

Kaehr, Shelley. *Edgar Cayce Guide to Gemstones, Minerals, Metals and More.* Virginia Beach, Va.: A.R.E. Press, 2005.

Katz, Michael. *Gemstone Energy Medicine: Healing Body, Mind, and Spirit.* Portland, Ore.: Natural Healing Press, 2005.

Leavy, Ashley. *Crystals for Energy Healing: A Practical Sourcebook of 100 Crystals.* Beverly, Mass.: Fair Winds Press, 2017.

———. "Don't Cleanse These Crystals." Love and Light School of Crystal Therapy website.

Lilly, Simon. *The Crystal Healing Guide: A Step-by-Step Guide to Using Crystals for Health and Healing.* London, U.K.: Thorsons 2016.

Melody. *Love Is in the Earth.* Wheat Ridge, Colo.: Earth-Love Publishing,

Pearson, Nicholas. *Crystal Healing for the Heart: Gemstone Therapy for Physical, Emotional, and Spiritual Well-Being.* Rochester, Vt.: Destiny Books, 2017.

———. *Crystals for Karmic Healing: Transform Your Future by Releasing Your Past.* Rochester, Vt.: Destiny Books, 2017.

———. *Foundations of Reiki Ryoho: A Manual of Shoden and Okuden.* Rochester, Vt.: Healing Arts Press, 2018.

———. *The Seven Archetypal Stones: Their Spiritual Powers and Teachings.* Rochester, Vt.: Destiny Books, 2016.

———. *Stones of the Goddess: Crystals for the Divine Feminine.* Rochester, Vt.: Destiny Books, 2019.

Permutt, Philip. *The Crystal Healer: Crystal Prescriptions That Will Change Your Life Forever.* New York: CICO Books, 2007.

———. *The Crystal Healer Volume 2: Harness the Power of Crystal Energy.* New York: CICO Books, 2018.

Raphaell, Katrina. *Crystal Enlightenment: The Transforming Properties of Crystals and Healing Stones.* Vol. 1 of the Crystal Trilogy. Santa Fe, N.Mex.: Aurora Press, 1985.

———. *Crystal Healing: The Therapeutic Application of Crystals and Stones.* Vol. 2 of the Crystal Trilogy. Santa Fe, N.Mex.: Aurora Press, 1987.

———. *The Crystalline Transmission: A Synthesis of Light.* Vol. 3 of the Crystal Trilogy. Santa Fe, N.Mex.: Aurora Press, 1990.

———. *Crystalline Illumination: The Way of the Five Bodies.* Kapaa, Hawaii: The Crystal Academy of Advanced Healing Arts, 2010.

Simmons, Robert. *Stones of the New Consciousness: Healing, Awakening and Co-creating with Crystals, Minerals and Gems.* East Montpelier, Vt.: Heaven and Earth Publishing, 2009.

Simmons, Robert, and Naisha Ahsian. *The Book of Stones: Who They Are and What They Teach.* East Montpelier, Vt.: Heaven and Earth Publishing, 2007.

Singer, Beatriz. *The Crystal Code.* Carlsbad, Calif.: Hay House, 2019.

Walker, Dael. *The Crystal Book.* Sunol, Calif.: The Crystal Company, 1983.

Index

BOOKS OF RELATED INTEREST

Stones of the Goddess
Crystals for the Divine Feminine
by Nicholas Pearson

Crystal Healing for the Heart
Gemstone Therapy for Physical, Emotional, and Spiritual Well-Being
by Nicholas Pearson

Crystals for Karmic Healing
Transform Your Future by Releasing Your Past
by Nicholas Pearson
Foreword by Judy Hall

The Seven Archetypal Stones
Their Spiritual Powers and Teachings
by Nicholas Pearson

Awakening Your Crystals
Activate the Higher Potential of Healing Stones
by Sharon L. McAllister

Healing Crystals
The A - Z Guide to 555 Gemstones
by Michael Gienger

Stone Medicine
A Chinese Medical Guide to Healing with Gems and Minerals
by Leslie J. Franks, LMT

The Metaphysical Book of Gems and Crystals
by Florence Mégemont

Inner Traditions • Bear & Company
P.O. Box 388
Rochester, VT 05767
1-800-246-8648
www.InnerTraditions.com

Or contact your local bookseller